Dr. Jensen's
NATURE HAS
A REMEDY

Dr. Jensen's
NATURE HAS A REMEDY
HEALTHY SECRETS FROM AROUND THE WORLD

Bernard Jensen, D.C., Ph.D.
Clinical Nutritionist

KEATS PUBLISHING

LOS ANGELES

NTC/Contemporary Publishing Group

The purpose of this book is to educate. It is sold with the understanding that the publisher and author shall have neither liability nor responsibility for any injury caused or alleged to be caused directly or indirectly by the information contained in this book. While every effort has been made to ensure its accuracy, the book's contents should not be construed as medical advice. Each person's health needs are unique. To obtain recommendations appropriate to your particular situation, please consult a qualified health care provider.

Library of Congress Cataloging-in-Publication Data

Jensen, Bernard, 1908–
    [Nature has a remedy]
    Dr. Jensen's nature has a remedy : healthy secrets from around the world / Bernard Jensen.
       p. cm.
    Includes index.
    ISBN 0-658-00272-4
    1. Naturopathy. 2. Naturopathy—Cross-cultural studies. I. Title: Doctor Jensen's nature has a remedy. II. Title: Nature has a remedy.

RZ440 .J46 2000
615.5'35—dc21   00-069022

Published by Keats Publishing
A division of NTC/Contemporary Publishing Group, Inc.
4255 West Touhy Avenue, Lincolnwood, Illinois 60712, U.S.A.

Managing Director and Publisher: Jack Artenstein
Executive Editor: Peter Hoffman
Director of Publishing Services: Rena Copperman
Managing Editor: Jama Carter
Editor: Claudia McCowan

Design by Andrea Reider

Printed in the United States of America
International Standard Book Number: 0-658-00272-4
   01 02 03 04 VP 18 17 16 15 14 13 12 11 10 9 8 7 6 5 4 3 2

This book is dedicated to doctors and people throughout the world who are interested in healing as an art. The remedies contained herein are for those who would like to see that their body follows the holistic path; they are for the doctor who puts the whole of life together for his patients, using every appropriate remedy for the building and repair of the human body. Everything must be united in wholeness—a healthy body and mind lay the foundation for the serenity and peace we need as we develop a deeper appreciation of our Golden Days in God's Garden.

To my late wife Elsie and my late daughter Louise.

—Bernard Jensen, D.C., Ph.D.

Too many people still believe in cures, and in spite of my protest that I cannot cure anything, they come and assume the attitude, "Well, here I am and now it is up to you to cure me." They are foolish enough to believe that a cure should be made without any effort or any trouble on their part. Living haphazardly, guessing how to live when dependable knowledge can be had is a foolish and inexcusable hazard. I repeat, I cannot cure, but I can teach all who crave knowledge how to live to cure themselves and how to live and stay well.

—John H. Tilden, M.D.

CONTENTS

Preface   *xiii*

1. **The Nature of Nature**   1
   The Seven Doctors of Nature • On Beliefs and On Faith
   • Spiritual Aliveness • My Favorite Poem

2. **The World Around Us**   13
   The Air We Breathe • Climate • Air Pressure • Altitude
   • Humidity • Seasons • Environment and Body Heat
   • Which Climate?

3. **How Can We Live a Long Life?**   33
   • Youth • We Poison Ourselves • Learning from Other
   Countries • Pollen and Special Herbs • Invigorating
   Life Tonic • Small Meals Favor Old Age • Avoid
   Pronounced Changes • Spend Time Outdoors • Staying
   Healthy After Forty • Health Vacations • How to Avoid
   Unnecessary Surgery

4. **We Are in a New Age**   51
   Foods for Survival and Health • Nuclear Radiation
   Problems • Inventory of Supplies for Emergency Storage
   • Find A Philosophy

5. **Another Way—Another Direction**   **63**
Caring for the Whole Person • The Value of Natural Remedies
• Find Out What Is Right • Health Power • The Magic of
Foods • Changes We Can Make with Foods • Use What We've
Been Given for Health • About the Healing Crisis • Correction
of Body Tissue • Old Ailments Come Back • Watch Your Daily
Habits • Be Big—Lengthen Your Steps! • Fresh Air Heals
Wounds • Where Is the Cure? • The Law of Reversing • The
Disease vs. the Healing Crisis • Fasting • Nature Does Have a
Remedy • Fly from the Artificial • Nature's Way

6. **Heads Up!**   **85**
Eyes • Sinus • Throat • Mouth • Tongue • Gums and Teeth •
Ears • Headaches • Hair

7. **Primacy of the Brain**   **111**
Attitude and Brain Health • Food for Thought • The Brain
and Addictive Behaviors • Alzheimer's, Nutrition, and Brain
Function • Brain Food • Ways to Strengthen Brain and Nerve
Force • Building the Nerves • Best Brain and Nerve Foods

8. **The Blood**   **135**
Ways to Improve Circulation • Vein Problems • Understanding
and Correcting Anemia • Blood Pressure Problems • Angina
Problems • Sexual System in Relation to Blood • Food
Remedies for Blood Problems • Spiritual Strength

9. **Your Circle of Life**   **157**
Help for the Kidneys • Care of the Lungs • Bowel
Management • Foods and Bowel Problems • Abdominal
Exercises to Rejuvenate the Colon

10. **Beauty Starts with the Skin**   **181**
Care of the Skin • The Beauty Element: Fluoride
• Complexion Problems and Remedies • Suntanning • Air
Baths • Perspiration • Bathing • Showering • Skin Brushing

11. **Get Moving with Exercise** 193

Deep Breathing Exercises • Throat and Face Exercises • Special Eye Exercises • Organ Blood Circulation Exercises • Muscle Tension/Relaxation Exercises • Spine and Nerve Exercise • Prolapsed Organs Exercises and Solutions • Slant Board and Other Exercises • Draining the Neck Lymph Glands • Water Treatments and Baths • Tai Chi • Overcoming Tension • The Need for Minerals • Posture Wise • Our Attitudes Are Killing Us

12. **The Catarrhal Runoff** 217

Why and How Do Catarrhal Conditions Develop in the Body? • Symptoms of a Catarrhal Condition • What to Do • Diet and Catarrh • Asthma and Remedies • The Common Cold and Remedies • Flu and Remedies • Skin Care for Catarrhal Conditions • Other Catarrhal Remedies

13. **Building a Healthy Body** 241

Vitamins • Macro Elements and Trace Elements Needed • Carbohydrates • Cholesterol • Supplementary Foods • Supplements and Fortifiers

14. **The Health Food Store** 281

It's Time for a Change • Your Life is in the Label— How Much Do You Know? • Reading the Label • Foods from Animal Sources • Grains, Cereals, and Baked Goods • Fats • Fruit Juices • Ice Cream • Canned Foods and Their Effect on the Diet • Cleaning Products • Salt • Some Items You'll Want from Your Health Food Store

15. **Natural Food and Health Tips** 297

Special Nutritional Tips • Foods and Their Influence on the Body • Special Health Tips

16. **Natural Remedies**   307
Diseases and Remedies • Abnormal Foods, Abnormal
Bodies • A Natural Body Handles All Foods Well • Sodim
to Stay Young • Silicon for the Nervous System • Manganese
for the Brain • Magnesium for the Bowel • Honey for the
Heart • Potassium for the Muscles • Lecithin for Brain
and Nerve Energy • Salts for the Feet • Iodine for the
Thyroid Gland • Raw Foods • Dried Fruits • Food
Allergies • Proteins • Learn from Your Ailments

17. **Know Your Liquids**   321
How Much Should We Drink? Water Remedies • Water
Facts • The Wonders of Raw Vegetable Juices • Health
Cocktails • Milk Substitute Drinks • The Benefits of
Blending • Broths and Soups for Specific Conditions
• More Valuable Health-Building Tonics • Special Drinks

18. **All About Foods**   349
Foods That Serve a Purpose • Food As Medicine • Foods to
Limit in Your Diet • Unfavorable Foods • Foods for Arthritis
• Brain Food • Calcium Tonics • Foods for Cholesterol
and Other Deposits • Foods for the Heart • Foods for
Hydrochloric Acid Deficiency • Foods for Hypoglycemia
• Foods for the Nerves • Foods for the Liver • Acid/Alkaline
Balance • Good Food Combinations

19. **My Health and Harmony Food Regimen**   375
Balanced Daily Eating Regimen • Rules of Eating
• Impositions for Getting Well • Food Healing Laws
• Before Breakfast • Breakfast • 10:30 A.M. • Lunch
• 3:00 P.M. • Dinner

20. **Special Diets**   387
The Brown Rice Diet • Diet and Diabetes • Dietary
Considerations • Elimination Diets • Transition Diets
• Diet for Hypoglycemia • Stomach Ulcers • Nervous

Indigestion • Bland Food Diet • Reducing Diets • Bulk
Program for Cleansing • Cleansing Grape Diet • Internal
Water Treatment • Table Supplements • Vegetable Juices
• Special Broth for Sick People • Normalizing Weight
• Signs of a Chemically Balanced Body

21. **Healing and Cooking with Herbs** **425**
Herbs for Healing • Catalog of Healing Herbs • Cautionary
Notes About Herbs • Herbs and Spices for Cooking

22. **Conclusion** **449**

Index *453*

PREFACE

Nature has a remedy—and that is a concept now accepted by most scientists, doctors, health researchers, and government agencies. Natural healing has achieved a prominent place in the healing arts of our time because it has succeeded. We have learned much about how to use nature. It is the great provider—and healer. Still, there is much we don't know. And many of the remedies we now use may become out of date as conditions change and as we learn more in the years to come. Electricity, for example, may come in and supplant many of the remedies we use at the present time. Our understanding of many other aspects of nature will develop and mature. But in the meantime, there is a great deal we can do to promote our own health.

I want to emphasize that these remedies are not given with the idea that they provide a complete cure, but they are the little assists that a doctor may use who is interested in the use of the natural healing art.

Before we can live right we must first learn the proper methods. But where do you get the information to guide you in learning how to live? Today, as a rule, doctors are too busy taking care of the extreme cases; however, it has always been my belief that every doctor should spend one-half of his time educating and lecturing his patients so they will avoid some of the problems that build up in their environment, in their thinking processes, at the table, at their jobs, in their marriages, while handling finances, or whatever their paths carry them into.

The consciousness of man today is not a healthy one. He comes to the office with bad habits; he knows practically nothing about the care of his body. As long as things are white, sterilized, clean, and made by a well-known company, most people think the product should be good for them. This is a mistaken idea. We must consider our bodies as loyal servants depending upon our decisions, and know that everything that goes into the mouth has an effect upon the body. Also, the body is affected by what we hear and see, by our feelings—and it can all add up to our good or to our destruction. All of these things should be understood.

The remedies that are brought out here surely will only touch a small percentage of that which the average doctor or patient needs to know. Some of these remedies will not fit certain patients because of their temperament or feelings, because of inherent dysfunctions or weaknesses, and possibly because of their climate or attitude or occupation.

These remedies are approved by God and nature. They are not fast working. But when patients have been given guidance and instruction, these remedies can sometimes do a great deal toward reversing a disease or improving the body's natural defenses. Many times the patient's hopes will be raised; their path becomes easier because they are doing some work besides what the doctor requires; possibly it is what nature demands. It is a matter of cooperation among the doctor, the patient, and nature that helps us to win.

The success of my work has been due to the use of many of these remedies throughout my sixty years of practice. I have worked with over 350,000 students and patients. I did my best work when I considered caring for the whole patient and not "fighting" the disease. I looked to everything possible in the natural healing arts to help me raise the level of the health in my patients. And it was at those times that I saw the patient leave the disease and come into good health. My work centered around nutritional support for repairing and renewing damaged tissue, not just alleviating symptoms.

This book sums up my sixty years of practice, traveling, learning, and seeing what other people do—bringing it together in written form.

It is to raise the health level that we use these remedies. And if you have to do fifty things better than you were doing before in order to get well, you have the privilege of doing that in this age. There is no reason for anyone not to have all the success he wants in any direction he may wish to go, if it is a matter of education, because education is open to everyone these days. There was a day when only the wealthy, only the nobility, only the royal family had education, and the rest of the people were serfs or slaves. In this day we have broken that bondage and we can all be kings and queens, and no one has to be a serf or a slave. It is my understanding that these remedies will not be misconstrued as a cure for any disease but will be used as part of an overall effort to take the path to higher values, better health—physically, mentally, and spiritually—and greater happiness.

Above all things, these remedies are not given to use without considering the basic principles of life. For instance, a good diet is necessary in support of most remedies. A person with a beer in one hand and a cigarette in the other will find little or

no relief with a natural remedy. These remedies are not for people who insist on living a degenerative lifestyle, whose purpose
in taking a remedy is only to help them hang onto their
lifestyle. This book is meant for the sincere student, for the person who is sick of being sick, who wants to elevate himself,
who wants a finer path for going through life—and is willing
to live according to nature's principles and use some of the simple remedies described in this book.

None of these remedies is to take the place of a doctor's
treatment. We need doctors. A doctor can be your best friend
in times of problems and troubles. I think we should always
have somebody who works along with us, a doctor we can call
to find out whether a natural remedy is consistent with a therapy he or she may have prescribed. But with serious conditions
like meningitis or high fevers, don't try to heal yourself. The
remedies in this book are not meant to be applied to potentially dangerous, acute symptoms, or sudden episodes of
extreme pain.

Let me emphasize that. Suppose you look to the index at
the end of the book for "prostate trouble," turn to the specified
page, and see that pumpkin seeds are recommended for prostate
gland trouble. Do you take a few pumpkin seeds and consider
yourself healed? No! Don't think for a moment that if you have
a stoppage of urine and take a few pumpkin seeds that you're
going to cure it. Each of these remedies should be used as part
of a total health plan. This is why I suggest that you have a good
doctor to work with.

These remedies are for those who are interested in learning
about the natural healing arts and should be used along with all
other help possible. A good diagnosis, a good lab analysis, and a
good talk with your doctor are advisable in all of our problems.

You will find in working with nature's creative power that it exceeds man's inclination to destroy, in part, by demonstrating our need to avoid lifestyle habits destructive to our health, mental attributes, and relationships with others, and by providing a natural means for better physical health.

So be patient with nature, be patient with your fellow man, but, most of all, be patient with yourself.

CHAPTER 1

THE NATURE OF NATURE

Nature has been here a long time. The Earth is nature; the sky is nature; the water is nature. All our resources and all of our building and repairing, whether it be in the body or out—all comes from nature. And nature always has a remedy.

The Armenians say it well: "There is not a disease for which nature doesn't have a remedy right next to it." I believe that. I also believe that we are currently aware of only 8 to 9 percent of the natural remedies that will eventually be discovered. I see a wonderful future for the natural healing arts.

THE SEVEN DOCTORS OF NATURE

Number One: Sunshine

We know that without the proper amount of sunshine, an animal cannot have healthy fur on its back. Humans need sunshine, too, of course. Authorities found a child who had been in an attic for five years. His teeth were soft and loose in the gums because of a lack of sunshine. Sunshine is necessary to develop natural vitamin D, which is necessary for us to assimilate and use calcium in the body. You can have all the best foods, but without sunshine you will not be healthy.

We are all children of the sun, whether our skins are light or dark. We find we must have a definite amount of sunshine. Sunshine is an essential part of our existence. We live in the sun. We are not meant to live in houses with closed doors and shaded windows that block the light of the sun. The sun is for the good of the planet and everything on it. It is for everyone's good. However, overexposure to the ultraviolet radiation in sunlight can have harmful effects on the skin and increases the risk of cataracts.

Number Two: Water

We can live only a few days without water. Our bodies are 85 percent fluid—a water mixture. Even our teeth and bones have water in them. We need this fluid. Without it we would become dehydrated, dry up, and die. Tissues cannot receive nutrients without water. It is water that carries off toxic wastes from living tissue and brings rebuilding elements to damaged or aging tissue.

Nature doesn't require distilled water to promote health. I have traveled through many countries in search of the oldest men and women, inquiring about the secrets of their longevity. Yet, I have never found one that uses distilled water. They use natural water, pure water, usually from mountain springs or streams. I believe that cold, natural water is alive. I'm positive that there is usually more calcium in natural water than in filtered or chemically treated water. Water high in calcium is called "hard water."

However, I feel there is a use for distilled water. An arthritic patient needs to dissolve and get rid of the heavy calcium salts deposited in the joints and muscle structure. The wise doctor knows he can use distilled water to help such patients.

Water is not just a fluid within our bodies. We are beginning to realize that the vibratory forces in water and foods are influential.

Water carries a vibration. The salts contained in water carry a vibration, an electromagnetic influence. In distilled water, we don't find that influence; the salts and other elements have been removed. I'm convinced the electromagnetic influence in water that is high in either sulfur, calcium, or sodium can help balance a person's body chemistry.

I would say that in extreme cases of arthritis, arteriosclerosis, or cholesterol deposits, use distilled water. You may use pure spring mountain water, if you wish.

Vibratory water may contain inorganic material. But this material is naturally being removed from the body as metabolic wastes are processed and eliminated. Your perspiration tastes salty because it's high in sodium. Salts are thrown off in the urine and by the bowel. When your chemical supply is depleted, the vibratory rate, the electromagnetic quality, is gone. These are what we live on. I have found that live foods are also necessary.

Number Three: Oxygen/Air

We've got to have oxygen. We can live only a few minutes without it. Oxygen breaks up the waste material in the body. It gets rid of garbage and helps to produce energy in our body. We need energy to process and break down our foods so that micronutrients can be absorbed and delivered to the tissues properly. Without oxygen, we cannot build any structure in the body.

Oxygen can be increased by adequate exercise and by getting enough iron in our foods. Many people in the United States, especially premenopausal women, are deficient in iron, which carries oxygen to all the cells.

Carbon dioxide is constantly being thrown off into the air and purified by plant life, so that the air is kept in proper balance. Greens growing around us are also doctors. It is best to live where there are trees and an abundance of green plants. People with lung troubles have sometimes gotten beautiful results by breathing the air around pine trees.

Number Four: Mother Earth

Mother Earth is doctor number four: the origin of every chemical element our bodies need. We should rely on and take care of Mother Earth in order to have fully mineralized soil and food crops, so our bodies can have every nutrient they need from the foods we eat. We must fertilize the soil to make sure it always has the chemical elements needed to support food crops.

There is a saying that if something has the approval of God, it can be used. God supplies the sunshine, rain, and soil. It is up to us to till the soil, plant seeds, water them, and harvest the crops. If we identify ourselves with nature and work with the processes of nature, sustaining the fertility of the soil and doing our part, we shall find that we have the approval of God.

Number Five: Food

I consider food as our doctor number five, especially fully mineralized foods that come directly from nature's rich soil. What did God provide for us in the beginning? He gave us whole foods, such as peas with pods to use so that we get the whole food. You don't have to eat the pea pods, but you can make a juice out of them. Put the juice in your broth, and you will get all the chlorophyll you were meant to have. We should also not throw away the seeds of the watermelon. When we do, we throw away some of the valuable nutrients. Watermelon seeds have chlorophyll, lecithin, vitamin K, vitamin E, and iron. They are very good for kidney troubles, hypertension, and high blood pressure.

We are meant to eat mostly unpeeled foods. If the peelings are unpleasant (as with citrus or avocados), we can put them into teas and make drinks from them; we can make them into soups. There's a way to do these things; there's a way we can stay close to nature.

Life is a circle. We go from birth to adolescence, youth, middle age, old age, and have children and grandchildren who repeat the cycle. We go from summer to fall to winter to spring and back to summer. Our food routine should be different in the winter than it is in the summer season. We should have dissolving foods in the beginning of summer. Sodium foods such as whey and cucumbers are cooling foods. Cucumbers are high in sodium. (Remember the expression "cool as a cucumber"?) Cucumber juice mixed with pineapple juice is pleasantly cooling on a hot day.

Barley heats the blood. Such heating foods are winter foods. Barley and kale soup, for example, is a good warming food for a winter's day.

We also must consider the acid/alkaline balance of the foods we eat. I recommend an 80 percent alkaline foods and 20 percent acid foods requirement based on the assumption that a person is active, creating many metabolic waste acids in the body in order to balance at 50/50. The pH or acid/alkaline balance is a very important and very subtle balance to maintain in the body. From time to time, the blood may be a little too alkaline or a little too acidic. Of course, no two people are exactly alike, even regarding body chemistry. There are some people who can hold the alkaline condition in their body better than others. There is a possibility that dietary differences make for different conditions. But you must create a projected norm as a guideline. Not everyone should be a dray horse and not everyone should be a race horse.

There is a uniqueness in nature. You can't expect the same food program to fit every human being. You can't expect everyone to have the identical acid/alkaline balance. There are wide variations in skin and hair.

Whole foods are necessary in all seasons of the year. We must build a reserve. We may build a house in six months, but it can burn down in about ten minutes. *Building takes longer than burning.*

When sufficient chemical elements are in reserve, the body can continue to work in building a good sound structure, despite the ups and downs of particular nutrients in the intake.

One of the most important considerations in rebuilding the body is to allow ample time. Don't expect an overnight miracle. Plan on a minimum of one year—each of the four seasons—to get the benefits of all the seasonal foods. The wise doctor uses foods as medicine and works with the patient in attaining chemical balance.

Nothing in nature's realm is more healthful than proteins. However, some protein foods are heavier than others. In general, protein foods are much heavier than the complex carbohydrates containing mineral salts and vitamins. Fats must be taken in moderation and are used as an energy fuel reserve.

Fruits contain more vitamins than vegetables. Some vegetables, such as turnips and carrots, may be very high in vitamins, but, as a rule, we find the vegetable kingdom is higher in mineral salts than fruits. Fruits tend to stir up body acids. Vegetables help carry off acids. In the instance of kidney trouble, fruit juice can be aggravating. Fruits work on every organ, stirring up the toxic acid wastes present in those organs. How are the acids removed? The kidneys carry them off. The kidneys must be strong to handle any overload.

Number Six: Color and Vibration

There are definite laws of nature that lead us to health. We need exposure to color and beauty to be as healthy as we should be. Sunlight is actually a combination of red, orange, yellow, green, blue, and violet light, each with its own vibration or frequency. Add all the frequencies together and we get white light.

One of these days science is going to seriously study color and vibration as related to health and the seasons and foods a person needs.

There's a vibratory state of the body. The vibratory state is determined by the body's electrochemical structure and the relative state of health. When the chemical structure is perfectly balanced and functioning properly, the normal vibratory rate indicates the body's catabolic (building) function and anabolic (tearing down) function are nicely balanced. During a fast, the body is not balanced as well as it can be because it is tearing down and eliminating toxins. Once the body is cleansed, if the person returns to the old way of living, he is worse off for the effort. Maybe he is rid of some of the toxins, but he is back to creating inflammations and underactivity in inherently weak organs, glands, and tissues.

Many people are constantly fasting, or on all-cleansing diets, so to speak. The program I recommend is divided into three stages: cleansing, transition, and building. The body constantly goes through these cycles, moving into the various changes normal to the human body.

Number Seven: Emotions

People can try to kill us, warp us, disturb us, yet if our emotional nature is secure we have a natural doctor. It gives us the ability to relax even when external circumstances are unstable or even threatening. We can know how to feel at peace even during distressing times. During relaxation and quietness, tissue repair takes place in the body.

The mind has to have a harmonious balance for the body to be healthy. We need to be surrounded by and immersed in freedom, peace, and joy. We find that some kinds of people interfere with that joy. We run into people with financial problems, marital problems, children problems, school problems, and many other disturbances. But we don't have to enter into their distress.

Emotional balance and a good mental philosophy help keep the body repairing and rebuilding itself as fast as you break it down. But a proper food program, including appropriate brain foods, is essential. Without such a program, the brain force may go down, resulting in a nervous breakdown or a mental depression.

ON BELIEFS AND ON FAITH

It is impossibile to learn everything there is to know in this lifetime, so we go through much of life believing and having faith. We all live within some kind of belief system.

When I say you can trust in nature, I go back to original beliefs. I go back to certain primitive beliefs, such as giving spiritual significance to the sun, the moon, and the stars. Without the sun, no life could exist on our planet. All light gives life and interacts with our planet and the life forms it supports.

There are many reasons for returning to nature. God and nature never let a man down. I've seen that proven many times. We have to believe in things according to their past performances. I believe that my apple trees will blossom again in the spring because they did it before. I believe I can get well because I have seen people healed of the same thing before. I believe I can continue to have good joints because they have served me well for many years and I continue to take care of them.

I believe that the body is in a state of flux. You can't hold anything still. The only thing that is permanent in life is change, and the body is always changing. I believe this because I see it working right before my eyes. I work my beliefs into what I am experiencing. I cannot believe in devitalized foods. I cannot believe in white flour because I have seen what white flour can do. I've seen experiments in which dogs were fed with flour. Researchers have found that dogs can live longer on water than on white flour. In other words, there are a whole lot of people believing in the wrong things. They are misled. They are believing in what others have told them. But what others say can be wrong.

You don't have to believe in God, but I'll say you have to believe in nature, because you live in the midst of it. You can see it, hear it, feel it, smell it, and taste it.

I realize a lot of people don't want to believe in the God described in the Bible. But man, by his nature, is a being that must worship something, and if he doesn't worship the biblical God, he will invent his own god or gods. Man knows something very intelligent and creative is actually behind it all, responsible for all growth, all life, all the laws science has discovered. He knows that something gave a first shove to get things started even before the first human beings were around. We have to believe that if we look at the geological and archeological records.

Personally, though I have doubted many times that God was around, I can't say I've ever been an atheist. I've had experiences that have led me to believe in prayer and God. Now I want to live out the godly principles of truth, joy, and happiness in having a loving heavenly Father. I know He wants His children healthy and harmonious. I try to live according to His teachings, but I don't put it on a religious basis.

The universe itself teaches us these beliefs. Dr. Wernher von Braun said:

> Anything as well ordered and perfectly created as is our Earth and universe must have a maker, a master designer. Anything so orderly, so perfect, so precisely balanced, so majestic as this creation, can only be the product of a Divine Idea. There must be a maker. There can be no other way.

Astronaut Eugene A. Cernan looked at this Earth a little differently than we do. He said:

> When you get out there—a quarter of a million miles away from home you look at Earth with a little different perspective. The Earth looks big and beautiful and blue and white, and you can see from the Antarctic to the North Pole and the continental shores. The Earth looks so perfect. There are no strings to hold it up, no fulcrum upon which it rests. You think of the infinity of space and the infinity of time. I didn't see God, but I am convinced of God by the order in space. I know it didn't happen by accident.

SPIRITUAL ALIVENESS

A person must be spiritually alive. I'm not speaking of religion; but we do need the spiritual things for our health.

To be spiritually alive is to be truthful. To get the truth we shouldn't look for *who* is right, but *what* is right. A person of integrity goes with truth because it feels good inside, because he knows he is doing the right thing, even if he has to go alone. We find out by doing the right thing that we have relief of tension in the body, relief of animosity, relief of anxiety.

If we do the right thing before God, we can (and must) leave the rest to God. In our humanity, we need to realize that our life is limited to a sphere with specific boundaries, and we can live only from day to day, even though we may plan and schedule our time for months ahead. Some people can't think past tomorrow afternoon.

The spiritual life has to be developed. Some people have more spiritual awareness than others. If you have this special spiritual awareness, you will experience spiritual phenomena and be moved by such events. Some people are so coarse, so calcified in their thinking, that they have walled out any spiritual experience or phenomena whatsoever. Their awareness has to come through some great extremity—like the man who was buried in a mine for thirty-one days recognizing for the first time in his life his need for God. Eddie Rickenbacker, the famous fighter pilot ace in World War I, was stuck on a raft for twenty-one days on the Pacific. Before that time he did not believe in God. Yet he finally changed his mind as he was facing death.

When a person desperately needs water, needs help from people, needs to have his life spared, then he looks up. He looks up for a moment hoping for something that will save him. And that moment comes along. The sight of a ship to a castaway gives greater joy than all the money in the world, greater than any other joy he has ever experienced. The ship becomes the greatest event in the world to the rescued person. Some people would say that God intervened; some people would say God appeared; some people would say that man's extremities are God's opportunities.

So we need to believe in these things and be grateful for the lovely things that come to us each day. This is part of good health. We live to be grateful for each day; this is healthy. A healthy spiritual attitude is just as important as having a good working body.

MY FAVORITE POEM

I asked God for strength that I may achieve;
I was made weak that I might learn humbly to obey.
I asked for health that I might do greater things;
I was given infirmity that I might do better things:
I asked for riches that I might be happy;
I was given poverty that I might be wise.
I asked for power that I might have the praise of men;
I was given weakness that I might feel the need of God;
I asked for all things that I might enjoy life;
I was given life that I might enjoy all things.
I got nothing that I asked for but everything that I had hoped for.
Almost despite myself my unspoken prayers were answered.
I am, among all men, most richly blessed.

(Author Unknown)

CHAPTER 2

THE WORLD AROUND US

M any experiments have been performed to show that certain environments are better than others for our good health. For instance, studies with rats and other animals show that different altitudes and climates have definite effects on lung structure, heart movement, and the water balance of the body.

Certain types of people do better in one environment than in another. With high blood pressure you should not go to a high altitude, and sometimes a too dry climate is not good.

Each person is different, and will be uniquely affected by his particular environment: climate, altitude, temperature, humidity, and so forth.

THE AIR WE BREATHE

The air is composed of one part oxygen and four parts nitrogen. There is 1 percent of a gas called argon, and small percentages of neon, krypton, and xenon. Our air contains close to 21 percent oxygen; if the oxygen is increased very slightly, we do not thrive well. Nitrogen exists in our air to the amount of a little more than 78 percent. Of course, the air can also contain dust, insect wings, water vapors, smoke, coal tar, fumes, ammonia, nitrous acid, sulfuric acid, nitric acid, bacteria, odors, and other impurities.

We need to learn to breathe properly. Oxygen, when inhaled into the lungs, is attracted to the iron in the hemoglobin of red blood corpuscles and is carried by the blood into every organ, tissue, and cell of the body for purposes of oxidation and energy production. Blood also carries carbon dioxide from the tissues to the lungs, where it is released to be exhaled from the body. When the breathing function is not efficiently developed, the carbon dioxide in the tissues and blood is not carried away rapidly enough. This results in an overacid blood, and reduction of oxygen supply to the heart and brain. This is why it is necessary to breathe deliberately and vigorously in high altitudes. I highly recommend aerobic exercise on a daily basis to assure abundant oxygen to all body organs and efficient elimination of carbon dioxide.

A man at rest uses about 580 to 1,000 liters of air. A heavy man of 250 to 300 pounds doing physical work uses more than 1,000 liters in twenty-four hours. An office worker who uses only about 400 liters of air each day will soon suffer from bad blood, acidity, bloating, brain fatigue, and sleeplessness.

Respiration can vary from three breaths a minute to thirty breaths a minute. The respiration can vary in the same person at different times according to his state of health, the development of his chest and brain, the presence of gases in his system, the amount of food in his stomach, the condition of his lungs, his state of mind, his age, his level of daily activity, and many other conditions. The more powerful the lungs, the more reposed the individual will feel at any given time, and the fewer breaths required each minute. But the weaker the person and the more emotional, nervous, and sensitive he is, the greater the number of breaths each minute.

We know that the air in an unventilated room is unfit for breathing. But did you know that those who have a lot of sugar, starch, and fat in their bodies produce more carbon dioxide in the blood and tissues and therefore need more oxygen? The more carbohydrate foods we eat, the more carbonic acid we make, and the more carbon dioxide we exhale. The accumulation of carbonic acid does not allow the proper amount of oxygenation to take place in our bodies. Eventually, oxygen hunger develops and disease results. When we begin to need more oxygen in the body, we should leave sugars, starches, and fats alone and seek a higher altitude with dry air.

Without air, light, heat, moisture, and plants, animals would not exist. We should realize that the vegetable kingdom is a manufacturing concern that gives us a new supply of oxygen—and therefore life. People, birds, and animals utilize oxygen and exhale carbon dioxide. Plants need carbon dioxide and nitrogen and give off oxygen for us to breathe. Here we can see the wisdom of the great world builder. The more abundant the garden around us, the more trees, plants, and flowers, the more oxygen and ozone in the air. Wind and light help to purify the air and are therefore great blessings to us. Carbon dioxide and oxygen both gradually decrease in concentration as we ascend to higher altitudes. Mountain air is cleaner but contains less oxygen, whether or not it is heavily forested. Although pollution increases in urban environments and the trees and vegetation are not as plentiful, the ratio of carbon dioxide to oxygen remains stable.

Human health is compromised by air pollution. Carbon dioxide, a normal by-product of plant and animal respiration, has increased by 82 percent since 1940, but it is still only 365 parts per million of air (less than four-hundredths of 1 percent), harmless to humans and beneficial to vegetation. But its near relative, carbon monoxide, is very dangerous.

Carbon monoxide is formed by incomplete combustion of wood, coal, natural gas, diesel, fuel oil, gasoline, and anything else that burns. Most of it in our cities comes from auto exhaust fumes and coal-dependent manufacturing processes. At 200 parts per million (ppm) in air, headaches may begin after two hours of exposure. When air contains 12,800 ppm (1¼ percent of carbon monoxide), immediate unconsciousness and death take place within four minutes. This gas is invisible and odorless, and people die from it every year, usually from being in confined spaces with a gasoline engine running. Carbon monoxide aggressively replaces oxygen in blood hemoglobin and shuts off our oxygen supply. This literally suffocates people overexposed to it. Most such accidents occur in closed spaces, but there is a little carbon monoxide in most urban air, and that's not good. Even trace amounts can diminish brain function and harm the heart muscle. Carbon monoxide is only one of the thousands of chemicals that pollute urban air, and over six hundred of them are known to be harmful to health at certain concentrations. Most occur in such tiny amounts that they are measured in parts per million of air, but some are present in amounts that cause serious health problems.

Of the thousands of chemicals that pollute the air over planet Earth, most come from industrial processes and auto exhaust emissions. These chemicals mix with natural pollutants such as ozone, dust particles, smoke from forest fires, insect debris, and other organic matter, and make up the kind of air pollution people are exposed to who live in industrial nations, especially in urban areas. Air pollution is known to cause environmental damage and specific health problems like asthma, cancer, neurological damage, and birth defects. In response to this danger, the U.S. government passed the Clean Air Act in 1990, in which 188 chemicals were designated "hazardous to health" and safety standards and cleanup goals were established. In recent years, studies have been made of the relative risk of cancer due to high pollution in urban areas.

Studies made of Los Angeles and the San Francisco Bay area were published in 1999. Earlier studies of New Jersey and Pennsylvania were examined. The most dangerous pollutants are 1,3-Butadiene, benzene, carbon tetrachloride, chromium VI, formaldehyde, 1,4-Dichlorobenzene, methylene chloride, and perchloroethylene. A House of Representatives report issued in March 1999 claimed that the air in Los Angeles was 426 times more hazardous than the air quality standard established by the 1990 Clean Air Act. A similar report for the San Francisco Bay area found the air 208 times more hazardous than it should be. Serious cancer risks from air pollution were estimated from data gathered in New Jersey and parts of Pennsylvania, which mentioned ozone, sulfur dioxide, carbon monoxide, nitrogen dioxide, and lead among leading pollutants. Since lead was eliminated from gasoline in the 1980s, it has almost disappeared from the air.

Indoor air pollution is another major problem. Chemicals from rugs, furniture, electronic equipment, and household cleaning supplies get into indoor air. Recently Scotchgard discontinued use of 1,1,1-trichloroethane in its carpet waterproofing product because trace amounts were found in people who had Scotchgard-treated carpets in their homes. Radon, a gaseous breakdown product of radium in the earth's crust, seeps into homes in certain parts of the country and can cause lung cancer. Secondhand cigarette smoke is a major cause of asthma and bronchitis in children whose parents smoke in the home. House mold, pet dandruff, and particles of house dust can trigger allergies. Air filters and other protection systems can help, as can taking care to keep the home clean. No one should smoke around children. If you do, you are creating the potential for tobacco addiction in your children later on in life, and you are exposing them to chemicals that cause lung diseases, including cancer, asthma, bronchitis, and emphysema. Make a conscious effort to keep indoor air pollutants out of your home.

What you breathe, indoors and outdoors, powerfully influences your health level from childhood on. Make every effort to avoid polluted air, indoors or outdoors.

CLIMATE

The forces of nature are very important in maintaining good health. Sunshine, rainfall, wind, and the four seasons are all important to our health. So are the finer forces, such as the beauty in nature, the electricity in the air, the sounds of birds, crickets, and wind. Lightning during storms discharges from clouds to the earth, sometimes starting forest fires. Sunlight is necessary for photosynthesis in plants, so they can make carbohydrates from carbon dioxide in the air together with water from the ground. Sunlight is necessary for the food we eat, for the natural control of bacteria, and for stimulating production of natural vitamin D in our bodies.

Some people's health is at its best at the mountains, while others are healthier living near the sea. There are people who thrive in a dry climate but sicken rapidly in a high-humidity tropical climate—and vice versa. There are people who can't stand long periods without sunlight, a condition called seasonal affective disorder, or SAD. If you are depressed during prolonged periods of cloud cover and no sunshine, you may have SAD. The farther north people live, the longer the days are in summer and the longer the nights are in winter. People who live along a seacoast may have months of cloud overcast weather.

We find out there are diseases that thrive in the tropics but nowhere else, but there are also people who thrive in the tropics and don't get those diseases. Parasites, however, are almost always a major problem in tropical regions. In many third world countries, parasites are the number one cause of death.

Variations in barometric pressure affect many people. I believe some people are able to sense the coming of storms because their bodies are sensitive to changes in air pressure. Snow, ice, and cold weather in general can have a profound effect upon health. Pneumonia cases in the elderly always increase in the winter months in more severe climates. Spring and fall usher in colds and flu as the immune system adjusts to rapidly changing ratios of day-to-night hours, while the pollens and other natural substances carried by the wind vary with the season, causing rises and falls in allergy reactions.

Weather conditions such as wind, air pressure, electricity in the air, humidity, and temperature are all sensed by the human body, causing subtle or not-so-subtle changes in the brain and nervous system, alertness, reaction time, body tension, skin sensitivity, moods, and emotions. How well we sleep can be influenced by weather, as well as our rate of healing from wounds or a disease. I feel that people who tend to live with a lot of tension in their lives should not live in places where there is a lot of electricity in the air and turbulent weather. These things are not good for their nerves, mind, and senses. This is especially true for nervous people and for those who are inclined to develop fears easily.

Mountains are wonderful for a vacation. They are usually full of pine scent and have cleaner, purer air. People with a low red blood cell count should live at a higher altitude where more red blood cells are produced. Invigorated, toned up to the point of friskiness, we feel new after a visit to the mountains. Health resorts owe their curative power to such natural agents as air, exposure to the sun, vigorous exercise, massage, clean air, climate, altitude, relaxation, luxuriant vegetation, peace, and a change of scenery. Before you go on a vacation, consider the health-related benefits of your options and choose a season and location that will be good for you.

Natural electricity has a very positive effect on the soil. "Lightning helps fertilize the soil by producing up to ten million tons of nitrogen annually," according to Dr. Martin A. Uman, author of the book *Understanding Lightning*. When a thunderbolt streaks through the air, it creates a nitrogen compound, or natural fertilizer, that falls to the earth in raindrops.

AIR PRESSURE

The barometric pressure is not the same at different times of the day. It rises toward sunset; it usually falls as heat increases. Warm air expands and ascends, and cooler air takes its place. This produces the air circulation or air motion called wind. Sea breezes are cool air flowing from the sea in response to low pressure systems over land heated by the sun. The land heats up faster than the sea in the daytime, the heated air rises, and sea breezes blow landward. In the evening, the land cools faster than the surface of the sea, so the breeze blows seaward.

Storms are nothing but air in motion. When the wind blows at the rate of three miles an hour or less, we call it a stand-still, a calm. When air moves at eight miles an hour, the wind is hardly noticeable. But in a hurricane, the air travels approximately 88 to 130 miles an hour.

Rain is man's best friend in the sense that it purifies the air, but it can be his enemy, too, because moisture increases germ life. Microbes increase enormously when moist organic matter begins to warm up after a rain. In dry weather, great clouds of dust are found in the air. The best time to breathe freely, fully, and most enjoyably is after a cool rain.

Rain decreases inorganic substances in the air, but it increases microorganisms almost unbelievably. Dust, dirt, and impurities, however, are more dangerous than germ life. Pathogenic bacteria never stay long in the air because of light, rain, and wind. Such bacteria are thrown to the ground by the rain. A salt moisture is found in the air to a certain extent, evaporated from the ocean, and it floats about as little salt globules and particles. Salty air has a soothing effect upon sleeplessness, nervousness, hysteria, temper, and restlessness.

The weight of air is considerable when we realize that there is an air pressure of from 11 to 15 tons bearing down on us daily, yet no one is conscious of it. Moist air is much heavier than dry air.

Gases expand upon heating, and rise. Atmospheric pressure therefore diminishes as we ascend into the air. The higher we go, the less pressure. The air is thinner, rarified; the air molecules are farther apart. And it is cooler because as gases expand, temperature drops. When we travel over higher elevations, we should ascend slowly, gradually.

ALTITUDE

The more red corpuscles we have, the more oxygen we can utilize. At sea level, people are known to have about five million red blood corpuscles per cubic millimeter, but those living in high altitudes of five to six thousand feet have seven or eight million corpuscles per cubic millimeter. In the Andes Mountains in South America, many people at some ten to twelve thousand feet have blood counts of 7,500,000, which is unheard of with those living by the ocean. There may be much truth in the old Bible saying, "Go to the hills for thy strength."

Divers and others who work in dense air suffer from pain in the limbs, grow weak, and become anemic. Oxygen under high air pressure becomes toxic, and the red blood count decreases alarmingly. Mountain sicknesses, on the other hand, are peculiar to people who suddenly go to high elevations. At first our nervous system is irritated by high altitude: temper increases, we become more violent, fussy, morose, and hunger and thirst increase. If the altitude is excessive to us, our digestive functions suffer. If, however, our vital functions can respond to the change of altitude, we soon feel as wonderful as if we were born anew. We become active; our functions are sharpened; the brain is clearer. We think right, concentrate better, create better, feel more important, accomplish greater deeds.

At a higher altitude and in a drier climate, we breathe differently. We have a greater expansion of the chest, oxygenation takes place more rapidly, metabolism is quickened, and the thyroid gland works at a more rapid pace.

If we go too high, however, new symptoms and ailments appear. Our red blood cells are the oxygen carriers in the body. Our lungs are actually an oxygen pantry where the red corpuscles go for their oxygen supply. In a higher altitude, we can become more active in spirit, more willing to work, more inventive, and less tired. But in *too high* an altitude, we can become dizzy from insufficient oxygen. Some people become accustomed to a higher altitude in a matter of weeks. Others may require as much as a year.

Unusually high elevations produce a high nervous pulse and increase the number of respirations per minute to the point of fevered breathing. Nervousness is increased at a high altitude and decreased at a low altitude. Unusually high altitude produces a rapid pulse and respiration, which makes the heart beat faster. It makes many people nervous. Work that is easy at low altitudes becomes difficult at a high elevations. At an excessive elevation, people may develop heart disease, lung trouble, and especially hypertrophy of the heart, owing to the fact that the blood is not sufficiently charged with oxygen. This throws an extra strain upon the valves of the heart.

HUMIDITY

Humidity is the invisible water vapor in the air, not snow, fog, rain, or dew. Relative humidity is the vapor present in the air as compared to the vapors the air *can* hold. Cold air holds less humidity. The higher we go, the less humidity. The more the air expands, the less water vapor it can hold. If air cools after reaching its saturation point, precipitation results.

Dry air permits the sunbeams and light to pass through it. Moist air absorbs heat and sunshine. When moist air moves briskly and is cold, we lose body heat so rapidly that the next day we are "under the weather" with a cold, and our nasal membranes are congested. A dry climate has many changes of temperature caused by the sun's heat in the daytime and the great heat radiation at night.

There is more heat where there is more vegetation, which is especially true around the equator. Abundant vegetation moderates both heat and cold.

Moisture intensifies both heat and cold, while dry air decreases heat. Dry air makes tissues more alkaline than any diet will. When the skin evaporation is poor, the kidneys are overworked. When the skin is sluggish, the kidneys work double shift. A moist, warm, congenial climate relieves the kidneys, but a cold climate does not. An active skin relieves the kidneys. When we have a high or slightly high humidity, the skin function is always more active, as more water vapor is removed by the skin from the body. Evaporation of bodily heat decreases as the water vapors of the air increase. Thus, we feel uncomfortable in warm, stuffy air. A high temperature and muggy air always lower respiration and functional activities; they also increase the carbon dioxide in blood and tissue. In cold weather, more carbon dioxide is exhaled and breathing has a wider, deeper range.

The advice of Dr. Clarence A. Mills (author of *Climate Makes the Man*) to some of his patients in cases of sinusitis and high blood pressure is to seek a warmer climate. In another case, he told one of his patients with high blood pressure to leave Wyoming, where he was trying to get well, and seek the relaxing warmth of southern Florida. He says that most physicians in the tropics now appreciate the importance of lowered vitality in hot climates and send their patients out to more invigorating regions as soon as tuberculosis is detected. The wise doctor will take care that this move does not plunge his patient into the respiratory hazards of winter cold and storms. Here again, the dry, nonstormy Southwest is an ideal region.

Dr. Mills's research showed that the blood pressure of an American usually falls during a few years' stay in Peking, and that of a Chinese rises when he comes to the northern United States, even without any change in dietary or living habits. He tells how two of his Peking faculty colleagues, both native Britishers, experienced a 30 percent fall in blood pressure within a year after returning to China from furloughs spent in England or the United States. In Peking, it was difficult to find enough cases of hypertension (high blood pressure) for teaching purposes. But in Cincinnati, almost a third of the hospital beds were occupied by this type of health problem.

So it is easy to see that temperature, altitude, humidity, winds, and electrical differences in the atmosphere can create a profound effect upon us, especially where disease is present.

SEASONS

Wintertime

In the wintertime, we should consider taking large amounts of vitamins A and C: 30,000 milligrams of vitamin A daily, and from 1,500 to 2,000 milligrams of vitamin C daily.

During the wintertime, many people living in foggy or smoggy areas spend too much time indoors and do not get enough winter sunshine. Heavy clothing is worn and longer hours are worked than normal. Consequently, around the month of March, lack of resistance allows colds and bronchial troubles to develop. To build natural resistance, eat plenty of oranges, grapefruit, sulfur vegetables such as broccoli, cabbage, cauliflower, and turnips to produce heat, and tops of vegetables such as beets, carrots, or turnips. Then you are adequately supplied with winter sunshine. Sensitivity to weather changes indicates a need for potassium and calcium foods.

It is well to give children a little cod liver oil. This contains the sunshine vitamin material and will help us remain healthy if we do not get enough sunshine and are not outside enough. The best cod liver oil is obtained from Norway, and I would suggest that you take one teaspoon daily, or two capsules daily.

If you suffer from chilblains, a good remedy is to apply lime water several times a day until there is relief.

Summertime

Most people get well in the summertime. Every disease is helped during the summer because this is when nature works best with all human tissues. In the summer, we either naturally get well or are able to utilize a natural environment that helps us get well.

We should seek two summers in a row; one summer where we live, then fall and winter in a place where the winters are more like summer. There's no reason to build ourselves up 50 percent and then drop down 25 percent again in the wintertime. A lot of people who are sickly ought to go south like the birds do. If we're using natural remedies, natural foods, and so forth, let us use all the natural means we can to hasten our getting well.

Summer sunshine stimulates vitamin D needed to fix the calcium required by the body during the coming winter. It should be a recreative time in which we build up the body to carry on our life's activities.

Calcium is the healer, the knitter in the body. All sores require calcium to bring healing; therefore, get those "greens" into your food program.

In the summer, more greens are available. This is the time to eat greens because next winter you are going to need them.

We must be careful about exposure to the sun during the summer. The rays of the sun are very powerful in the summertime. Skin cancer is on the rise since the ozone layer in the atmosphere was damaged. If you work in the hot sunshine, protect your head with some type of covering. Wear a sweatband inside your hat. To maintain a good temperature, your bloodstream must be kept more fluid by increasing your intake of water in the summer to at least three quarts daily.

Sodium is a wonderful summer cooling element. Powdered whey is the most important food for the summer. It is highest in sodium. Sodium is eliminated through perspiration, which has a salty taste. We need to replace the salt thus eliminated, especially if one perspires freely. We can use okra and celery, which are high in sodium. Celery juice combined with pineapple juice is splendid. Juice of comfrey leaves may be added, using one-third of each with a little whey powder. Combining comfrey and strawberries is also very good.

Strawberries are high in sodium. Eating strawberries ripe does not cause hives. If you have berries that are not fully ripened, put them in a sieve under hot water. This will remove the fuzz on their skin. Rinse immediately with cold water. This should prevent any occurrence of hives. Try to get ripe berries. In fact, get all fruit as ripe as possible. Our choice of foods in the summer should be those that are the most easily digested and low in carbohydrates. Maintain a low starch and sugar intake during the summer months. The natural sugars of fully ripened fruits are most easily handled in digestion. Drink plenty of juices. If you are on a high intake of juices and you are losing too much weight, add a tablespoon of nut butter or sunflower seed meal (from freshly ground seeds if you use a liquefier).

Air baths are just as important as sunbaths. In privacy, practice this vital air bathing as much as possible. Men can wear shorts and women can wear shorts with a suitable top. This may be enjoyed indoors with benefit if you have adequate ventilation.

Today many people have thyroid disturbances. This results from an overbalance of those things that affect the mental side of life. To balance this, get out in the air. Get a lot of fresh air upon the skin. Wear as little clothing as suitable for the occasion. This will help the nerves more than anything else. Mental and nerve depletion may be overcome by air- and sunbathing.

Iced drinks are one of the worst things we can use in the summertime (or anytime). They cause the villi (the tiny fibers lining the walls of the intestines) to contract, thus impairing one's digestion. Ice cream can be good if it is made from nutritious ingredients, preferably in your own kitchen. But don't mix it with other foods, and eat it slowly, allowing each spoonful to melt in the mouth. The coldness of ice cream contracts the stomach wall so that we don't secrete the hydrochloric acid needed for digestion.

For cooling the blood in the summertime, use cucumbers, lettuce, celery, parsley, tomatoes, and a low-calorie diet.

ENVIRONMENT AND BODY HEAT

We need to be aware of our body heat and careful that it is at the right level. People whose internal heat is low have very sluggish skin. This is why purification of the system falls so heavily upon the liver, lungs, and kidneys. These organs become overworked and result in disease. Some 7 to 8 percent of body heat is lost through the evaporation process performed by the lungs.

Muscles are the great oxidizers and heat producers in the body. When the cerebellum is weak, we suffer from cold feet, cold hands, chilly sensations, colds, catarrh, and perhaps pneumonia.

It is good that the heat generated in the body is dissipated easily. More than 70 percent of body heat is lost through the skin. If we did not radiate this heat continually, internal chemical reactions requiring a very narrow temperature "window" around 98.6 degrees Fahrenheit would not be able to take place. Excess body heat is lost through radiation, evaporation of perspiration, elimination of urine, and convection. We find that this takes place better at certain altitudes.

WHICH CLIMATE?

A cold, bracing climate and high altitude (that is, from 2,000 to 6,000 feet) tone our functions, increase appetites, build new red blood corpuscles, and promote oxidation in the tissues and blood. However, in high altitudes our hearts must be sound.

Weak people, old people, lazy people, and paralyzed people thrive in a warm climate; but healthy people, people of high production, muscular people, and great workers are comfortable in a cool climate. Cold increases energy, but heat decreases it. Some people are subject to infectious diseases in hot climates. Breathing is decreased in hot weather, and the removal of carbon dioxide is more difficult. People in hot climates are less energetic and more sociable. People in cold climates are greater fighters and less sociable. Cold winters lead to muscular action. Hot weather favors indolence. Moderate exercise of muscles and nerves and a breezy climate favor the muscular and nervous systems.

Normal cold increases the elasticity of arteries and the heart, but heat decreases these. People in a cold climate have a slower pulse and higher blood pressure. People in the tropics have a higher pulse and a lower blood pressure. Small people have a quicker pulse than larger people. The skin pores are always active in hot climates, but they are sluggish in cold climates. Perspiration carries off heat and moisture through the skin in a hot climate.

Some people can withstand more heat than others. Dark-skinned people can endure it better than light-skinned people because they have more melanin in their skin.

Temperatures affect the sex functions. Warmth develops sexuality, unless heat is excessive. Heat increases the generative function. There is more sexual excess in hot climates than in cold climates. The menstrual function begins earlier in a hot climate. Child-bearing is attended with greater difficulty in a hot climate because of a tendency to hemorrhage. Warmth develops the sexual system and increases sexual power. Heating foods, on the same principle, also develop sexuality. Wind is bad for the sexual system and for people who suffer from sexual weaknesses.

Excessive heat destroys tissue, as does excessive cold. Great heat can result in sunstroke. Sunstroke kills; excessive cold also kills. If the cold is excessive, all vital processes suffer, and unfavorable results follow. Cold, as you know, constricts the surface blood vessels beneath the skin, lowers skin activity, and affects the capillary function of the circulation, resulting in inadequate skin nourishment. Then the skin is robbed of its fatty principle, sebum; it cracks, and chilblains form. Wounds fail to heal because of lowered vitality and faulty circulation. Such an excessive cold climate is too severe for our well-being. Regenerative functions suffer in a very cold and windy climate. Male reproductive capabilities are seldom at their best. Female processes act under lower pressure, giving rise to menstrual difficulties and female ailments.

Extremes Are Dangerous

Going to extremes in climate is always dangerous. It is not wise for anyone to change climate and stay there for good. A man who goes from a hot climate to a cold climate and lives there the rest of his life may be healthy, but his offspring may suffer and die early. This holds good also for one who goes from a cold to a hot climate. A climate can be a tonic to one man, depressive to another, and even death to a third.

There are many books written on climate, but I think one of the best is the one written by Clarence A. Mills, M.D., *Climate Makes the Man*. He answers a great many of our questions about what climate does to us. Dr. Mills is one of the leading men in the field of experimental medicine and has studied climate for many years. He demonstrates that climate plays a dominating and startling role in all that we do. He shows that it affects our growth, speed of development, resistance to infection, fertility of mind and body, happiness, and length of life. He also shows that it lulls the people of the tropics into passive complacency and drives those of the temperate zone into restless activity. According to Dr. Mills, sexual development is actually retarded by extremes of heat and cold. He has experimented with many rats and mice and other animals and has concluded that caffeine, alcohol, and nicotine have differing effects under different climatic conditions. He shows that hardening of the arteries, tuberculosis, sinusitis, and many other ills are related to man-made weather, air conditioning, and so on. He believes that different diseases are related to various types of weather.

CHAPTER 3

HOW CAN WE LIVE A LONG LIFE?

The first forty years of life give us the text; the next thirty supply the commentary.

—ARTHUR SCHOPENHAUER

A prominent San Jose pioneer was celebrating his eightieth birthday and also his fiftieth wedding anniversary. The reporters gathered around him to express congratulations. Then they asked, "What do you attribute this long span of successful living to?" He reflected for a moment and replied, "When I got married, my wife and I had an agreement that anytime we saw an argument coming on, I would grab my hat and walk four times around the block. You'd be surprised what fifty years of outdoor exercise will do for your health."

That's not the only method of having a long life. Dr. Frank Gallup polled 29,000 Americans who were ninety-four years old and older and concluded that the way to have a long life is to: 1) be a woman, 2) be born in Norway; 3) be of long-lived ancestors; 4) not worry; 5) not smoke; 6) eat wisely and lightly; 7) have enthusiasm; and 8) have a strong religious belief. Sounds good—but what if you aren't Norwegian?

YOUTH

The secret of a long life can be learned. But all is not always just as it seems. The paradox is that in regions of the world where sanitary conditions are often primitive, many persons reach a span of life beyond one hundred years. How can they do that? A major reason is that their lifestyle makes them healthy, and a healthy body is immune to infections; harmful microbes are scavengers existing only in putrefying matter.

If a child is introduced to a natural diet after weaning, his intestinal flora closely resembles that of the milk diet. Fresh, uncooked, organically grown food provides the ideal nourishment. Cooking reduces food's ability to give us resistance. Raw foods harden the gums; chewing stimulates digestion. Raw foods are often the only ones supplying the vital enzymes that protect us.

WE POISON OURSELVES

Anyone who lives on an unnatural diet of artificially grown and processed foods, who overeats meat and carbohydrates to the exclusion of fresh fruits and vegetables, who fills his mind with negative thoughts and overworks at the expense of adequate rest, who floods his body with acids (the home of pathogenic bacteria) is bringing trouble to paradise. His bowels become a sewer from which poisons seep into the blood and are carried to all parts of the body. No wonder so many people try to regain health by taking strong purgatives! But they are no cure. Prevention is the wisest medicine. And prevention means finding a natural way to live, the way we *by our natures* should live. When we do, nature will reward us with a healthy, active body—a long living body. One means of finding the natural healthy lifestyle is to study peoples around the world. Is a particular people healthy? Why—or why not?

LEARNING FROM OTHER COUNTRIES

I have made many travels in my sixty years of practice, and I have gleaned something from each country that I believe will help you in your "health search," to put your health on a higher level.

Armenia

The people here are most gracious, receive you royally, and make you feel at home. This is a necessary characteristic for good human relationships. A good idea I saw here was to fold rice in grape leaves and steam them. One elderly lady, 127 years of age, told us that rose hip tea kept her well.

Bulgaria

Bulgaria has traditionally had more people over one hundred years of age, per capita, than any other country in the world. They claim the reason is that they use a fair amount of a clabbered milk that contains the *Bulgaricus acidophilus* bacteria. Everybody with any bowel trouble should take a course in acidophilus culture for at least one month, three times yearly.

China

There has been considerable talk about ginseng, gotu-kola, and fo-ti-tieng. These three herbs have been used in China for many centuries and are purported to promote longevity. For instance, Taoist master Li Ching Yuen in Szechuan Province lived to the age of 252, according to the *New York Times* of May 6, 1933. It is reported he gave some twenty-eight lectures at the University of Sinkiang when he was over 200 years old. It is claimed that the three herbs of ginseng, gotu-kola, and fo-ti-tieng were used in his daily diet. He was known to be a master herbalist and teacher of Tao yin, internal health practices. Before he died he was asked to what he attributed his long life. He left a sermon for us when he said, "I attribute my long life to *inward calm*."

Colombia, Heleconia

The average life expectancy here in the 1950s was thirty years due to a lack of protein in the diet. But when industry moved into the area and introduced soy milk powder into the local diet, life expectancy increased dramatically. I believe soy milk powder is a great protein and a great food.

Denmark

Here they have a wonderful broth that increases the calcium content of the body and helps growing children in proper bone development. It is made from barley and green kale.

Ecuador

This country taught me that gravity affects our health. Gravity hinders blood flow to the brain, which controls the rest of the body. Here I found a man over 130 years of age, and there were many other very old people here in Ecuador. You have to have good health to resist the pull of gravity. The poorer the health, the more effect gravity has on one, interfering with proper circulation in the body.

Egypt

The greatest energy-giving food is the date. I found dates and milk to be an ideal combination for people suffering with stomach trouble.

Finland

The great lesson here was the value of using rye to build muscle, versus wheat, which builds fat. Since 1906, the first year they competed in the Olympics, Finnish athletes have won 19 gold medals in track events; more winners than any other nation. Four more gold medals were won in Nordic skiing relays, showing the high endurance of Finnish athletes.

France

I think the most wonderful thing to come out of France was their Roquefort brand cheese. This is a cheese that crumbles, originally made from sheep milk and goat milk. It is a great calcium builder in the body. Always use cheese that breaks and is aged.

Germany

In a sanitarium here, they were using sauerkraut and tomato juice as a slight laxative. This was taken daily by people who were constipated, as part of an elimination diet program. In Worishofen, we saw the great Kneipp baths (water treatment). The same circulation you have in your legs, you have in your head. To improve the circulation in your head, take care of the legs and feet. Use the Kneipp leg bath at home as follows: Go out into the yard and run cold water from a hose up the back of the right leg, from the toes to the groin and down again. Repeat the same motions on the left leg. Then walk on grass or in the sand until dry. Do this once a day.

Hawaii

All fruits grown in Hawaii are high in iodine because they grow close to the ocean. The people who had the best teeth chewed the natural sugar cane. Hawaii's greatest contribution is fruit and fish.

Hunzaland

One of the greatest secrets of Hunzaland (an area west of Tibet) is the apricot pit. After breaking open the apricot seeds, the Hunzas string the pits and eat them whenever they wish. They are rich in protein and taste almost like an almond. To make an apricot drink, squeeze the dried apricots in water with your hands until they are completely dissolved. This is a splendid fruit drink. Apricots and apricot pits give one a good carbohydrate and protein combination. The Hunzaland people stuff apricots with apricot pits and eat them during the winter. They make an apricot and apricot pit soup that is very tasty and provides them with a lot of the energy they need for the heavy work they do. The oldest man we met in Hunza was 120 years of age and still working.

India

Sri Aurobindo Ashram is the greatest Universal Center I ever visited; there, a balance of the physical, mental, and spiritual are taught. The integration of all three was deemed most important. Sai Baba was one of the greatest teachers my group ever met. His teachings and philosophy lift everyone. He said, "Money may bring comfort, but it cannot bring you contentment; however, your spiritual attitude can bring you contentment."

Iran

Here they have a variety of soils, both good and bad, and they also have longevity. I believe the chemistry of our body depends on the chemical balance of the soil and the foods we eat. Elderly people here live where the soil is black. Try to eat foods from black soil, free of fertilizer or pesticide.

Italy

Sun-dried olives from Italy are the highest potassium containing foods. Olives are cured in sea salt in Turkey and in Italy. The heart needs the potassium. A potassium broth can be made from ten sun-dried olives steeped in two cups of hot water for ten minutes. Strain and drink the liquid. Another excellent heart tonic is honey and water. Mix one teaspoon honey into a glass of water two or three times daily. A wonderful potassium broth is made from potato peelings. We use it for extreme acids in the body and for rheumatism and arthritis. It is made this way: cut peelings of six potatoes, ½ inch thick, simmer twenty minutes in water in a covered pan. Strain off liquid and drink every two or three hours. Do not make too strong in a convalescing diet.

Celery may be added for flavor. Add powdered okra if the stomach is irritated.

Japan

A wonderful soup, high in iodine, can be made with many varieties of seaweed. In Japan, they make many things from seaweed—soups, candy, and salads. There are over five hundred varieties of seaweed that can be used.

Mexico

The word *siesta* would help to make famous men even more famous by helping them live longer. Regular relaxation is a key to a longer, healthier life. To crowd too much into one day will kill anybody. Do what you can today, but don't do tomorrow's work, too. Don't try to get a quart out of a pint bottle.

New Zealand

In New Zealand, they all have a weekend holiday for rest and recuperation and for happy hours. Arthur Lydiard, the great Olympic champion (and later Olympic coach) from New Zealand, takes people jogging through the country. Jogging began there. Jogging is a great sport to keep one in fit condition. Every school in New Zealand has a swimming pool. Swimming is another of the finest of all exercises.

Norway

Beauty is brought out in Norway so much because of its past culture. There is beauty surrounding everything—the fjords, the mountains, the green pastures, the people—and the feeling is wonderful, which helps beauty to act as a healing factor.

Peru

In the Peruvian Andes, I learned that altitude helps to create a better blood count. This is where squash originated. Squash is one of the greatest of all foods. Winter squash is excellent for intestinal disturbances.

Philippines

Soak coconut pieces in honey in a jar for one week. It makes a wonderful sweet for the children.

Russia

We met many of the oldest people in the world here. The last man we met was 153 years of age, a Mr. Gasanov. The secret of these men living to great age is the altitude, climate, a simple life, and plenty of protein. The protein they use most is clabbered milk. It is a wonderful food—a complete protein and a whole food that is easy to digest. Put a little concentrated apple juice in clabbered milk and use daily in your diet. How to make clabbered milk: Heat two quarts raw milk to lukewarm. Stir in one cup yogurt or buttermilk. Set in oven with only the pilot light on or set to lowest temperature. Leave overnight. Remove from oven, leave in the same pan, and place in refrigerator to thicken. If you use a starter from a health food store, follow the directions included with the starter.

South Seas

Coconut milk is a perfect protein and should be used more in the diet. Dried papaya seeds make a wonderful tea that helps in digestion.

Spain

In Barcelona, we were entertained by the mayor, who served a delightful almond milk drink. This gave me the idea of making milk out of seeds and nuts. I have developed what I call "my drink." It is a complete vitality-giving protein drink. It is non-catarrhal forming and a delightful body-builder for vegetarians. My drink: Take one tablespoon of any good brand of sesame seed meal or butter, one glass of liquid (may be raw milk, fruit juice, vegetable juice, soy milk, rice milk, broth, or water), one-quarter avocado, and one teaspoon honey (or add honey to taste), and blend thirty seconds.

Sweden

The great thing here is gymnastics. Outdoor exercise and massage are both necessary to keep people balanced. Everyone here is very health conscious. In many places, groups go for a weekend of swimming or to the mountains to ski. They have lithe, athletic bodies and are in good condition due to their participation in athletics. Swedish sports doctors recommend cod liver oil for their athletic clients.

Switzerland

The greatest food here is yogurt. This is good protein food that builds friendly bacteria in the bowel. Yogurt with fruit makes a good combination. One of the finest things they did in Switzerland during World War II was to establish a place in the country where each person could grow his own foods. Everyone should grow some foods for himself. The Swiss grow their herbs in window boxes. These are used for flavoring salads, soups, and various other foods used in their daily meals. You could grow your own parsley, chives, rosemary, anise, and so on. Everyone should grow comfrey and dry it for a winter tea. Whatever herbs are not used fresh can be dried for winter use.

Tahiti

Relaxation and absorbing the sun was the highlight in Tahiti. They were healthier without clothes. I believe that wearing clothes is the beginning of every disease. Those who wear clothes must get acquainted with skin brushing to keep the skin clean and healthy. You make new skin every twenty-four hours, and the skin is only as clean as the blood is. No soap can wash the skin as clean as the new skin is, so use a skin brush to remove the top layer of old skin. This helps to eliminate uric acid crystals, catarrh, and various other acids in the body. The skin should eliminate two pounds of waste acids daily. Keep the skin active. Use a dry vegetable bristle brush with a long handle. (Do not use a nylon brush.) Use the brush dry, in the morning before dressing and before bathing. Use over the whole body for about three minutes.

Turkey

In Turkey, they use sesame seed mixed with a concentrated grape juice as a candy. Use sesame seed butter in one-half glass of grape juice as a tonic. Use sesame seed daily for building a strong body. They have men of great strength in Turkey. A man seventy-five years of age was head of Turkey's wrestling team.

POLLEN AND SPECIAL HERBS

Much is to be said about bee pollen helping glands in the body. Many experiments on animals show it prolongs life and helps to keep the glands in good order.

Ginseng, gotu-kola, fo-ti-tieng, and damiana have been considered long life herbs, as is the commonly known sage.

INVIGORATING LIFE TONIC

In the pericarp, or outer hull, of barley, we find a principle that is very invigorating to the functions of life. The same is true of the pericarp of oats.

When that pericarp essence can be extracted and mixed with the fresh raw juices from celery, parsley, thyme, beets, and spinach, it becomes a remarkable restorative in time of lassitude and fatigue.

Soaking barley—or better still, barley bran—in cold water to prevent fermentation until the oily substances come to the top allows us to extract some of this barley pericarp essence. A cupful of the juices mentioned and one-third cup of the barley skimming, but not the scum, gives you this pericarp essence called *avenin*. Parsley and celery contain *apeol*; beets contain *betaine*. Such food essences are a tonic and sanative for the weak and aged.

SMALL MEALS FAVOR OLD AGE

Small meals favor old age because of a weaker digestion, sluggish bowel action, low nerve force, and reduced secretion of the digestive juices.

Use clabbered milk as you get older rather than whole milk. Older people should never, under any circumstances, eat until they are hungry. Eat slowly and masticate foods well. Seek fresh air and breathe it deeply. Elderly people should sit and tempt their appetite at meals for some five to ten minutes before they eat in order to secrete gastric juices in abundance for good digestion.

As we get older, we must have the food salts to carry out the functions of life. These are found mainly in goat brown cheese, in berries, and in greens. We should eat some of these foods each day.

In old age, digestion and elimination (especially elimination) need constant attention.

Uric acidity, which causes neuritis, rheumatism, and arthritis, is best treated by dry, intense, local heat applied with electric heating pad or hot water bottle.

AVOID PRONOUNCED CHANGES

Vacations can favor our health if we go to the right altitude and right climate and have the proper comforts. Pronounced changes do not favor old age. As soon as our feet or knees or head, or any part of our bodies become cold or damp, we should do something to regain the normal heat equilibrium. Even if we have to change footwear, bedclothes, underwear, or gloves, we cannot afford to chill any part of our body, or become damp as we advance in years. We should dress so that we are comfortably warm and dry at all times. We should not stay long in sultry heat, severe cold, or strong winds.

SPEND TIME OUTDOORS

Outdoor life among trees, shrubbery, and flowers, life in the fresh air and sunshine favor health in both young and old. As we get older we should spend at least six hours outdoors each day. If it is possible, go on horseback rides. This is vibratory and promotes circulation, elimination, respiration, oxidation, tissue metabolism, and nerve generation. Sleep in abundance. If you are restless, use abdominal applications, take a Swedish massage, and eat a combination salad with your evening meal.

Take pleasurable walks each day after each meal to promote the vital functions. Do not sit in a rocking chair after meals. Don't work hard after meals, and don't use the brain energetically after meals. Find a genial climate that is neither humid, arid, nor windy, and which is not too sunny. Avoid glaring sunlight: It can be trying on the optic nerves. The Swedish massage from a trained masseur has a wonderful effect on the tissues and function of all people, whether young or old.

It is especially important to know and live in the climate that is good for you. There you can feel pleasant and relaxed.

STAYING HEALTHY AFTER FORTY

Men and women over forty should realize that they now have the opportunity to start enjoying the special richness of a full life that only time can bring.

There are many interesting hobbies and rewarding occupations. One of the best is gardening. (If the joints become the least bit stiff and hard, use lots of sodium and drink potassium broths.) Never retire from work—find something interesting to do, then never lose that interest. Tissues will become flabby if you do, and circulation will decrease. Use iodine in the diet— one to three Nova Scotia dulse tablets daily. The dulse tablets not only help flabby tissues but also will help weight conditions. Cut down on starch and add a little more protein. Go to a temperate climate, usually at an altitude of 2,000 to 3,000 feet.

For men, if prostate gland trouble develops, if you have difficulty urinating, or if you have to get up several times in the night, consider hot and cold sitz baths. They are very good for these conditions.

Use a slant board for any prolapses of abdominal organs, if no high blood pressure exists. Consider getting a vibrating bed for internal circulation. Add vitamin E—taking 400 IU (international units) to 1,200 IU capsules daily or as recommended by your doctor.

Walking (in clean air) is one of the best exercises for people over forty. Spend much time in the open air, partake of natural foods, and avoid work in the city. Papaya and mint tea will help the secretions of the stomach to digest proteins. Avoid extreme changes in temperatures; don't become "chilled to the bone." Use distilled water when the joints become hard.

A good tonic is to use lecithin and lots of vegetable broths in the diet. Fresh goat's milk adds to the youth of the body. Drink black cherry juice along with bitter pungent salads. Eat dark cherries and strawberries. When you need fats in the diet, raw sweet cream and avocado should be used as a source of fat. Try a celery juice cocktail with wheat germ in it. Have warm drinks. Eat gruels made from barley and wheat. Plan light meals for morning and at night. Take one egg yolk in black cherry or Concord grape juice daily.

Strive for a simple life with freedom from economic pressure.

HEALTH VACATIONS

Sometimes we need to take a vacation to improve or to restore our health. Seek a health vacation that rests the mind and the body. It must be a total change from the type of work you are getting away from. Seek a complete change in climate. Eat the right foods. Sometimes elimination foods are desirable.

During the vacation, you should be surrounded by people who are easy to get along with; the vacation environment should be enjoyable. Spend your health vacation with people who are happy and companionable.

This vacation should be one that allows for recuperation to prepare the mind and body for the job that's waiting for you when you return.

HOW TO AVOID UNNECESSARY SURGERY

To help consumers combat a wave of unnecessary surgery, Herbert Denenberg, Pennsylvania Insurance Commissioner, prepared "A Shopper's Guide to Surgery: Fourteen Rules on How To Avoid Unnecessary Surgery" in *National Health Federation Bulletin*. Denenberg's "rules," in checklist form, follow:

1. Don't go directly to a surgeon for medical treatment; go to your regular family doctor, a general practitioner, or internist for any initial diagnosis.
2. Make sure any surgeon who is to perform surgery on you is Board Certified. This means his competence as a surgeon has been certified by one of the American Specialty Boards after vigorous oral, written, and clinical examinations.
3. Make sure the surgeon you are to engage is a fellow of the American College of Surgeons.
4. Even if your family doctor and surgeon agree that surgery is necessary, consider getting an independent consultation.
5. Make sure any surgery is performed in an accredited hospital and, if possible, select a hospital that gives staff privileges (i.e., the right to practice in the hospital) to both your doctor and surgeon.

6. Don't push a doctor to perform surgery on you. If you insist on surgery, even if it is unnecessary, you are likely to find a surgeon willing to perform it.

7. Make sure your doctor and surgeon explain both the alternatives to surgery and possible benefits and complications of surgery.

8. Frankly discuss the fee for surgery with your doctor.

9. Check out the surgeon with those who know him or have used him. This includes other patients as well as associates.

10. Make sure the surgeon knows and is willing to work with your general practitioner or internist. If they can't work as a team, you may be the loser.

11. Consider a surgeon who is a part of a group practice and preferably a group that includes internists, surgeons, and other specialists. With a group practice, you are more likely to have a doctor available at all times who is familiar with your case and you have the built-in benefits of consultation.

12. Select a surgeon who is not too busy to give patients enough time and attention.

13. Be especially on guard if some of the operations that are most often unnecessarily performed are proposed for you. These include hysterectomies, hemorrhoidectomies, and tonsillectomies.

14. The patient, not the doctor or surgeon, is supposed to, and is entitled to, make the decision on whether to have surgery. Listen to the experts. But it's still your decision.

CHAPTER 4

WE ARE IN A NEW AGE

T his is the age of the atomic and hydrogen
   bomb, and of strontium 90, through which
tremendously powerful forces have been released. We are coming into a new day of culture. We have an entirely different outlook on life.

In his social behavior, man is just a child. We throw rocks at
each other, just as childish pranksters do. It has been said that
never has a wise old man been known to declare war. The wise
avoid fighting. But the human race has not learned to solve its
problems peaceably. So far, man has gotten away without
destroying himself. But I think it is necessary for us to consider
the principles of survival.

I am interested in the nutritional side of survival more than
the political or financial. However, the nutritional side also
embodies the religious side. Just what is going to survive? Our
businesses, our homes, our money? What do we want to save?
What is really most important? I am sure that if people really
thought about survival and what it means, they would be more

interested in nutrition than ever before. Nutrition and health are the survival principles; even a rich or powerful man may not survive certain adverse conditions if he is not healthy. Survival means keeping the best body—one that will overcome disease and rejuvenate and repair properly. This is the thing man has neglected. It is only those who have lost their health who are seeking and crying for the vital life they had. It is the survival principle they are looking for. We have been pranksters, and it is time we woke up, all of us!

Anything that does not nourish the body is taking away from the survival principle. A stomach full of nutritionless food has nothing to do with survival. It just means temporary existence. That person who doesn't realize the laws of nutrition is ignorant of the survival principle. Unpolluted air, unpolluted water, sunshine, good food—these make up survival. We have to get closer to these things. But we have to do it correctly. If we eat too little, we starve; if we eat too much, we kill ourselves. We have to have a certain amount of bulk, vegetables, fruit, proteins, and starches every day; we need variety in good proportion.

We need to learn how to prolong life, how to get strength and energy, how to get vitality. If there is one way better than another, it is the way of nature. We will all have to go back to nature, to "the beginning," eventually. Man's inventions provide a lot of comfort, internally and externally, but too often they also work negatively. When man turns a food that could be nourishing to the body into one that is disease-forming, lacking in vital materials that are needed to build a good body, he has gone too far.

Because of what we too often do to our food, thinking is very necessary to survival. To go to a popular supermarket and buy indiscriminately may not even be safe! Though foods may be made of the best ingredients, they could be improperly prepared and could hinder the body in its attempts to repair, rebuild, or regain health once it has been lost. You have to be careful in what you buy. The survival principle demands that we *think*.

This way of looking at survival requires a change in consciousness. We need to look at things in a new way. A short time ago, a newspaper reporter going through India noticed that the women had a lot of back trouble because of curves in their upper spines. He made the suggestion that they use longer-handled brooms so they would not have to bend over. Many did so, with the expected results.

We need to make similar changes in our way of thinking if we hope to survive. But many of us refuse to do so. Our thinking has deteriorated; we are not thinking about what is best for our own bodies, we are looking for bargains.

When you go camping, what do you take along with you? Frankfurters? Marshmallows? When you stop and think about the bread we buy, puffed up, white spongy stuff, do you imagine that is good bread? Is that the bread that is the "staff of life"? No! We've traded survival for a bargain. And that bargain destroys rather than builds our health. And if you lose your good health, you are going to lose your family and your job and be no good to yourself or your spouse. It all comes back to principle in foods. Health isn't everything, but without health, nothing else counts.

It is still a matter of the survival of the fittest. Who is the "fittest"? The one with big muscles, the massive fellow who lives on hot cakes and prepared cereals? Or is it the man who is wise enough to do the right thing? The "fittest" is the man who knows the right thing to be done and does it. He is fit in every way: moral, mental, spiritual—*and* physical.

We need to develop ourselves in all these areas. I think we have to be much more conscious of what we are doing or we will be lost. Most of us are on a "sentimental journey." We are not using our intelligence to have the best life possible. We are having "too little, too late." Ultimately, the only thing that counts is the growth of our souls and our minds. A good life lived should be long enough. A long life lived is not necessarily good enough. Life must be earned from the inside rather than the outside. We are told that we die for a lack of knowledge, that without vision we perish. I even saw a sign outside a church offering candy to children to attend Sunday school. Do we have to be bribed to do the finer things in life? Do we have to be frightened into wisdom? How long will it be before we recognize what has to be done?

FOODS FOR SURVIVAL AND HEALTH

Some people have become very interested in putting food away. What should we put away and how much? Suppose you had to store food supplies for two years, how would you do it? The storage place must be dry and cool. The food may be stored in airtight vessels where it cannot oxidize or spoil. Concentrated foods are best. We might put away ten loaves of bread, but in the same space we could store enough wheat to bake fifty loaves of bread. This wheat must be "alive" for our survival, not milled. You cannot afford to have any other kind of wheat. Other good grains are oats, millet, brown rice, yellow cornmeal, and some legumes—lentils or garbanzos. The importance of concentrated foods is one of the first principles we need to recognize.

Though we need to think first of an immediate food supply, we also need to prepare for our future food. Nature gives us a 300 percent return on whatever seed we choose to plant. We should therefore think of seeds to grow a garden. Have a variety of some fifteen vegetable seeds—beet, carrot, green kale, and lettuce, for instance.

For immediate food, we can store perishable vegetables in a dehydrated form. Celery and okra powders are available. Green kale is one of the vegetable foods high in calcium, which is especially needed when we are under strain and stress. One who anticipates extreme stresses should also consider putting away a definite amount of rice polishings, which are very high in vitamin B, one of the stress vitamins.

We should use vegetable broth powder for seasoning, as this will supply the salt we should have. Some people want to have real salt. If so, they should use sea salt, taken from evaporation ponds near the sea. We should never eat anything that has been exposed to extreme heat. This is another survival principle.

Then we have to have a certain amount of sweets on hand. Honey is a concentrated sweet; also, pure maple sugar can be put away and used very well. Date sugar is fine. Dates are one of the highest foods in sugar content. Dried fruit must be sealed airtight.

Have on hand powdered whole milk, soy milk powder, dandelion root coffee, herb teas, and sunflower and sesame seeds left in their hulls to prevent deterioration. Alfalfa seeds are excellent—be sure you know how to sprout them. Keep nuts in the shell. It might be well to have a few liquid concentrates of both vegetable and fruit juices; also have concentrated fruit powder that can be stored well.

Make sure the foods you store are nourishing. Remember to consider the protein and starch content. Vegetables may be in sprouts; and fruits can be dried. This will give you the proper variety. We should also have herbs. Different herbs take care of various parts of the body. Consider herbs for the kidneys, digestive system, and muscular system. We should have a variety of herb extracts to take care of all parts of the body in case of stress. Some food supplements, such as vitamins A and C, and especially vitamin B-complex, are needed. It might be well to have a green vegetable powder, such as blue-green algae, chlorella, or spirulina. Have a good source of bulk, such as powdered psyllium or flaxseed, which is high in vitamin E and can be used for any skin disturbances. Flaxseed may be boiled for making tea. For any kinds of burns, consider peanut oil. Peanut oil also is high in vitamin E and is good for the outside of the body.

Another thing to consider is water. It should be distilled water. In case of emergencies, use what liquids you have stored until you're able to establish a good water supply. If you plan to dig a well, obtain a purification unit that will treat the water to make it fresh and remove any contamination.

Finally, be sure you have a meal plan for thirty days, with directions and recipes for using all the food you've stored. Also have details on how many persons a can or container will feed (a given weight will feed a given number of people for a certain number of days). Have matches, a few extra resealable plastic bags for storage, a first aid kit, and soap.

NUCLEAR RADIATION PROBLEMS

Although threat of nuclear war between the Eastern Europe and the West is now minimal, the use of nuclear weapons by terrorists cannot be discounted.

If a disaster occurs that forces us to use our food supply, it might well bring with it the problem of radiation exposure. It may be wise, therefore, to have foods that give the body the greatest resistance and rebuild it most effectively. Bone marrow has been used with animals that were exposed to atomic radiation, and it proved to be one of the greatest foods for preventing malignancies. Iodine tablets could protect the thyroid from radioactive iodine. Chlorophyll rich foods would be valuable, including alfalfa tablets and the algae previously mentioned. Blue violet tea has great powers for ridding the body of toxic materials. I stress detoxifying foods, realizing that at the moment of any critical action you want the very best that is available. It is possible that if you don't have them, you may not survive.

We should be applying the survival principle to our *everyday* living and eating. If you are sick, you are not surviving well. The U.S. government tells us that a high percentage of the American people are sick now. Illness is all too often the result of not using good nutritional principles.

INVENTORY OF SUPPLIES FOR EMERGENCY STORAGE

Following is a summary of foods to be stored in preparation for emergencies. For protection against radiation, supplies can be stored in steel boxes, completely airtight and waterproof, and buried ten feet below the surface of the ground.

1. Water, preferably distilled.
2. Seeds for planting. Include a variety of vegetable seeds, including those of shortest growth periods; grains (for those who may have use of land); herbs; nuts; fruit stones (begin to save a variety of these from ripe fruits—from year to year—it could be the means of starting trees bearing fruits and nuts); and seeds of different varieties of melons and squashes.

3. Seeds for food. May be ground or liquefied. Include sun-flower (with some unhulled to avoid deterioration in case of oxidation), sesame, flaxseed, pumpkin, and peptoria (a variety of squash).

4. Seeds for sprouting. Especially alfalfa seed. In the absence of fresh vegetables, sprouts are our best source of the vita-mins and chlorophyll, which are essential to life. (Store the items of equipment that you would expect to use for sprouting. Also, have complete instructions for sprouting).

5. Whole grains. Whole grains can be stored indefinitely with-out spoiling. Good grains are wheat, oats, millet, corn, brown rice, barley, and rye. If possible, store a mill for grinding—a hand mill could be used in the absence of electric power (some mills work both electrically and by hand); also have thermos bottles for use in preparation of cooked grains, either whole or ground.

6. Nuts. Unshelled—almonds or other varieties.

7. Legumes. Lentils, garbanzos, beans of all kinds, peas—these may be used in sprouted form, especially for persons who can't digest the dry kind.

8. Root vegetables. May be kept for some time if properly buried in the earth (supply should be renewed periodically if these are to be available for emergency use).

9. Dehydrated vegetables.

10. Vegetable broth powder. Very essential in case of scarcity of fresh vegetables.

11. Dried herbs. For nutritional and medicinal needs, especially to take care of the vital organs of the body, the kidneys, the digestive system, and the muscular system, in particular.

12. Dried fruits. Every possible variety. Store in airtight containers.

13. Extracts. Vegetable and fruit juice concentrates (these are especially valuable and practical for storing).

14. Supplements. Minerals and vitamins, especially vitamins A, B, C, and E.

15. Intestinal lubricants. Especially flaxseed (high in vitamin E; beneficial in cases of skin disturbances). May be ground, or use whole seed in tea.

16. Oil. Peanut oil (one of the foods highest in vitamin E, it may be used on the outside of the body).

17. Rice polishings. These are high in B-complex vitamins, particularly beneficial under stress conditions.

18. Antiradiation foods. Bone marrow, blue violet tea (good for ridding the body of toxic material), and green algae.

19. Powdered whole and skim milk and soy powder.

20. Sweets. Honey (a concentrated sweet), dates, and pure maple sugar.

21. Salt (if desired). Use earth salt, which has not been subjected to any heat process.

FIND A PHILOSOPHY

One thing that helps in survival is to have something larger than yourself to look to. The source of my strength is belief in a Supreme Being. I believe He gives us our all and will help us in times of trouble—emotionally and spiritually, at least, if not physically.

The eighth chapter of Deuteronomy in the Bible in some ways summarizes this belief:

> All the commandments which I command you this day you shall be careful to do, that you may live and multiply, and go in and possess the land which the Lord swore to give to your fathers.

And you shall remember all the ways which the Lord your God has led you these forty years in the wilderness, that He might humble you, testing you to know what was in your heart, whether you would keep His commandments or not.

And He humbled you and let you hunger and fed you with manna, which you did not know, nor did your fathers know; that He might make you know that man does not live by bread alone, but that man lives by everything that proceeds out of the mouth of the Lord.

Your clothing did not wear out upon you, and your feet did not swell these forty years.

Knowing then, in your heart that, as a man disciplines his son, the Lord, your God, disciplines you.

So you shall keep the commandments of the Lord, your God, by walking in His ways and by fearing him.

For the Lord, your God, is bringing you into a good land, a land of brooks of water, of fountains and springs, flowing forth in valleys and hills.

A land of wheat and barley, of vines and fig trees and pomegranates, a land of olive trees and honey.

A land in which you will eat bread without scarcity, in which you will lack nothing, a land whose stones are iron, and out of whose hills you can dig copper.

And you shall eat and be full, and you shall bless the Lord your God for the good land He has given you.

Take heed, lest you forget the Lord your God by not keeping His commandments and His ordinances and His statutes, which I command you on this day.

Lest, when you have eaten and are full, and have built goodly houses and live in them, and then your herds and flocks multiply, and your silver and gold is multiplied, and all that you have is multiplied, then your heart be lifted up and you forget the Lord your God, who brought you out of the land of Egypt, out of the house of bondage,

Who led you through the great and terrible wilderness, with its fiery serpents and scorpions and thirsty ground where there was not water, who brought you out of the flinty rock.

Who fed you in the wilderness with manna which your fathers did not know, that He might humble you and test you, to do you good in the end.

Beware lest you say in your heart, "My power and the might of my hand have gotten me this wealth."

You shall remember the Lord your God, for it is He who gives you power to get wealth; that He may confirm His convenant which He swore to your fathers, as at this day.

And if you forget the Lord your God and go after other gods and serve them and worship them, I solemnly warn you this day that you shall surely perish.

Like the nations that the Lord makes to perish before you, so shall you perish because you would not obey the voice of the Lord your God.

CHAPTER 5

ANOTHER WAY— ANOTHER DIRECTION

W herever there is disease, God has put a remedy right next to it. We have remedies that will help us in every illness, but we cannot depend on just a remedy to get our problems solved; we have to take care of the whole man first.

We must recognize that the whole body's health is not to be found in any one remedy. You may take a remedy, but it will give you only temporary results. Some remedies are stimulating and some have a sedative effect; some cease to have an effect if they are used constantly. Remedies are only part of good health. They are unbalanced, like part of a diet. Good remedies have to work hand in hand with correcting the body, building new tissue to replace the old while the old body undergoes changes.

CARING FOR THE WHOLE PERSON

It takes a year to convert broken-down organs into healthy ones. It is a gradual thing, like putting clean water into dirty water; finally you have a good body. A person who does not take into consideration the whole person—body, mind, and spirit, using a wholesome variety of foods—is not doing the right thing for his or her body.

THE VALUE OF NATURAL REMEDIES

Natural remedies do not mask symptoms while the cause is still there. Symptoms such as discharges and ulcers are natural processes for the elimination of acquired and hereditary disease matter. If a poisonous drug is used as a remedy and suppresses the initial lesion, the disease matter will be diffused throughout the system, and the problem will show up in the next weakest organ or organs. Suppression may go on for months or years, resulting in a chronic disease condition; the disease does not heal because the life force and immune system are so compromised that they can no longer produce an acute reaction. As the diseased tissue dries up, it sets up a cumulative reaction that acts as a time bomb, and you are on your way to an abnormal growth. If the initial disease is not taken care of through the elimination organs, it may appear again either in the patient or in his offspring.

It's often true that one operation leads to another. The cause of the trouble was not taken care of in the first place, and it was bound to show up some other place in the body. When people come to me, I always make a record of the surgical operations they have had. They invariably had enlarged tonsils as a child. Why were they enlarged? Because catarrh, toxic materials, phlegm, and mucus were overtaxing the lymph glands.

These patients had too much white flour and white sugar products. This produced an overload on the tonsils. The tonsils are lymph glands; they become enlarged when they are overworked. The problem was that they were not cared for before they were overworked, and that is where the remedy should start!

We must move the whole body into good health; then the symptoms will begin to leave. Nature has stored away foods for our bodies and put certain chemicals in these foods. When our body chemistries are balanced, we rid ourselves of most of these symptoms. I don't know of anyone who doesn't need a healthy change in his body.

If we eat what nature has supplied, we begin to follow the natural preventive laws. That means we eat pure, whole food; use the right proportions of six vegetables, two fruits, one starch, and one protein every day; and include variety in our diets.

One of the most important preventive remedies is to avoid overeating. Overeating will kill you. When you find how much you need to eat, eat no more. You will find this is the successful way of living.

You are endowed at this moment with a certain amount of energy to do a specific amount of work. That energy helps digest the food you put into your body. It heats your food. It absorbs, distributes, and eliminates your food. If you use more energy than you have stored in your body, you will become depleted. And one of the quickest roads to depletion is to overeat, which causes your body to expend energy—processing food it doesn't want.

You can also starve from the food you eat. Malnutrition often accompanies the eating of devitalized, demineralized, processed food.

FIND OUT WHAT IS RIGHT

The first step in taking care of ourselves is to find out what is right. How did God intend us to live? What foods are approved by God? How should we live physically, mentally, and spiritually so that all things will be put into their proper places? Pain and discomfort are nature's warning that we are not doing the right thing; we haven't been doing the right thing, and the coffee and doughnut habit is catching up with us.

Something is wrong, and you must awaken! It's a matter of toxic blood, overacidity, a growth stagnation pressing you on the shoulder, squeezing you, bending you, pulling, producing acute sharp pains, muscle weakness, memory loss, nerve exhaustion, decline in vision, anything to stop you in your tracks. Think for a moment! Take care of yourself. It's not time to carry on, go on, look outside, chase a cure, or replace this old body for a new body with a pill or any other cure. If it did cure you, you would be sick again tomorrow if you didn't learn to live correctly and maintain good health.

All species of animals live on foods they should have for their particular bodies. We find that horses and sheep in the pasture will pick out different grasses for their particular kind of body. Neither the horse nor the sheep has ever studied what to select for a good life and for various levels of his development. It's all done by a basic wisdom they never lose. We should apply more wisdom and selectivity in foods for our good health.

HEALTH POWER

Civilization is late in taking care of this, and if something isn't done now, it may become too late. There should be a definition of health given to people so they can sort out these problems. We have a health department in our government where everybody is working on quick solutions and nobody is working on the basic problems.

We are using up the resources of the Earth, wearing it down, burning it up, and we are also doing the same thing to our human systems. Our body is self-rejuvenating, self-repairing, self-building, yet we do not supply proper fuel for our bodies to repair and rebuild properly. Health education is sorely neglected with regard to building a good body.

Health is an important part of our life. In fact, it is *the* most important factor in our life. I will say that while health is not everything, without health, everything else is nothing. We should get on a good nutritional program *now*. Then, if it turns out you need a constructive operation a year from now, and there is such a thing as constructive surgery, you will be ready for it.

My interest in nutrition lies mainly in the healing arts. To say a person needs help, or needs one element especially, is not enough. To be able to properly feed the whole body and see to it that food is contributing the essential chemicals to that body is truly an art. It is also an art to look into the eyes of a patient and see the causes that are brought on by a nutritional depletion in the body, and then determine what is necessary to build the body back toward physical and mental health.

THE MAGIC OF FOODS

If I were going to recommend one particular food to cleanse and rebuild the body, it would be greens. If you are green inside, you are clean inside. Greens control the calcium in the body and are high in iron and potassium. The more bitter they are, the more potassium they contain. Greens are one of the finest things known for neutralizing the acids in the body. The chlorophyll in greens is high in vitamin K, the antihemorrhagic vitamin. Also, there are a lot of vitamins C and A in any of the green vegetables.

We can absorb greens into the digestive system faster than any other food. Less digestion is necessary for getting chlorophyll into the blood than any other form of food. There is nothing more wonderful to use than greens to strengthen the body, to clean the mouth, sweeten the breath, and take away odors.

The individual who does a lot of physical work should have plenty of iron, calcium, and silicon. He needs a lot of sodium if he perspires a lot. I can look at anyone and tell if they are lacking in at least four chemicals—namely, iron, calcium, silicon, and sodium. I will watch him walk, watch his facial expressions, and take a look at his hair. Nearly everyone of us is lacking in these four elements to some degree, many of us gravely so. We must do something about it or lose our health. We need these elements for future health insurance. It is every man's job to give attention and serious consideration to the business of maintaining good health. Isn't it better to pay the cost of keeping well (*prevention*) rather than pay costly bills trying to cure yourself until you die? Think about that!

CHANGES WE CAN MAKE WITH FOODS

The impact of a healthy diet is evident in the following report:

> London, England—Can Diet Cut Juvenile Delinquency? A survey of 17 maladjusted or delinquent girls between the ages of 11 and 15 in a Salvation Army hostel seems to prove that diet makes good girls from bad ones. Previously the girls lived on the poorest possible types of meals, white bread and margarine, cheap jam, lots of sweet tea, canned and processed meats. Fish and chips had been one of their most nutritious meals. A year later their diet was changed to raw fruits, nuts, vegetables, salads, whole wheat bread, dates, prunes, figs, honey, cheese, meat, fish, eggs, oatmeal, crushed wheat. This is what happened: The girls quickly became less

aggressive and less quarrelsome, bad habits seemed to disappear, "problem children" became less of a problem and the bored ones lost their boredom. Physically they improved almost beyond recognition. A spokesman said, "It is amazing to see the difference in their complexions, general brightness and poise, but the difference in their behavior is the most significant. The part the diet played in their personalities is undeniable."

In another similarly related instance, two doctors in charge of a mental institution in Oklahoma changed the diet of problem patients, and the patients stopped screaming at night. They also stopped fighting at the tables, skin conditions improved, thyroid disturbances were improved, and women patients became quiet and complacent, permitting their hair to be combed.

I did a study at the penitentiary at San Quentin, California. We found that in some men the lack of iodine seemed linked to the triggering of their brute tendencies—kill the other fellow before he gets a chance to kill you! Yet when they got iodine, they changed completely. Without iodine we cannot think properly; we cannot be level-headed. Certainly, there are other causes; but iodine deficiency is one of them.

Many of the subnormal expressions of our thinking can be cleaned up if we take care of the deficiencies of food elements that the body needs. Prisons have often served food lacking in nutritional value, which only reinforces criminal tendencies.

I am not saying that the family environment is not important in teaching children to be responsible adults. Moral values are important and necessary, as necessary as laws in a civilized nation. But I also feel that without balanced nutrition, exercise, sufficient rest, and other health needs being met, most people will exhibit abnormal behaviors as well as symptoms of deficiency or disease.

USE WHAT WE'VE BEEN GIVEN FOR HEALTH

With the wondrously created body we possess, do you think we have missed out on some of the natural things that we require? Do you think we have a Creator who has put His children here and forgotten the means to sustain life?

Everything we need is here. From the very highest plane it gives the Father great pleasure to give from His kingdom. The power that He has is ours. From the grass on the hills to the iron in the hills, it is there for man's consumption. It is up to us. If we leave out what God has given us, we end up failing to meet our total needs and with one or more of the deficiency diseases of today.

There is something about "doing the right thing" that is good for your health. Try doing the wrong thing and see what it does to your mind. What does it do to your thinking? How does your conscience feel, especially when you know better? It's true—you know better!

If you're interested in natural remedies, you're not going to get rid of a headache right now. You are going to start a natural way of living so that those headaches diminish and leave.

Find a good, healthy way to live. If you don't live right and set the body up properly, you can take a remedy and no matter how good it is, it will never work. You will never get anything good out of a natural remedy if you do not live a wholesome life.

Go with clean living, eat good clean foods, have a right pattern for right living. The main thing in life is to find the right path, a path that God would approve of, because the body molds to that path. It molds a little bit to the mind, a little bit to the spiritual, some to good companionship, good climate, and good air. These are partial remedies for people who are on the right path.

I am sure that when you get closer to the garden, closer to nature, and further away from pills that sedate, stimulate, or tranquilize, you are going to be in much better health.

But you are not going to get well overnight. You will never get well from anything in less than a year. You need "two summers" in a row for this healing. Climate and altitude may be your answer. Remedies that work overnight can be detrimental because they put you under their control.

A person who is living on constant resistance and resentment cannot ever be well. This person cannot digest his food. He will be chasing remedies for his acid stomach, rheumatic joints, and a host of other acidic ailments. Correct his present condition, and further troubles will never occur.

ABOUT THE HEALING CRISIS

As part of the reversal process, we must go through the healing crisis. This is a process the body goes through to eliminate accumulated toxic waste. At the time of the healing crisis, we have new tissue replacing old tissue, and this is responsible for the elimination. The new tissue is strong, virile, young, and active. It is able to cope with any of the disease processes that have been built up through wrong living habits. In a chronic state of affairs, you will always find toxic-laden old tissue.

CORRECTION OF BODY TISSUE

Disease is when a degeneration of tissue has taken place, when toxic materials have accumulated and you are not capable of getting rid of them. Then there is a manifestation of symptoms developed in the body such as boils, rheumatism, joint disturbances, or headaches, foot troubles, and so on. A correction is brought about only when the condition is reversed. In other words, we have to have better functioning tissue than we had before. We have to have cleaner tissue than we did before. This brings about correction. When there is more vitality in the tissues to get rid of toxic material, we are working toward cleansing.

OLD AILMENTS COME BACK

Now, if we are becoming younger as we become older by reversing the process of tissue repair, many times we go back over the old diseases we have had in the past. The healing crisis always gives you symptoms of some of your past diseases. Anyone who can bring on a healing crisis, or who develops a healing crisis, is going through a reversal process as expressed in Dr. Constantine Hering's Law of Cure, which states, "All cure is from the head down, from the inside out, and in reverse order as symptoms first appeared."

Rheumatic conditions, discharges, pains, and aches in various parts of the body are brought back, but they last only a very short time. The average healing crisis lasts three days, although it can last longer in elderly people. The average person develops a healing crisis during the third month of coming onto a good, strict nature regimen. With children, it comes on much quicker, for children have not built up a chronic form of disease.

To bring on the healing crisis, be sure the diet is proper. It may be that a fast is indicated for the first few days to ensure that the body is rested enough to have the vital energy to work on the foods. We must have quiet. We must also have rest, psychologically and physically. The more rest we have, preferably in bed, the better the cure.

A lot of liquids and juices in the diet are indicated, especially vegetable broths. Potato peeling broth is one of the best to use. Water treatments are important in reversing any disease. There is a water treatment that can be used for every part of the body, for every condition. We should learn which water treatments are indicated for our particular problem. The next thing indicated is to find the herbs most suited for a specific condition that you may be expressing or for any one organ that is not functioning properly. As my old professor said years ago, water can be used internally, externally, and eternally.

When you love, you recuperate. You do not recuperate in misery, depression, and resentment—only in love, understanding, and agreement.

We must eliminate all negative influences from our lives. Pick up all the positive things and thoughts. "Neglect the weeds and nourish the roses." Organize your life. Reorganize your mind. Healing is impossible when the mind is in turmoil.

Pursuit of the ideal is another remedy for mental health. The only thing that will keep you young and youthful is an interest in life. If you have lost an interest in life, you're dying. If you have something to accomplish, to do, finish, or overcome, you have youth.

I make a hobby of collecting spoons from around the world. When I look at the thousands of spoons I have, I notice that every handle is different, and each represents a man's imagination and inspiration. It is in man's mind that we look for creation. Each creator was in pursuit of an ideal when he fashioned his spoon. In India, they say a man should go through life giving to the world something of his own. That's what creation is all about.

If you are stopped at every opportunity, you will never be well. If you have no activity in the brain, you will have no activity in the body either, because the brain leads the body.

WATCH YOUR DAILY HABITS

If you want to learn one of the big secrets in life, look closely at what you do every day and see if you are spending your time wisely. If it is the least bit wrong, or less than it should be for perfection, or for your best health, you will find that eventually it will break you down. I do not believe that one cigarette ever hurt anybody, but I think a cigarette every day for eighteen years will finally get you. I don't think one cup of coffee will hurt anybody, but one cup of coffee every day for eighteen years will give you a weak liver. So watch your daily habits. If there is one thing you do every day, watch it! This is one of the greatest remedies that I can tell you.

BE BIG—LENGTHEN YOUR STEPS!

Few occupations give us all the health essentials we need for a strong body. Working indoors, sitting, or standing all day in one position, commuting in poorly ventilated buses and streetcars, grabbing quick lunches, working under tension of noise and time, all tend to jeopardize our health. We coddle our comforts and forget that we need fresh air, sunshine, exercise, and good, wholesome food.

Most people huddle into themselves when walking along the street. Their heads are down, their hands are in their pockets and their thoughts are dwelling on the worrisome events of the day. Be big—lengthen the stride of your step, throw out your chest, breathe in fresh air, look upward to the sky, and think outwardly on bigger things. The blood will surge through your body, feeding it and making it warm. You will be happier and healthier.

FRESH AIR HEALS WOUNDS

Never neglect the value of fresh air in healing. As Dr. Charles Rollier, a Swiss doctor best known for his treatment of tuberculosis at high altitudes, says, "It is a well-known fact that wounds exposed to sunshine and fresh air heal more rapidly than when bandaged. In fact, no wound will heal *without air.* In order for wounds to heal quickly, it is most important that they be exposed to a constant supply of pure, fresh air."

What if you live in a smog-ridden city, and there is no fresh air? Use a combination of these foods and vitamins: vitamin C, 500 milligrams daily; vitamin A, 30,000 units daily; green alfalfa—juice or tablet form; or any green juices (these attract oxygen from the air). Also, take more of the oxygen-giving foods. Sprouts are the best of all! And, of course, all the green vegetables. Eat lots of salads, all the water-bearing fruits, and those that have a lot of iron in them. You must have iron to attract oxygen from the air. Drink a lot of black cherry juice. Use black cherries. This is necessary to regenerate the lung supply and to prevent many of the catarrhal conditions we develop in the wintertime and/or in the polluted air of the city.

WHERE IS THE CURE?

Many people feel that everything is just in the physical body. Actually, the whole man is at stake when we treat the body to make it better. No part of the physical body or cell in the body can be divorced from the spirit, that life force that flows through us. Too many people have the idea that all we have to look for is a chemical reaction in order to find the cure. The more highly evolved man becomes, the more he recognizes that changes in consciousness rid him of sickness and make him "whole" once again. We have to return to nature and intelligent living. The physical in most cases cannot see what is going on in the spiritual realm. It takes a lot of studying to recognize the value of friendship, the destruction of emotion, or the involvement of what money can do to the heart, kidneys, and stomach. It seems we are involved more in *solutions* than taking care of *causes.*

We must follow the proper path for corrections to be made and true health to manifest itself. It must be an upward path, a better way of living; otherwise, whatever correction we make won't last. We cannot continually go against God and nature and expect this violation to maintain good health.

THE LAW OF REVERSING

Everyone wants a quick cure, "Get rid of the problem immediately!" They want to get back to work, to be able to walk or run again. They never seem to realize that most quick cures will keep people from having lasting health. It is better to take the slow way of improvement over a year's time and develop good tissues and better functioning. At the end of the year you'll look back and say, "I am better today than I was five years ago." This is the true way of healing.

Dr. Constantine Hering gave us the law that we must reverse and atone for our sins and go back over our problems and troubles no matter what has been built into the body. Then we can have good health once again. Whatever has been built into the body can be replaced by doing better things in its place. How could you expect a person who constantly does wrong in his life to have a good body? We have said many times, you *earn* your health, and *learn* your health. Hering's Law of Cure says that all cure comes from above, down from within, out, and with symptoms reappearing in reverse order of their original development. That is why the doctor must work with and teach his patient. The patient has the obligation of learning to undo what he has done. He must weave into his body (the rug of life) new threads, giving him the healthy body he wants.

We must have the desire to live a better life; otherwise, there would be no reason to improve, no reason for us to go on. We must recognize that there *is* a better way. In the dictionary, the doctor is rightfully called a teacher. A person should learn from his doctor the proper way of living so he can correct his present condition and prevent further troubles.

THE DISEASE VS. THE HEALING CRISIS

People, as a rule, will die in a disease crisis but not in a *healing* crisis. When we think of a crisis, we think of something that is for the better or the worse. Usually, a healing crisis comes after we feel best. Nature tries to show us how good we can feel, and then a healing crisis comes to us. A healing crisis comes when we have developed enough of the vital energies in our body to throw off the toxic materials. Hippocrates, the father of medicine, has said, "Give me a fever and I will cure any disease." I believe that in the reversal process we bring a higher temperature in these crises and burn out much of the toxic conditions in our bodies.

The healing crisis should be studied by everyone who is interested in perfecting his body and having good health. In the healing crisis, we eliminate this toxic material through discharges, extreme contractions, convulsions, pains, and eliminations from various parts of the body. It can be of a catarrhal nature, such as mucus phlegm from the bronchial tubes, sinus, ears, and other orifices of the body.

My old professor used to say that to pollute is to impair. Now, I believe this is true about the air we breathe, the water we drink, and the foods we eat. This is also the same as far as our body is concerned. We pollute our body with heavy toxic materials, bad foods, soft drinks, fats, fried foods, and so on, to the point that when cleansing takes place, it comes on in a violent reaction or a fever. This can be termed as a healing crisis.

There is no foreign matter that can stay in your body during a healing crisis because the blood is making new tissue. New tissue takes the place of the old, and in the vitality of that new tissue, the old has to go. Even in a disease crisis, it is an elimination of toxic material and we should favor it. We find that most people suppress this, driving the cold back into the body, suppressing various eliminative processes. When we suppress a discharge in the body, we are on our way to a chronic disease.

FASTING

Fasting brings the crisis on more quickly. The crisis can occur either during the fast or many months afterward. Crises develop much faster in the summer than in the winter. There are times we need more than one crisis to have a complete body elimination. They may develop one after the other—first in the bronchial tubes, then later in the bowel, and still later in the knees or wherever our problem might have settled.

It is a very interesting thing to observe how the body reverses itself in the process of healing, picking up first the problem you had several years ago, then the one you had five or six years ago, and if you continue with proper living habits, even retracing troubles as far back as ten or fifteen years. Again, it shows the wonderful working of the body and proves that the

---

 ∽ **Remember This . . .**

A long fast should always be under the supervision of a doctor.
Detoxification is like tearing down the walls of an old building.
There comes a time when you have to rebuild, and that results
from a new eating regimen afterward. *Eventually you have to get off
this diet idea and go on to a healthy way of living.* It is good to go
from the elimination diet to a healthy way of living, then after a
month or so on an elimination diet, and then . . . back to a healthy
way of living.

---

body works according to law. Without a doubt, we earn the diseases we have, but the wonderful part is that we may also earn
our way back to health.

Fasting can also bring other good results. Dr. George Weger
of Redlands, California, who was one of my first teachers, showed
me what fasting can do. I had a boy who had been scheduled for
surgery. The doctors were going to amputate one of his legs
because the circulation was so bad. He had ninety boils on his
legs, and I couldn't cure these boils with all the infection that had
been set up there. He came to my office one Friday night and
the following Monday he was going to have his leg amputated.

I called Dr. Weger (I didn't even know him at the time), and
said, "Doctor, I have a young boy; they are going to amputate
one of his legs. I'm wondering if it is possible to save this boy's
leg." Well, we put him on a thirty-day fast, and I *did* see this
boy's leg saved.

Fasting is like having a life preserver thrown to you, something
to pull you out of danger. I have fasted no fewer than 25,000 people, so I do know the effects of fasting. But we should always seek
the counsel of a doctor if we wish to fast for more than a few days.

∽ Important Crisis Note

A crisis comes usually after you feel your best. It is the will of nature. No doctor, no patient, no food can bring a crisis on. It comes when your body is ready. It does it in its own time. It goes through slow or fast according to the patient's constitution, nervous system, and what you have earned. You *earn* this crisis through hard work. It comes through a sacrifice, giving up bad habits, taking a new path, cleaning up the act that you've been in when your life wasn't working with the laws of nature. A crisis can come harshly, small, violently, softly, according to what is possible for the body to control and take care of. Some crises come in with backaches, skin rashes, teeth on edge, diarrhea, or joint pains. I have seen people have all of these symptoms; however, they do not usually come at the same moment but move from one part of the body to another and wherever the body is placing its energy for cleaning, rejuvenation, and getting rid of the old tissue and acids that probably have accumulated over a period of years.

There is one thing about fasting that may seem a little foolish to some of you. Fasting is only like squeezing your body like a sponge. You get rid of toxemia, but you have a building job along with it, or following it. To accomplish the rebuilding and regeneration of tissues, glands, and organs recently cleansed, you will need a food regimen that takes care of both the building of the damaged tissue and ongoing cleansing of the whole body.

NATURE DOES HAVE A REMEDY

Scientists are trying to invent a pill to eat instead of a meal; they are looking for an injection to take instead of giving up coffee and doughnuts. They are not interested in changing their habits. If your wife can't cook, eat "TUMS." It's an unnatural life today.

But if you want to go this unnatural way, you will be following the majority of people.

The government tells us that a high percentage of the people in this country are sick, even though they are still working. I am convinced that the masses are messes. I am convinced that a large percent of people who are sick do not know the value of nature, the value of living a good life. There is an old saying that man's extremity is God's opportunity. It is possible that when we have increased our sickness to about 98 percent and have broken down to the place where the prevention of virus disease by antibodies doesn't work anymore, we will have to look for another way out. Did you know that they are now using new antibiotics to take care of the infections that old antibiotics no longer cure? Flies get so used to the DDT spray that something else has to be found to kill them. One of these days, we also might get hardened to all of the injections we have taken in the past.

FLY FROM THE ARTIFICIAL

We have to find another way out. I think there is going to be a flight from the city—a flight from the artificial. There has been a "back to nature" movement since the sixties. People are finding places in the country to enjoy, sometimes just a "bed and breakfast." Many people have begun to follow healthier lifestyles—vegan, vegetarian, or simply cutting down on meats, fats, and junk foods with little nutritional value. Natural food stores have increased in numbers in our cities, and even the federal government has recognized the significance of nutrition in preventing or reversing diseases. School lunches are healthier, and many adults have given up cigarette smoking. Natural health supplements sell in the range of billions of dollars annually. Things are changing.

NATURE'S WAY

The wonders we find in nature are something to be studied. We have to work closely with her in order to be well. In fact, my old professor used to say that we must pick the vegetables right out of the garden to be well. I was not brought up like that. I had to come to this like most people. I haven't met many who can sit down to spinach and say, "This tastes good." None of these things tasted good to me! I don't know about other people, but I came from a family that really sugared everything and fried things to a nice golden brown, that really sold you the sizzle in the steak. It was wonderful, too. Then you come into this health work, and they talk about coffee substitutes. There is no substitute for coffee—that's the real stuff!

The idea of studying this natural way, although wonderful, has been difficult for me. But the more I became aware of how wonderful and bountiful nature has been to my body, the more I go along with her. Nature is wonderful both to our minds and our memories. Our hearing depends upon our assimilation. Smell depends upon our respiration; respiration depends entirely upon the muscle activity of the body; muscle activity depends upon potassium found in green leaves. We are inseparable from nature: her greens; her yellows, which have vitamin C; and her reds (e.g., tomatoes), which are high in vitamin D and fix the calcium in our bodies, thus giving us tone, energy, and power to work. We can't get away from nature, as much as we strive to find a way to live without her.

So many of us are looking for the substitutes. I have a letter from a lady who said "I find I can't drink coffee anymore, my stomach can't take it. What should I do?" Do you know what she should do? Quit!

I am convinced that today, more than ever before, we live in a disturbed, psychological, subjective world. I feel that the individual has to be more balanced today than ever before. You have to "stand" more because of today's pressures, today's competition, today's communications, which are constantly bombarding us. We have gone back to a kind of "caveman-like" existence with our weatherproof, air-conditioned houses and penthouses, our automobiles and subways, huge offices and factories, and our inside living that often removes the necessity of ever going out into the fresh air. We hang landscape pictures on our walls and fill our vases with imitation flowers. But nature brings us entirely different suggestions, and when you live out in nature, the ever-changing scenery is a complete wonderment, beyond all imagination. If you have ever lived near the Grand Canyon, you know that there is never any day or any moment when you look at the canyon that you see the same scene. The lighting effects present you with an ever-changing view.

MINISTRY OF HEALING

The physician needs more than human wisdom and power that he may know how to minister to the many perplexing cases of disease of the mind and heart which he is called to deal with. If you are suffering with poor health, there is a remedy for you.

Young children can grow into almost any shape by habits of proper exercise, and positions of the body obtain healthy forms.

The living organism is God's property. God is the owner of the whole man.

The physical organism should have special care that the powers of the body may not be dwarfed, but developed to their full extent.

—ELLEN G. WHITE

CHAPTER 6

HEADS UP!

The eyes and teeth are nature's barometer of health. They are the two things in your body that first begin to diminish when the rest of your body is starting to go downhill. When your eyes or teeth start getting bad, that is an indication that something more general might be wrong with your health.

The head itself also tells us much about our health. Do you have headaches? How about dandruff? We can find remedies in nature for all these problems.

EYES

Circles Under the Eyes

Circles under the eyes are caused when the veins fail to get rid of the sludge blood, because the blood is lacking in iron.

Our bodies have their poorest circulation under the eyes because the underlids seldom move. When we blink, we use only the upper lids.

Here is a nice exercise to increase the circulation under the eyes and thereby help fight those circles: While facing straight ahead, with head level, roll the eyes upward as far as possible without undue strain. Then blink your eyes. Repeat three times; then close your eyes and rest them, covering them with the palms of your hands.

Infected or Irritated Eyes

Taking carrot juice helps eye infections. Vitamin A in carrot juice prevents and gets rid of eye infections. Every 8-ounce glass of carrot juice contains up to 24,750 units of vitamin A.

Honey. A drop of honey in the eyes is said to be beneficial. It must be running honey that has not been heated. If the full-strength honey is too strong, mix it half and half with distilled water.

Linseed Oil. Linseed oil is one of the best cleansing agents we can use in our eyes. Putting drops in the eyes (one in each) is the best thing for eyes irritated by smog. We find that linseed oil has been used many times in the past, even for cataracts. (Sterilized linseed oil can be found at a drug store).

Milk Pack. A warm milk pack is a fine remedy for the eyes.

Potato Pack. A grated potato pack is good for irritated eyes. Leave on for twenty minutes. Select a potato that has not been treated with chemicals in growing or storage.

SINUS

Horseradish. Put a little horseradish on the tongue and take a deep breath.

Sage. Sage is a wonderful thing for the sinus. Rub it in the hands and breathe in. It stimulates sinus drainage.

Bay Leaf. The bay leaf is a wonderful stimulus for the sinus. Just rub it in your hands and breathe the scent. Also, you can do the same with mint and eucalyptus leaves.

THROAT

For sore throat, use ½ teaspoon of liquid chlorophyll in ½ cup water three times a day.

MOUTH

Do you chew tobacco? How about gum? Both of these have a definite adverse effect on the digestion. Constant chewing causes excessive salivation, and the prolonged stimulation of the salivary glands results in an inactive juice with little effectiveness. A very small amount of starch is digested in the mouth. Most starchy food is digested in the stomach and intestine.

While fruit acids, such as malic and tartaric acids, exert very little effect on the saliva, citric acid stimulates its flow greatly, aiding in mastication. Acetic and oxalic acids (rhubarb and spinach) interfere with calcium assimilation. Too much fiber intake interferes with the assimilation of minerals in the small intestine.

The saliva possesses modest antiseptic properties. Although typhoid fever, tetanus bacilli, colon bacilli, or pus-producing organisms are not destroyed, many other pathogenic bacteria cannot survive in human saliva. The saliva of goats and other ruminants, especially parotid saliva, has been found to have distinct bactericidal properties. Apparently, saliva maintains mouth conditions unfavorable for the growth of certain microorganisms that might otherwise remain there and cause decay or ulceration. It is well known that wounds in the mouth heal rapidly.

Disease can affect the saliva. In cases of diabetes, cancer of the stomach, leukemia, pernicious anemia, jaundice, and sometimes chlorosis (iron deficiency anemia), the saliva becomes acid.

The quantity of saliva is also affected by disease. It may be very scant when profuse sweating, vomiting, dropsy, diabetes, anemia, cachexia (accompanying carcinoma of the stomach), fever, uremia, and cirrhosis of the liver are present. The saliva in such cases is usually cloudy and acid, with a peculiar sweetish odor. In excessive salivation, the saliva is clear, thin, and alkaline. Pregnancy is accompanied by a marked increase in saliva. This is also the case in many painful stomach ailments.

The taste of food does much to influence digestion. The pleasure of food in the mouth stimulates the stomach, pancreas, liver, and other organs of digestion to secrete their juices. This is accomplished by the nerves of taste, sending messages to the reflex centers of the brain. The longer food stays in the mouth, the more gastric juice will be in the stomach to receive it. Thorough chewing is another prerequisite to the effectiveness of our built-in feed intake regulator, especially with regard to quantities. The uvula, or soft palate, at the back of the mouth is sensitive to solid food, rejecting any such particles and routing them back to the teeth for further breaking down. It also protects the opening of the esophagus from the entrance of any foreign or injurious articles.

TONGUE

Why is it that a visit to the doctor invariably involves a look at the tongue? The tongue may not indicate the disease, but the state of the patient.

The mouth and the nose are vulnerable parts of the body, coming constantly into contact with microorganisms. It is only the action of the saliva that prevents the tongue and all mouth surfaces from being continually coated with microorganisms.

In the average-sized healthy individual, about 30 billion leucocytes (white blood cells) are constantly active, destroying bacteria. Freshly secreted saliva contains many white blood cells, as well as opsonins and alexins (other agents hindering the growth of bacteria), which help to keep the mouth clean. If the mouth becomes dry due to fever, disease, or sleeping with it open, the tongue gets thickly coated with molds, yeasts, and bacteria.

But a much more common cause of coated tongue is autointoxication. The saliva is incapable of supplying its normal protection of the mouth against uneven odds. So when putrefactive products and virulent bacterias are present in greater numbers than its germicidal action or that of the blood can handle, the tongue becomes thickly coated and the breath has a bad odor.

Most often the colon is at fault. With intestinal sluggishness, body wastes are retained in the bowel, sometimes for days, and are not properly eliminated. Thus, quantities of toxins find their way into the bloodstream. Invariably, the coated tongue is a sure sign of a toxic condition of the body and a lowered resistance to bacteria; it is practically always coated in fever, whatever the cause of infection.

GUMS AND TEETH

Bleeding Gums

The herb calendula can have a wonderful effect on the most chronic cases of bleeding gums. Calendula should be used in a tincture and can be held in the mouth for two or three minutes upon arising and before retiring. A teaspoonful is enough, mixed with a small quantity of water.

Liquid chlorophyll is another fine thing for bleeding gums. Use it as a mouthwash, holding it in the mouth for two or three minutes until the effect of chlorophyll can come about through the absorption of this fluid.

Other remedies are bonemeal, taken in four tablets, twice a day, and vitamin C, taken in 1,000 milligram doses every three hours for one week.

Breakdown of Gum Tissues

Many people have pyorrhea, gum disorders, and mouth disorders. The teeth are only as good as the gums.

A papaya tablet is recommended where there is a breakdown of gum tissues. Immediately following a meal, place a papaya tablet on each side of the mouth and let it soak for ten or fifteen minutes or until completely dissolved. This will rid the bacteria and dead tissue that have gathered around the teeth. Papaya eats dead tissue but does not hurt live tissue. It is a digestant and a wonderful remedy for getting rid of old structures that most of us have in our mouths. This same method of using papaya is good for people who find that tartar forms easily on their teeth.

Loose Teeth

Loose teeth are a problem today because many people do not chew any hard foods. If you cannot chew hard foods and cannot enjoy the salads we use today, the teeth become loose. It is recommended that you chew a carrot before breakfast, before lunch, and before dinner. It will not only tighten the teeth, but it will also strengthen the gums so that the teeth will harden. It is hard to believe that we can set our teeth in the gums by chewing the carrot before meals, but this is absolutely true. Spit out the pulp, you do not have to eat the pulp. You can then eat your regular meals, but be sure to chew your food well.

The dentist wanted to put braces on my son's teeth at the age of ten. However, I told my son to chew a carrot before each meal, and it actually straightened out his teeth so that braces were not required. You can expand the jaw on some children, who are born with narrow jaws by making them chew a carrot before meals.

Canker Sores

For canker sores, use calcium lactate.

Toothache

When you have a toothache, you can use cotton wool saturated with oil of clove. There are packs we can get from the drugstore to use alongside the gum for an abscess. Sometimes using flaxseed meal packs will help a toothache. Put it into a little bag inside the mouth, alongside the tooth.

Tooth Surgery

To speed recovery following tooth surgery and to lessen the pain, use one teaspoon liquid chlorophyll, straight or diluted in one-half cup water, about five times a day. Work the liquid around the teeth and hold it in the mouth for two or three minutes. This is very soothing as a mouthwash.

Tooth Decay

There are innumerable research programs being conducted in laboratories all over the world with just one idea in mind—the prevention of tooth decay. Most of these research programs have recognized that the most glaring fact discovered to date is that decay is caused by faulty diets and nutritional deficiencies.

Dr. Michael J. Walsh, when he was director of clinical nutrition courses at the University of California Dental Extension in San Francisco, said, "Americans are waterlogged and are suffering from dietary deficiencies—but don't know it. What the public must look upon as three square meals a day is likely to be a starvation diet and one that will decay the toughest tooth." Instead of calling up your neighbor and inviting her children to come over and have ice cream and cake with yours, you should ask her to send them over so that you can drill holes in their teeth! The result *is* the same. Chinchilla breeders, dog fanciers, and even poultry breeders give more thought and attention and pay more money to learn how to feed their animals than the average American does to learn how to feed his own family.

False Living—False Teeth

One of my own recent experiences brought this home to me. An eleven-year-old boy was sent to me by another doctor. The boy had a complete set of dentures. When we have to face the fact that a boy of eleven has to have dentures, it is time to start doing something about this horrible scourge! Every sincere and thinking medical man or healer today should be devoting a great deal of his time and energy to this problem.

Another dentist sent a young chap to our office with most of his teeth gone. He was only twelve years old. The dentist claimed he could not do anything with his teeth; that it was a body condition. What a shame to see these teeth, the beautiful pearls of the mouth, broken down when, after all, a good diet could have prevented their ruin.

We know that teeth are broken down and deteriorated when a person does not live right and follow a proper diet. In our diet, greens are most important; they control the calcium in the body. The Hunzas, who had such beautiful teeth and kept them until they died at over 100 years of age, followed a diet in which they ate a lot of greens including the tops of vegetables. We should eat more parsley, beet greens, watercress, spinach, and the many different greens that we can get for salads daily. These will help to keep our teeth in tip-top condition.

Chlorophyll

We have also found chlorophyll effective in halting tooth decay. Chlorophyll is best known for its mysterious action in the process known as photosynthesis, which is the complicated chemical process in which a green plant converts the energy of the sun's rays into stored food energy in the form of carbohydrates. Science has never been able to break down this process and discover exactly how it works, but it has long been known that without chlorophyll, neither plants nor animals, including humans, could live. Chlorophyll is the substance that gives plants their green color. We can get chlorophyll by making juice drinks from the tops of vegetables. The liquefier comes in very handy for this purpose. Green kale, turnip tops, carrot tops, beet tops, and other green vegetables run through the liquefier and made into a drink should be part of your program for the entire family. It is much easier to do this than to suffer with an aching tooth or to pay the dentist's bill.

Learn to Feed Yourself and Your Smile

We cannot give the best to our job if we are suffering from an aching tooth. This, of course, goes for all dietary deficiencies as well. It has been stated by health authorities that billions of dollars could be saved by employers each year if the employees were better fed through improved nutritional programs. Better-fed people work more efficiently because they have stronger minds and bodies, including teeth! Americans can be better fed if they will only take time to learn how to use better foods.

We know that millions of dollars are spent each year to improve personal appearance by having teeth whitened, straightened, or capped. Our mental attitude is much better when we are satisfied with our personal appearance. Is it not smarter, then, to learn how to produce these beautiful teeth we so earnestly desire by finding out which chemical elements and vitamins are required in our diet to make them what we desire?

Vigorous Chewing

The average person does not chew his food thoroughly enough. He does not have the habit of chewing in the first place. Many children's jaws have not been developed fully and the teeth are crowded because they have not had hard foods to chew. Give the child nuts to chew, or a raw carrot every day, while his teeth are growing and developing. To make gums well, hard, and to keep them from bleeding easily, chew hard, crisp foods. Eat dry starches and keep away from mushy, soft foods.

EARS

General Remedies

Deafness may be caused by the toxic effects of some drugs and antibiotics on the auditory nerve. Hearing may be improved by hot applications, neck exercises, massage, and cleansing of the blood, liver, and eliminative organs. Strong garlic juice dropped into the ear a few times alleviates colds and catarrh. Wax may be removed by application of a few drops of warm glycerine. Live insects will be forced out of the ear with a little oil (one or two drops). If children have placed beans, peas, buttons, or other small objects in the ear, take them to your doctor. (Do not use oil or water in the ear for object removal.)

Eardrum Hardening

The ears change gradually and many times we do not even realize that changes are taking place. This is not uncommon in the body. For instance, when a hardening occurs in the tissues of the body, it sometimes takes twenty years to develop. It may be twenty years before a handicap in the ears shows up in a lack of response. Twenty years may pass before hardening develops in the arteries.

When the eardrum has become hardened, it usually has a long-standing cause. Some theories about this hardening include the eating of too much salt, poor circulation of blood to the head, or a lack of nerve supply from the spinal cord. For poor circulation to the head, common sense and nature tell us to lie down or get on a slanting board. I am sure that will rejuvenate the brain tissues.

Catarrhal Conditions and the Ears

Lymph drainage is important. Whenever a catarrhal condition is dominant in the body, especially in the bronchial tubes, a certain amount of catarrh will be backed up into the lymph glands, which are numerous along the spine and the neck. A sedentary occupation sometimes does not provide enough activity for normal emptying of these glands, which leads to a congestion that backs up into the smaller tissues nearby. The eardrum is one such tissue. Earaches may signal such a malady and hot packs (or a hot water bottle) are advised. Persistant earaches should be checked out with your doctor.

Also, when things are not working properly within the abdominal region, toxemias develop, resulting in an excessive elimination of catarrh. This catarrhal elimination can spread to all the orifices of the body. In this case, the ears in many cases develop what is called a *mastoiditis,* a running ear, and over a period of time catarrh can cause loss of hearing in the ear.

Symptoms such as buzzing in the ears may come from an anemic condition and can come also from high blood pressure.

It can be due to emotional strain, indigestion, or excessive gas pressures in the bowel.

In taking care of these problems, the first thing we should think about is exercise that helps to get the blood into the area of the ear (making sure first, of course, that the blood is high in quality and quantity). An extra rush of blood can be brought about by getting as nearly as possible in an upside-down position, so that the blood can flow easily into these upper areas. The slant board exercise, with the feet above the head, the feet and legs performing "bicyling," will help to get extra blood into the head. While in this position on the slant board, pull the knees down to the chest and hold for five minutes. This also helps to stimulate the lymph drainage in the neck, reducing heavy catarrhal conditions. In time, this helps the ears.

Using vitamin B-complex, especially niacin, will also drive the blood into the extremities of the body. For instance, taking rice bran syrup, a product high in niacin, on an empty stomach may cause even the ears to become red. Use the rice bran syrup directly after a meal to enjoy the benefit while avoiding symptoms of local manifestation.

There are ways of entering the mouth to drain the catarrhal settlements in the back of the uvula. From there, drainage of the sinuses can be forced—especially if any excessive tissue has developed and adhesions are keeping the catarrh from flowing freely from the sinuses. This is done through the manipulation called finger surgery.

Cleansing and eliminating nutrients, such as those found in vegetable juices, are best for the ears. Parsley and shave grass teas work miracles on the kidneys, and that has real benefits for the ears. Cucumber juice and whey are good foods for dissolving processes. A combination of these two helps tremendously in dissolving any hardness of the eardrum. Okra and celery are also very good for hardness in the eardrum. And they have the added effect of helping those with high blood pressure conditions.

Neck exercises, thyroid exercises, lymph gland drainage exercises, and tension and relaxation exercises that deal with the head and neck are important when we have any ear trouble. The best nerve foods for taking care of the ears are found in desiccated liver, powdered yeast, wheat germ, amino acids, lecithin, and gelatin.

Whenever we treat one part of the body we must treat the whole body. A lack of vitamin C can lead to hearing problems, especially during the winter months, when the body's reserve is limited because of a lower intake of fresh vegetables and fruits. And that same dietary deficiency in vitamin C can often invite the *common cold*. So, as we build up the liver, the stomach, the digestive powers, the elimination ability, we find that the ears will improve. Always take care of the whole body when you take care of any one of its organs.

Hearing Problems

Hearing problems can come from clogging of the eustachian tubes; pressure on the nerves, basal membranes, or some other part of the inner ear; thickening growth around the ear; stiffness or ossification of the ear bones; and exposure to excessively loud noises that have damaged the inner ear. When we have a weak development of the faculties that pay attention to sound, music, melody, and speech, the hearing may depreciate.

Boxing the ears also many times causes injury to the nerves of the ears; deafness is the result. Putting hairpins into the ears to clean them can also injure the ear mechanism and lead to deafness. Nothing hard should ever be put into the ear.

Episodes of flu and catarrhal discharges in other parts of the body will sometimes harm the ears, for the ears are an organ of catarrhal discharge, and the settlement of catarrah in this area could in time affect the hearing. Catarrhal conditions in the throat can migrate into the eustachian tubes.

A lot of vitamin C should be used at all times to help the ears. Vitamin C reduces infections and the various types of catarrhal conditions that may settle in the ears. Dr. William Evans has shown that when the vitamin C level is high, bacteria are less likely to be found in the nose, throat, and ears, and, if present, seldom become virulent. Experiments conducted abroad demonstrate a direct relationship between vitamin C and infection of the middle ear, which is often a factor in loss of hearing. Eighteen cases of examined middle ear infections showed a high vitamin C deficiency with chronic pus secretion. Administration of vitamin C stopped the secretion completely.

Dr. Edmund Prince Fowler, a prominent research physician who specializes in ear, nose, and throat disorders, shed much light in recent years on hearing problems. In examining schoolchildren in slum areas, he found their percentage of ear troubles much higher than that of children in nonslum schools. The children in slums repeatedly suffered from infectious diseases, due in part to insufficient diet, especially nonvariety of foods and vitamin deficiencies, which reduced resistance to infection. Vitamin A was found to be lacking in many of the people who had ear disturbances. It is deficient in many who have frequent nasal discharges and in patients with abcesses of the middle ear. Surveys show large doses of vitamin A to be effective in reducing the duration of colds.

In checking some people, it has been found that intake of vitamins A, B, and C has been deficient a good part of their lives. In one case, for instance, subjects were given treatment of these vitamins along with some endocrine substances for one year; the result was complete relief from fatigue and marked improvement of nervous condition. The women's audiograms showed a definite change, and whispered voices that could not previously be heard at all were audible at a distance of six feet after the treatment.

Based on these findings, it may be necessary to add vitamin concentrates to your regular diet if you have hearing problems. These should be evaluated by a well-qualified doctor.

Dr. Fowler also found that excessive sweets and starches could be responsible for bringing about lowered resistance of the nasal membranes and, in turn, aggravate existing ear conditions. Clear up your nervousness; do not hurry through your meals. A highly nervous person very seldom eats properly; they eat too fast; they eat under stress; and in the long run this can bring on ear conditions.

HEADACHES

Causes of Headaches

There are many causes of headaches. President Theodore Roosevelt once said, "We have to be very careful going to a surgeon with a pain in a toe because the surgeon might want to cut it off." The same goes for a pain in your head—you could lose it! It is possible that many headaches are caused by troubles quite remote from the head. There are acute headaches and chronic headaches, the latter including migraines.

Acute headaches (they come and go) can be caused by diseases or infections of the eyes, ears, nose, throat, teeth, or sinuses. A blow to the head can cause a headache. Exposure to cigarette or other smoke, allergens, or chemical fumes are sometimes at fault. Certain drugs (quinine, morphine, and so on), furnace fumes, use of alcohol, and dehydration may also be at fault.

Chronic headaches may accompany diseases, nerve dysfunctions, worry, brain tumors, and other physical, emotional, or psychosomatic disorders. Fevers and changes in metabolism may be at fault.

A headache that is twisting, boring, burning, or jumping is possibly caused by aching nerves. We must provide nutritional support to the nervous system in order to get rid of this kind of headache. Headaches that are dull, heavy, and persistent are either of the brain, periosteum (the membrane covering the skull and other bones), scalp, or base of the brain (cerebellum).

Headaches can come directly from an acid stomach when the hydrochloric balance is off. Whenever we have heartburn, it can cause reflex conditions, including headaches throughout the upper part of the head. Bowel stagis, constipation, and imbalance of the acid/alkaline system may trigger headaches. Cardiovascular disturbances, endocrine problems, premenstrual syndrome, fibromyalgia, menopause, over exposure to heat or cold, pregnancy, and almost any disturbance of the body or mind can cause headaches. We could go on and on naming causes of headaches.

Nerve conditions such as anger, fear, worry, excitement, disappointment, nervous exhaustion or tension, and stress can cause headaches as bad or worse than those that have physical causes. Bad news can cause headaches very quickly.

Migraines are the most extreme headaches and may begin in childhood or any time during adulthood. They may come with visual images—spots, lines, stripes, light flashes, and so on. Migraines may start with mood changes, fatigue, slowed thinking, depression, thirst, hunger, or nervousness. Light and noise become painful. Twice as many women as men experience migraine, and about half of all those who experience migraines report that it runs in the family. Some researchers report magnesium deficiency in their study of people with migraines.

Disappointments in love, excessive bile, a sluggish liver, pressures on the pneumogastic nerve, or splenic nerve, and diseases of the scalp can initiate headaches. Other causes are loss of blood, excessive use of the eyes in reading and studying, poor glasses, improperly fitted glasses, diarrhea, menstrual disorders, or too much sun.

Many people have headaches when giving up coffee, tea, and other addictive foods, because the withdrawal process involves changes in the nervous system as well as release of toxins. This withdrawal process is often the cause of headaches.

Prolapsus (a dropped transverse colon), pressure on the kidneys, the excessive use of starches and proteins, or too many fruits that stir up acids, all cause headaches of various kinds and patterns of pain.

Remedies for Ordinary Headaches

First, drink two glasses of water to see if dehydration is causing the problem. If you still have a headache an hour after drinking the water, try thyme tea. Put a handful of fresh thyme into a quart of boiling water, let steep (covered) for twenty minutes, then drink a cup every four hours. The following herbs have helped people with headaches: rosemary, peppermint, ginger, basil, and blessed thistle.

Chronic headaches may be due to toxins from the intestinal tract. So make sure you get the proper diet, use acidophilous culture and get 25 to 30 grams of fiber daily. It would be best for you to cleanse your colon to detoxify it. Use enemas made with baking soda or lemon juice and water. If the bowel is irritated, use flaxseed tea enemas. Sometimes food allergies are the cause of chronic headaches, and your doctor can help you if that is the problem.

Physical work helps nervous headaches; good activities are swimming, outdoor exercise, morning walks, bending exercises, and skipping rope.

Some headaches are caused by climate conditions. Seek those parts of the country conducive to healthful living. An altitude of about 1,700 to 3,000 feet is usually best. If headaches come during hot, humid weather, you may have to move to a place where the climate is dry and breezy-cool.

In some cases, headaches will disappear when we improve our marriage relations, our communication with our children, or our dissatisfaction on the job. If you live in grief, sorrow, fear, disappointment, or depression, you must get a new outlook on life to be healthy and headache free. If you have lost a lover, find another. If you have had a disappointment, find a new avenue of growth and self-satisfaction. Every experience will turn out to be a blessing, though you may not see it at the moment. Do not live in grief; do not live in resentment. You may have to change your environment and change your personal philosophy. Get into a set of suitable exercises, perhaps aerobics. Or get into games and learn to play to forget your troubles.

Hot teas such as lemon grass and chamomile may be helpful for headache distress. Some of these teas can be taken every hour; you can have quarts of them every day. Use them for improved elimination, to clean the bloodstream, and reduce sources of toxic substances from the body.

Cool applications to the head, hot foot baths, manipulation, massage, working on the spinal nerves, warm applications to the body, a warm sulfur bath, lots of fresh air, foot exercises, sand walks, and early morning grass walks will develop the circulation and also help reduce headaches.

What should we do in general? Get on a good sleep schedule, going to bed before midnight. Trade destructive lifestyle habits for healthy ones. You will find that living a peaceful, serene life will help most chronic headaches.

Sleep with your head to the north; sleep on pine needles; sleep on the ground; sunbathe, but do not overdo it. Use the Kneipp leg bath, spraying cold water up to the knees for one minute at a time. Skip a meal once in a while.

Take on new associates in your job, in your home; seek new companions—whatever you do, balance your day to live well.

Migraine

Migraine is one of those increasingly prevalent maladies of our day. Distressingly painful and crippling, it is often shrugged off as being incurable. But there is much help for the migraine sufferer. The herb feverfew has provided significant relief to many migraine sufferers.

Evidence shows that sometimes it could be psychosomatic. That is, it has a basis in nervous and emotional stress and strain as well as physical causes. It is this correlation that enables us to achieve good results by raising the physical level of fitness.

Diet has tremendous implications for the migraine victim. With a stronger, less fatigued body, anxieties automatically fall into proper perspective. A basic, regular, balanced daily diet is essential for our well-being. Research has shown that most chronic migraine cases are linked to magnesium deficiency. It may be advisable to take a short fast, in spite of the natural cleansing action of the vomiting and abstinence from food usually accompanying migraine attack. Juices are excellent for cleansing. The carrot, beet, and apple combination should be tried, along with liquid chlorophyll drinks.

Manipulative therapies also help. They tend to relax the nervous system as well as correct the functional organs of the body. Adjustments to vertebrae out of alignment may be necessary.

All efforts to improve blood circulation will help. Sand and grass walking, plus regular use of the slant board, should be an integral part of the daily routine.

Stretching the abdominal area, drawing in at the upper solar plexus, helps release tensions in the digestive tract. Moderate exercise, including walking (out in fresh air and sunshine if possible) without overdoing it, helps raise the health level and thus helps the migraine sufferer.

Besides building bodily strength, the careful avoidance of exhaustive reactions, such as worry and tensions, will hasten recovery. Get an interesting hobby to relieve the strain of work. Then change your diet: drop bread and baked goods for your head's sake.

Many famous people have been migraine sufferers, according to Dr. Diamond, a prominent Chicago physician. They include writers Alexander Pope, Rudyard Kipling, Edgar Allan Poe, Leo Tolstoy, and Lewis Carroll; composers Frederic Chopin, Peter Tchaikovsky, and Richard Wagner; scientists Sigmund Freud and Charles Darwin; and such political figures as Julius Caesar, Peter the Great, Thomas Jefferson, Ulysses S. Grant, and Karl Marx.

"Migraine sufferers tend to be hard-driving, hard-working individuals," said Dr. Diamond.

HAIR

Hair Culture

In taking care of the hair, we have to recognize that the hair is dependent on the bloodstream. It belongs to our body, just the same as our skin, nails, and eyelashes. It must be fed by the digestive system. It lives. It has its roots in the scalp. In order to get a good plant to grow, we must nourish it, care for it, and see that it has a balanced ration of sunshine and water. This is also true of the hair. It has to be nourished and cared for.

There are many things we neglect in our body and in our daily habits. And there is good evidence that hair is one of them: People are losing their hair because they do not take care of it in the way they should. Hair must have more care than just a daily combing or brushing.

As we consider care of the hair, let us remember that the hair is functional as well as ornamental. It is a receptor, it helps to keep us magnetically balanced. It holds the greatest amount of silicon in our body, and silicon is the "feeling" element of our body; silicon is also the magnetic element in the body.

I know of many doctors who take care of their hair, and they all have the same idea: the hair must be taken care of the same as the teeth. When the hair begins to deteriorate, it is due to neglect. Women tend to take better care of their hair than men, brushing it, using special shampoos and rinses, and going to hair salons for special care. There may be a genetic component to male pattern baldness and to women's more luxurious hair as they grow older.

Every hair has a hair-bed in the skin, with a bulb at the end of the hair root, through which the hair draws its nutrition from the blood. The hair contains a food substance called keratin, which contains great quantities of sulphur. The scalp, which is made up of muscular material, should be relaxed so blood will circulate well beneath it. A tight scalp keeps the blood from circulating to the hair root. Many people find that in old age the top of the head is not properly nourished because their tissues do not allow proper circulation of the blood.

We also neglect the hair and the scalp when we do not sleep enough. Sleeplessness is one of the causes for a lack of hair growth as are overstudy, worry, and insufficient oils and nutrition in the blood. Baldness can come from a lack of lecithin, which is a brain and nerve fat. When we lack sulphur, silicon, and iron in our food, the hair shoots will not develop and grow properly. Typhoid fever and many of the diseases found in childhood can bring on a loss of hair.

The thyroid gland has a lot to do with hair also, for when the thyroid becomes underactive, the circulation is slow, and the tissue is flabby. An extra amount of iodine in the diet can help this condition, and that in turn will help the hair. Strong acids and alkalines, when applied to it, can destroy the hair. Dandruff can smother the hair shoots and the scalp in general. This is caused by a lack of moisture in the sebaceous glands.

Beautiful Hair

To have a beautiful head of hair one must give it care and attention. Learn what diets are good for the body, and find out how to feed the weaknesses in the body that prevent it from circulating good blood. Live on nutritionally balanced foods. Stay

away from devitalized foods, especially demineralized starches
such as white flour products and white rice. The demineralized
starches take away the outside layer (or silicon layer) of the
grain, which is specifically needed for hair growth. The finest
foods to use for healthy hair are found in the following: oat-
straw tea, rice polishings, rice bran syrup, wheat bran tea, shavegrass tea, radishes, horseradish, sprouts, sole, black bass, smoked
bluefish, whitefish, shad roe, bran bread, strawberries, avocados,
cucumbers, steel cut oatmeal, graham bread, seaweed, wheat
germ, nuts, fruits, dandelion, leeks, romaine lettuce, parsnips,
whole barley meal, tender raw carrots, marjoram, collards, caraway, whole rice, and wheat.

It is best not to use a nylon brush on the hair. One hair in
the head is worth two in the brush. For brushing, a natural bristle brush helps keep the hair clean and shining.

Graying and Thinning Hair

There are many things we can use in the diet to help the hair,
but the one thing that seems to get the best results is Nova
Scotia dulse tablets. Also good are three or four parsley tablets
taken three and four times a day, or one-half glass of parsley
juice taken daily.

Alfalfa tablets and alfalfa tea are especially good for helping
the hair regain its original color.

These things, along with a scalp massage while on the
slant board, will change the hair considerably in a period of
six months. You will find that you can bring a good supply of
blood to the hair if you massage your scalp while lying on the
slant board, head down. Massaging the scalp with the tops of
the fingers about twenty minutes three times a week helps
tremendously.

One shampoo that is very stimulating to the hair and to the scalp is made of an egg yolk combined with a quarter teaspoon of sea salt. Rub this well into the scalp and let it set for some ten or fifteen minutes, then wash it out with castile soap. This can be done twice a week.

Watch your elimination; make sure that the kidneys and the bowels are functioning well. Be sure that the skin is cared for by brushing it. It might be well to stimulate the circulation in the head areas at times by using hot and cold packs while lying on the slant board. Use the packs one-half minute hot, one-fourth minute cold. Make about six or eight changes while on the board. Do this once a day.

To revitalize our hair we must conserve our energy, control our imagination, stop working when we are tired, and use a lot of silicon foods. Give your scalp a thirty-minute massage twice a week for at least six to eight weeks, and a noticeable result will be observed; however, scalps that are put under extremely hot hair dryers and subjected to the use of some of the dandruff cure-all remedies available are having much of the hair growth destroyed. The itching of dandruff can also be relieved through the use of regular scalp massage.

If there is a fungus growth on the scalp, a good remedy is to use sheep fat and a little garlic oil. Leave it on the hair for a period of twenty minutes, then shampoo. Washing the hair in soft water and castile soap is wonderful. The gentle friction of the massage, as we mentioned, will bring the proper heat and blood to the surface and help the hair shoots to develop and grow in the proper head of hair.

An egg yolk in grape juice is a great tonic to help the glands and to help the circulation. Whenever there is any hardening of the arteries, it is advisable to use whey and grapevine root and leaf tea.

I had an interesting experience at one time with a man who was billed as the strongest "upside-down man" in the world. His name was Joe Tonti, and he used to live in Oklahoma City. He told me that years ago when he was a child he had a severe fever and lost his hair. He also had blemishes on his face, an eczema that was very difficult to get rid of. As he grew older he went into weightlifting work and athletic activities. He did a good deal of his work upside-down and found that in getting more blood to his head in these upside-down activities, the blemishes on his face left and his hair returned. Onions, horseradish, and the sulfur foods will also help drive the blood to the brain areas and to the scalp.

Dr. V. G. Rocine, a Norwegian homeopath, used a wash made of the roots of the ordinary grapevine once a week. He believed that drinks made of honey and tonics made of celery with Concord grape juice were good for the hair. Weak tea made of the roots of the grapevine can be taken occasionally.

CHAPTER 7

PRIMACY OF THE BRAIN

The brain is probably the most neglected and underrated organ in the health sciences in terms of understanding its importance in health and disease. For that reason, its care and nourishment are seldom given adequate consideration, and if you asked your doctor what you need to do to keep your brain in top condition, he would probably be caught by surprise and unable to give you helpful instruction. Yet, unless we take care of the brain, the brain cannot adequately monitor, protect, and interact with body tissue and activities that not only determine our quality of life, but that may mean the difference between life and death. The brain is the orchestra conductor that harmonizes all of our body functions and guides us in our journey through life, and if we don't take good care of it, it can't take good care of us.

The brain and spinal cord make up the central nervous system that takes in sensory information, learns from experiences, operates the body, and constantly balances all the activities and processes of the body, most of it at a subconscious level. It is constantly checking out and reacting to hundreds of thousands of bits of information from different tissues of the body—things like blood pressure, muscle movement, acid/alkaline balance, temperature, oxygen level, hunger, thirst, osmotic pressure, metabolic rate, organ functions, glandular secretions, and much more. It also takes in data from the senses—vision, hearing, taste, touch, and smell—reacts to the environment, evaluates it, makes new memories, and stores them with existing memories.

In order to do everything it has to do, the brain uses 25 percent of both the oxygen and glucose in the blood, despite the fact that it takes up only 2 percent or so of the body weight and is made up of 80 percent water. Even though it uses a great deal of energy, the brain never moves. At any given time, 20 percent of our total blood supply is in the brain. If our bodies go into a starvation mode from not eating, storage reserves of glucose are released from the liver, and the brain may use up to 75 percent of that stored glucose for its own functions, while reducing body metabolism to a basic survival level.

The brain contains 100 billion neurons that interconnect with each other by means of 60 to 100 trillion connections called synapses. It is generally divided into several parts, the largest being the cerebrum, which handles communication, conscious learning and thought, organization, and social behavior. Under it, the cerebellum is involved with the operation and coordination of muscles, including walking, running, posture, balance, and fine muscle movements, like those involved with playing a musical instrument. The brain stem is considered the most primitive part of the brain, responsible for breathing, heart rate, blood pressure, swallowing, coughing, sneezing, vomiting, and the sleep/wake system. The eyes are actually parts of the brain, connected to the visual cortex at the back of the head.

I am not going to get into how the brain interreleates with the endocrine gland system, or how importantly the brain is dependent upon liver function. But I want to draw your attention to the fact that if the brain is undernourished, not only are the nerves that it uses to communicate with the rest of the body less efficient and the constitutionally weakest parts of the body more vulnerable to disease, but its own control centers for specific functions, such as appetite, sex, and alertness toward danger may be severely compromised. We have every good reason to take the best care possible of our brain and nervous system.

We can be good to our brain by 1) keeping the blood well nourished with the foods it needs; 2) keeping the blood charged with oxygen through regular exercise and exposure to fresh, clean air; 3) keeping the blood clean by taking care of the eliminative channels—bowel, kidneys, lungs, and skin; and 4) giving it sufficient rest. You will not be able to do this if you are too lazy or are running too fast trying to keep ahead in the rat race. Pay attention to your need for motivation in all this. Find out about nutritious foods and learn the art of making them delicious. Select forms of exercise that you really enjoy and look forward to (exercise to music you love). Get into a high-fiber diet, drink at least two quarts of water daily, and follow a special cleansing diet at least twice a year to keep your elimination channels clean and healthy.

ATTITUDE AND BRAIN HEALTH

Don't clutter up your mental landscape with garbage. Focus on the good things in life and practice thinking in productive and enjoyable ways. Refuse to hold grudges, develop ill will, or seek out revenge on anyone. Practice kind and wise thoughts about people. Learn to switch your anger onto safer, healthier tracks. (If you need assistance with anger abatement, there are lots of classes and counselors around who know how to help you change.) Develop a wholesome, enjoyable sex life, which always involves learning ways of better pleasing your partner than yourself. Are you laughing enough? If not, do something about it. Do you dam up sadness or grief? Learn to cry and let it out. Study to improve yourself. Hang around with interesting, lovable people. Healthy forms of pleasure build up vitality. Sadness, grief, and depression lower immune system effectiveness.

FOOD FOR THOUGHT

Remember what I said earlier about the importance of glucose to the brain? Researchers have rediscovered the need for a healthy breakfast in order to enhance learning ability. In an April 22, 1999, United States Drug Administration seminar, Paul Gold told an audience, "Cognitive abilities might be expected to be enhanced by breakfast, and perhaps optimally enhanced with a sufficient carbohydrate load to elevate [blood] glucose for several hours. Appropriate snacks, including moderate carbohydrate content, should be incorporated . . . so that brain glucose reserves are not depleted by complex [mental] tasks." Glucose makes remembering easier and more accurate, even for people with Down's syndrome or Alzheimer's disease. In one experiment, elderly subjects were found to be more creative after a good cereal-and-milk breakfast. Their minds worked better. In another experiment, low levels of glucose reserves were found to limit remembering. This suggests that snacks designed to replenish brain reserves of glucose would expand the time limit factor for making and storing new memories. These findings work for both children and adults of all ages.

The ideal breakfast, then, would be a whole grain cereal topped with a little honey, maple syrup, or sweet dried fruit, along with goat's milk, soy milk, seed or nut milk, or rice milk, and some fruit. This is the kind of breakfast I have encouraged my patients and students to adopt. It is well to keep the breakfast low-fat, because there is some indication that fats interfere with the brain's assimilation of the highest amount of carbohydrates. I want to make clear that simple sugars like sucrose or fructose are available to the bloodstream most quickly, while more complex carbohydrates like vegetables and whole grains take longer for digestive enzymes to break down into glucose.

THE BRAIN AND ADDICTIVE BEHAVIORS

We find out that biochemical deficiencies in the brain are now considered a major cause of compulsive behaviors such as drug and alcohol addictions, or even compulsive overeating. According to Dr. Kenneth Blum of the Division of Addictive Diseases at the University of Texas, the neurotransmitters dopamine and GABA (gamma-aminobutyric acid), when present, produce a feeling of well-being or calm, while a shortage of dopamine can cause discomfort or craving (for drugs or alcohol), and a shortage of GABA can produce feelings of restlessness, tension, or anxiety. Apparently, that's when the urge to drink or use drugs takes over. Neurotransmitter deficiencies may be due to genetic defects, severe stress, or destruction by previous excessive use of alcohol or drugs.

The amino acid D-phenylalanine doesn't come in food, but it can be used to compensate for the genetic defect that reduces dopamine receptors, and it can prevent the breakdown of brain endorphins (which provide a feeling of well-being). L-tryptophan, another amino acid, can be used to stimulate production of more dopamine. L-tryptophan is involved with serotonin production. Serotonin reduces cravings for drugs and alcohol and makes sleep easier. The trace element chromium assists getting food tryptophan into the brain, which helps restore amino acid balance, favors relaxation, and reduces addiction.

Alcohol addiction destroys or depletes vitamin A, all the B-complex vitamins, vitamins C and D, calcium, iron, zinc, magnesium, and selenium. Alcohol destroys liver cells by dehydration, gradually creating scar tissue, a condition called cirrhosis. This reduces the liver's ability to store important vitamins, minerals, and glycogen, the storage form of glucose. In turn, these deficiencies cause damage to other tissues and organs, and the lack of glucose handicaps brain function.

Nutritional restoration of the alcoholic often requires nutritional supplements together with a balanced food regimen to compensate for long-term deficiencies and tissue damage due to lack of vitamin-dependent and mineral-dependent enzymes.

ALZHEIMER'S, NUTRITION, AND BRAIN FUNCTION

The latest research on Alzheimer's disease implies that information stored in the brain isn't destroyed by Alzheimer's, but the transmission of that information is blocked. Short-term loss of memory is linked to deficiencies in vitamins B_{12} and C and glucose; poor cognition is believed to be due to lack of folic acid, vitamins B_6 and B_{12}, iron, and glucose. Poor results in problem-solving tests indicate loss of riboflavin, folic acid, vitamin B_{12}, vitamin C, and glucose.

It is hard to get Alzheimer's patients to exercise, but it is crucial to get oxygen and glucose to the brain. Taking walks may be the best way to improve oxygenation and circulation of the blood. I have found that ginko biloba and ginseng are excellent brain stimulants, and I would advise fresh, warm, raw goat's milk to the person suffering from Alzheimer's or dementia.

Socialization tends to hold back Alzheimer's. One study showed that persons who isolate themselves, as compared with those who visit and interact with friends and relatives are more than twice as likely to get Alzheimer's. Some people keep busy with knitting or crocheting or braiding rugs. Others do cross-word puzzles, play checkers or chess or other games. I think the main idea with the brain is "use it or lose it," the same thing we say about exercise and the body.

BRAIN FOOD

The brain requires a significant amount of proteins, which are made of amino acids, every day. It may require certain amino acid supplements in abundance to compensate for genetic weaknesses in the brain.

WAYS TO STRENGTHEN BRAIN AND NERVE FORCE

Self-esteem

Each person needs a positive sense of identity. Self-recognition is imperative. Most persons do not know themselves; each of us is more than we realize. Praise other people and you become popular and influential whether you want to be or not. They notice your own higher qualities and this gives you a sense of your own significance. It all depends on how you feel. Feel great and you become greater; feel noble and you enable yourself;

feel honest and you grow into greater honesty; feel bashful and you look like a sheep, act like a sheep, and talk like a sheep. Attitude is everything, as they say.

Sentiments and thoughts can also be cell builders, brain builders, and soul builders. You may just as well dwell on your own significance as upon your own insignificance. Imagination is one of the greatest forces we have. It is a great constructive force. You will find that imagination helps to develop the potential within you.

If you lack courage, imagine a few times a day that you are a courageous person, that you can stand up to anyone—the devil included. In less than a year you will feel a remarkable change.

Save your nerve force until you need it. Tempers, arguments, anger, resentment, gossip, worries, strife, anxieties, jumpiness—each and all of these are negative mental and physical energies. When nerve force is not used nobly and usefully, it should be held in reserve. This will make you greater, more useful, more popular, better composed, and more self confident.

Learn to be your own company, learn to value your own selfhood. It is the highest, noblest power you possess. Never stay too long with others. Be your own companion as long as you are building brain cells within. All have genius slumbering within. To discover it is your greatest mission.

Learn to Live with Change

There is nothing permanent in life but change! It is unfortunate to get into a groove and be unable to get out. Be flexible enough to take on the new practice and become new.

As soon as we realize we cannot go through life with everything always the same, we will find that things begin to work out better.

I have reached the point where my days are slowing down, while once they were full of change. Extra responsibilities were often forced upon me, and I did them well while I was able. One of the finest things I learned is to gracefully anticipate the unannounced, the unexpected, which includes the awareness that I am ninety-two years old! I am learning to appreciate a slower, more peaceful lifestyle. I still do all that I can do within the limits of my energy and mobility, but I am still able to deal with the unexpected.

Work with Joy

Another thing that will help give you more vitality is to learn to enjoy your work. There is no such thing as getting out of doing work. You will always have work to do, and you might just as well accept that fact now. So, work we shall do. But we can work with joy. Joy makes time go by swiftly. Many persons say they have time on their hands; they say they don't know what to do with all the time they have. Well, any job that causes you to feel there is time on your hands is not an enjoyable one. For the happy man, there is no time. In my eighties, I faced both prostate cancer and paralysis from the hips down. First, I beat the cancer, then I worked my way out of paralysis, walking with a pronounced limp, but walking without a cane. I gave several public lectures at that time and received standing ovations. After a year or so, my hip gave out and I was back to my bed again, with occasional outings in my wheelchair to speak to audiences or show someone my work. I can't tell you how much I missed my work and my audiences during the time I spent fighting cancer and paralysis. Pitting my brain force and willpower against the disease and the paralysis *became* my work. I didn't (and still don't) like it, but I suppose this is my ultimate challenge—to be the best doctor I can, on the one hand, and the best patient I can, on the other. Meanwhile, I am trying to finish up two or three more books. Am I happy? Not always. But I'm as happy as I can be, considering the circumstances.

Find Joy in Music and Color

Besides a pleasurable job and a good hobby, two other things contribute to happiness: music and color. Wherever there is color, wherever there is music, you will find happy people. Music can make people ecstatic; color can delight as well.

Music Affects Every Mood. Music can do the glands a lot of good. Within music there are so many variations of consciousness that everybody can be reached. Music works through various levels of feeling, and this feeling is sparked in the glands more than in any other part of the body.

We have all heard music that makes us want to cry, and we have felt joyous with upbeat music. We find that in drawing us close or inspiring us, music plays on the full gamut of senses in the body, from the lowest to the highest. Fish and other animals turn away from certain kinds of music, yet those same fish and animals will turn toward other types of music.

Music has an effect upon the human body, just as it has on fish, animals, and even plant life. Certain plants will turn away from rock music but will actually bend toward such music as a Strauss waltz. There is something about music that either repels you or draws you to it.

Music resonates with a level of our consciousness, a level of response, a level of feeling, a level of enjoyment, empowerment, and upliftment. Of course, music is not the only way we get a response from the body. We react to words and color, just through their associations with our memories.

We usually pick a type of music for our mood. Classical music has a soothing effect. When a person is tired, soft music can be quite pleasing and uplifting, just as some people enjoy music that makes them want to dance. When music is playing at a certain tempo, look around and you will see toes tapping. It does something magical to the body. We are carried along with it; there is spirit in music.

We have all witnessed the effect of a band playing a stirring march. Men have come under the influence of martial music and have done amazing things. I had a friend in the British army, Captain Murdo McDonald Baine. He told of seeing men in wartime practically dead come alive suddenly and stand up on their feet at the sound of Scottish bagpipes playing their national anthem. These men, with their energies miraculously restored, would pick themselves up and start marching to this music. It gave them a surge of spirit that nothing else could have mustered into their depleted bodies. We find that music can bring tears, joy, and laughter. It can affect the entire gamut of feelings.

Color Affects Our Emotions. There is also spirit in color. We find some colors stimulating just as we find certain music stimulating. Other colors are sedating and tranquilizing to the body. Colors are cold or warm, exciting or subduing. A lot of work can be done by some people in a room painted red, but by the end of the day they could very easily be fighting with each other. Red is a stimulating color. When a matador enters the bull ring you do not see him carrying a blue cape; he brings in a red cape. Red also can affect breeding. Flies that do not breed in a blue box will quite readily breed in a red box. We are all guided by the red light that means "stop." It draws attention. There is rarely a lethargic response to the color red.

In certain religious faiths, the believers are not allowed to wear red. In Spain, all the Catholic pomp and ceremony is found in very bright colors. In Scotland, Presbyterians and Lutherans use only the cold, quiet colors.

We find entirely different colors are worn in different climatic regions. The same colors are never used when it is warm as when it is cold. The cheerful, wild colors children wear disappear as they become adults. Perhaps grownups grow up too much.

We select our clothes as much for the color as we do for the style. I've had some suits that I liked and others that I didn't, yet they were all practically the same style. A brown suit, for instance, I wore only two or three times and then gave it away. I didn't feel good in it. Many people go through life in a spectrum of colors, but they don't realize its effect. We even have what we call "colorful moods." People can look at the world through rose-colored glasses or be green with envy. Just think about it. We all live in color.

Different colors call forth different responses in people. Pay attention to how color affects you.

Remedies With Color. There is a lot we could see and use in nature if we knew the value of color and its effect on the body.

1. Yellow-colored foods generally have a laxative effect. Yellow apricots, peaches, castor oil, and eggs are all laxative. Senna leaves and senna flowers are yellow, as well as other laxatives in nature.

2. We should know not only the laxative foods but also the constipating foods. For instance, blackberries are normally constipating, but they are one of the foods that can be used

when a person has diarrhea. When we understand nature, we can use this knowledge for a good purpose.

Energies in Sexual Union

We know that sex is used for procreation and the continuance of the races, but there are many more values the average person does not know about. Recreational sex is used too much by men and women as a mere physical expression. It could become an uplifting experience. One of the greatest regeneration factors comes when the unclothed body is in contact with another without overindulgence. Some people take energy and others give it. The energies can be rebuilt in each other this way. The powers of life flowing through the body can be increased. All the physical powers as well as mental powers can grow and develop in proportion to the feeling and contentment that a person has in this contact.

AIDS and other STDs have not destroyed the value and power of sexual intimacy, but they have forced us to consider how our sexuality may be safely and responsibly expressed. Disease is always as much a message about our lifestyle, survival, and personal choices as it is an entity that disrupts, somehow, the flow of our lives.

Pure Fragrance: Food for the Soul

There is much talk today of the healing value of color, music, and fragrance. These three are all related in their harmonics, but I believe fragrance is the higher octave of the spectrum. Aromatherapy can be traced back to ancient Egypt. More recently Roland Hunt of California wrote a book on the subject entitled *Fragrant and Radiant Healing Symphony.* Hunt also wrote

The Seven Keys to Color Healing. Many people believe fragrance is vital in promoting health, claiming it is "food for the soul," just as beauty is. They say without it the visible body will follow the spiritual into a decline. Strengthening aromas, however, must be genuine. No artificial perfumes can replace the scents of nature in influencing the mind. There is healing value in a garden, its perfumes and colors.

Bring floral or herbal fragrances inside. Put them in your window boxes and planters. Decorate your home often with cut flowers. Use sachets of dried lavender in your closets and thyme in your kitchen. Their fragrance will delight you, and some herbs act as insect repellents, too. For your evenings out, wear natural perfumes made from essential oils.

Sleep to Rest the Brain

Many people do not understand sleep. Everybody is looking for an insomnia remedy; hundreds of gadgets have been patented; sleeping pills galore have been developed. People tell me that if they could only relax they could sleep. You can learn to relax by listening to soft music, reading a book, having warm feet when going to bed, drinking a little warm milk, or having a small snack of crackers or bread. Melatonin, a natural sleep aid, may help; or try a cup of valerian tea.

But if you still can't sleep, don't despair. It has been found that good resting is nearly 90 percent equivalent to good sleep. So if you are in wonderful contemplation, free of anxiety, living in joyful thinking, and allowing harmonious thoughts to pass through the mind while your eyes are closed and completely relaxed, 90 percent of that time is equal to good sleep. Just remember that sleeping is mainly for resting the brain.

Music before sleeping helps a person to relax. Dr. Fournier Pescay used the music of a flute for insomnia in the case of his own son. Dr. Stephen Halpenn of Belmont, California, uses pure sounds to assist in healing. His audiotape *Zodiac Suite* is a wonderfully relaxing work of musical healing art.

See that hypersensitive children have rest in the afternoon by lying in a dark room with no disturbances. Whether they are asleep or not makes no difference. Do this in the afternoon when they come home from school. Some moments of quiet rest will give their metabolism a chance to slow down after all the mental and physical activity of the day. Then allow them to go out and play. Slow music is also very good for a hypersensitive child.

We should try to get a hard mattress for our sleep. If necessary, put a board between the mattress and the springs. This is better for the back and for postural support lying down. There are some people who sleep better in the presence of a different atmosphere and even with a perfumed atmosphere.

I remember once while in Austria that when my wife and I pulled down the covers of the bed one night to go to bed, there was a lavender sachet bag in the bed. The sachet added a very pleasant aroma to the atmosphere, and we fell asleep very quickly.

Make sure your bedroom is painted in a pastel color, using greens and blues. They are cooling colors and do not stimulate the mental or nervous system.

Warm feet are very important for sleep. Walking ten minutes in sand or grass to build up the circulation in the legs will help you to have warm feet. Warm feet allow for perfect relaxation when you go to bed.

Insomnia can sometimes be caused more from bowel troubles than anything else. Other causes are late hours, excessive mental labor, close study, sluggish liver, and having too much protein (especially meat) late at night. Remedies include hot foot baths, warm drinks, a light supper, quiet, and cultivation of uplifting thoughts in the evening.

Nightmares or unpleasant hallucinations may be caused by too much food at suppertime, or what you've been watching on television.

Some good herb teas for sleeping include valerian, hops, catnip, and black cohosh. A combination herb tea that helps to promote natural and refreshing sleep can be made from hops, valerian root, and scullcap.

A good juice tonic is a combination of celery and lettuce.

Sleeping Nude or Comfortably. People should sleep in the nude, or, at the very most, in loose pajamas. We get into clothes in the morning to hold ourselves together; we jump out of our clothes at night, and before we can drop them to the floor, we jump into pajamas and more clothing.

Our bodies should be kept loose and free at night so that we can turn and move in any direction without any restrictions. You will get more rest and better restore the brain force for the next day. It's impossible for the body to rest properly with corsets, garments, or bras in the way.

Snoring. Sometimes snoring hinders good sleeping. A good remedy is to place a small quantity of sesame seed oil or peanut oil in each nostril before retiring. This prevents drying out of the nose. Drying automatically opens the mouth, and snoring begins. It is claimed that this oil treatment is very effective.

Do not sleep on your back. Have polyps in the nose broken down through massage. Stop using heavy starches. Taking the time to have peaceful and restful sleep will make a new person out of you. Avoid negative and destructive thoughts at all times, but especially before going to sleep. You should pack up such thoughts and send them off into the purifying light of exalted thinking.

A Mental Formula That Works. To increase serenity for sleeping, on going to bed, relieve yourself of the day's problems and accept the last thoughts you have at night as the thoughts you want to ring through your subconscious mind all night. Say to yourself: "My nerves are strong and calmer. I feel in harmony with myself, with the universe, and with everything around me. I am rich with inner powers that give me harmony, security, and serenity. No one—nothing—can separate me from unity with Higher Powers, which protect me from all evils. The Higher Powers make me invincible."

New Vitality to Start Your Day

You can bring vitality and energy into the body through your mind. For new vitality, say this at the beginning of the day, repeat it three times, say it consciously, think it deeply each time you repeat:

> I am filled with health and the joy of living.
> There is sunshine in my soul today.
> The clouds have rolled away and I feel
> Confident, reassured—ever so confident.
> I feel young, ever so young.
> Every day in every way I feel younger and younger.
> I feel like a new and wonderful personality,
> And I can overcome everything with the greatest of ease.
> I feel wonderful—truly wonderful!

BUILDING THE NERVES

Nerves must be fed—mentally as well as physically. Behind every function of the body, nerve action is needed. Your eyes, for example, are an extension of the brain. Many times the eyes may be affected when the nervous system is under stress. Many different kinds of conditions can harm the nervous system. Nutritional deficiencies, prolonged stress, trauma, neurological diseases, tumors, and chronic depression are a few of them. But by caring for your nerves through specific, nourishing activities, you can avoid some of these conditions and build healthy nerves.

Outdoor Activity

Dr. Rickly, one of the great naturopaths of the past, found that he could normalize the thyroid gland by putting a person outside in the fresh air. The late Bernarr McFadden was a great champion of exercise in the great outdoors a generation before jogging became popular. Outdoor activity normalizes the metabolism quicker than anything else. We need fresh air, and to a nervous person it is the most soothing massage to give to the nervous system. Get fresh air into the lungs every day.

Warm Baths

The legendary actress Sarah Bernhardt, said she never could have carried on her wonderful work without warm baths. Sometimes I think warm baths are overdone, but when we work under tension, we need relaxation. Napoleon, in order to carry on his work, always brought a bathtub with him. He felt the need to have a warm bath during his campaigns.

Skin Brushing

Massage is also wonderful for the nerves. A good massage can be obtained by skin brushing. Use a dry brush and brush the entire body. Do it every morning for five minutes before you put on your clothes. It will do more for the nerves and the body than anything else I can tell you. Use a natural bristle brush, never nylon.

Avoid Excessive Noise

Noise can break down the nerve force and leave a person weak and depleted. A recent news article, headlined "Nerve Ailments Linked to Airport," explained:

> People who live near the Los Angeles International Airport suffer a higher rate of nervous breakdowns than people who live further away from the constant jet noise, according to a 1992 University of California at Los Angeles study.
>
> Dr. William C. Meecham, a UCLA engineering professor who conducted the three-year study, found that mental hospital admissions for residents within three miles of the airport were 29 percent higher than for residents about six miles away.
>
> The findings of this report reinforced an earlier British study which showed a 31 percent increase in the nervous breakdown rate above England's national norm for neighbors of London's busy Heathrow Airport. The subject of "noise pollution" is relatively new in terms of actually being able to measure the harm done to people.
>
> Dr. Meecham analyzed the geographical distribution of residents referred to mental hospitals by South Bay Mental Health Service in reaching his conclusions.
>
> He numbered mental health patients living in what he considered a "maximum noise area" in Inglewood, where a decibel level of 90 was not uncommon from jets nearby. For comparison he selected a control area in El Segundo three miles to the south.

"The 90-decibel level in the maximum noise area is considered by acoustic experts as hazardous to mental and physical health and may trigger social tensions and a wide range of physical health problems," explained Dr. Meecham, who has also published a paper titled "Increase in Mortality Rates Due to Aircraft Noise" in Proceedings of Inter-Noise, 1993.

BEST BRAIN AND NERVE FOODS

How can we best strengthen our brain and nerve force through food?

We need lecithin and the nerve salts, both found in egg yolk and prune juice. We need phosphates as found in yellow corn meal. We need animal proteins, including cheese and dairy products. Phosphorus is necessary for building brain and nerve energies as well as bones and teeth.

We can get brain-building material from all of our foods, but there are some mental faculties that use more of one kind of food for repair than another. Those mental faculties that are used for love, veneration, and similar feelings require lecithin and cholesterol foods.

Among the best brain foods are those containing silicon such as oat straw tea, barley gruel, shavegrass tea, and bran tea, all used between meals. Manganese is found in high quantity in Missouri black walnuts and is wonderful for the memory centers. The high phosphorus content of North Atlantic fish is also considered a wonderful brain food. It is beneficial to use fish broths and clam broth or juice often.

I know there are some vegetarians who will disagree, but if you want to build nerve and brain structure, you need to have amino acids, the highest concentration of which come from animal products. (We can also get them from tofu.)

A good herb drink for the brain and nervous system can be made by boiling together one ounce each of vervain, mistletoe, and valerian in two quarts of water for twenty minutes. Drink two or three glasses per day.

For poor memory use ginko biloba, manganese-rich foods, vitamin B-complex, and RNA-rich foods such as sardines, cod-fish roe, and chlorella. Also good is a juice tonic of carrot, celery, and prune, with rice polishings; rosemary and sage teas; and slant board exercises.

An alert, quick mind needs phosphorus, calcium, and magnesium foods. Heavy mental work requires selenium. Phosphorus and sulfur foods improve ability to make decisions.

Egg Yolks

I want to tell you about a tonic that is splendid for the nerves. In the early 1900s, Nobel Laureate Alexis Carrel made a tissue culture of fibroblast cells from a chicken heart and kept it alive for thirty-four years in a nutrient medium derived from egg yolk. The longest any chicken had been known to live was twelve years. Dr. Carrel's experiment gave birth to the idea of the immortality of cells, if properly fed. The concept of cellular immortality was later disproved, but it is evident that proper feeding has a great deal to do with promoting health and longevity.

I consider egg yolk one of the finest foods for the nervous system. You don't have to have it raw. You can have it cooked, but I don't believe it should be fried. There are many ways to cook eggs. The part of the egg yolk that is so good for the nervous system is called vitellin, which goes along with lecithin, a brain and nerve fat also found in egg yolk. Egg yolk is a far richer source of lecithin than any other food, although soybeans, avocado, and olives also contain liberal amounts of lecithin.

We must recognize that egg yolk is one of our fattiest foods. The liver and gall bladder must take care of that fat. Whenever you serve egg yolk, be sure to serve with it a food for the liver. The best liver and gall bladder food is greens. The most specific food is dandelion greens or dandelion tea. One of the finest nerve tonics is magnesium chlorophyll, available in your health food store. Another splendid tonic is a teaspoon of chlorophyll in a little cherry concentrate or grape concentration base (foods high in iron and good for the liver). Put egg yolk in this for a complete nerve food. Don't overdo it. Have it only once a day. Just add it to your regular way of living.

In Italy, many doctors use this tonic for treating patients going through the change of life. It helps to control hot flashes and other disorders caused by the change of life.

The egg yolk may be slightly cooked and eaten separately, but be sure to have something green at the same time. Do you remember how Grandmother served poached eggs on spinach? That was a good combination. Serve poached eggs on beet greens, Swiss chard, or with a salad. Then, when it is carried to the liver, it will not cause trouble.

Sprouts

One of the finest sources of protein is the sprouted seed. Alfalfa seeds, wheat kernels, and even garbanzos are wonderful when sprouted. You can eat them raw or grind them and put them into various dishes. Have them in your salads. Sprouts are wonderful for the nerves.

In Germany a short time ago, doctors experimented with about one hundred patients who had multiple sclerosis, which is a degeneration of the nervous system and the spinal cord. In some of the cases, medical treatment could do nothing. They were given green juices and sprouts as the main part of their meals. Every one of them improved; fifteen totally recovered. Food not only affects the nervous system, it affects our entire body.

THE GOAL OF THE DISCIPLE

The goal of the disciple is within himself—it is God.
Many in the world seek outside of themselves;
That is why their lives are full of discontent.
Everything is within,
Be always content,
Then there are no obstacles on the way to attainment.
Never desire more suffering or joy than is necessary.
No one is measured by the number of sufferings
He goes through,
But by what he has learned from them.
Have Peace internally, externally, and eternally.
If love cannot give Peace, it is not Love.
He who lives in Love is always young,
Calling the powers of Heaven to his aid.
Go in Peace . . .
Then healing enters into the body.

(AUTHOR UNKNOWN)

CHAPTER 8

THE BLOOD

A person can't be healthy without healthy blood. The blood distributes and stores food, collects waste throughout the body and helps eliminate it, regulates the heat in the body, kills germ life, and above all, carries its secretions to the various organs that are in need of them.

We respond immediately to the adrenal gland substance carried by the blood through the lymph stream to every cell in the body. Every bit of blood in the body travels through the thyroid glands every hour and a half. Silicon in the blood speeds through the body to reach the toenails, the hair, and other extremities that require it. The same blood that is depositing the calcium in the bone will also deposit whatever calcium is needed in the transverse colon to keep it from developing a prolapsus.

The blood travels through the body at a rate of thirty feet per second. It constitutes about one-twelfth of the body weight. When normal, its white blood cells and antibodies resist all disease.

Chronic colds, pneumonia, bronchial troubles, and catarrhal disturbances lower the resistance of the body and take away the vital values of the blood. And those ailments get a foothold when the body is weakened by improper care. Bad food is one culprit: It takes away the good from our body. Salt draws in the water; and distilled vinegar and whiskey are literally embalming.

WAYS TO IMPROVE CIRCULATION

There are many things we can do to help our circulation. It's always best to take care of the heart first. The heart is one of the strongest organs in the body. Many people develop fears about a weak heart, but there are many things you can do to make it strong again.

To begin with, start a program of slow walking. I specifically prescribe slow walking, because overexertion can break down a weak heart. Build it up gradually each day.

There are also natural foods that help strengthen the heart. Try liquid chlorophyll, vitamin E, magnesium, and hawthorne berry tea, for instance. Avoid beef.

A fast pulse is usually caused by a thyroid condition. Many times the thyroid controls the heartbeat, and if we would take care of our nutrition and stress levels, we wouldn't have thyroid trouble that eventually leads to heart trouble. Our mind gets to the heart by way of the thyroid gland. Of course, thyroid dysfunction affects many other systems in the body.

Higher Altitude: More Oxygen in the Blood

High altitude is a great help in building a healthy bloodstream. It quickens the thyroid gland so that oxygen can enter the bloodstream. We must remember that oxygen clings to the iron in hemoglobin. You could breathe from now until infinity and never have enough oxygen in the body unless you have enough iron in the blood. The tissues will never be oxidized without iron.

The higher the altitude above sea level, the less oxygen we take in and the more red blood cells we need. At ocean level, our blood count can go as high as five million. For example, those living on the shores of Norway average a blood count of five million. In Peru, where elevations reach about 12,000 feet, the average blood count can run from seven to eight million. While we need a high count for good oxygenating, our heart does not respond well to extremely high altitudes. We would most likely end up panting, nauseated, and perhaps vomiting. We must therefore be careful in choosing our altitude. We should not overlook or ignore it.

Breathing Outdoors

Breathing out in the fresh air is excellent for circulation. Massage of the body, massaging toward the heart, is good. Quick inhalations and slow exhalations are good. Make sure the peristaltic action in the bowel is good. When this action is slow, activity in the bowel and circulation of blood are also slow.

Cheerfulness

We must develop cheerfulness for good circulation. Cultivate your love emotions; they're a necessary function. This doesn't necessarily mean sexual love, but it does mean love for people, love for surroundings. Love has many connotations and we should try to see all the facets of life affected by love. Each of us knows that we love to be loved. Go where you are loved and live so that you love others. Love is important to all our lives.

As my mother used to say, "Hate and fear only hurt the people who use them." You don't have to love your enemy for his sake; you don't have to love your neighbor for his sake; but you *must love for your own good.* Most of us are our own worst enemy. That's where love has to begin. Love is your best friend.

Exercise

Our circulation improves when we learn to contract the muscles in all parts of the body. There are many forms of exercise that are good for the whole body. I'm not recommending strenuous exercise that builds big muscles and strains the heart, but rational muscular activity that keeps the cells of the body alive and vigorous. Such an exercise is walking; but I think we should learn to hike, not just walk. Hiking is going into the hills, going up hills and down. Remember to avoid overexertion. Walking on ground that is not flat helps to develop the small muscles in the legs. We develop only the long muscle structure when we walk on sidewalks or the street. Anytime we are using the muscle structure in the arches of our feet on uneven ground, we develop the small muscles. That is why we have the sand and grass walk. There isn't anything finer to build up circulation in the body, especially the legs and lower extremities, than the sand and grass walks.

Swimming exercises every muscle in the body at one time. It is the finest exercise known, developing good circulation while we are in a prone position. Golfing is also an excellent exercise. It entails much walking and gives the mind needed relaxation. Not all of us are so situated that we can spend several afternoons a week on the golf links.

Walking, on the other hand, does not require expensive equipment or membership in a club. Everyone who is able to be up and around can get in some walking every day, even though it may be only walking to and from your work. Walk from two to five miles a day, and at the end of three months you'll feel like a different person.

People who have sluggish circulation have to quicken it; this is done through quickening their thoughts and body through exercise and work. Some people have to slow down, to learn to rest, to be still and quiet. Being quiet sometimes is very important, too, and to breathe slowly controls emotional strain.

Kneipp Baths

The Kneipp bath is a wonderful water treatment for better circulation in the legs. It also relieves heart pressure. The bath consists of splashing through a 25- to 30-foot walk in cold water up to the knees, then a barefoot walk in grass or sand until you are dry. Do not wipe dry; if you do, you lose the value of the bath. The value is in warming your own circulation and working to make sure that the circulation takes care of that cold water. This builds up the resistance in the body to take care of ordinary drafts and ordinary problems.

Another way of taking the bath is with a common garden hose, without the sprinkler attachment. Run cold water starting at the farthest point from the heart, which would be the ankle of the right leg, move the water in a stream from the toes to the groin, then around and down the back of the leg to the ankle. Spray first the right leg front and back, two or three times; then do the left leg in the same manner. You should be able to count to six while running water up and down each leg. This is very good for circulation of the entire body. Again, don't dry off. Run or walk until dry and warm. Do it once a day.

Grass Walk

In the early morning, while the dew is still on the grass, get out in your bare feet and shuffle up and down a few minutes. This will do wonders for the circulation, and, if begun in summer, can be carried through most of the winter in temperate climates; thus one can sleep with warm feet.

Sand Walk

Walking barefoot in sand is excellent for the feet and helps the circulation. Walk on the beach without shoes as a before breakfast exercise or set up a long "sand box" in your own yard to use as a "walk." If possible, walk in four or five inches of water while at the beach along with walking in the sand.

Hot and Cold Water Baths

If you cannot take the Kneipp bath, you can take hot and cold water baths. Put your feet in hot water for one minute then into cold water for half a minute. Make this change five times. It helps the circulation tremendously.

Sitz Baths

Sitz baths or foot baths are very conducive to good circulation. They get the blood moving. We use hot and cold foot and sitz baths for moving blood along. Warm water brings the blood to the surface and cold water drives it away again. In this way, good circulation is developed in the bloodstream.

Warm Feet

Cold feet affect the entire body and we cannot sleep, or for that matter, do anything comfortably. The entire circulation is dependent upon keeping the feet warm. Living in the sunshine, breathing plenty of good fresh air, sleeping where the air is active, and in other ways getting close to nature are the life-building principles. Children especially should keep their feet warm. Particularly keep children's ankles warm, since the ankles are a very vital center in the body and definitely should be kept warm.

Breathing

There are various techniques for driving blood into different parts of the body. This can be accomplished through taking in full breaths and applying pressure to the specific organ or area you are trying to affect. Then relax while exhaling. Inhaling a full breath and holding drives blood into the liver area. Quick inhalations and slow exhalations are good for the body and help the development of the lungs. Rue herb tea helps with difficulty in breathing.

Sniff Breathing Exercise. Walk three steps sniffing deeper at each step. Exhale on the fourth step. Do not breathe for the next three steps. Then repeat.

Breathing benefits good circulation in many ways. The Valley Forge Heart Institute revealed that cholesterol and triglyceride levels of joggers and long-distance runners were lower than those of the average man.

Specific Foods

There are a few foods that work well to increase the vitality of the circulation. Make sure that the liver is not overworked through the ingestion of too much coffee, sweets, and starches. Keep the liver clear and clean by taking iron foods; vegetable juices are best. Of course, herb teas are also good. If you know you have liver trouble, take dandelion tea, dandelion root coffee, liquid chlorophyll drinks, and cherry juice.

In the wintertime, keep the venous congestion down— congestion evidenced by blue flesh, a blue discoloration under the eyes, or blue fingernails. Get those cold feet and hands warm by drinking sage tea. Raw cucumber juice is wonderful for any venous congestion, and don't forget parsley juice.

There is a wonderful food for people called rice bran syrup. It's made from the polishings of rice. It's one of the foods highest in the vitamin B-complex; it is also high in niacin. Doctors have found that the use of niacin can drive the blood into the ear structure and help those who have difficulty hearing. The same principle—and remedy—works with the eyes. Sometimes the eyes fail to function properly because the circulation in the head is poor. Through the use of niacin, doctors can quicken the circulation and drive the blood into the head, into the arms and hands, and down into the leg structure.

VEIN PROBLEMS

Venous Congestion

When the arteries or veins become clogged, high blood pressure can develop. Blood does not pass through the capillaries as fast as it should and anemia begins to develop in the brain. Proneness to strokes increases. This is why it is so important to keep the blood on the move. Soreness and pressure on the nerves of the legs can be a sign of venous congestion. Whenever we have cramps in the legs, we should look first to venous congestion. Look to the veins and see that they are draining the blood well.

Superficial Veins in the Lower Extremities

The superficial veins of the lower extremities bear a heavier burden than any other vein in the body. They carry along a heavy column of blood extending almost perpendicularly from the sole of the foot to the heart.

In persons with weak connective tissue, the valves and the walls of these superficial veins yield to this heavy pressure. The valves become incompetent; the blood ceases to flow toward the heart and stagnates in the veins. Nodes form in tubes or veins with wide flocculations. These are known as varicose veins. The circulation is impaired when the blood stagnates. The surrounding tissues are damaged by the waste products that collect in the area (veins carry the toxic blood). The tissue around these areas breaks down many times faster and ulcers are produced. The best remedy for varicose veins is prevention.

If you have weak veins, try to pick out an occupation that does not require you to be on your feet continuously for hours. You should not be a baker, motorman, conductor, grocer, postman, or laundry worker.

Gymnastic exercises help to strengthen these veins. The barefoot sand walk, barefoot grass walk, and the Kneipp baths are exceptionally good. Leg baths, massage, slant board, leg exercises, and wearing lower heels could also help greatly.

Remedy for Varicose Veins

In dealing with varicose veins, savoy cabbage can be used as packs. Take the pithy vein from the center of these cabbage leaves and roll the leaves out flat with a rolling pin or something equivalent. After you have flattened the leaves to make them soft, lay them directly on the varicose veins. You can walk around, leaving them on all day if you wish. If you are working in the daytime, put them on every night. In my experience, it is a wonderful remedy for many persons with heavy varicose veins.

It would be helpful if you put your legs up at every opportunity, and if you took an exercise break every hour, if possible.

Another remedy for these veins uses 20 Mule Team Borax: take one tablespoon of Borax to about one gallon of hot water. Soak for approximately ten minutes or longer if possible. This mixture is also good for packs on the legs. Dip cloths into the mixture, wrap them around the legs, and leave them on all night. When you use hot water packs on varicose veins, do not walk around—stay off your feet! Use cold water on legs if you are going to walk around after a hot bath.

Still another treatment is to keep your feet above the rest of the body at night. This doesn't mean to elevate the foot end of the bed, because we don't want all the soft organs of the abdomen pushing against the heart area all night. Simply elevate your feet by putting a pillow under them.

Remedies for Fragile Veins

One of the best ways to help veins that break is rutin, which is found in buckwheat and has what they call the antifatigue factor. Rutin, however, should always be taken with vitamin C. Vitamin E is also good in all muscular conditions, since the veins are part muscle. We must also use silicon to back up the treatment. This is the chemical element that makes veins stronger. Oat straw tea and the daily use of rice polishings are also very necessary. (To make oat straw tea, cover ordinary clean oat hay, oat straw, or chaff with cold water. Bring to a boil and boil gently for ten minutes. Strain carefully.)

Use more vegetable broths and less fruits. Potato peeling broth is one of the best broths to use. Consider the liver and toxins in the blood and my elimination program. Using my elimination diet will also benefit.

It would also be wise to consider quick inhalation; slow exhalation; games; laughter; change of scenery; change of occupation; pleasing companionship; proper glandular release; developing a strong feeling of love and good will for one another; clearing the mind of worry, fretting, and stewing; and stopping the production of fatigue acids.

Ulcerations Inside the Legs

Ulcerations can be formed on the inside of the blood vessels and calcium can deposit in the form of microscopically small granules and combine to form plaque. In extreme cases, the entire vascular wall may become cemented with a hard mixture of calcium, cholesterol, and other substances.

Several things can interfere with the passage of blood through the legs and result in ulcerations and plaque. Some possible causes are prolapsus of the bowel, prolonged crossing of the legs, wearing garters, constipation, spinal distortion, bad arches in the feet, the wearing of shoes of the wrong size, pregnancy, overeating, and prolonged sitting.

UNDERSTANDING AND CORRECTING ANEMIA

Most anemia responds well to iron foods. Iron attracts oxygen—all the oxygen you could breathe would never do any good unless you had iron in the blood. We have breathing specialists going about telling you how to breathe, but we must have iron in the blood to attract the oxygen. Anemia, however, can also be caused by a deficiency of vitamin B_{12}, folic acid, copper, and a stomach protein referred to as "intrinsic factor."

The food that we have to consider most is the food that will take care of and build a good bloodstream. If the blood is not healthy, it won't do an adequate job of taking remedies to other parts of the body. If a condition of anemia exists, therefore, it should always be handled first.

In treating anemia, the best iron food is a mixture of black cherry juice and blackberry juice. These are two of the highest iron foods. (As a drink, blackberry juice is constipating, and as a drink, black cherry juice is a laxative. Together, they neutralize each other.) Eat strawberries and wild cherries, too.

Remember, anything green always has a lot of iron in it. Most foods grown above the ground have an abundance of iron. Use green and leafy vegetables, spinach, concentrated chlorophyll from alfalfa, wild clover honey, Concord grape juice, watercress, romaine lettuce, eggs (either raw or cooked under very low temperature), red pepper used in marrow soup, cod liver oil, and sweet cream.

Watercress is a powerful blood purifier. It is very delicious, although it is peppery. Whether eaten as a vegetable or made into a tea, you can get good results if it is used regularly over an extended period. Also good are pungent bitter salad greens. (The bitter taste means they are high in potassium.)

Other tonics for blood building: foods that contain silicon, iron, sodium, and chlorine. Red cabbage, coconut, fish, fish roe, oat and barley preparations, beets in abundance, Chinese cabbage, and salads are especially good. Include in your diet parsley juice, dandelion juice, dandelion greens, wild lettuce, tomato juice, desiccated liver, tops of vegetables, sarsaparilla tea, nettle tea, and raw juice from onions, cucumbers, and lettuce.

BLOOD PRESSURE PROBLEMS

Low Blood Pressure

Normal blood pressure ranges from 100 to 140 systolic reading and 60 to 90 diastolic reading. When the adrenal glands become underactive, we find that the blood pressure is lowered. Normally, adrenalin coming from the adrenal gland raises the blood pressure. Adrenalin is one of the most powerful hormones known to us. It is released when we are stressed or in danger, and it constricts blood vessels in the skin and viscera while increasing heart activity and dilating blood vessels in the muscles. It dilates the bronchi to increase oxygen intake, and stimulates glucose release for instant energy, drawing on glycogen stored in the liver and transforming it to glucose. This provides emergency energy and strength to meet any circumstance. Norepinephrine, also released from adrenals (along with dopamine), increases blood pressure. Chronic low blood pressure is often a sign of a strong, healthy heart and may predict greater longevity. Abnormal low blood pressure can result from the underactivity of the adrenal glands, but also from the kind of strong heart developed by long-distance runners and bicycle racers.

Bringing Up the Blood Pressure. We find that protein stimulation seems to quicken the body and will raise the blood pressure. In all cases of low blood pressure, an extra amount of protein is indicated. This is one time when, if permitted, we add meat to our diet. On the other hand, if we need just extra protein we should use cheeses, milk, eggs, and so forth.

The Sun Raises Your Blood Pressure. The action of sunlight on the skin also produces a substance which contracts the blood vessels of the skin and thus raises the blood pressure. On this account, persons who must avoid any rise in blood pressure, such as cardiac and pulmonary patients, should be very cautious when taking sun baths.

Chronic Fear Dilutes the Adrenal's Function. Chronic fear and resentment will wear out the adrenal glands more than any other thing. The adrenal glands are responsible for the hair standing erect in time of fear and troubles. If a person lives in constant resentment and fear, his body will eventually dilute and break down the adrenal glands and hormones to such an extent that he will develop an unhealthy chronic low blood pressure.

Low blood pressure can also develop from extreme enervation in the body or when our bodies are debilitated from overwork.

Things to Do for Low Blood Pressure

1. Add protein to the body. Sometimes you need animal proteins to bring up the blood pressure.
2. Have enough hydrochloric acid.
3. Make sure you also take a good blood-builder, like high iron foods.
4. Get into something you love to do.
5. Use cold water treatments, which build up the blood pressure.
6. Get exercise and be with stimulating friends rather than those who are depressing.

High Blood Pressure

Many people have high blood pressure. How can it be dealt with?

Lowering the Blood Pressure. Whey and other sodium foods can be used to bring down blood pressure if there are no heart complications. Sodium is one of the elements that is so necessary for relaxing the arteries, dissolving cholesterol, and any hardening of the arteries; however, we cannot use an excess of sodium in the diet if there are heart problems. When this hardening in the body must be dissolved by the slower process, we can resort to the extra amount of potassium found in our foods. The use of many of the herbs that help the kidneys to act and take out hard excretions from the body are buchu leaf tea, shavegrass, and cornsilk tea.

Nine times out of ten, if you will get rid of your excess weight, high blood pressure comes right down. The best way to start this process is to increase your water intake to at least two or three quarts of water daily.

High blood pressure is called hypertension in medical terminology. It is usually found in a person who has an overactive mind; too ambitious, too critical, too serious, too driven, usually an extrovert. There are many factors that can produce high blood pressure, and we always check on the mental status first. It is important to know that a person has a good philosophy and uses his philosophy—that he lives a more placid life.

Blood pressure can be altered by glandular conditions; for instance, the pituitary gland can bring up a blood pressure. An aggressive, outgoing person in many cases has an overactive thyroid, which can raise blood pressure. The adrenal glands can also be responsible for blood pressure disturbances. Kidney disease can cause high blood pressure. People with high blood pressure are more likely to have coronary artery disease and/or cerebral vascular disease. Taking corticosteroid can drive up the blood pressure, and dosage should be carefully monitored.

Diet has a lot to do with blood pressure. Meat is one of the things that keeps blood pressure up. A meat meal stimulates the heart and circulation 26 percent while a vegetarian meal stimulates the heart 6 percent. When we have extreme high blood pressure, a fast for a few days may help. But don't go longer than three days if you are not under a doctor's supervision. You can also go on either fruit or vegetable juices for a few days, making sure that the bowels are regulated. During a fast or juice regimen, we must take enemas to make certain that the bowels are free of any toxic waste, if they're not moving. Use carrot juice diets or the grape diet; they are both capable of bringing down blood pressure. Cut out citrus fruits also. At least one meal a day should consist of cooked brown rice and vegetables or rice with stewed fruit. You could have this at lunch every day, then follow my regular diet.

In many cases, where blood pressure has been very high, I encourage two brown rice meals a day. If we want to bring down the blood pressure very quickly and still allow a person to eat, we give them as much as three rice meals a day. This is sometimes a good help for women who develop high blood pressure in the last trimester of their pregnancy.

We need to make sure that the environment is right. Make certain that your occupation is not too demanding, that the boss doesn't keep you under too much pressure. Make sure you are not overworking, putting in too many hours at work. Make sure you are living in harmony with your family, that your children are not disturbing you to the point where you need to have a watchful eye on them even when you are sleeping. When we get excited, blood pressure always goes up, but this is not dangerous or abnormal in most cases.

We should get to the point where the body works under tranquility, serenity, and calmness.

Take care of the skin. Brushing the skin helps reduce the load on the kidneys, and many high blood pressure cases accompany weak or diseased kidneys. When we have this type of high blood pressure, we should be sure to seek the help of a doctor.

Wherever blood is needed in the body, the fibers relax and the vessels dilate. Actually the caliber of the vessel is determined by the degree of tone or the state of tension. We have a good example of the tension and relaxation of blood vessels in the blanching and the blushing of the face.

When the muscle fibers of the blood vessels underlying the skin of the face relax, the vessels dilate and the individual blushes. When the muscles contract, the vessels become narrow and the face becomes pale. When we have chronic spasms of the vascular muscles, it causes high blood pressure. When we have spasms of the cerebral arteries, we can develop fainting spells. Spasms of the coronary arteries can also cause angina pectoris. It is well to realize that our attitude of mind has a lot to do with the spasms, tensions, and relaxation of the muscle structure of the body.

ANGINA PROBLEMS

For angina troubles, pains in the left arm, or pains in the center of the chest, seek a doctor's care. Find out if you actually do have heart trouble, or if the pain is caused simply by gas pressures or other causes. You may have to take care of the cholesterol deposits by reducing the fat intake in your diet, increasing lecithin-rich foods and lecithin supplements, and taking up an aerobic exercise program (or at least walking half an hour each day). Cholesterol can be reduced safely by taking 1,000 milligrams of niacin (not niacinamide) with each meal.

SEXUAL SYSTEM IN RELATION TO BLOOD

The blood-making capacity of the system depends upon the strength and development of the sex brain and the condition of the sexual system. The red blood cells are very important for good health, sexuality, youthful appearance, and personal magnetism. There are many agents that increase the red blood cells: a good married life, cultivation of the affections, a strong sexuality, outdoor exercises, cheerfulness, foods coming immediately from nature, spending some part of the day in the free and open air— in the sunshine where the vegetable kingdom is in a flourishing condition, and living where there is an abundance of greens around you. (There is a life principle in the oxygen given off by the vegetable kingdom.) Again, I remind you that living at higher altitudes (5,000 feet or more) brings an increase in red blood cells.

FOOD REMEDIES FOR BLOOD PROBLEMS

There are certain remedies that have become standards for certain problems with the circulatory system. Here are a few.

For Circulatory System and the Heart

GREEN DRINK

Blend a small handful of parsley and alfalfa sprouts in a cup of unsweetened pineapple juice. Sip slowly.

For the Heart

POTASSIUM COCKTAIL

¼ cup celery juice
½ cup carrot juice
¼ cup of the following, combined in equal parts: spinach juice, beet top juice, and parsley juice

Blend all ingredients.

HONEY TREAT

Drink 1 teaspoon honey in a glass of water. Drink two or three times a day.

For Venous Congestion

ELDER FLOWER TEA

1 teaspoon elder flower herb
1 cup boiling water

Steep three minutes, strain, sweeten with honey if desired. This tea brings on perspiration and is also good for the skin.

For Varicose Veins

OAT STRAW PACKS

Make up your oat straw tea in the usual manner, strain it, but keep the straw. Make the straw into a warm pack and wrap it around the congested area, leaving it on all night long. Do this for a period of thirty days. Drink the tea, which is high in silicon.

For Other Blood-Related Problems

Hemorrhages. Increase iron intake. Use Vitamin K. Use burnett, comfrey, plantain, nettle tea, shepherd's purse. Consult your physician if blood loss is due to unusually heavy menses. Make green drinks, take chlorella or blue green algae, or use dessicated liver capsules.

Iron-poor Blood. Use greens to build, as well as black cherries and strawberries.

Circulation Problems. Spinach and celery juice with sulfur foods.

For Cleanser. Use sage and watercress. Use bran tonic for one month.

Poor Coagulation. Use chlorophyll, chorella tablets, green vegetables.

Low Blood Count. Will increase with chlorophyll supplement, living at higher altitudes, use of organ meats.

Discharges. Increase manganese intake; get your doctor's advice on dosage.

Clotting Problems. Increase calcium intake. Use figwort.

SPIRITUAL STRENGTH

That's the food side of it. But we can't neglect the mental and spiritual side. On the spiritual side, St. Paul put it very nicely when he said, "Set your mind and heart on higher talents, and even higher paths. I will go on to show you." (see Colossians.) In other words, allow no stagnation in your life. Life is eternal; it is forever; it never quits. You never die, but are born again. There is no sunset, but what a sunrise follows!

We are meant to live and go on; yet, for the overactive and for those who are fighting themselves and their way through life, it is said, "Be still . . ." One of the greatest things for the person who wants to be quiet is not to engage in battle with what is going on in this world. It is truly an irrational world. It is a rapidly changing world, and we tend to eat too fast and too much. It is an overactive world. It is an overpowering world.

So we have to face the fact that if we're going to be well physically, we must deal with this world from a spiritual standpoint, too. Don't forget, you can't have sweet thoughts with a sour stomach. The physical body is a manifestation of the invisible. It is the

∞ A Doctor's Diagnosis

No one can appreciate so fully as a doctor, the amazingly large percentage of human disease and suffering which is directly traceable to worry, fear, conflict, immorality, dissipation, and ignorance—to unwholesome thinking and unclean living. The sincere acceptance of the principles and teachings of Christ with respect to the life of mental peace and joy, the life of unselfish thought and clean living, would at once wipe out more than one-half the difficulties, diseases, and sorrows of the human race. In other words, more than one-half of the present afflictions of mankind could be prevented by the tremendous prophylactic power of actually living up to the personal and practical spirit of the real teachings of Christ.

—Dr. William S. Sadler, Director
Chicago Institute of Research and Diagnosis

end result. It is the effect of our thoughts. Thoughts are things. Our bodies are made by Divine thinking and broken down by humans. To get acquainted with it is to begin to control it.

The nicest thing I can remind you of is this: "Thou shalt have dominion over all that flies." And have we got the fussy and flighty things to take care of. "Thou shalt have dominion over all that swims." Ah, there are troubled waters to go through! "Thou shalt have dominion over all things that can get into your consciousness; all things that get into your life." They can disturb and distort you to such an extent that you wake up a wreck—seven mornings a week.

Get out of the ruins! Lift up your head! Lift up your consciousness and walk, walk the upright person! Find the good life and live that life! Let life flow through you, don't *make* life happen. Then you will have no underactivity and no overactivity. Balance your activities and you won't live in misery, pain, depression, and false hopes, either physically, mentally, or spiritually!

CHAPTER 9

YOUR CIRCLE OF LIFE

You must keep the bloodstream and the blood circulatory system clean in order to keep your organs alive and healthy. The organs can only be as clean as your bloodstream.

The blood is kept clean through the eliminative processes of four major organs—the skin, the kidneys, the lungs, and the bowel. These are generally the most neglected organs in the body. If too much attention is given to food and drink and not enough to the eliminative processes, we create an imbalance in the body that leads to disease.

The skin is treated at length elsewhere in this book. In this chapter, we will deal with the kidneys, lungs, and bowel.

HELP FOR THE KIDNEYS

If you have kidney troubles, cut out citrus fruit. We stir up the acids in the rest of the body and the extra liquid of the citrus fruit has to go out through the kidneys. The kidneys are overworked with the extra toxic materials that we are breaking loose in the body.

We cannot expect a weakened, or many times diseased, kidney to take care of all that extra work. Move from fruits to vegetables.

Many times, in helping the kidneys and helping the skin, you must have the vegetables in a cooked broth. Even raw vegetable juices can stir up the acids too fast. This irritates the skin and kidneys and makes them act too quickly. Try to keep away from that irritability as much as possible.

For health in general and the kidneys specifically, we sometimes advise using extra water. A good remedy is to take two or three 8-ounce glasses of water every morning before breakfast. It might be good to use a little liquid chlorophyll in one of those glasses. Liquid chlorophyll does not cause kidney disturbances as do the fresh vegetable juices. Then make sure you drink at least five more glasses of water during the day. On hot days, drink an extra quart of water.

CARE OF THE LUNGS

Catarrh Elimination

The lung structure is a vital one to take care of because it is a great catch-point for catarrh, phlegm, and mucus that settle in the chest as part of the elimination process. This material is thrown off by the mucous membrane, where excess acids are collected from the body.

Accumulated toxins in the bowel are thrown back into the body, absorbed by the blood, and finally go to the lung structure. This is where we have large amounts thrown off in a hurry. I have seen some people throw off teaspoons of catarrh through the bronchial tubes. This is something I never try to stop. I try to bring out more of it, if possible, to cleanse that lung structure. How do we do that?

We must start eating noncatarrhal foods. One of the greatest remedies for getting rid of catarrh in the lung structure is to cut out milk and wheat. Cut out bread and citrus fruit. They stir up the acids and force all of this heavy toxic material into the lung structure to be eliminated. Use more from the vegetable kingdom and liquid chlorophyll.

Chest Breathing

Anytime you can concentrate on your chest, it will develop. Anytime you can do some of this while you are on the slant board, you will get more blood into the medulla, which is the part of the brain that helps you to breathe well. Chest breathing is dependent upon the brain. This is why a person gets tired and mentally fatigued. He is always yawning. He has depleted his nerve supply. The chest will breathe as much as you want if the nerves are good. Make sure you have enough iron to oxygenize the blood; then make sure you use your chest through exercise to get that oxygen to the brain. Laughter exercises the chest and recharges the medulla.

Plant life throws out oxygen, the very element we need to keep us alive. Deep breathing; hiking in the mountains; and dry, warm air will help the lung structure the most.

Take a hundred deep breaths before dinner and a hundred breaths afterward. When you breathe out, flex your hands. This stimulates circulation throughout the system.

Food for the Lungs

Turnips are excellent for the lungs. I have also used garlic or, in many cases, a garlic and onion combination, with considerable success. Like the turnip, these odorous vegetables are a wonderful thing for catarrhal problems. When taken along with a regular health diet, they can be used for packs on the chest and throat, or they can be chopped, mixed, and eaten.

BOWEL MANAGEMENT

The bowel and the liver work together as a team. Detoxification of the whole body works through them. No matter what treatments, no matter what doctor, no matter what kind of special diet, be sure the bowel is clean. Nutrition is first among the healing arts, and healing takes place first through the bowel.

We can have a lazy bowel and not know it. The bowel is one of the softest tissues in the body, and it has the poorest nerve supply of any organ. It does not tell us when we have real problems. We can have gases and not know it. We can have obstructions, constrictions, spastic conditions, and still not know it. Feelings in the bowel are very poor.

There are certain things we can do, and things we should not do, to have healthy bowels.

Bowel Bacteria

Acidophilus bacilli create an acid medium in the intestine where unfriendly disease-producing bacteria do not thrive. In most people, the ratio of unfriendly bacteria is 80 percent to only 20 percent good acidophilus bacteria. This ratio can be reversed by using an acidophilus culture to destroy the causes of constipation, autointoxication, and other intestinal disorders.

There are many brands of acidophilus culture available in most health food stores. There are brands made from broth if you do not want to use those made from milk products.

You can take the acidophilus by mouth the first thing in the morning and the last thing at night. You can also use it in enemas and in colonics. To get the best results, it should be used for two months straight without stopping. If you have bowel troubles, use it for two months, skip two or three months, then use it again for two months. Do this three times a year until the bowels are under control.

Yogurt is a good protein food that builds the friendly bacteria in the bowels. Friendly bacteria are also fed by using whey, high sodium foods, salads, greens, sprouts, and other natural foods. Raw foods help the bacteria to grow best.

Some foods break down the friendly bacteria. Coffee destroys the friendly bacteria, and it is a detriment to the bowel and the liver. Chocolate also is bad. Too much meat in the intestinal tract also destroys friendly bacteria by putrefying, allowing harmful bacteria to multiply and overpower the others. If you have a good intestinal tract, you can handle a little meat. People who have meat three times a day are building up too much putrefaction, and the harmful bacteria take over. Even cooked food is not the best food for friendly bacteria; 60 percent of your daily diet should be raw.

Antihistamines, penicillin, and sulfa drugs all destroy the friendly bacteria in the bowel. This is of great concern to the gastrointestinal specialist these days. It is good to use kefir or several bottles of acidophilus milk to sweeten the intestinal tract and to give food to the friendly bacteria.

Formula for Feeding the Bowel

I had given to me an excellent formula for feeding the acidophilus bacteria. It uses 8 ounces of powdered buttermilk,

8 ounces nonfat milk powder, and 2 ounces pure fruit pectin. Then add 1 quart fresh buttermilk, and 1 quart water, and sweeten each cup with 1 teaspoon milk sugar. Take 2 table-spoons of acidophilous milk four times daily, and drink 2 quarts or more of the formula for several days.

Clabbered Milk

Many old men in the Balkan countries make this high protein, high enzyme, easily digestible food an important part of their diet. When prepared, clabbered milk undergoes one of the enzyme actions that would naturally occur in the stomach when hydrochloric acid is present. Clabbering the milk before ingestion, therefore, gives the stomach an easy way to absorb the milk proteins. Most people over the age of fifty lack hydrochloric acid, so preparing clabbered milk is a good deed they can do for themselves.

To make clabbered milk, all utensils should be clean. Heat 2 quarts raw milk to lukewarm. Powdered milk (½ cup) may be added *before* the milk is heated, if desired. Blend the powdered milk well with 1 cup raw milk to make a thicker clabber. After the milk is heated to lukewarm, take 1 cup of it and mix with 1 cup yogurt or buttermilk. Stir well and add to the rest of the warm milk. Place in the oven with only the pilot light on (or at the lowest temperature setting), or in a warm place where it will go undisturbed until it sets. The time needed may vary from four to eight hours, depending upon the culture and the temperature (90 to 115°F). When ready, refrigerate in the same pan. It can be eaten by itself or mixed with fruit four hours after being refrigerated.

Alfalfa Tablets

Alfalfa tablets are among the best cleansing agents for bowel pockets (the small, weak spots in the bowel wall called diverticula). These pockets fill with fecal material and then interfere with the health of other organs in the body. Alfalfa tablets provide the bowel wall with a fibrous material that can get into these pockets. It gives the bowel muscles something to work against while cleaning out these settlements. Alfalfa tablets help get this stagnant, gas-forming, toxic material moving along, and start developing tone in that part of the bowel that is not working right. The tablets are slightly laxative, and there are some people who cannot take them.

Take four to eight alfalfa tablets at each meal. Be sure to break each tablet before using. The tablets are tightly compressed, and should be broken so they will disintegrate.

Take a Good Digestant

Along with the alfalfa tablets, I recommend adding a digestant of some kind to take care of the gas. There are many digestants on the market that have a little pancreatic substance, hydrochloric acid, papain, bile salts, and probably a little protomorphogen stomach substance. There are also enzyme digest-aids available. These help in the digestion of fats, starches, and proteins, and helps get rid of the gases. We do this until the bowel is well enough to take care of itself.

In some patients, it takes as long as a year for the bowel to be well enough to function properly. You can start taking care of the bowel overnight by the food you eat right now. But the bowel will not be well overnight. You must develop tone in it over a period of time.

If Elimination Is Poor, Prefer Vegetables over Fruits

Fruits stir up the acids in the body and vegetables carry off the acids. Many people who are having discharges from the body, where elimination channels are not working properly, should use less fruit and add more vegetables to their diet. In this way, acids are not stirred up so fast and are carried off more safely.

There are some foods that should be avoided in cases of bowel disorders. For example, head lettuce is very gas-forming and slows down the digestion. See others on page 173.

Aloe Vera

Aloe vera is one of the oldest remedies known to man. It is the source of a well-known, drastic purgative drug, Barbados Aloe, which is a solid extract obtained by evaporating the plant juice. It is also one of the ingredients in the famous "Sacred Bitters" of ancient Egypt.

The aloe vera is an old tropical plant. It is sensitive to cold and thrives in the tropics or adjacent subtropical areas. It was not until 1935 that it came into popular usage. Its reputation as a new "wonder herb" spread quickly. It is cultivated commercially in Florida, Texas, Arizona, and other states, and acreage is rapidly being increased to meet the growing demand.

The aloe vera is the only true medical aloe referred to so often in magazine articles about the healing aloes used by Native Americans in Florida. It is a mucilaginous plant. Most of its tissue does not contain any medicinally active substance, but when the leaf is peeled back, you find the crystal clear, jelly-like juice of the plant which is the reputed healing "gel." This aloe gel is soothing and rapidly relieves pain, burning, and itching. It acts quickly because it is speedily absorbed. It seems to reduce scar tissue formation, does not stain, and has no unpleasant odor. Its popular use ranges from treatment of ulcers, arthritis, constipation, boils, skin eruptions, chapped lips and hands, asthma, coughs, and to body beautification. Many southern Floridians claim it is a "cure-all." The gel-like fresh juice is of a highly perishable nature after it is cut from the mother plant, but for home use, it can be used as an ointment for insect bites, barber's rash, burns, sores, and swellings by merely spreading it on the afflicted area.

The juice can be taken and bandaged onto afflicted areas by slicing the leaves open and placing them over the wound. Unused portions of leaves may be laid aside for future use. It will keep for many weeks.

To obtain the juice, cut the matured leaves at the base, then place the cut end downward in an inclined trough or receptacle so that the juice, in trickling from the leaves, may be collected. The leaves may also be crushed to a pulp and the juice strained out through a closely woven thin cloth. The juice may then be dried by evaporating off the water at a low temperature. This produces the dried aloe of commerce.

The fresh juice is also used by incorporating it into an ointment and applying it locally, or by diluting with water and selling it as a drinkable tonic.

Aloe is good for any burn, especially X-ray burns, sunburn, and friction, electrical, chemical, hot fat, fire, and steam burns. Doctors have used aloe vera in the treatment of burns of all degrees of seriousness, and several large hospitals have tested aloes in the treatment of X-ray and radiation reactions. The "aloe gel" is also used as a household remedy for burns, skin disturbances, sties, cysts, and other external disorders.

The gel can be used as a shampoo. It is also a good body lubrication for arthritis and crippled arms and legs. Recently, the healing properties of the aloe vera have been incorporated into medications, suntan preparations, and cosmetics. To apply, use the gel liberally on the affected areas, or spread on waxed paper and bandage in place. Replace before it dries out.

The gel-like fresh juice of the leaves is also taken internally in place of the drastically concentrated aloe pills, which often cause gripping pains. This juice is much milder in action. For stomach, liver, and kidneys, try this efficient method: Cut up leaves into small pieces and place a cupful in a quart of cold water. Place in the refrigerator and drink a small juice glassfull on an empty stomach, morning and evening. Add more water as it is used until one cupful of the cut leaves makes 2 quarts of aloe water. Be careful not to take too much or you will experience a dull feeling in the neck of the bladder. When this occurs, merely dilute the aloe with more water.

For stomach ulcers and constipation, thoroughly wash about three aloe vera "prongs" or leaves and cut up the flesh into a quart-sized jar. Fill the jar with water and refrigerate. The water will blend with the mucilaginous substance and form a thickened liquid. Take a small glass half an hour before each meal. The quantity should be regulated according to the laxative effect on the user. An easier way is to put the fleshy cubes in an electric blender (cut off the outer green skin first), add a small amount of water, and blend the mixture into a foamy liquid, which can be poured into a jar and refrigerated. Shake before using.

Assume a Squatting Posture

Assuming a squatting position for evacuation of the lower bowel is very important. It is helpful when having elimination to keep the hands above the head. In this position, a more complete bowel elimination will be accomplished. The extensive use of the modern toilet seat, a contrivance of civilization, is responsible for most of these troubles: It is not conducive to elimination by nature's method, the squatting position.

If you use the customary sitting position, place your hands palms up on your knees, incline the body forward, and rest your forehead against your cupped palms. Then rest the forehead on the knees and bend the arms over the head and massage the neck area to relieve tension, which is beneficial and also accomplishes the purpose of raising the arms upward. This is generally helpful.

Hemorrhoids

Many people have developed hemorrhoids as the result of sedentary occupations. Constipation, sitting on the "civilized" toilet, eating too many foods that dehydrate before they eliminate, and straining at the stool produce a pressure that results in hemorrhoids, protruding varicose veins, painful at times of elimination. These protruding hemorrhoids at the edge of the rectal opening can stand only so much pressure, then they begin bleeding.

These protrusions may enlarge and produce external nodules. Many times this tender tissue becomes so mutilated that it is necessary to see a doctor.

In trying to overcome these conditions and alleviate simple hemorrhoids, the following natural means and exercise routine can help.

For Inflammation with Hemorrhoids. In acute inflammation accompanying hemorrhoids, a garlic oil capsule or clove may be placed in the rectum each night. In many cases, the use of an enema is an aid in the healing of damaged tissues.

A Healing Enema. The best enema for *lower rectal problems* of a simple nature is flaxseed tea with a teaspoon of liquid chlorophyll. This allays inflammation. Use the chlorophyll in ¼ cup of flaxseed tea, to be retained in the bowel, until the next bowel movement. If the urge to eliminate develops, hold the liquid for ten minutes before getting on the toilet.

Benefits of the Slant Board. One exercise that will help these tissues most is the use of the slant board. The abdominal exercises as described for the slant board are of the utmost importance in all rectal conditions.

Adopt a Bland Diet. It may be necessary to adopt a bland diet, eliminating seeds, skins, rough foods, and raw vegetables until the rectal condition is improved. It is advisable to be under a doctor's care. The above suggestions are given only as a home treatment. A specialist in the treatment of your specific condition should be consulted to determine the most effective means of improvement and possible correction.

Constipation

In dealing with constipation, we must deal with the individual. A highly nervous person can produce constipation from nervous reactions and the tensions he may carry during the day. His workload must be considered, both physically and mentally.

Also, some people are just plain dehydrated. They do not have enough water in their systems because they do not drink enough water. The result is a hard stool. Some people become more constipated living in a high altitude and dry climate. They must learn how to combine their foods properly. They may eat too much starch without the water-carrying vegetables. Without looking into the trouble, they turn to laxatives. This can be dangerous. It is unfair to the health of the intestinal tract. More harm than good can result from taking laxatives.

Correction of Constipation. If the history of an adult patient reveals no apparent reason for the onset of constipation, we would suspect an organic disorder of the colon. There are over thirty million people taking laxatives regularly, but this does not mean that it is the proper procedure for treating constipation. In our practice, we discontinue the use of laxatives. We teach people to have natural bowel movements through eating properly. We restore the defecation through reflex, by teaching people to answer nature's call, not "put it off." Our main object is to reestablish the peristaltic action to a normal rhythm. This is done through exercise, the use of foods laxative in nature, and giving up those foods that are constipating.

Fibrous Residue Is Essential. We must have a certain amount of fibrous residue in our diets, otherwise we have a decreased frequency in bowel movements. Insufficient fluid intake can cause many disturbances. A diet low in vitamin B_1 is found to produce a balloonlike bowel. This is a bowel that has lost much of its capacity to react to normal stimuli. Many times the nerve stimulus through the spine must be cared for through physical manipulation to bring the bowel back to normal reaction. A lack of bile flow may also produce constipation.

Stomach Washes. In washing out the stomach, tepid water should be used. Drinking water is good for constipation, providing it is warm and taken upon retiring and arising. A person who suffers from kidney trouble should drink much pure water, reduce his intake of protein (meat, fish, poultry, and dairy products), increase fiber intake, and exercise to work up a sweat. Distilled water can be a solvent in the body and can penetrate every cell of the organism, carrying away impurities providing the water is pure. Pure spring water and fruit juices are the best liquids.

Internal Water Cleansing Treatments. A water treatment can help constipation, eliminating toxemia in the body and cleaning out the kidneys:

First Day: 1 glass of water 1 hour before breakfast;
                1 glass of water ½ hour before breakfast; and
                1 glass of water immediately before breakfast.
Second Day: 2 glasses of water 1 hour before breakfast;
                2 glasses of water ½ hour before breakfast; and
                2 glasses of water immediately before breakfast.
Third Day: 3 glasses of water 1 hour before breakfast;
                3 glasses of water ½ hour before breakfast; and
                3 glasses of water immediately before breakfast.

The water should be warm and exercise should be taken each half hour before drinking water. Stay on your regular health schedule diet. The water is just in addition to regular meals. This water treatment should be taken for one month.

Bowel Wall Inflammation. Bile is the fluid that stimulates peristaltic action. Inflammation of the bowel, which occurs when a person has not eaten the right foods to feed the bowel walls properly, may result when harsh, rough foods are taken.

Diverticulitis. Diverticulitis refers to the large bowel when it has a number of small pockets or sacs protruding. Diverticulitis describes a condition of inflammation in the bowel sacs. Metal poisonings from substances such as lead, phosphorous, mercury, or arsenic can be responsible for spastic constipation, although nervous tensions are usually more responsible for hypertoxic colon conditions. Never neglect the need to have a bowel movement. Develop a regular time to go to the bathroom each day, to reestablish the defecation reflex. Laxatives should be used on a temporary basis only. Tight girdles and improperly fitting trusses are some of the mechanical devices that can disturb the normal function of the bowel. Adhesions, foreign bodies, fecal impactions, and prolapse can also disturb the normal flow of toxic waste in the colon. We have to make sure there are no obstructions. We may need to see a doctor to be certain. Those who have this ailment may receive a temporary special diet from their doctor.

Diarrhea

Some people have a hypersensitive bowel, and the least little roughage or the least irritation to their nervous system will cause a loose bowel movement. There are foods that will balance and control it if we know the proper constipating foods to use for this condition. You can use blackberry juice to flavor a gelatin dessert and add pineapple juice to cut down the strength of it. Consider a variety of juices in your diet. Blackberry and black cherry juice can be used several times over a period of a month.

Blackberry juice and black cherry juice are wonderful mixed with gelatin. Most people can take gelatin very well. Many people complain about the aching joints in their bodies. Gelatin is made from the joints of animals and is a good material to use for aching joints. Gelatin mixed with black cherry juice is sweet enough; you won't have to add any other sweetening. If you are going to use any other sweetening, make sure it is honey.

There are ways of mixing prune juice with blackberry juice so that you have a laxative juice. In cases of diarrhea, we use blackberry juice to control it. The juice has been used for ages for this purpose. Blackberry compound can be purchased in a drugstore today for the control of diarrhea. Another good remedy for diarrhea is a potato, cut into one-inch squares, and boiled in a quart of milk for ten minutes. Sip it like tea.

FOODS AND BOWEL PROBLEMS

Learn the Foods to Use

There are a number of things we can do to avoid gas in the stomach and the intestinal tract:

1. Too many rough foods can cause a great deal of disturbance in the bowel. You would not run sandpaper over a sore, would you? You would not run lemon juice or citrus fruit over a sore, would you? Whenever there is an accumulation of gas, there is a sensitive bowel.

2. One of the remedies for gas is putting a little lemon juice in milk.

3. Clabbered milk is a wonderful remedy. If milk is difficult for you to take, then leave it out.

4. Barley gruel and rice gruel are wonderful for those suffering with gas problems. These foods are high in vitamin B-complex, necessary to solve gas problems.

5. Sometimes it is best to avoid too many liquids, like just before bedtime, or when you are very gassy.

6. Eating drier foods will often help. Dry graham toast or soybean toast may ease a gas condition.

7. Flaxseed tea is wonderful for dissipating gas. If it is difficult to take by mouth, use it as an enema.

8. A warm pack over the abdomen for half an hour or so after eating will help to bring relaxation to the body; relaxation is a wonderful aid in dissipating gas.

Cautions: Food to Avoid

Here are some foods that we should leave alone if we are having bowel problems:

1. Although tops of the vegetables and other greens are good and necessary foods, sometimes they can be very gas-forming. Many are too rough as, for instance, are the strings in turnip greens.

2. Sometimes the sulfur foods, such as cauliflower, broccoli, Brussels sprouts, cabbage, and onions have to be avoided for a short time, and more bland foods added, such as carrots, beets, string beans, spinach, collards, endive, and watercress.

3. Sometimes salads must be cut down.

4. Even vegetable juices, when drunk alone, can cause gas.

5. Adding a little milk or a little vegetable broth to the juice will reduce the activity in it.

Foods That Digest Easily and Act as Remedies

Here are some foods that will help us:

1. Soaked and peeled dates in milk is a wonderful combination.

2. As a soft food, grapes are wonderful if skin and seeds are eliminated. Acidophilus culture to help change the intestinal flora is a wonderful aid. Whey is also good. If it's powdered, take a tablespoon three times a day. Massaging the abdomen with olive oil will sometimes help until a good balanced system is established.

   Exercise is necessary also. You cannot get well without exercise. One of the finest exercises for the bowel is to take an orange or a lemon, or a tennis ball, and work this around the abdomen fifteen to twenty-five times, until a good balance is established in the body.

3. Be sure to always use green leaf lettuce, such as Bibb, romaine, or red-tipped. Bread causes a dry, hard stool, because the heat used in baking it dries up the oils in the grain. Use cereals instead, and vary these to include brown rice, yellow corn meal, millet, rye, and ground wheat. Ground wheat is a wonderful food for good bowel activity. Prepare it by placing ½ cup ground wheat in 2 cups hot water. Put this in a thermos bottle, cork it, and leave overnight to soak. In the morning, it is ready to eat. Sweeten only with dried fruits, never with sugar.

4. Beets are good for the gall bladder and the liver. They are good for building blood. Stemmed, shredded beets are one of the best tasting vegetables. Use raw, shredded beets the size of a golf ball once a day. If fresh beets are not available, use beet tablets.

5. An ingredient in black horseradish is one of the best helps to get the bile flowing. It cleans out the gall bladder and the liver.

6. Dandelion is good for the gall bladder and the liver. The fresh leaves can be used in raw salads in early spring, or they can be steamed. Dandelion root coffee is an excellent remedy for the liver.

7. Flaxseed tea contains vitamin E and is one of the finest teas for the mucous membrane of the bowel. The tea is fine boiled, but for the best results, add ¼ cup flaxseed to 1 quart hot water and let it stand overnight. Strain off the seeds before drinking. This method preserves more of the vitamin E. Never reuse the seeds after you have boiled or soaked it. In cases of constipation, you can use the whole seed by putting it through a grinding mill.

8. Winter squash is another great food for intestinal disturbances.

9. Flaxseed is one of the best remedies for ordinary constipation. Take 1 or 2 heaping teaspoons of ground flaxseed meal twice a day, every day, for several weeks or even months. Be sure to mix it with a liquid so that it will not stick to the roof of your mouth.

   Flaxseed contains 30 percent vegetable oil by weight. Introduced into the colon, it acts as a laxative by softening the feces and lubricating the canal. For years, doctors have recognized that flaxseed tends to stimulate peristaltic action (bowel action) of the intestines. Flaxseed tea also works well.

Whole flaxseed swells to approximately three times its own size when water, milk, or other liquids are taken. Because of this expansion, whole flaxseed furnishes added bulk, which is so important in cases where there is a lack of bulk in the diet. Flaxseed is not a harsh irritant or purgative.

A smooth laxative of flaxseed meal and slippery elm can be made by combining 1 tablespoon flaxseed meal, 1 teaspoon slippery elm, and 1 tablespoon whey in a glass of apple juice. Take first thing in the morning.

A laxative of slippery elm helps us in mild forms of constipation. Blend 1 teaspoon slippery elm and ¼ cup water two or three minutes. Take before breakfast.

10. Figs are excellent for the bowels if taken when fresh (one to three days old). They contain a high amount of magnesium, potassium, oxygen, and papain. I have obtained excellent results in the treatment of arthritis and rheumatism with fresh figs and raw goat milk. Figs, ripe from the tree, are wonderful energy foods. They are high in a natural sweet, and the seeds have a natural laxative coating, which is important when a patient is in distress.

11. Other laxative foods are agar-agar (Irish moss), used for constipation, containing manganese, nickel, iodine, copper, and vitamin D; peaches, containing phosphorous, sodium, and mangenese; yellow fruits and vegetables; alfalfa tablets, whey, mulberries, cherry concentrate; liquid chlorophyll, mixed 1 teaspoon to a glass of water and then taken three times daily; and herb combination for lower bowel system: barberry bark, cascara sagrada, red clover, lobelia, ginger, and capsicum.

12. For a dried natural fruit laxative, which also aids in overcoming arthritis, the following formula has been recommended by a doctor from the famous Mayo Clinic:

21 prunes

14 teaspoons raisins

14 halves of apricots

7 halves of pears

7 halves of peaches

7 figs

Put fruit in a large pan and pour boiling water over fruit to cover entirely. Cover with loose lid, let stand for four days at room temperature, adding water to keep fruit covered, then store in lower compartment of the refrigerator. Makes enough servings for one week. Each day take three prunes, 2 teaspoons raisins, two halves apricots, one-half pear, one-half peach, and one fig. (If desired, grind these dry with senna leaves.)

13. A coffee enema was used a great deal by Dr. Max Gerson, a New Jersey medical doctor in the 1930s. Many of his patients would set alarm clocks to get up in the middle of the night to take coffee enemas. They would take two or three a night to get rid of toxic wastes that the body was breaking down and throwing into the colon. He made sure the toxic waste was eliminated consistently. The formula for making the enema is as follows: Take 3 tablespoons ground (drip) coffee (not instant) to 1 quart of water; let it boil three minutes and then simmer fifteen minutes more. Strain and use at body temperature. The daily amount can be prepared at one time. This enema can be used three to four times daily or anytime to relieve pain in any part of the body. It is good for helping the liver eliminate stagnant bile.

14. Retention enema. In a blender, mix 1 teaspoon apple cider vinegar and 1 tablespoon slippery elm powder. Use as an enema with 1½ quarts warm water.

15. It is helpful to know the effectiveness of different enemas. A water enema can irritate the bowel. Flaxseed tea makes a soothing enema. Buttermilk feeds the friendly bacteria when used as an enema. Coffee used as an enema stimulates the bowel and brings down the bile.

ABDOMINAL EXERCISES TO REJUVENATE THE COLON

All abdominal exercises are recommended when you want to overcome bowel problems. Here are just a few of the best.

Chest-Leg Pull-Up

In the chest-leg pull-up exercise, you sit on the edge of a chair with your feet straight out in front, toes pointed upward, and body straight toward the back of the chair. In this position, you are almost in a straight line. Now lift your heels slightly above the floor, just an inch or so. You will find it took all the abdominal muscles to lift those legs when they were straight out. Your abdominal muscles become solid and tense—and stronger. As you keep your body in that straight line, lift the legs slightly. Hold onto the arms of the chair, pull up the legs, with the knees up to the chest; then bring them down to the floor without touching the floor and repeat. Do this two, three, ten times if you can. This develops tone in the bowel. Within three months, you will have developed the tone of the muscles in the bowel to match the better food you have been eating for the past three months. You will also help rejuvenate your abdominal tract.

Slant Board

Use the slant board for stretching the abdomen and rejuvenating the colon. While lying flat on your back, stretch your abdomen by putting your arms above your head, then raise and lower them to the sides. This stretches the abdominal muscles by pulling them up toward the shoulders. Do this exercise ten to fifteen times daily.

To rejuvenate the colon, lean to the left side and stretch. Pat the stretched side of the abdomen vigorously with an open hand. Change sides and lean to the right. Stretch and pat vigorously fifteen to twenty-five times each side. Reverse sides three to four times.

The slant board is one of the best remedies I know for getting the dropped transverse colon back into position. The basic position on the slant board is the best position for resting to compensate for overwork, especially when you are mentally tired. Exercise is an important part of any health program. Food will not do you any good unless you exercise to get the blood to the place where it is needed.

Twisting. Standing alongside a chair, twist your knees from side to side. Squat, put your arms out to the side, and twist side to side.

Stretching. Put your left arm high above your head and reach down and touch the right foot with your right hand. Then throw your right hand straight up and go down with the left hand, touching the toes. This stretches one side of your abdomen and then the other.

Rest. The good of all exercise is developed in rest. Exercise can be good for you, but you can't exercise twenty-four hours a day. A time comes when you need absolute rest. I think everybody should have one day a week of absolute rest. It could be a fast day, or a juice day, but do nothing on that day!

Resting from food while you see how hard you can work physically is not fair to the body. When you cut out food for one day, lay yourself out prone and don't do anything. Let your body recuperate. That is the day when you take the phone off the hook; that is the day you don't gossip; that is the day when the outside world comes to an end. We should learn how to rest. Very few people really know how to rest. Some people would get well if they would just keep quiet for a whole day. I remember hearing my professor say, "If you want to be a success in life, keep your mouth shut and your bowels open."

CHAPTER 10

BEAUTY STARTS WITH THE SKIN

The skin—the most diversified and the largest organ of the body. The other organs are compact and take up as little space as possible. The skin on the other hand is like "dough." It is rolled out as extensively and as thinly as possible.

The skin weighs twice as much as the liver or the brain. It receives one-third of the circulating blood and its surface extends over 3,100 square inches (20,000 square centimeters). Each square centimeter contains 100 sweat glands, 15 sebaceous glands, and hundreds of signal apparatuses.

The skin is sometimes called the third kidney. We actually throw off toxic materials through the skin. The skin aids in the elimination of all toxic wastes in the body. It is one of the body's most important organs: it has 120 billion cells, 2 million perspiratory glands, 400,000 points of pressure, 300,000 oil-yielding glands, 100,000 minute hairs, and 150,000 feet of underlying capillaries.

On hot days when the skin eliminates a great deal, the kidneys do not have to eliminate as much, and the urine usually is quite concentrated. The opposite is true in the wintertime. The urine is very heavy and we do not eliminate much through the skin. The skin and kidneys work hand in hand.

CARE OF THE SKIN

The skin needs water (not just from bathing or showering). Insurance statistics show that an average of five years longer life belongs to those who drink an abundance of water. We all need it.

A shriveled appearance of the skin may indicate a manganese deficiency or chronic dehydration. Scaly skin indicates a fluoride deficiency; to correct it, increase your intake of fluoride as well as vitamin A. If your skin is sticky, you have a sodium deficiency. Rashes or pus may indicate a silicon deficiency. Itching sometimes indicates a phosphorus deficiency; and to help soothe this condition rub aloe vera juice on the skin and take nasturtium juice, which helps to purify the blood. Scar formation can be reduced by rubbing aloe vera on the skin and by drinking marigold herb tea. For skin sores, use a flaxseed poultice, a grape pack, a salve made from garlic and lanolin, and wash with apple cider vinegar solution. Runny sores indicate a calcium deficiency. For skin eruptions, use a chlorophyll ointment.

With any skin problem, remember to take care of the kidneys first.

We must recognize that the skin has to have silicon. This element is found in sprouts, particularly alfalfa sprouts, oat straw tea, and many other natural foods. Barley, tomatoes, spinach, figs, and strawberries are all good sources of silicon.

Good herb teas for the skin include horsetail tea (high in silicon), bay herb tea as a stimulant (or basil and bay combination), oat straw tea, sweet marjoram, and tarragon.

THE BEAUTY ELEMENT: FLUORIDE

Beauty is not possible without fluoride (the mineral form of fluorine gas). The body requires a reserve of this "beauty element" for good health.

Fluoride is one of the most important chemical elements to the human body, even though it is not essential to life or health. It is liberated into air by cooking or heating. If the system lacks fluoride, trouble may arise with the spleen and blood, especially the red corpuscles. Other symptoms include infection and toxins in the body, and kidney and skin problems.

I call fluoride the "resistance" element of the body. When calcium becomes calcium fluoride by joining with this highly reactive element, the teeth and bones are hardened, and long life and resistance are encouraged. Germ life is combated in the body and disease is unwelcome. Tooth decay is prevented by the proper amount of fluoride. Uncooked foods contain more fluoride, as heating breaks it down to its gaseous form, fluorine. The outside of bones is hardened because of the fluoride-containing portion of the bone structure.

Raw goat's milk is one food that is high in fluoride. Raw black bass is the highest. Green quince, rye flour, avocado, raw sea plants, sea cabbage, goat's cheese, cream, whey, cottage cheese, and Roquefort cheese are all high in fluoride, too.

COMPLEXION PROBLEMS AND REMEDIES

For a clear complexion, drink cocktails made of apple juice concentrate with cucumber juice. This is a very good summertime drink: Cucumbers are high in sodium, which helps to keep the body cool. Sodium also helps to keep the skin from wrinkling. Another very good treatment for wrinkles is to use a Honey Pat ten times a day for two months (using only your fingers, pat the face with honey to exercise the facial tissue); comfrey root poultice is also very effective. For dry skin use lecithin balm.

Apricot kernel oil is one of the finest things for a lovely complexion. This is what the Hunzas use in that extreme cold they live in. They have lovely complexions. It can be used as a cleansing oil for keeping the skin free from wrinkles. It also can be mixed with aloe vera to give it astringent qualities.

Brown Spots

Many people complain about the brown spots on their hands and body. In most places, it comes from sun damage disrupting the melanin distribution on the skin. We have used aloe vera with some effect.

Skin Ulcers

A good remedy for skin ulcers is one green pepper cut into ½ cup strong oat straw tea to 1 quart of water; simmer for forty minutes; strain off and drink 1 cup of the tea two or three times daily. A mixture of equal amounts of lanolin and garlic oils is the best salve for skin ulcers.

Whiteheads

Whiteheads found on the forehead, around the nose, and on the face are usually caused by poor starch digestion. A pancreatic substance added to the diet will help immensely. Using clay packs on the face or using aloe vera as a lotion or a salve may help. Start from within, with the pancreas. Cut down on the heavy starches, breads, and wheat cereals for a while. There are a few starches that especially bring whiteheads on: wheat, oats, rye, buckwheat, and potatoes. Eliminate these for a while. Turn to millet and brown rice.

SUNTANNING

Ultraviolet light acts on the tyrosine in the skin, transforming it into the brown pigment melanin, which is deposited in the superficial layers of the skin, protecting the skin against further action of the light rays. Excess exposure results in dark skin spots often called aging spots or liver spots. They are deposits of lipofuscin in the skin.

In order to understand the problem of the sunbath, one must remember that sunlight not only acts on the parts of the skin that are directly exposed to it, but it also produces substances in the irradiated skin, which pass with the blood into the interior of the body and act on the entire organism. If one's feet are exposed to the sun's rays, the blood pressure may be elevated, and cholesterol is transformed into vitamin D, which acts to deposit calcium in bones or teeth. Exposing one's skin to the sun's rays can be compared to swallowing 1 teaspoonful of medicine every five minutes—a medicine that is by no means harmless. For this reason, one must be careful. For the average person, ten minutes of sunbathing a day is all that is needed. Sunbathing is necessary only to keep up the vitamins D and A content of the body. A deep suntan may be considered attractive, but it is not beneficial to the skin.

When too much sun is taken, the resulting suntan is simply a defense pigment that filters out further harmful rays of the sun. Since the damage of the ozone layer in the atmosphere, skin cancers have radically increased. From 1975 to 1995, the number of melanomas has doubled, and the total number of skin cancers diagnosed in the year 2000 is over one million in the United States. Use a sunblock if you have to be in the sun for more than twenty minutes. The highest risk group for melanoma is older white males, 17 percent of whom die from skin cancer.

AIR BATHS

The daily air bath is a definite aid to good health, toning the skin and improving its texture. Body air baths in the privacy of your own room gradually build up your resistance to a cooler temperature; they may then be taken throughout the year. Limit outdoor air baths to twenty minutes to assure protection from skin cancers.

PERSPIRATION

Under normal conditions an individual loses 500 calories daily, one-eighth of his total heat loss, as a result of perspiration evaporation. The skin contains two million sweat glands. If all the sweat glands were placed end to end, we would obtain a tube six miles in length. Perspiration is acid. It contains sodium chloride, potassium, iron, sulfuric acid, phosphoric aid, lactic acid, and above all, urea. The skin excretes a small amount of urea, so it has been correctly described as a third kidney. If we prevented the skin from giving off heat, sweat, and waste products, the body would suffer from the resulting buildup of toxins and from overheating.

Methods to Remove Toxic Wastes

Steam baths, saunas, and electric blanket–induced sweating are a good means of eliminating toxic wastes from the system. As a means of reducing weight, they are only temporary. It is a good idea to detoxify the body before starting a reducing and health diet routine for best results. Doctors warn of spending too much time in steam baths or saunas—twenty minutes is sufficient—and more than an hour is dangerous. You will lose a pint of perspiration every fifteen minutes, so it is best to drink at least two 8-ounce glasses of water at the start.

Consider baths as workers of good health. The skin brush bath, the sunbath, and the air bath are daily *musts* in your health-building and weight-reducing programs. Any other baths you may choose are an added bonus.

BATHING

The body should be bathed and cleansed three or four times per week. The process of respiration not only goes on in the lungs but in the skin cells (and all other cells of the body). Impurities and poisons find their way out through the skin pores. Dirt and sebum (a fatty skin gland substance) clogs pores. Internal eliminations can also cause clogged pores. Over three million skin pores cover the body. If they were closed, a person could possibly die within one hour. This is one reason why many people today have problems with fatigue—the skin is neglected. Skin brushing is invaluable in caring for the skin.

The temperature of the room, drafts, the temperature of the bather, the time of day, the relative exhaustion of the bather, and the amount of food in the bather's stomach are all important considerations. Never take a hot bath in a very cold room or your system will be filled with moisture, which may trigger lung problems. The temperature of the room should never fall below 68 degrees Fahrenheit when you're bathing. Neither should the temperature exceed 96 or 97 degrees Fahrenheit except in extreme cases. Always let the body accustom itself gradually to extreme measures. Local applications or baths assist the part to which it is applied but do not affect the general body.

Never bathe within two hours after eating, nor when exhausted, nor before you cool off after perspiring. Never bathe in the open air when chilliness follows the plunge. Bathe when the body is warm, and lose no time in getting into the water— never chill yourself while undressing before a bath. Bathe before retiring and take your cold sponge bath when you arise. Those who are strong may bathe early in the morning on an empty stomach. Those who are very young or weak should bathe three hours after a meal, or about three hours after breakfast.

Cold Baths

Cold baths stimulate greater internal oxidation in the tissues, providing sudden and vigorous friction is taken after the bath. A cold bath increases the absorption of oxygen and the elimination of carbonic acid from the system. A cold bath increases urea elimination.

Sheet baths or compress baths may be used in fevers for stimulation of the skin and pores, for soothing inflamed and irritated nerves, or for reducing abdominal inflammation, and so on. This procedure consists of wringing out the water from a large linen sheet previously immersed in cool (not cold) water, then wrapping the sheet around the body while lying on a rubber blanket for bed protection. Cover up well with blankets to rest or sleep for a while, perhaps about forty minutes to one hour. If chilled, remove the compress and your normal body temperature will return. This sheet bath or compress is variously used: water, milk, liquid whey, brine, alfalfa, water, starch water, red clover water, or clay water, may be used either warm, cold, or lukewarm as the case may require. Such packs, sheets, and compresses are often highly beneficial either for reducing bodily heat, inflammation, fever, or for increasing body heat, in which case either hot fomentations or hot packs are used.

Russian Baths

The Russian vapor bath is the same as a Finnish sauna. Water is thrown upon red-hot stones, bricks, or metal, filling the room full of vapor for us to breathe and perspire in. Then follows a cold shower and a vigorous skin friction. If a person feels chilly, he should never take a cold bath. If he takes a cold bath, he should always have his feet comfortably warm before and after taking the cold bath or it will affect the chest.

Sunbaths

The more delicate a person is, the less vitality he may have. It is dangerous for such persons to even undress in a cold room.

Neutral baths, sponge baths, and sunbaths with massage are the very best for them. In the sunbath, increased metabolism and more efficient nutrition take place in the nervous system when the body is naked—provided that the sun is not too hot, the air is not too cold, and the person's privacy is protected. There is nothing better for the nerves than a sun tent in a big luxuriant tree with massage in the sun, sleep among the branches, and fresh air, along with a brain-and-nerve-building diet.

Special Baths with Cold Water

Eye Bath. Take cold water in your cupped hands, gently lower your head until your eyes are in the water, then open and close eyes in the cold water two or three times. Do this twice a day.

Mouthwash. Take a mouthful of cold water, swish it around in your mouth until it is warm, then spit it out. Repeat. Do this twice morning and evening after meals or before and after brushing your teeth. It is very good for the gums. Follow this by flossing your teeth with unwaxed floss thread.

Abdominal Disorders. Wet and wring out a small Turkish towel in very cold water and fold into a square large enough to cover your abdomen. Wrap and pin a large Turkish towel snugly around back and abdomen, covering the small towel and holding it in place. This top towel is dry, and it is vital that it be wrapped so the air does not go in under it. Leave this on for one or two hours daily, or all night, according to doctor's instructions.

Foot Baths. To overcome stagnant circulation, use the hot and cold foot baths. The alternating effect of hot and cold foot soaks with the temperature of the waters not too extreme wakes up a lagging bloodstream and helps the skin.

SHOWERING

A warm, then a cool shower is an invigorating start for the day. The full force of the spray is like a gentle prick of needles on the skin, stimulating the body until it fairly glows with health. After you have turned down the warm water and the cooler water hits your body, there is a moment when your breath will quicken. When you first begin to take the breath in sharply, that is the moment to complete your shower. Your reaction is good then. If you remain longer, the prolonged cold may be detrimental to your health.

SKIN BRUSHING

Daily dry friction brushing, or skin brushing, creates greater activity for the pores of the skin, is far more cleansing, eliminates more waste material than any soap and water bath, and lets the skin retain its natural oils. Soak a dry Turkish towel in cold water, wring out the excess water, and then rub the towel vigorously over the entire body. The friction of rubbing the skin after the skin brush bath tones the skin, develops good circulation, and aids in eliminating mild skin conditions.

To become accustomed to the dry rub, use a soft natural bristle brush at first. Then change to a *soft scrub brush,* which you can purchase in most variety stores. The bristles are stiffer and the friction is more satisfactory. Use a soft face brush on the face, since the blood vessels that lie near the surface are easily broken down with too harsh rubbing. Do not use a nylon brush, but rather a long-handled dry bristle vegetable brush.

Use both face and body brushes without water. With your face brush, start at the forehead and work down over the eyes, along the nose, cheeks, chin, ears, and finally the neck, using a firm, brisk, rotary movement. With the body brush, brush the limbs with an upward movement, or toward the heart, brushing the entire body gently at first until the skin becomes conditioned. Avoid brushing the breasts entirely. Devote at least three to five minutes, morning and night, to this type of bathing. Your skin will become stimulated to better function and actually becomes softer; your health improves without question, and you will have lasting returns in both health and charm. Rubbing the body with salt is also a fine health measure; rinse it off as you shower.

I believe skin brushing is one of the finest of all baths. No soap can wash the skin as clean as the new skin you have under the old. You make new skin every twenty-four hours on the body. That new skin is as clean as the blood is.

Skin brushing removes the old, dead layer of skin. This helps to eliminate uric acid crystals, catarrh, and various other acids in the body. The skin should eliminate 2 pounds of waste acids daily. Keep the skin active. No one can be well wearing clothes unless they brush their skin. It is the best method to remove the surface layer of dead skin pores, dried perspiration salts, urea, and external dirt and accumulations. Do your brushing first thing in the morning when you arise, before your bath or shower.

CHAPTER 11

GET MOVING WITH EXERCISE

Due to the high tech world in which we live today and due to the abnormal processes and often sedentary occupations under which we work, it is necessary to enter into some form of compensatory exercises if we choose to stay well.

Physical activity of the body is an absolute necessity. Our bodies were made to move. If they are not kept supple and exercised they will deteriorate, giving poor service. Through actual experience with patients, we have found three objectives extremely advisable to work toward in all cases. We must keep the abdomen in good working order, the spine limber, and the blood circulation efficient. To keep the spine limber, muscles must be developed evenly on both sides of the spine, then a perfect lymph supply is able to get into the cartilages between the vertebrae. Lymph is necessary since we have no blood vessels to keep these tissues alive. Exercise helps to develop greater room for the nerve liners that pass through the foramen in the spine.

This chapter presents a variety of exercises that improve circulation, muscle tone, and flexibility for a healthier body and mind.

DEEP BREATHING EXERCISES

Few of us breathe deeply enough to oxygenate the blood. The deep breathing exercises explained here are highly concentrated to drive the oxygen into the bloodstream, benefiting the nerve, muscular, and glandular systems. These exercises benefit all ages. They are especially good for those over fifty, when one leads a less active life. Through these exercises, you receive the equivalent of two and one-half to three hours of the usual form of very active exercises.

To Benefit the Liver and Spleen

The liver is the detoxifier in the body. The correct posture for this exercise is to sit up straight with no curvatures in the spine. Take a deep, full breath in through both nostrils. Hold your breath. Drop head gently back (don't strain). Then bring head forward, expelling breath through the nostrils strongly. Do this from ten to fifteen times.

To Benefit the Heart

Close the right nostril using the thumb of the right hand. Take a deep breath in through the left nostril. Close both nostrils using the thumb and fingers and hold your breath as long as it is comfortable—then open the right nostril halfway and let the breath out slowly. This is highly concentrated and need be done only once.

To Benefit the Thyroid Gland

This exercise normalizes weight through correctly balanced metabolism; it also calms the nerves. All the blood in the body goes through the thyroid every one and one-half hours. The thyroid influences the cellular oxygenation rate. The thyroid produces two hormones, referred to as T_3 and T_4, the T standing for thyronine, the numbers indicating how many iodine atoms are attached to each molecule of thyronine. The thyroid regulates energy production in the body through the amount of hormone released. Thyroid hormone controls the rate at which foods are used as energy fuel, influences blood sugar level, cell respiration, and body temperature.

Start by sitting up straight. Using the thumb of the right hand, close the right side of the nose. Take a deep breath in through the left nostril. Close both nostrils for a few seconds, then open right nostril halfway and let the breath out slowly. Now reverse the order. Close the left side of the nose, and take in a deep breath through the right nostril. Close both nostrils for a few seconds, then open the left nostril halfway and let the breath out slowly. Do this alternately ten to fifteen times.

To Benefit the Neck and Parathyroid Gland

Keeping the spine straight, drop head slightly forward. Then place the three center fingers of both hands at the top of the neck. Take in a full breath and hold as you pull both hands, slowly but hard, around to the front of the throat just above the Adam's apple. Let the breath out by slowly blowing.

The second time, vary the exercise by beginning the hard pull from the center so that the neck shows red; blow out, and relax.

The third time, begin at the base of the neck and pull the fingers around the collar bone. Release arms, blow out, and relax.

Excessive mucus is the beginning of all disease. All these exercises stimulate the eliminative processes in the entire system and help get rid of excessive mucus.

To Benefit the Pituitary, Thyroid, and Adrenal Glands

Put feet together and stand erect. Take in a full deep breath, with hips forward and no swayback; pull up the stomach and abdomen; bow arms by slightly raising out to the sides. Turn head full sideways to the right; hold a few seconds; then bring head forward and relax arms down while slowly blowing breath out through the mouth. Relax. Repeat this two more times. Then do it three times turning the neck and face sideways in the opposite direction. Relax.

Remember: The glands function more efficiently when they are supported by constructive mental emotions: joy, love, beauty, peace, music, and so on, which we must consciously practice. The glands must also be fed nourishing food. As soon as you stop destructive thinking you will eliminate one cause of thyroid trouble.

To Purify and Strengthen the Lungs

This is a way of getting rid of all stale air in the lungs. Close right nostril with right thumb, take a deep full breath in through the left nostril, close both nostrils, expelling breath out through the mouth with a "HA" sound. Alternate this same procedure, first one side, then the other, for approximately ten to fifteen times.

To Strengthen the Abdomen and Bowel

Exercise of the bowel is very important, on an equal par with diet. These exercises strengthen the bowel and its entire digestive and assimilative role. We must have good muscle structure support for the abdomen to keep the intestines in their proper place.

These exercises strengthen the abdominal structure, revitalize internal organs, stimulate peristaltic action, and hold the ascending colon in place.

An excellent practice is to hold the abdomen in at all times; discipline yourself to do this and you'll see an improvement in your digestive and bowel action. Also keep the chest up.

1. Stand up, taking in a deep, full breath through both nostrils. Hold the breath while pounding with closed fists the abdomen below the navel, in a circular right to left motion. Do this thirty times and then let the breath out by blowing it out through the mouth slowly and gradually.

2. Sitting down, sit up straight. Pull in lower stomach or the abdomen. Pull it way in, then let it out. Do this ten times; then relax. Now pull in the left side of the abdomen ten times. Relax. Now pull in the right side of the abdomen ten times. Relax. Now roll the entire stomach/abdomen around right to left twenty-five times, while holding breath, then blow breath out.

To Benfit the Pneumogastric (Vagus) Nerve

This exercise supports a complex cranial nerve that has to do with hearing, speaking, heart function, lung function, and the digestive system.

Standing, take a deep full breath and while holding the breath, circle head from right to left all the way round. Beginners do ten times each way—slowly at first. One who is thoroughly accustomed to this exercise can do it thirty times rapidly, with shoulders participating in the same circular movement. Relax. Now do the same exercise the reverse way, left to right. Always let the breath out through the mouth slowly or gradually after holding it. If you get dizzy, bend backward and forward from the hips. Any grating feeling in the neck is good: you are breaking up calcium deposits (called "gravel").

To Improve Sleep

This induces peaceful sleep and helps eliminate snoring. This exercise also helps balance thyroid gland function. Fear, sorrow, and extreme negative emotions immediately show their effects on the pancreas and thyroid glands, and break down enzymes that have to do with hormone release in both glands.

Close the right nostril with right thumb, while repeatedly and rapidly opening and closing the left nostril halfway with the index finger of the right hand. Do this seventy-five times. Repeat, closing the left nostril with left thumb, while opening and closing rapidly the right nostril with index finger of left hand. Do this seventy-five times. Breathe normally throughout. All these exercises develop muscular tone and flexibility in the abdomen.

To Improve Circulation

Sit forward slightly in a straight chair. Place hands on knees, head forward, and pant with open mouth in and out one hundred times. When just beginning, pant only fifty times, and build up gradually to one hundred times. This also stimulates the salivary gland juices.

To Benefit the Pituitary Gland

The pituitary gland is the master gland that controls all the other glands in the body. This exercise feeds the brain by improving circulation and toning the thyroid gland. It acts as a beauty treatment by bringing blood to the neck and face. It produces flexibility in the spine by stretching vertebrae and spinal nerves. THIS EXERCISE IS NOT FOR PEOPLE WITH HIGH BLOOD PRESSURE.

Stand with feet wide apart. Close right nostril, take in a deep, full breath through left nostril, close both nostrils, bend knees slightly. Place right hand on head, then bend slowly down, concentrating on each one of the spinal vertebrae all the way, letting the neck drop loosely. Hold the breath in this position as long as you can. Come back up still holding the breath and feeling each one of the vertebrae pull up. When you are straight up, open the right nostril halfway and gradually let the breath out. Do this exercise only twice, since it is highly concentrated.

To Benefit the Pancreas Gland

The pancreas supervises digestion of all the body's proteins and starches.

Close right nostril with right thumb, take in a full breath through left nostril, close both nostrils, and moisten lips, letting the breath out gradually through the lips while vibrating them, pulling up the diaphragm at the same time. Relax, then repeat twice.

This next exercise is for greater confidence, increased energy, and chest expansion. Standing up, in one breath, sniff in four times so that the chest is fully expanded while alternating arm and knee raises; then let the breath out in one snort through the nose. Raise the right arm shoulder high in front and left knee to take in the first sniff. Then raise the left arm and right knee on the second sniff. Raise the right arm and left knee with the third sniff. Then after the fourth arm and leg lift, snort breath out through both nostrils. Rest for three counts. Keep this up for fifteen to twenty-five times. This same sniff breath can be done while walking. These exercises help you to breathe deeply, which promotes good health.

To Benefit the Throat

Another excellent vibratory throat exercise is to take in breath through both nostrils. Bend head to right and tap up and down the throat while you HUM the breath out through the mouth. Reverse and do the other side of the neck.

To Improve Breathing Capacity

Sitting up straight, with no swayback or front droop, sniff breath in and out through both nostrils in rapid succession from seventy-five to one hundred times. Beginners who have to can do it twenty-five times, then stop and relax, then repeat twenty-five times more, then stop and relax, and so on until you build up your breathing ability and capacity.

To Benefit the Vocal Cords

This exercise works out and clears up mucus and energizes the entire abdominal region. Sit up straight, take in a full breath through both nostrils, and hold. Put three fingers of the left hand on the right side of the frontal mid-throat, pulling the Adam's apple to the left. Turn the head full to the right; hold it for a few seconds, then bring the head forward and let the breath out gradually, blowing through the mouth. Relax, then repeat this same exercise twice more. Reverse the exercise, taking in a full breath through both nostrils, putting the three fingers of the right hand on the left side of the Adam's apple (or "Eve's apple"). Pull the apple to the right as you turn your neck and head full to the left, hold for a few seconds, bring head front, and let breath out slowly, blowing through the mouth. Relax; and repeat two more times.

THROAT AND FACE EXERCISES

These four special throat and face exercises improve circulation and muscle tone.

1. Sitting down, smile very exaggeratedly, stretching the throat cords and upper chest fifteen times. Relax.
2. Alternate each side of the mouth the same way. Tense right side, then relax. Tense left side. Relax. Repeat fifteen times.
3. Tilt the chin upward and move it in a chewing motion. Stretch the throat thirty times. Relax.
4. Close the mouth and squeeze the facial muscles under the skin, up to thirty times. This is good to keep the under-face muscles firm, which keeps the skin from sagging and lifts the mouth muscles.

SPECIAL EYE EXERCISES

To Develop Quick, Keen, and Alert Near and Far Eyesight

Put the right index finger up directly 1 foot in front of the eyes. Pick out the smallest object you can—at least 100 yards away, look at the finger tip, then quickly look at the distant object. Do this twenty to thirty times, looking only at the tip then directly at the distant object. This exercise keeps the eye muscles flexible.

To Improve Eye Circulation

Place the left middle finger over the right eye, lightly tapping the first joint of the middle finger with the index and middle fingers of the right hand, moving the left middle finger joint all around the right eye. Then repeat the same procedure with the right middle finger over the left eye.

To Show Your Optic Fusion Is Good

Hold up the right index finger about a foot and a half in front of your eyes, look way out in the distance until the finger makes two, then look out between the two fingers.

To Tone Eye Muscles

Put the right index finger up in front of the eyes and, while looking at the finger tip, move it in close to the eyes, feeling the eye muscle pull in, then move the finger out two feet, feeling the muscle relax out as you do this fifteen to twenty times. Relax arm down.

Keeping the head straight ahead, throw the eyes way up to the upper right, then down lower left, swing them fully up and down. Then reverse procedure, upper left down to lower right, fifteen times. Relax.

Raise the eyes up to the sky, also lifting the lower lids upward, then lower the eyes to the ground, always keeping the head straight ahead. Do this fifteen times. Relax.

Roll the eyeballs around in the eye socket from right to left in a full circle, feeling the muscular action, then reverse the eye action. Do each fifteen times. Relax.

To Test Peripheral Vision

Put the two index fingers out in front of the eyes about two feet apart, bringing them slowly back toward the ears, until you can no longer see the fingers from the sides of the eyes. Keep the head and eyes straight ahead. Do this procedure fifteen times.

ORGAN BLOOD CIRCULATION EXERCISES

To circulate blood through every organ of the body is the second most important requirement in getting well. This is done through exercise.

Walking and hiking stimulate the flow of blood throughout the body. Swimming is the best form of exercise for those who have back problems. It requires movement of the whole body evenly in a prone position and promotes excellent circulation to the brain, which controls all body functions.

There are many forms of exercise that may be used. I believe that tensing and relaxing the body (isometric exercise) is very good. Any time we tense a muscle in the body we force the blood into the more relaxed nearby muscles. If we follow this tensing with relaxation, blood automatically refills these relaxed tissues. Many times muscles can be squeezed and contracted without bending the joints.

MUSCLE TENSION/RELAXATION EXERCISES

These exercise the entire body, especially the spine from top to bottom. A strengthened spine opens all nerve lines and aids the thyroid gland. It gives poise to the body and causes true, right relaxation.

1. Raise arms up over the head, claw hands, and with great tension draw arms down to the chest as though you are doing a chin-up. Hold very tense for a few seconds, then relax completely. Do this three times.

2. Arms to sides, claw hands, tense arms, and bend up toward chest. Hold tension for a few seconds, then relax completely. Do this three times.

3. Arms out front, claw hands, and pull arms into chest. Hold tension a few seconds, then relax completely. Do this three times.

4. Arms stretched out at sides, claw hands, and bend tensed arms up to shoulders. Drop arms and relax completely. Do this three times.

5. Fingers interlaced, raise arms out front to the left and level with the head. With both hands tensed and pulling against each other, gradually bring left hand down across chest with the right hand as far as you can and relax.

   Do this same exercise but on the opposite side. Keep body straight as you pull the arms across the chest. Do this three times on each side.

6. Interlace fingers behind you. Tense the muscles and pull one arm against the other. Then raise the hands up toward the shoulders, keeping your hands locked and tensed.

Slowly bring them down to position and relax. This can be done under tension three or four times.

7. Abdominal exercise: Knees stiff, bend forward, put hands together way out to right side and push one against the other, resisting all the way to the left side, then do it the other way to right side, feeling the pull in the abdomen.

8. Put right leg slightly in front of the left. Tense calf, then thigh. Relax both. Then repeat with the other leg. Do each leg eight times. Excellent for building and strengthening circulation and leg muscles, giving correct contour to the leg.

9. Hands together in prayer position at chest, push from left to right side, then from right to left, resisting each direction.

10. Hands together in prayer position at stomach, push against each other all the way up over the head while pulling the entire stomach way up; then relax.

11. Bend left arm over left shoulder, reaching down back, while the right arm and hand is bent up the spine. Clasp fingers together if possible. Gently pull up with left and down with right; let go and relax. Then do opposite hands and arms.

12. Lie on the floor or a bed, arms at sides and legs and feet straight. Bending at the hips, bring the head and feet up toward ceiling, tensing all the muscles of the body, including the arms, legs, and stomach. Stretch arms out toward feet to help maintain balance. Hold for three seconds in this position and relax. Do this three times.

SPINE AND NERVE EXERCISE

Standing, place feet apart. Turn toes in pigeon fashion, get a good, firm gripping stance, so hips are held absolutely straight. Bend at waist and swing loosely from hips up, from left to right, letting arms, hands, and neck go very free and relaxed. Do this twenty times. This is a wonderful spinal exercise, and if done properly, will cause the spine to make its own correct adjustment.

PROLAPSED ORGANS EXERCISES AND SOLUTIONS

Many persons experiencing ill health have a prolapsed to converse colon. A prolapsed colon may be caused by devitalized foods, occupations that keep us from exercising properly, not enough sleep, too much standing, improper posture, overeating, and lack of fiber in the diet.

To overcome prolapsus, which can cause bladder and kidney irritations, pressure on the sex glands, pressure on the heart, improper breathing, acidosis, and painful menstruation, it is absolutely necessary that we learn how to live properly. The best way to start is a cleansing process, a tearing down of old cell structure material and a rebuilding of new. It requires a real physical housecleaning, which sometimes is not pleasant. But years from now you may recognize it as the greatest thing you have ever done for yourself.

It is important with prolapsus to empty the rectum while squatting. This can also be done by using a toilet that is no higher than 14 inches (for an adult) and putting the feet on a 4- to 6-inch stool. It also helps to hold both arms over the head while having a bowel movement. It is also appropriate to take enemas for a good cleansing of the rectum. By following my Daily Diet Regime over a period of time, your body will absorb the chemical elements that will give your flesh tone and firmness, while providing the necessary fiber (25–30 grams daily) to strengthen and tone the bowel. If you do the right exercises and learn the proper posture, the abdominal organs will go into place where they belong.

In extreme prolapsus, raise the foot end of your bed about two or three inches so that when you are lying down the organs will fall toward the shoulders and stay there during the sleeping hours. A useful exercise is to lie across the bed with the shoulders on the floor, allowing the organs to fall down toward the chest cavity. You may also use slanting board exercises once or twice daily to bring the prolapsed transverse colon back to its natural location.

SLANT BOARD AND OTHER EXERCISES

Use ankle straps while doing the following exercises:

1. Lie full length, allowing gravity to help the abdominal organs into their proper position and letting the blood circulate to the head. For best results, lie on board at least ten minutes. The basic position should climax all slant board exercises.
2. While lying flat on the back, stretch the abdomen by putting arms above head. Bring arms above head ten to fifteen times; this stretches the abdominal muscles and pulls the abdomen down toward the shoulders.
3. Bring abdominal organs toward shoulders while holding your breath. Move the organs back and forth by drawing abdomen upward, then allowing it to go back to a relaxed position. Do ten to fifteen times.
4. Pat abdomen vigorously with open hands. Lean to one side then to the other, patting the stretched side. Pat ten to fifteen times. Reverse sides three or four times.

5. Bring the body to sitting position, using the abdominal muscles. Return to lying position. Do three or four times, if possible. *(But do this only if doctor orders.)*

Hold onto the handles, feet out of straps, while doing the following:

1. Bend knees and legs at hips. While in this position (a) turn head from side to side five or six times; (b) lift the head slightly and rotate in circles three or four times. Reverse. Repeat each set two or three times.

2. Lift legs to vertical position and rotate outward in circles eight or ten times. Then change direction to inward circles. Increase to twenty-five times after a week or two of exercising.

3. Bring legs straight up to a vertical position and lower them to board slowly, first right leg, then left, keeping each straight. Then raise and lower both together. Repeat three or four times. Bicycle legs in air fifteen to twenty-five times.

4. Relax and rest, letting the blood circulate in the head for ten minutes.

The Side Roll

The side roll is especially good for conditions of sciatica and lower back pains, for relaxing nerve tension in the lower and middle back, and for directing nerve supply to the lower abdominal organs.

Lie upon a firm bed so that when the leg is extended in this exercise it will be at a lower level than the body. Turn on left side, raise the right leg to a 45-degree angle across the body.

Grasp ankle with left hand and pull leg up toward the head and at the same time away from the body. Stretch right arm up and back, pulling the spine in the opposite direction. Reverse and repeat on the other side.

This is an extreme spinal stretch with the greatest amount of muscle pull on the lower back.

The Mule Kick

The mule kick is done best by standing in back of a chair and grasping the chair with both hands. Raise the right leg backward, bending the knee so that the heel touches the buttocks. Kick back with a fast jerking movement, like a mule would kick. Then extend the same leg straight back as far as possible and parallel with the floor and kick back with a sharp thrust. Alternate the legs, kicking three times each leg.

Wrestler's Stance

Stand with feet apart and knees bent. Twist from side to side, from the hip up. Bend arms at elbows.

Gradually do a knee bend, going down as close to the heels as possible. Come up slowly, tighten the buttock muscles, and continue the same twist. Do this up and down motion four or five times.

The twisting motion helps develop the muscular structure on each side of the abdomen so that hernias and ruptures will not develop. Tightening the buttocks when rising to a standing position also helps to get a better circulation of blood into the rectal area and the prostate gland.

Sitting Exercises

1. Sit upright—feet and knees well apart—and stretch arms straight over head. Bend body forward, swinging arms well under the chair, keeping your chin on chest. Put head as far under chair as possible, stretching back muscles. Return to sitting position with arms still above head and the upward stretch tensing the abdominal muscles.

2. Sit upright—knees and feet well apart—arms sideward, shoulder height. Bend over and turn trunk to left while left hand touches right toes and right hand stretches well above the head to produce tension on side of abdomen. Turn trunk in opposite direction and reverse exercise.

Standing Exercises

1. Look straight ahead and lean head over on shoulder while keeping eyes straight front. First lean to one side, then to the other.

2. Turn head from side to side, stretching as far as possible.

3. Drop head forward. Turn head in circular motion, keeping face and eyes straight ahead. Do this three times in each direction.

4. Drop head straight backward and forward as far as possible, omitting circular motion.

5. Stand with feet 12 to 14 inches apart. Looking down toward right foot, bring right arm up and place palm of right hand at the back of head and draw steadily toward right foot. Do the same on other side and with left arm.

6. Clasp both hands behind head and pull straight down toward feet.

7. Feet apart—arms to side—twist body at hips, swinging around first to one side and then to the other.

8. Bend forward allowing hands to drop down to toes, and throw arms together, first up to one side and then to the other.
9. Raise arms sideward, level with shoulders, and make circles with hands (backward) about 15 to 16 inches in diameter.

The Calf Stretcher

1. Stand up straight, putting one leg directly behind the other, toe touching heel.
2. Keeping erect, bend slowly at the knees. Do this ten times. This pulls on the long muscles of the leg.
3. Change over so the other leg is in front and repeat another ten times.
4. Repeat.

DRAINING THE NECK LYMPH GLANDS

1. Press thumbs behind both of the ears at the base of the skull, then push under the skull into neck with firm pressure, slowly going down toward the collarbone.
2. Press thumbs 1 inch further in on both sides.
3. Press thumbs still further in alongside vertebral column.
4. Repeat.

   Be sure to press under the skull with the thumbs, then down into the neck to shoulder level. Do the above exercise once or twice a day to relieve head and neck congestion.

WATER TREATMENTS AND BATHS

Water treatments are excellent for improving circulation. They are effective at getting blood into the various organs of the body without exercise. Cold water forces the blood away from the tissues, wherever the cold pack is used. Warm water relaxes the tissues, allowing blood to return to the tissue wherever the hot pack is used.

By using alternate hot and cold packs, we are then able to drive the blood into and draw it out of the various organs of the body. Using hot and cold packs on the shoulders, knees, feet, and abdomen is very beneficial. It moves along the stagnant blood. In using the alternate packs, consider one-half minute cold and one minute hot, with eight changes.

Of all the baths that we use, I believe the sitz bath to be the best. It is best used alternately hot and cold. There is a very wonderful bath called the cosmo-vital bath. The method is to lie on the back in 4 inches of cold water from one-half to one minute, while the exposed part of the body is in the hot sunshine. The blood will thus be drawn to the upper parts. Then turn over so that you are face down in the water, back exposed to the sun, and the blood will quickly be drawn to your exposed back, while the front parts are now being cooled in the water.

Stay in this position one-half to one minute. This is the most natural of all baths. Lie with the head to the north. A shallow cement basin can be made just for this purpose, with walls four inches high and large enough to allow the human form to lie stretched out in it.

TAI CHI

Tai chi—short for tai chi chuan—is an exercise used in Taiwan and the internal parts of mainland China. It is used in the morning before going to work as an exerciser and a conditioner for the body. Tai chi does not give you any heavy breathing or exhausting gyrations such as we have in our typical calisthenics. It is a very graceful, pleasant conditioner. It is similar to the martial arts, but it has been slowed down to a balletlike activity that the average person can do and enjoy. It helps to develop the small muscles of the body that we use so much in our daily activity and to take care of the internal arterial and venous blood system.

Many people don't do enough from a physical exercise standpoint. The majority of the people in America seem to have sedentary jobs, exhausting mental activity; they need a hobby or exercises to balance this out. Tai chi could be used every day by everyone. The Chinese use it for all ages, from when a child is young right on through to seventy and eighty years of age.

You will find that tai chi is a well organized program and takes in the development of the whole body. I personally believe that tai chi is the greatest emotional balancer that we have for the body. It is a wonderful exercise in developing the longevity pattern in a person and for producing the best of health.

Tai chi also exercises the joints and helps to keep the circulation going in all parts of the body. It is a very wonderful exercise because many exercises just go forward and backward, side to side, and do not give the circle exercises to the joints.

OVERCOMING TENSION

Renew the mind. Relaxing and revitalizing the mind has to come from within. The source of all change and improvement is within us. If we learn the right principles, the physical body will respond in well-being. The physical body is the temple we live in. The stones are set according to our relationship to life. That is going to determine the condition of every cell in our bodies. Every thought will finally find an expression in the physical body. By thinking the very best thoughts, we can have the best kind of body possible, consistent with our genetic inheritance.

In other words, physical perfection is accomplished by the renewing of the mind. This has been a largely neglected factor in our lives. We have been unaware of its relation to our state of health. In the future, we are going to call this neglected factor "life." You are the richest person in the world if you can live by right principles, keep your body well, and enjoy peace of mind.

You must advance in knowledge, beyond the belief that whatever you eat makes no difference to your health. You have got to know there are such things as good food, good health, and a good mind. Without all these, you are not going to get anywhere. Let us be inspired to live a better life. "When good men do nothing, evil comes in." There are a lot of people who talk about things but do nothing about them.

THE NEED FOR MINERALS

Normal relaxation is impossible if the body is starving for mineral elements. Magnesium, a mineral found in yellow cornmeal and nearly all fruits and vegetables, is essential. Obtain it from these sources at least five times daily. "Milk of magnesia" is used for the bowel as a medicine. Why not get your own biochemical magnesium from the food you eat? Phosphorus, a required nerve food, is also found in yellow cornmeal and in meat, poultry, and fish.

Silicon is another of the elements needed by the nerves and is found high in oat straw tea, rice bran, rice polishings, and rice bran syrup, which is also very high in vitamin B. The B-complex vitamins are a wonderful food supplement for those who have nervous disturbances. Vitamin B is found in whole grains, wheat germ, and rice polishings—along with various mineral elements. If you want to overcome mental and nervous disorders, lecithin is a wonderful food. Vitamin B will not stay in the body without it. Vitamins alone will not do any good. Don't buy vitamins without minerals. Get all the minerals possible. Vitamin and mineral supplements must be natural. However, if you can keep the body healthy and relaxed, your vitamin consumption won't have to be as high. We burn up vitamins through tension.

The richest source of calcium in the vegetable kingdom is green kale. Calcium gives tone and steadiness. The very best source of calcium is milk products, such as yogurt. Good sources of calcium include green tops of all vegetables. Other sources are cereal grains, of which I believe barley is best. You should not use this grain in the summer, as it is a heating food. However, in the winter, use barley/green kale soup often for its high calcium.

POSTURE WISE

Standing tall, sitting tall, and walking tall should be our uppermost thought for good posture. Posture habits are formed early in life and these three points should be considered in training and raising our children. The following rules will help in this training:

1. Learn to stand tall, sit tall, and walk tall.
2. Follow a few simple daily exercises to preserve strength and tone of the ligaments and muscles which support the spinal column.
3. Learn to relax completely.

Good posture is the foundation of good health. With correct posture we allow the different organs of the body to have free movement with one another, and no pressure symptoms are produced on one organ more than another. The knees do not become buckled, prolapsus does not set in, shoulders will not droop, and the Adam's apple will not be pressed forward to put pressure on the thyroid gland. Our breathing becomes deeper with good posture. Our chest is carried higher. Good posture does away with lower back curve and the consequent curves that develop in the upper spine. With good posture we walk with our feet straight ahead, the muscles of the legs are strong, the veins and arteries carry the blood more freely, and the nerves in our body carry the messages from our brain to the different organs without any inhibitions or stimulation. Digestion and elimination are improved through good posture.

OUR ATTITUDES ARE KILLING US

I am convinced that people's attitudes are killing them faster than anything else. We should control our thoughts and keep them positive. We should control our speech; there is great power in the spoken word! Keep well by seeing the good. If you need to get well, be spiritually minded about your disease. Dedicate yourself to finding a deeper realization of oneness with all life. This will bring relaxation, and harmony will express itself in your life and affairs.

CHAPTER 12

THE CATARRHAL RUNOFF

What is catarrh? A catarrhal condition is nature's method of ridding the body of waste materials not handled in the normal elimination process. (The word *catarrh* means "Flow down.") When these elimination processes reach the "running" stage, it means that the body is waging an all-out fight against the centers of infection.

The elimination process should never be stopped, since any discharge is the natural healing effort of the body to get rid of that which does not belong to it—excess waste material, fatigue acids, and so on. Discharge cleanses the body of toxic materials before they harden and become even more difficult to remove from the system. In other words, if we use unnatural methods to stop these acute processes of elimination they will manifest themselves in subacute ways. If the policemen of the body are thwarted in their efforts to oust the petty criminals, the detective may have to be called in later to find the hardened criminal. When we stop a catarrhal discharge we have not effected a cure or conquered a disease; we have merely prolonged the day of reckoning.

WHY AND HOW DO CATARRHAL CONDITIONS DEVELOP IN THE BODY?

Why do we develop catarrhal conditions? There are hundreds of "little reasons," but basically it all goes back to several major causes, such as inherent or constitutional weaknesses in certain areas of our individual bodies. When we know we have an inherently weak colonic system or that our bronchial system is inclined to be affected by adverse weather, we should as a matter of common sense guard against unnecessary attacks—just as we would put a fence around our yard to keep out stray dogs.

One reason for the existence of catarrh in any part of the system may be fatigue, because a tired body develops acids that irritate tissues and mucous membranes. This fatigue may be due to habits of work that place undue strain on certain portions of the body. It may be due to overeating or indulging in wrong combinations of food over long periods of time, or the use of narcotics, drugs, or any factor that depletes our normal energy beyond the natural power of the body to resist and throw off such attacks. In short, fatigue may be due to repeatedly breaking the laws of equilibrium or balance that maintain a healthy body.

When we break a public law once, we get off with a small fine or a light sentence. So it is with the body. We may be able to get away with one cold, but if we continue to break the law that resulted in that penalty, we will develop a chronic condition and pay for our negligence just as the habitual criminal pays for his law-breaking. If we have already become habitual offenders against the laws of nature, then it is up to us to correct our habits and to establish law and order again. We need to rehabilitate ourselves! By doing so, we can avert serious stages of catarrh as manifested in chronic diseases such as asthma, arthritis, bronchiectasis, diabetes, heart trouble, hardening of the arteries, and cancer.

Getting the Right Start

Much of the ill health in adults has its beginning in childhood. Colds and children's diseases, such as mumps, measles, discharges of the ears and nose, and so on, should be taken care of by natural methods. We should remember that body cleanliness, correct foods, normal activities, and a happy environment, with plenty of *love,* will prevent most of the ill health found in children. Even those with inherent weaknesses will, if properly cared for, escape most of the ills of childhood and become healthy adults. Are you giving your children the care that is their birthright?

SYMPTOMS OF A CATARRHAL CONDITION

There is such a thing as innocently breaking laws that we are unaware of until we are caught, but the body has its policemen who write tickets to enlighten or warn us. These are known as "symptoms." They are in the form of discharges, irritations, pains, and inflammations that occur when we have an accumulation of dead matter or poisons in any part of the body. These symptoms usually appear first in the mucous membranes. The signposts grow as we progress down the road to a complete breakdown of the body. From the common cold, which we suppress, we go on to hay fever, which, when dried up, becomes asthma or even arthritis or some other chronic disease.

A weakened body and a sluggish bloodstream and lymph system react to every change in temperature. Every little breeze that blows becomes an ill wind for us. What should be normal adjustments to changing weather conditions such as temperature, humidity, or atmospheric pressures become violent reactions. We can't take them in our stride. We get summer colds, winter colds, attacks of asthma, hay fever, sinusitis, bronchitis, and our joints, which have become corroded with arthritic accumulations, are painful. Accumulations in the arteries cause a strain on the heart and slow the circulation, causing coldness in the extremities. These are symptoms of subacute and acute conditions; they are the result of neglect of small symptoms or the suppression of catarrhal conditions. We are only storing up misery for ourselves and our children when we suppress these small ailments, first discharges, first colds. When we understand that, we have gone a long way toward maintaining good health.

Nervousness and depression often accompany catarrhal conditions. Many people today have nervous breakdowns, which affect the mental capacity as well as injure the physical body beyond its power to recuperate. This may be due to the strain of living, but disease usually follows tension, and vice-versa.

Fatigue can be a symptom of catarrh, as well as a cause. We feel tired all the time. We can't quite "cut the mustard" at work and we just don't feel like playing. We haven't the energy to carry on our normal activities, much less the extra vitality needed at times for special occasions. Life becomes dull and burdensome.

Catarrh manifests itself in many other ways. Some of the most common are bronchitis, sinusitis, and tonsillitis.

The symptoms of *bronchitis* are a raw, stuffed feeling in the membranes of the bronchial tubes; poor circulation of the blood; slight inhalation of the breath; weak voice; suffocation, soreness in the chest, developing into a rattle; and a contraction and tightness in the chest that is often accompanied with a hollow cough.

The symptoms of *sinusitis* are similar to those of bronchitis except that they develop in the sinus area, causing pressure pains in the ears, eyes, and head, with a raw feeling in the sinuses.

Sinusitis affects the various cavities of the head, but we do not treat it as a local condition but as a general thing. When we want to treat the face or the nasal membranes for a local condition, we can use the nasal chlorophyll douche, the saltwater nasal douche, or the chamomile tea douche. We could also use hot and cold packs or hot epsom salt packs on the face, along with our catarrh treatment.

We treat *tonsillitis* the same way as we do all catarrhal conditions of the body. We do not consider tonsillitis a local condition to be taken care of without considering the whole body. We must build good health. It is part of our work to recognize that what cures disease is found in the prevention of disease, and whatever works to prevent disease can also be used in the eradication of a disease.

When we reach these extreme conditions, we know we are old offenders against the laws of nature. We know we have created an abnormal composition of the blood and lymph systems through improper foods or the addition of drugs. Or perhaps we have blocked the normal flow of the blood or lymph by some occupational or recreational habit that puts abnormal pressure on the colon and those portions of the body that act as waste disposal areas. When we block their normal flow, these wastes may eventually get into other areas of the body and cause mastitis, appendicitis, colitis, or any of the many forms of "itis" with which we mortals are commonly afflicted.

WHAT TO DO

When we get that kind of backup, the first thing we must do is give the body as much rest as possible, because a tired body cannot eliminate, nor can it function. It requires all the energy it is producing to throw off its excess accumulations. Just as it took an abnormal amount of strain to break down the body, so will it take more than an abnormal amount of rest or relief from stress to rebuild it to a normalcy. Any undue stress or strain must be compensated for by extra relief and rest for that portion of the body that is affected. Any accumulations must be taken care of by giving the body the right combination of foods, water, air, sunshine, a normal amount of work, and a plentiful supply of joy. Why joy? Because the body is physical, mental, and spiritual, and the well-being of one is dependent upon the well-being of all the others.

Watch Your Breath

Too many of us do not understand the importance of correct breathing, possibly because we do not know much about this vital function of the entire body. The medulla of the brain is the nerve center that controls the respiration of the lung structure. When we wear down the nervous system, this particular center of the brain cannot control the breathing well. There are many people who cannot breathe as they should and who actually lose their lives from nervous breakdowns.

Our breathing capacity has a direct connection with the spinal cord, the muscles and nerves in the neck, and the medulla of the brain. An arthritic spine or tight neck muscles will impair breathing capacity and eventually weaken the brain control over our breathing. Some people with depleted nervous systems and weakened medullas will breathe way down low as little as six times a minute. This is scarcely enough to sustain life, much less enable them to work, play, and enjoy living. Those who are subject to fears will develop a very fast breath. Under emotional stress, such as fear, anger, and hatred, the breathing will become staccato, short and quick, as high as thirty times a minute. Watch your breath!

Air that is laden with dust, industrial chemicals, car exhaust, carbon monoxide, and other offending materials cannot feed the lungs or the bloodstream with a healthful supply of oxygen, nitrogen, and other essential elements. The body is fighting a losing battle when it tries to extract from such poisoned materials the small amount of good that remains in them, and it cannot help but develop acute, then subacute catarrhal conditions, then finally chronic ailments.

Keep Clean

In order to have true freedom from any disease, it is essential to have a *clean body*. Keeping the body clean is a must in maintaining good health. Whenever we have debris or an excessive amount of catarrhal congestion in the body, germ life is attracted. It has been said that nearly everyone has tubercular germs in the throat area. This doesn't mean that nearly everyone has tuberculosis, but it does mean that if the body is allowed to become nutritionally unbalanced and filled with catarrhal settlements, this germ life can become more active and may develop into a serious condition.

I have never felt that we should treat this germ life. I believe we should treat the *cause*. I believe we should cleanse the liver, the gallbladder, and the intestinal tract and thereby increase the resistance of the body to germs. The eliminative organs will throw off the catarrh and with it the germs, because they have no breeding grounds. We do not consider germ life the primary negative condition in the body or the primary cause of disease; rather, it is the secondary effect—it is the effect of a catarrhal buildup in the body.

The enema can be very helpful in preventing a catarrh buildup, but it should be used principally in an eliminating and fasting regime. It should be used for cleansing the lower bowel only, serving as a slight stimulant to peristaltic action. One pint of plain, lukewarm water is sufficient for the enema. If there is an extreme colitis condition, flaxseed may be boiled in the water; flaxseed is both soothing and healing. A warm milk enema will relieve internal hemorhoids. For severe constipation, a thorough cleansing of the lower bowel may be accomplished by using a coffee enema four times daily, every four hours. Coffee stimulates a sluggish bowel. Use three tablespoons of ground coffee to one quart of water; boil two or three minutes; then simmer ten to twenty minutes. Strain and use at body temperature. Do not dilute.

To develop a clean intestinal tract, we must have what I call the proper acid/alkaline balance. We have over four hundred species of bowel flora. If they are in balance, we have 80 percent friendly bacteria, mainly acidophilus bacteria, and 20 percent unfriendly bacteria, including E. coli, proteus, klebsiella, and others. Along with acidophilus, we have bulgaricus, B. bifidum, and B. longum. The ratio of the germ life within us determines our health. One mix produces a lot of gas in the bowel. Until we get the proper balance, we are going to have gas problems. There are very few people who have perfect balance. In nearly every case we have tested, we have found that the sick person has about 20 percent friendly and 80 percent unfriendly bacteria in the bowel. It should be just the opposite. Research has shown that acidophilus bacteria can kill 50 percent of twenty-seven different disease-causing bacteria.

If we combine our food properly, it will build up the friendly bacteria in the bowel. Whey is one of the finest foods we have to multiply the friendly bacteria. Soybean milk is also good for feeding the acidophilus bacteria. We can also use acidophilus fortified milk, but it does not have the same potency as does an acidophilus culture. I estimate that it takes about 365 glasses of acidophilus milk to equal one bottle of culture. Using both regularly is one way to break up a prolonged deficiency of beneficial bacteria that can exist in our bodies.

Acidophilus milk is made in many different ways. We have a culture that can be put into the milk and as it grows, we can add another glass of milk, skimmed or whole. The culture can be kept growing for many years.

Bathing, of course, is of utmost importance in keeping the body clean, both inside and outside. We eliminate a great deal of toxic material through the skin every day. This is a form of catarrhal discharge, which is why the skin is referred to as an elimination organ.

Let us remember, "Cleanliness is next to Godliness." We cannot hope to attain perfection, either physically, mentally, or spiritually, unless we keep our "temples" clean.

Remedies for Catarrh Buildup

Black horseradish contains a chemical called raphanon, which is a wonderful eliminant for catarrh that has settled in the gall duct and in the gallbladder. Mix it with a little lemon juice and put some on the tongue, then breathe the fumes. It may lift the top of your head off, but it will open those passages beautifully. This is one of the remedies that naturopathic doctors are using for gallbladder disturbances. Powdered horseradish in its natural form may also be used in the way I have mentioned.

Another good "catarrh chaser" is a pinch of cayenne pepper in soup, or soft-boiled eggs, or in a hot cup of vegetable or chicken broth. Cayenne pepper is good for coughs.

A "cough syrup" that is effective is made by placing six cut white onions in a double boiler. Do not add water. Add a half cup of pure strained honey. Cook slowly over a low fire for two hours and strain. This mixture will stop a cough if taken at regular intervals. The onions act as a bowel cleanser and the honey aids in building up the bloodstream. Keep the mixture warm. It is more effective if slightly heated, and it will relieve the irritation that induces coughing.

DIET AND CATARRH

The habit of overeating develops a state of chronic gastric fermentation. This fermentation is normally thrown off directly by way of the mouth, but it can, through absorption in a body that is not working properly, be thrown out through the elimination of the lung structure. In people who are troubled with a chronic catarrhal condition, it goes through the nose many times, attacking the nasal membrane. The nasal membrane and mucus become very sensitive in those conditions. When particles of inert dust, lint from clothing, pollen of flowers, odors of all kinds (in fact, anything capable of having an irritating effect on the mucous membranes) are inhaled, they will bring out a highly sensitive, irritated, and inflamed state of the nose, eyes, and throat. If this irritation continues, hay fever results. For example, in dry, dusty weather, or in the season of the year when the pollen of certain trees, flowers, or weeds is filling the air, these persons are made very uncomfortable; but dust is not the cause. Those who have taken care of the cause of catarrh in most cases do not have these seasonal problems. What hay fever really means is that during the haying season, when the atmosphere is full of fine, particulate plant matter and pollen, those with an established catarrhal inflammation history experience irritation and swelling of mucous membranes of the nose and sinuses in response to certain allergens. The problem is not the pollen or dust, the problem is their health. Often the health problem underlying hay fever is a dietary deficiency in iron and chloride.

Diet can help us with catarrhal problems. Two salads a day, as the major part of the meal, would be beneficial. We do this because it takes some time to overcome a catarrhal condition— we may spend a solid year getting the body cleaned up. Those who feel they cannot miss any of the good things in life and must indulge in all kinds of food will find it difficult getting well. While trying to cleanse the body, we may have to lose weight, which might be a little disturbing to some people. But as soon as we have gone through the transition and building stages, we are on our way up. Each case is unique, and we should find out as much as we can about ourselves to learn about and deal with any constitutional or inherent weaknesses we may have. It has been said that catarrh is the beginning of all diseases, and to get rid of the root of all our physical troubles is not an easy job.

Catarrh-Producing Foods

Heavy starches: cereals, bread, potatoes

Dairy products

Eggs (eggs occasionally cause catarrh)

Non-Catarrh Producing Foods

All vegetables

All fruits

Meat—fish

Nut butters

Seeds

Milk substitutes (soy, sesame, almond, sunflower, rice)

Teas

ASTHMA AND REMEDIES

Asthma is considered a catarrhal disease. It is a heavy catarrhal condition of the bronchial tubes and other lung passages. Asthma can develop from various causes. Bronchial asthma is most often started by the effects of cigarette or cigar smoke—especially in children exposed to secondhand smoke. On the other hand, there is the asthma that is caused by the heart being unable to pump enough blood. It is called cardiac asthma.

Bronchial asthma is not usually connected with heart disease, but is often associated with hay fever, a catarrhal condition of the mucus lining the membranes of the bronchial tubes, and with allergies to such airborne substances as ragweed pollen, animal dandruff, or house dust. It is characterized by sudden attacks where the person has great difficulty breathing, has a terrible sense of constriction of the chest, sometimes along with choking, wheezing, a great deal of coughing, and, as a rule, with a thin, viscid sputum that later on becomes purulent in character. In this bronchial asthma, there is very little or no expectoration except during the end of the attack, when, considerable mucus or muco–purulent material is coughed up.

Bronchial asthma can almost always be helped, no matter how old the patient may be. There is a strong correlation between parental cigarette smoking and children developing bronchitis or bronchial asthma. Inhalers may provide temporary relief, but they do not cure. There are indeed few efforts that a man is called upon to make that are more wearisome than the toil of almost impossible breathing found in bronchial asthma. In almost every other illness, relief is obtained when lying down in a recumbent position. In bronchial asthma, the recumbent position is utterly impossible and the patient is compelled to sit up constantly day and night, until either relief is given or the attack subsides. In most cases, they cannot even have their feet placed horizontally on a chair or some other support, but they must hang down or be placed on a low stool or on the floor for the sake of mere comfort. Even the head of the patient cannot be laid backward on his chair nor can it be kept erect. It must be bent forward so it will rest on the arms in front of him or on something that will support his head. The patient's arms must be in a position where it will take the least possible effort to hold them.

Some patients have a constitutional vulnerability, an inherent weakness in some of their organs that tends to encourage a catarrhal condition in the body. When the sinus and bronchial membranes become inflamed, colds, hay fever, bronchial asthma, or other catarrhal conditions may take hold. These people are the ones who have to be careful of certain foods. They are the ones whom allergy specialists spend most of their time with, trying to find what foods bring on such a hypersensitive condition in the body.

Most allergies develop from preceding catarrhal conditions. Wheat and milk substances usually trigger the greatest number of allergic reactions in catarrhal-producing people. Cut out dairy products and substitute soy milk or goat milk products. Cut out wheat products and substitute other grains. If we have a tendency toward these conditions, we should look to the cleaning up of the body, making sure that we develop a hearty one, a healthy one, eliminating all catarrhal-forming foods, watching our climate and altitude. We need mountain air and the oxygen given off by pine trees.

We must obey the laws of life! We cannot follow uncontrolled impulses or emotions. We must not let business or domestic worries disturb us. *We must have poise and control* and eliminate anxiety and fear from our environment.

We cannot sleep without ventilation. We cannot have sexual excess, overeating, improper eating, or constipation. We cannot have a body that favors gastrointestinal decomposition and that develops a state of enervation that always cuts down on the secretions and excretions of the body.

When we are tired, elimination becomes poor, which in turn produces toxemia. Instead of toxins being expelled properly through our eliminative organs, such as the bowels, skin, kidneys, and bronchial tubes, they become reabsorbed and settle in the weakest organs. In bronchial asthma, this would be the lung structure and bronchial tubes. When our blood becomes so overwhelmed with toxemia, we are not able to get sufficient oxygen, and carbon dioxide elimination cannot take place in the air sacs of the lungs. Our greatest hypersensitive weaknesses are aggravated by certain starches and proteins. For this reason, we make a good start in our treatment if we eliminate these items.

We can divide the treatment of bronchial asthma into two sections: the treatment of the paroxysm or the attack, and the treatment of the general catarrhal condition. In the acute attack, we should abstain from water for at least a day, and from food three days more (but not from water). When the attack is less severe, a half teaspoon of hot water, if given every five or ten minutes, will many times give great relief. Swiss Ricola lozenges may help reduce any dry, nonproductive coughing. We may also rub along the spine with the hand, especially between the shoulder blades. Wet the hand with cold water. This brings ease many times, providing the rubbing is not carried to the point of irritation. Heat is almost always indicated, usually moist heat on the lower extremities; rub the feet and legs so that we bring on a healthy glow. When the blood circulation is poor, the feet are always cold and may swell badly. If artificial heat is not applied, serious and grave consequences can follow. When we help the circulation in the lower extremities, we help the circulation throughout the body. This helps throw off excess waste matter in all the organs of the body instead of bringing it all to the bronchial tubes and the lungs.

Brushing the skin—making the skin more active—is always indicated. After the patient has gotten some relief, he can be put to bed, and he should go with as little food as possible for at least a day. The length of the fast will vary depending upon the condition of the patient and the degree of enervation and the extent of the toxemia. When eating is resumed, do not start in with an excessive amount of food. That will overwork the digestive system and use up the energies of the body.

A doctor with whom I studied at one time used the following dietary guidelines whenever a person had catarrhal conditions, especially asthma. Eat lean meat (no fat, no pork); fish with scales and fins; vegetables of all kinds, prepared in any way; canned tomatoes; tomato juice; and fresh grapefruit (to help digest the protein). Always have the canned tomatoes or tomato juice or grapefruit when you have the meat or fish. Otherwise, combine the foods in any way you wish: one at a time, two at a time, or all three together. Make all your meals on just these foods. Nothing else is allowed except water. No salt or vinegar must be used. Good results are almost sure to follow.

Another good diet requires omitting all dairy products, anything from a cow. Omit anything from wheat, especially bread. Use soy milk and soy powder instead. Coconut milk is also good. Use vegetables and fruits along with the soy milk, or even follow a cut-up vegetable leaves diet.

Onion packs on the head and throat are also good for asthma, used with garlic oil capsules. This, along with our regular diet and no dairy products, will help to remove the catarrh in the body. Also find a dry climate, high altitude, warm air, and do everything possible to build a high blood count.

Some herbs will help with asthma. A good combination for the respiratory tract is comfrey root, mullein, marshmallow, slippery elm, and lobelia. Another good combination is blessed thistle, black cohosh, scullcap, and pleurisy root. Or try ½ ounce of stem of balsam of Peru in hot water and inhale. A tablespoon of peppermint tea in a quart of boiling water provides relief to congested nasal passages and sinuses when inhaled.

Good herb teas for catarrhal conditions include comfrey leaves and roots, hyssop, fenugreek, horehound leaf, aniseed, mint, and sassafras.

Those with severe asthma must continue to live with the greatest care, avoiding large quantities of food and limiting themselves to such amounts as they can both digest and assimilate. We must take care of the constitutional derangement (the inherent weaknesses in the body) and work for as clean a body as we possibly can.

THE COMMON COLD AND REMEDIES

A cold is not a disease in itself but is the beginning of catarrhal elimination. It is a sign that the body is endeavoring to liquefy hard catarrhal settlements in the body and trying to eliminate them. Contrary to the usual attitude of regret—"I have caught another blasted cold!"—the waste thus unloaded is a blessed riddance of toxins.

The common cold is usually the first disorder of any human body trying to eliminate catarrh. If the condition is suppressed by drugs or other therapies that block catarrhal elimination, the patient is definitely on his way to future chronic disease. Most of the cold remedies have been found by government health agencies to be effective against symptoms only.

When you have a cold, you should get plenty of bed rest, take warm baths, and take the proper teas as indicated in this book or as prescribed by your doctor.

Taking a warm bath and sponging off with a little cool towel afterward is always the way to bring up the energies and to help the circulation. Bowel exercises should be used two or three times a day. Enemas or other bowel cleansing procedures would be helpful. Do not use laxatives except under supervision of a doctor.

Our emotional patterns must be controlled by positive thinking and a good philosophy. Retoning of the skin should be started immediately, according to the methods explained in this book.

At the first sign of a cold, make sure the colon is clean by taking an enema. Take plenty of fresh fruit or juice, but reduce the amount of solid food you eat. You may fast a day or two. (Consult your doctor.) You should break your fast with fruit juices. Vitamin C may be taken frequently, as many as ten 250-milligram tablets a day, but antihistaminic drugs should be avoided, since many can produce bad side effects. Also take from 100,000 to 200,000 units of vitamin A for several days. This must be a vitamin A oil as opposed to an acetate or a drug. Within a few days, you can reduce the amount to 25,000 IU (international units) per day.

I learned from Professor Charles H. Gesser (a doctor of homeopathy in Chicago) of a cold remedy that is quite effective; it helps with coughs by getting rid of mucus and phlegm from the body. Use 2 tablespoons each of the following herbs: mullein flowers, coltsfoot, slippery elm, and finely chopped licorice root, and mix together. Put in 3 pints of cold water. Slowly bring to a boil. Simmer for five minutes and strain. Drink ½ cup to a cupful of this concoction every few hours during the day. Use until the cough has ceased. This remedy should be made fresh every day.

Some other remedies include using vegetable broth every two hours. Whey drinks are very good. You can also bake a lemon for twenty minutes and put half of it in hot oat straw tea or boneset tea. Go to bed, since this will make you perspire. Another option is to use an onion-and-garlic pack on the chest.

Deep breathing should be undertaken whenever we have colds. The head cold, or catarrhal condition we call "a cold," generally develops when we have been exposed to chill, dampness, or something of that nature. We say that we contract a cold when our body cannot maintain good balance in the face of the elements. When a fluid or moisture evaporates, a chill is produced. For example, if you moisten your finger and blow against it you will see that the side you blow against will feel cold. The skin throws off a certain temperature. The average natural, normal skin should be moist, but if a cold wind comes along, dryer than the humidity of the skin area, the skin will be chilled. When our skin is in good working order, we have less likelihood of catching a cold than at any other time.

FLU AND REMEDIES

During any epidemic of influenza, stay out of inclement weather and try to avoid atmospheric changes. If you should fall victim to the flu, the first thing you should do is go to bed and rest. Keep well covered and perspire, if possible. To encourage perspiration and help drive the virus and congestion from the chest, drink boneset tea, to which the juice of a lemon baked for twenty minutes has been added.

Do not try to act as your own physician in any serious condition. If your condition becomes serious, you should immediately consult a physician and rely upon his advice. It is good, also, to have a doctor prescribe home treatments for you. Be sure to straighten out your kitchen at home to be certain there is nothing on the shelf that will produce the trouble you are asking the doctor to correct.

SKIN CARE FOR CATARRHAL CONDITIONS

To be healthy, skin must be kept clean. I believe skin brushing is one of the finest of all baths.

The heating and ventilating system of our bodies must be working properly. High humidity combined with high temperature is extremely depressing. However, if the temperature is kept below 70 degrees Fahrenheit, the humidity may be up as high as 70 and 80 percent without causing discomfort.

Excessive dryness always irritates the nasal membrane. When the membranes of the breathing tract are exposed to extremely dry air, they open up; when they are exposed to cold, moist air, they contract abnormally and become congested, which usually leads to a cold. The skin needs an opportunity to breathe. It should throw off moisture and should come in contact with air so that the moisture can be evaporated within a short time. We should not wear airtight clothing except for a short period of time, as when we put on rainwear to go out during a storm. A good rule is to wear just enough clothing to keep us comfortably warm.

In case you become chilled when resting, exercise immediately to stir up the blood circulation. If you cannot practice exercise at that time, try some forced breathing. When symptoms of repeated sneezing and especially when exposure chills the body, take a hot bath before retiring. Even a hot water bottle used at the feet and a hot drink will help.

Nerve exhaustion is probably the beginning of many contracted colds. We find there are very few people with 100 percent mental and physical efficiency. Every action in our body is dependent upon an abundant supply of nerve force. When the vital organs of the body are not stimulated by impulses of the nerve force, the blood becomes impoverished and the system clogs with poisonous matter. These two factors are the main cause of most ailments. This is the reason we consider taking care of the mind and emotions, one of the most important things in taking care of the body.

OTHER CATARRHAL REMEDIES

When a person has a catarrhal condition, how much milk can he use?

First, I don't think that milk is the only thing that produces catarrh. Don't run away with the idea that dairy products are the only things that produce it. I believe that starches can produce catarrh. I believe that wrong food combinations can also bring about catarrh. I believe that an enervated body can produce catarrh from the best foods in the world. Catarrh and acids are the beginning of every disease. Now, how much milk should we eliminate? I would say the elimination of dairy products can quite often help the person with serious catarrhal problems. Many times our bodies have been so loaded down with dairy products in the past that simply eliminating them from our diet can easily change the chemical balance. Experiment to see what works for you.

For Chronic Nasal Catarrh

Chronic nasal catarrh can be very uncomfortable and hard to get rid of. But there are a few remedies. Put one or two drops of eucalyptus oil in water. Dip a cloth into the water and drape it over your head. Breathe the vapor into your nasal passages.

A nasal douche can be made with two drops of eucalyptus oil in four drops of olive oil. Take this into the nose by sniffing.

Herb teas can be used, such as those made from the following herbs: boneset, ragwort, burdock, cascara, clivers, and goldenrod. Simmer in 3 pints of water for one hour. Strain after cooling. Use about 4 ounces after each meal.

For nasal catarrh with colds: A tea made with dried elder flowers and peppermint before going to bed will often nip a cold in the bud. If you develop a heavy cold, this mixture can help: Mix 1 ounce each of ground ivy, horehound, hyssop, and honey. Place in 1 pint of water and simmer for an hour. Strain and cool. Take 1 tablespoon frequently until the cold has subsided.

The Turnip Diet

The turnip diet is excellent for asthma, bronchial trouble, and all other catarrhal conditions. White turnips are higher in vitamin A than carrots and have a most wonderful cleansing effect.

In the turnip diet, use the juice, the greens, or the turnip itself—raw, cooked, or in soup form. Vary the diet by eating the turnips in various ways along with the regular health diet, or by having turnip combinations alone. The juice can be made very palatable by mixing it with pineapple or apple juice. The raw turnip can be used in salads with cut dates or steamed raisins.

The turnip diet can be taken for a period of from three days to two months. For the long period diet, you should seek the direction of your doctor, but anyone can handle three days on a diet of turnips.

One of my patients at the center suffered from asthma, catarrhal trouble, and a 240 systolic blood pressure. We put him on a thirty-day diet of nothing but turnips. We gave him turnip greens, turnip juice, raw turnips, and cooked turnips. Yes, nothing but turnips for one whole month. When taken off the diet, he no longer had asthma or catarrhal trouble; his blood pressure was normal (140 systolic), and he was down to his normal weight after losing forty pounds. He was a picture of health. Compare this with the pills and potions he had been taking for years. You see, nature has a remedy!

Bronchial troubles need calcium foods, iodine-containing foods (excepting in cases of tuberculosis), onion soup, onion tea, cream toast, honey, hot drinks, blackberry tea, hot foot baths, dry feet, flannel and warm moisture next to the body, hot applications to the throat, and a warm, moist climate.

There are several acceptable brands of liquid chlorophyll in most health food stores. Use this as a nasal douche (¼ teaspoonful to ½ cup of water). Sniff it into the nostrils. Drinking 1 teaspoonful of chlorophyll in a glass of water three times a day (the first time before breakfast) is a very effective treatment for sinus disturbances as well as inflamed nasal membranes.

For a Catarrhal Throat

A fine cough syrup can be made from chopped onions and honey. It is a splendid remedy. Put 1 or 2 tablespoons of honey in a dish of chopped onions; let it stand for three or four hours, then drain. Sip a teaspoonful every hour, or, if necessary, every half hour.

It may not sound like it, but this is a very soothing syrup and children will not object to it.

Eucalyptus Honey

Eucalyptus honey is a powerful honey for catarrhal problems, tuberculosis, or swollen tonsils if used with a combination of onions, as in the cough syrup above. This combination goes deep into cells to release harsh toxic materials that settle in the body. Failure to release this harsh material is the reason the skin breaks out so often during the healing process. That is why catarrh runs when we are cleansing the body. Remember that we are striving for a clean body in recommending all these foods.

CHAPTER 13

BUILDING A HEALTHY BODY

In the past three decades, a virtual explosion has taken place in biochemistry, microbiology, and knowledge of the working of the human body at the cellular level. Only recently has the first complete map of the genome in the cell nucleus been completed by researchers. By *genome* I mean the sum total of genetic material in a single cell. I suppose what will follow will be a deeper understanding of the sequences of events needed at the cell level to sustain the health and well-being at the micro-level of various types of tissues. We already know a good deal about cell function, but this new knowledge should result in new insights.

Our organs, glands, and tissues need proteins, carbohydrates, lipids, water, minerals, and vitamins to protect, sustain, and nourish the seventy-five trillion cells that make up our bodies. We can supply most of our nutritional needs by using whole, pure, and natural foods grown on nutrient rich soils. For your own good, you need to know what it takes to build and maintain a healthy body.

There are forty-six chemical elements, on the average, distributed in the human body. Twenty-two of them are essential; nine are nonessential but either known or believed to be useful to the body. Sixteen or so are nonessential and apparently useless, accumulated and stored in the bones or fatty tissue simply because they happened to get picked up in foods. The twenty-one essential elements make up the soft tissues, bones, nerves, ligaments, cartilage, blood, secretions, hair, nails, hormones, and vitamins that make up the human body (see Table 13.1). In this chapter, we will be discussing the vitamins, minerals, and trace elements needed in a healthy, balanced diet.

I believe that whole, pure, and natural foods grown organically on nutrient-rich, uncontaminated soils will have all the vitamins, minerals, and trace elements; all the protein, carbohydrates, oils; and all the special natural chemicals we need for the best possible health each of us can have, considering the genetic inheritance we were born with. That is, if we search for that kind of food, shop wisely, and learn how to preserve nutritional values by the right kinds of food preparation, we could fix meals that would meet all our nutritional needs—if our bodies were perfectly made. The problem is, there isn't any such thing as a "perfect body."

Everyone is born with at least some genetically weak organs, glands, and tissues, hereafter called inherent weaknesses or inherently weak tissues. When your doctor says you have a constitutionally weak stomach, he means that it is genetically weaker than the average stomach and you may expect trouble digesting certain foods, or you may lack sufficient hydrochloric acid, or have a tendency toward ulcer formation. Inherently weak tissues are often less efficient at picking up nutrients from the blood than normal tissues. They are slower in getting rid of

Table 13.1. **The 70–Kilogram Body**

Element	Content
Water (H_2O)	45 kg
Hydrogen (not in water)	2 kg
Oxygen (not in water)	2.9 kg
Calcium	1.1 kg
Carbon	16.0 kg
Cobalt	2 mg
Phosphorus	0.5 kg
Nitrogen	1.8 kg
Potassium	140 g
Magnesium	19 g
Silicon	18 g
Selenium	13 mg
Iodine	10 mg
Sulfur	140 g
Zinc	2.3 g
Copper	70 mg
Fluorine	2.6 g
Chlorine	95 g
Sodium	100 g
Iron	4.2 g
Manganese	10 mg
Molybdenum	9 mg

Tissue Type	Mineral Needs
Thyroid	Iodine
Bowel	Magnesium
Brain and nervous system	Phosphorus, manganese
Skin and circulation	Sulfur
Nails and Hair	Silicon
Spleen	Flouride, copper
Teeth and bones	Fluoride, calcium
Liver	Sulfur, iron
Tissues and secretions	Potassium, sodium

metabolic wastes. They act as though their metabolism is slower than that of normal tissues. I feel that inherently weak tissues need to be "overfed" the specific nutrients they need most, which may require dietary supplements.

An additional consideration is that our access to really excellent, nourishing foods is limited. Soils vary in their mineral content, producing food crops that lack whatever minerals or trace elements the soil lacks. We may breathe polluted air and drink contaminated water. We might have sedentary jobs and get very little exercise. We might live near a freeway or airport where noise is a stress factor we have to live with. We may not have even known about health principles and a more natural way of living until an encounter with disease early or late in life forced us to find out what we could do to bring about better health and a longer life. The best starting point is to find out what vitamins, minerals, and other nutrients you need for good health, what foods they are in, and what the best vitamin-mineral supplements are in case you can't get everything you need from foods available to you. We don't live in an ideal world, we don't have ideal health, and we can't turn back to the Garden of Eden, so let's learn to take care of ourselves.

VITAMINS

Over one-third of American adults use vitamin supplements or vitamin-mineral supplements, and vitamin sales for 1998 were over 4.8 billion dollars annually. The known vitamins essential to health are vitamins A, B-complex, C, D, E, and K. Vitamins A, D, E, and K are fat soluble, while vitamin C and the eight B-complex vitamins are water soluble. The word "vitamin" emerged from the term "vitamine," first used in 1913 by the Polish biochemist Casamir Funk (*vita,* from Latin, meaning "life" and *amine* from the German *amin,* referring to the ammonia molecule in amino acids). Funk mistakenly thought that vitamins contained amino acids. Vitamins are microscopic organic molecules found in foods or made in the human body. They are essential to life, normal growth, and the metabolism of the human body, in very small amounts.

The idea that higher doses of vitamins build better health than the RDA (recommended dietary allowance) is not necessarily true. However, currently scientists are examining the question of whether we should base the RDA of vitamins and minerals on the optimum amount for the best health instead of the minimum amount it takes for a healthy person to prevent deficiency plus some extra amount as a safety factor. Certainly, some diseases and inherited genetic weaknesses benefit from high dosages of particular vitamins. Additionally, the late Dr. Roger Williams insisted in his book *Biochemical Individuality* that there were significant differences in the vitamin and mineral needs of individuals.

The debate over the most appropriate amounts of vitamins to take seemed to originate in the 1970s when the late Dr. Linus Pauling advocated taking one or more grams of vitamin C at a time when 60 milligrams was considered an adequate amount by most scientists. In recent years, changes have been made in the RDAs of several vitamins and minerals and more changes are being considered as more is learned about the biochemistry of the human body. In the following vitamin descriptions, I have listed the RDAs in most cases, not because I believe they are the last word on the subject, but because they lend themselves conveniently as a baseline.

Vitamin A

This vitamin is found in two forms, carotenoids (provitamin A) and preformed vitamin A in animal tissue. The preformed vitamin A is made from carotenoids, colored pigments found in carrots and dark green or yellow vegetables. There are over five hundred known carotenoids, but only fifty of them can be converted into preformed vitamin A, the only chemical form that can be used by cells. Yet, provitamin A has an important role of its own. It is an antioxidant, a destroyer of free radicals, the electrically active broken molecules which are known to cause cancer. Preformed vitamin A is most concentrated in fish liver oils, but is also in whole milk, cheese, butter, eggs, and meat. It helps maintain vision and is especially important in night vision. It is needed for building bones and teeth, for reproduction, aids in RNA synthesis, and plays a part in forming healthy red blood cells. It protects mucous membranes in the nasal passages, sinuses, throat, lungs, stomach, uterus, vagina, and bowel. Vitamin A protects cells from infection. Zinc is needed to help mobilize vitamin A from storage sites in the liver. Symptoms of deficiency are night blindness, tooth decay, infections, scaly skin, and diarrhea. Symptoms of overdose are headaches, nausea, vomiting, skin sores, hair loss, appetite loss, nose bleeds, and itchy eyes. Adult men need 5,000 IU (or 1,000 RE—retinol equivalents) and women need 4,000 IU (or 800 RE).

B-Complex Vitamins

The eight B vitamins form a family, and rather than describe them all individually, I am going to discuss what they all have in common, then I'll mention important differences. All B vitamins are "team players," forming coenzymes that are essential parts of hard-working protein molecules we call enzymes. Enzymes are the "factory workers" that make cells function. They are the driving force behind human metabolism. They help break down old molecules and help assemble new ones. B vitamins are essential to reproduction, the development of the embryo, the health of hair and fingernails, and the production of energy. Studies have disproved the once popular notion that B-complex vitamins "fight" stress, but because they are needed by the brain, nervous system, and immune system for normal activity, I would suggest that they certainly assist in raising the stress tolerance threshold. Except for B_{12} and folic acid, the B vitamins are abundant in foods, but because they are water soluble they can be easily destroyed by overcooking, some more than others.

Individual B vitamins have certain unique characteristics as well as qualities they share with other B vitamins. Vitamin B_1, also known as thiamin, was one of the first vitamins to be discovered. The disease beriberi, common in the Far East, was found to be caused by a nutrient deficiency, which turned out to be thiamin. The process of refining whole rice into white rice involves removing the hull and germ, which contain thiamin. White rice is a favorite in Asia, while the whole grain rice is often referred to as "dirty rice." Lack of thiamin eventually leads to loss of appetite, fatigue, paralysis of the legs, and, if not corrected, death. Thiamin is critical to the functioning of four of the enzymes needed to produce energy. I always recommend whole grains, never refined grains. Organ meats and brewer's yeast are also high in thiamin. Men need 1.4 milligrams, women need 1 milligram of B_1.

Vitamin B_2 (riboflavin) is heat resistant but is destroyed by exposure to sunlight or ultraviolet light. Organ meats are the best source, followed by dairy products, eggs, and other meats. Legumes, whole grains, fruits, and vegetables have a little vitamin B_2. It is seldom deficient excepting in Asia. A sore tongue and cracks at the corners of the mouth are signs of deficiency. Men require 1.6 milligrams, women need 1.2 milligrams.

Niacin is the most commonly recognized name for vitamin B_3 but it is also called nicotinic acid. Deficiency leads to pellagra, once common in the United States. An early symptom is a swollen tongue, but one of its advanced symptoms resembles mental illness. As the deficiency progresses, rough red skin, bloody diarrhea, anemia, and impaired liver function appear. The cause of the bloody diarrhea is extreme irritation of the digestive tract. Niacin is necessary to the production of cholesterol by the liver, and I have found that taking a 1,000 milligrams of niacin with each meal reduces blood cholesterol by reducing the liver's production of cholesterol. (More cholesterol is made by the liver than is consumed even in a fatty diet.) Dr. Joseph Goldberg, head of a Public Health Service Team, finally proved that pellagra was a dietary deficiency, caused by insufficient niacin and tryptophan, an amino acid that can be changed into niacin in the body. By 1945, pellagra was rare in the United States.

There is no evidence that niacin helps allergies or improves athletic performance. Organ meats, dairy products, soy products, brewer's yeast, fish, and peanuts are all good sources. Men should have 1.8 milligrams, women should have 1.3 milligrams.

There isn't any vitamin B_4 but there is a B_5 called pantothenic acid. The name says it all—the word *pantothenic* is from the Greek and means "from everywhere." There is no known deficiency because it is in just about every food we eat. It is needed to form steroid hormones. Both men and women need 4 to 7 milligrams of B_5.

Vitamin B_6 is pyridoxine, which is a coenzyme in sixty or more enzyme reactions, some of which involve nervous system functions. Like other B vitamins, it helps convert food to energy, but it is also needed for the formation of red blood cells, immune system cells, and the conversion of the amino acid tryptophan into niacin. For these reasons and more, it is a very important vitamin. It can limit the severity of asthma attacks and has cut down the pain for some persons with carpal tunnel syndrome (nerve inflammation in the wrist). There are women who claim that high doses of B_6 helped their PMS (premenstrual syndrome), but medical research shows that most are not helped. I want to caution against using megadoses of any vitamin or mineral unless under the supervision of your doctor. Megadoses are not found in nature, and mega amounts of any vitamin can have undesirable side effects.

There is a "window" of acceptable intake of this vitamin (2–200 milligrams), which means that both too much or too little B_6 causes nerve damage. Symptoms of excess include loss of feeling in hands and feet, resulting in an odd, ducklike walk. There may be pains like electric shocks along the spine. Deficiency is even more dangerous.

Deficiency symptoms start with sores around the eyes and mouth, and an abnormally smooth tongue, symptoms that escalate into confusion, dizziness, nausea, vomiting, anemia, and convulsions. Vitamin B_6 is in whole grains, potatoes, vegetables, meat, fish, and poultry, but all these foods are usually cooked first, and heat destroys the B_6. Light and air also destroy this vitamin. Over half the people in this country are estimated to be deficient in vitamin B_6. Those most at risk are the elderly, alcoholics, pregnant and nursing mothers, infants, and people on weight-loss diets. If you heat baby formula with B_6 in it, the

vitamin is destroyed. Adults need about 2 milligrams daily. Up
to 200 milligrams can be tolerated by most persons, but the risk
increases with intake. Some women, hoping for PMS relief,
were taking 800 milligrams to several grams of vitamin B_6 and
suffered nerve damage. Fortunately, it was reversible. I want to
round out my views of vitamin B_6 by two warnings. First, to
make sure you are getting enough, take a vitamin B_6 supplement of at least two milligrams. Second, never take more than
200 milligrams unless your doctor approves.

Vitamin B_{12} (cobalamine) was often prescribed by doctors
in the 1940s and 1950s for people who were fatigued or run-
down in health or showed signs of pernicious anemia. Shots,
not pills, were given, because B_{12} taken as an oral supplement
is not assimilated in pernicious anemia. Its best natural sources
are liver and other organ meats. Vitamin B_{12} is also in seafood,
eggs, milk products, meat, and poultry. There are no good vegetable sources that I know of, and it isn't in brewer's yeast. The
edible algae spirulina and chlorella contain vitamin B_{12}, but
some nutritionists say it isn't in a form that can be assimilated.
However, some B_{12} is made in the bowel by microorganisms,
and soil scientists say there are sometimes traces of B_{12} in foods
grown on soil that contains animal manure.

Vitamin B_{12} and folic acid (another B-complex vitamin) are
structurally alike and both are essential to the formation of red
blood cells. B_{12} is required by growing nerves and in the fatty
nerve sheathing. Even when our intake of B_{12} is adequate (we
only need 3 micrograms per day), lack of the special transport
protein (called intrinsic factor) that escorts B_{12} from the small
intestine into the blood can cause anemia. Vegans, the vegetarians
that don't use milk products or eggs, are most at risk for B_{12} deficiency, according to Joanne Stepaniak, author of *The Vegan
Sourcebook*. Many vegans take B_{12} supplements to avoid deficiency.

Ongoing B_{12} deficiency can cause severe nerve damage. We only need 3 micrograms daily, and any extra is stored in the liver.

Folic acid, or folacin as it is also called, can normalize anemic blood even when vitamin B_{12} is deficient. If the deficiency of B_{12} is masked by the restoration of a normal red blood cell count by folic acid intake, death or extreme nerve damage may result. Normally, people get enough folic acid, but because very little is stored, blood loss, burns, cancer, and other diseases (like measles) can deplete all available folic acid in almost no time. Alcoholism blocks folic acid assimilation and so can certain drugs. Overcooking also wipes out folic acid. Groups most likely to show deficiency of folic acid are women who take birth control pills, pregnant women, burn victims, people who have lost a lot of blood, and people with digestive disorders. Deficiency in folic acid for any reason blocks the formation of folic acid coenzymes and prevents the development of nucleic acids. This mostly affects body processes involving rapid cell reproduction, like bone marrow production of red blood cells. Deficiency symptoms include swollen tongue, diarrhea, and anemia. We need 400 micrograms of folic acid daily.

Neither folic acid nor vitamin B_{12} overdose has ever been encountered.

Biotin is needed by adults in the amount of 100 to 200 micrograms daily. This B-complex vitamin, like folic acid, helps form nucleic acids along with transforming food to energy as all the other B-complex vitamins do. Infants with genetic problems and people with bowel problems are most likely to be deficient in biotin. There have been very few documented cases of biotin deficiency and no recorded cases of overdose. Symptoms like insomnia, appetite lack, rash, anemia, hair loss, muscle pain, and a sore tongue indicate increasing deficiency. This seldom happens except to people with digestive problems.

A product called "pangamic acid" was promoted several years ago as vitamin B_{15}. Dr. Varro E. Tyler, in his book *The Honest Herbal,* says pangamic acid is not a vitamin and calls it "totally worthless and potentially dangerous." He cites tests that expose its harmful activities, including lowering blood pressure, causing kidney stones, increasing cancer risk, and the toxic effects of calcium chloride, which it contains. Be careful about products labeled "B vitamins" that utilize numbers higher than B_{12}. Only the eight B vitamins described previously in this chapter are officially recognized as essential to health.

I want to make sure you understand that all eight of the B vitamins have their effects on our bodies and our health by being joined to enzymes. It is the enzymes containing the individual B-complex vitamins that accomplish the functions attributed to each B vitamin, not the vitamins themselves. I feel it is also of the utmost importance for you to make sure you are getting enough vitamin B_6 and enough folic acid in your diet. These are the two B vitamins that people most commonly lack. If you aren't sure if your intake of these two vitamins is sufficient, take a supplement.

Vitamin C

I don't think you will be surprised when I tell you that the most popular of the thirteen vitamins we need to stay alive and well is vitamin C. People spend about half a million dollars a year on vitamin C! Because vitamin C is a powerful antioxidant, it helps prevent cancer. However, it doesn't reverse cancer once it is in the body. It is often taken to prevent colds, but studies indicate that it doesn't help unless the person taking it was first deficient in this vitamin. Vitamin C accelerates tissue healing, cleans up infections, increases iron absorption if taken at the same time as the iron, helps synthesize collagen, and assists in the metabolism of amino acids. It is a cofactor in eight enzymes, three of them involving collagen metabolism. It is involved in the production of norepinephrine. Taking an iron supplement with a small glass of orange juice (rich in vitamin C) doubles the amount of iron assimilated by the body.

Vitamin C is defined as ascorbic acid, but the discoverer of vitamin C, Dr. Albert Szent-Gyorgyi, later argued that vitamin C should be recognized in the context of cofactors like bioflavinoids that normally accompanied it in natural sources such as citrus fruit and rose hips. That is, he believed that vitamin C should be redefined to include its naturally occurring cofactors. I feel that all vitamins in their natural settings in foods have cofactors that make them more biologically useful than if the cofactors were stripped away. Food scientists tend to ignore cofactors and focus their attention on the most "biologically active" substances in foods.

Vitamin C came to light originally in the attempt to find a cure for the disease of scurvy, a fatal disease that commonly developed in sailors on long voyages deprived of fresh fruit and vegetables. In 1747, James Lind discovered that oranges and lemons kept British sailors from getting scurvy, but vitamin C was not isolated and identified until 1932.

Deficiency in vitamin C is shown by sore or bleeding gums, easy bruising, restlessness, painful joints, lack of energy, and anemia. The first sign of overdose (it usually takes several grams) is most frequently diarrhea. After that, nausea and vomiting may take place, reduction in red blood cells, and kidney stones.

Fruits highest in vitamin C include melons, citrus, kiwis, mangoes, papayas, and strawberries. Best vegetable sources are

green leafy vegetables, snow peas, bell peppers, asparagus, broccoli, potatoes, brussels sprouts, tomatoes, cauliflower, yams, and
sweet potatoes. Many animals make their own vitamin C, but
human beings are dependent upon foods for their access to this
vitamin. The RDA for adults is 60 milligrams. Recent studies
have shown that body cells are saturated with vitamin C when a
100-milligram tablet is taken, but the blood plasma is not saturated until 1,000 milligrams (one gram) have been taken. I believe
it is alright to take up to a gram and a half of vitamin C daily.
Aspirin, oral contraceptives, antibiotics (and other drugs), and
smoking destroy vitamin C. So does overcooking foods, especially boiling them, because vitamin C is water soluble.

Vitamin D

This fat-soluble vitamin is called the "sunshine vitamin," because
twenty minutes of exposure to the ultraviolet radiation in sunlight is sufficient to change a close relative to cholesterol in the
skin into all the vitamin D needed for the day. We can get vitamin D by taking fish liver oil (also vitamin A) or by eating fish,
eggs, or liver. Too much vitamin D given to children may result
in loss of interest in foods, bone malformation, and poor growth.
Excess given to adults results in weakness, headaches, vomiting,
diarrhea, and possibly kidney stones. Too little leads to muscle
weakness and apathy, followed over the longer term by the bone
disease rickets, cavities, an enlarged skull (children), soft bones
(in children), and brittle bones (in adults).

Lack of sufficient vitamin D causes a bone disease called
rickets. Without sufficient vitamin D, not enough calcium
deposits on the bones. This results in knock knees, bowed legs,
and other malformed bones including those of the arms, chest,

and rib cage. This disease was epidemic until our government passed a law requiring that artificial vitamin D be added to all commercially sold milk. Cases of rickets are rare in the United States but not so rare in Third World countries. Vitamin D is needed to assist calcium in forming strong teeth and bones, regulating blood calcium and phosphorus, and preventing osteoporosis and osteomalacia (adult form of rickets). Adults need 5 micrograms daily, equivalent to 200 IU (international units).

Vitamin E

This name refers to a family of four tocopherols labeled alpha, beta, delta, and gamma. Only the form d–alpha tocopheral is abundant in certain foods, such as vegetable oils, whole grains, liver, fruits, vegetables, beans, soybeans, and raw seeds and nuts. Wheat germ oil has been a popular source for many years. This vitamin is fat soluble and body reserves are stored in the fatty tissues, as are other fat soluble vitamins. Some is stored in the liver and muscles.

Vitamin E is a powerful antioxidant, especially when used together with selenium, another excellent antioxidant. It is needed for healthy red blood cells. It protects vitamin A and fatty acids from breaking down, aids in cellular energy production, and works together with selenium to protect internal organs from free radicals.

Examples of vitamin E deficiency are rare (excepting in premature infants). However, one study showed that 45 percent of elderly Americans were getting less than three-quarters of the RDA for vitamin E. I might add here that often my elderly patients are more depleted in valuable nutrients than younger persons, perhaps partly because their taste buds and olfactory sense have deteriorated and food doesn't taste "as good as it used to." I teach them that if they eat better, they will be healthier, think clearer, and need less medicating. Studies have shown that vitamin E increases oxygen availability to the brain, which improves short-term memory and mental acuity in the elderly. Some of the diseases associated with a lack of vitamin E are biliary cirrhosis, sprue, biliary atresia, pancreatitis, and disorders of fat metabolism. Diabetics should consult with their doctors concerning use of vitamin E.

An RDA for adults of 15 IU is recommended for men, 12 IU for women. Intake of over ten times these amounts may interfere with hormonal balance, reduce blood clotting ability, hamper white blood cell activity, and alter fat transport in the blood of some people. However, doses as high as 400 IU daily seem to help those suffering from PMS. I feel that older persons need vitamin and mineral supplements more than younger adults because their ability to digest and assimilate nutrients seems to diminish with age.

Vitamin K

This fat-soluble vitamin is best known for its help in making blood clot and in contributing to bone formation. It is found mostly in green leafy vegetables, milk products, eggs, blackstrap molasses (real, not the cheap imitation—read the labels), fish liver oils, various vegetable oils, and liver. Vitamin K is also manufactured by beneficial bowel bacteria, which means that antibiotics disrupt the supply of vitamin K by destroying the bacteria that make it. (I must tell you, I only believe in antibiotics as a last resort.) While deficiencies of vitamin K are rare, there are some. Most are caused by colitis, drug interference, intravenous diets, celiac disease, and inability to assimilate fats. As you might imag-

> ∞ **What are the best natural sources for vitamins?**
>
> Vitamin A   Carrot juice, greens, cod liver oil
> Vitamin B   Rice polishings, brewers yeast, liver, blackstrap molasses
> Vitamin C   Rose hips, alfalfa sprouts, citrus
> Vitamin D   Cod liver oil, sunshine
> Vitamin E   Wheat germ oil, raw seeds and nuts
> Vitamin K   Alfalfa juice (chlorophyll), all leafy greens

ine, deficiency is dangerous, interfering with blood clotting. Bleeding from miscarriages and nosebleeds becomes dangerous because so much blood can be lost before external methods are successful in stopping the bleeding. On the other hand, extra vitamin K may be given to patients prior to surgical operations or to patients taking anticoagulant drugs, to give them a slight margin of safety from excessive bleeding. Toxic effects have never been recorded for excess natural vitamin K, but there is a manufactured artificial vitamin K that is definitely toxic in excessive amounts. The recommended amount of vitamin K for adults is 70 to 140 micrograms, which is well within the safety limits of the artificial vitamin. The risks of excess artificial vitamin K are red blood cell damage, jaundice, and brain damage.

From time to time, people come up with "new vitamins," mostly hoping for market promotion of their product based on peoples' favorable opinion of vitamins. These are not true vitamins. The actual definition of vitamin in *Taber's Cyclopedic Medical Dictionary, Edition 18,* is "Any of a group of organic substances other than proteins, carbohydrates, fats, and organic salts that are essential for normal metabolism, growth, and development of the body." Often, the key word here is "essential," meaning we can't have normal health without it.

∞ Daily Reference Values Required

Nutrient	Adults & Children Over 4
Carbohydrates	300 g
Fiber	25 g
Protein	50 g
Fat	65 g
Saturated fat	20 g
Cholesterol	300 mg

Natural foods have been the source of all the vitamins yet discovered. Scurvy, pellagra, beriberi, and many other diseases are the result, all or in part, of vitamin deficiencies. Cheat the body of vitamin-rich food and you are on a disease-producing diet. *Quality* foods count, *not* quantity. And remember, vitamins essential to our bodies are best found in natural foods.

After vitamins, we must consider the chemical elements the body is made up of. I hope I have made clear earlier in this chapter that vitamins themselves are made of chemical elements, as are the proteins, carbohydrates, fats, and liquids that make up our bodies. Vitamins interact electrically and chemically with the other chemicals that make up the body structure. The most plentiful substance in the body is water, a total of 45 kilograms in a 70-kilogram person. The bone structure or skeleton weighs about 14 kilograms, including the protein matrix. The soft tissue of the body—muscles, ligaments, tendons, fat, collagen, nerves, bone marrow, and more—not counting the water content—amounts to 11 kilograms. All the soft tissue is made of carbon, hydrogen, and oxygen molecules in the cases of fat and carbohydrates, and the same three elements plus nitrogen in the case of the amino acids that make up protein. Because these chemical elements work together as molecules, food scientists don't list them among the minerals we have RDAs for. Instead, we have the Daily Reference Values (DRVs) (see chart on page 258).

MACRO ELEMENTS AND TRACE ELEMENTS NEEDED

The following elements, with the exception of silicon, may be regarded as essential to health and well-being. The RDA was developed to meet the needs of healthy, normal adults, which means that it doesn't necessarily meet the needs of the sick, diseased, elderly, or those with genetic differences from the norm. I always recommended amounts that took account of my patients' health history and current physical condition. You will be able to get most of your essential vitamins and minerals from a good, health-building diet, but maybe not all. The elements I found most often lacking in my patients over a period of sixty years of health care were natural sodium, iodine, and silicon.

Calcium

Essential element. RDA: 100 milligrams.

Activity in Body: Needed mostly in structural system and body electrolytes. Essential for cell membranes. Aids blood clotting. Builds and maintains bone structure and teeth. Helps regulate osmotic pressure. Counteracts acids. Involved in nerve transmission.

Principal Sources: Cheese, milk, yogurt, sour cream, and everything made with milk products, vegetables, legumes, nuts, and eggs. Vegetables like kale, collards, broccoli, turnip greens, and cabbage are good sources of calcium. However, nothing comes close to milk and its products for meeting calcium needs.

Special Points: Calcium is the knitting element in healing. Blood-clotting problems indicate calcium deficiency. Calcium carbonate, citrate, or malate are the best supplements. Works together with vitamin D, phosphorus, magnesium, manganese, copper, zinc, and sodium. Every bone in your body is rebuilt every decade or so.

Calcium Tonic: 1 tablespoon of dry, powdered milk in a glass of raw milk once a day.

A good way to increase calcium in the body is to cut up a large leaf of kale and put it in any broth or soup or run it through the vegetable juicer. This is one of the easiest ways to build the bone structure of the body.

Chlorine

Essential element (*chloride* is chemically active form). RDA: 3,400 milligrams.

Activity in Body: Cleanser in the body, stabilizes electric potential at nerve synapses, helps transmit carbon dioxide. Constituent of stomach acid, aid to digestion.

Principal Sources: Milk and milk products, fish, cheese, coconut, beets, radishes, common salt, figs, endive, watercress, cucumber, carrots, leeks, and all fruits and vegetables.

Special Points: Deficiency contributes to sluggish liver. Goat's milk utilizes chloride to resolve kidney problems by means of its germicidal effect.

Chromium

Essential trace element. RDA: 120 micrograms.

Activity in Body: Found in the adult body in the amount of 6 milligrams total. Essential ingredient of Glucose Tolerance

Factor (GTF), along with niacin and amino acids. Stored mostly in spleen, ovaries, testes, bones, and kidneys, with lesser amounts in the brain, lungs, pancreas, and heart. GTF, with chromium its primary activating factor, enhances the effectiveness of insulin in increasing cellular uptake of blood sugar. Chromium circulates in the blood in the amount of 20 parts per billion. Some studies show chromium intake reduced low density cholesterol (LDL), the "bad" cholesterol, and increased high density cholesterol (HDL), the "good" cholesterol, but other studies show no effect on cholesterol. It is probable that chromium intake affects the cholesterol of persons previously deficient in chromium far more than people whose chromium level is normal. Chromium increases RNA synthesis. Malnourished children were restored to normal growth much faster when chromium was added to a balanced diet, as compared to a similar group on a similar diet but without chromium supplementation.

Principal Sources: Brewers yeast is the best natural source. Black pepper is also rich in chromium. Fair amounts are found in legumes, raw nuts, raw seeds, and dark chocolate. Meat, poultry, fish, and dairy products are poor sources. Fruits and vegetables are not reliable sources. Best supplements are chromium picolinate and chromium chloride. Taking 100 grams of vitamin C at the same time as chromium supplementation or chromium-containing food significantly increases assimilation.

Special Points: The majority of Americans get less than a safe and adequate daily dietary intake. Only 2 to 3 percent at most of dietary chromium is assimilated. Older persons and pregnant women are most at risk for chromium deficiency. Chromium supplements have not helped diabetics, according to repeated studies. Chromium supplements of 200 micrograms daily did not improve strength of weightlifters. May inhibit arterial plaque deposits.

Indications of Chromium Deficiency: Slowed growth in children, less energy, lower metabolism, increased risk of diabetes, increased risk of cardiovascular disease, slowed healing, increased blood level of "bad" cholesterol (LDL). Because of limited (2 percent daily) assimilation of chromium, it is almost impossible to reach a toxic level in the blood. Toxic effects have only been observed in industrial workers exposed to airborne chromium compounds, which caused skin and nasal lesions and, over the long term, lung cancer.

Cobalt

Essential *only* because it is in Vitamin B_{12}.

Cobalt is a structural part of vitamin B_{12} (cobalamin) and does not separate in liquid to become an electrically charged, chemically active element. The element cobalt by itself has no known function in the body, so it has no listed RDA apart from that of B_{12}. Most of the functions of vitamin B_{12} are as a coenzyme. Cobalt, apart from its association with vitamin B_{12}, is toxic to humans. Taking cobalt supplements can bring on goiter and dysfunction in bone marrow, producing an excess of hemoglobin. Food sources are those named for vitamin B_{12}.

Copper

Essential trace element. RDA: 2 milligrams.

Activity in Body: Copper is required to make red blood cells. It helps transport iron from the bowel to the bloodstream and delivers iron reserves from the liver to the bloodstream. It is involved in the repair and rebuilding of tissue, and helps make phospholipids, collagen, and the neurotransmitter noradrenaline. Copper is a necessary element in many enzymes. Taking too much copper drives down zinc, and too much zinc drives down copper. The zinc to copper ratio should be 10 to 1. Copper is needed in bone formation, RNA production, and interaction with vitamin C to make elastin.

Principal Sources: Oysters, liver and other organ meats, whole grains, shellfish, molasses, poultry, fish, meat, avocados, eggs, legumes, seeds, nuts, and cauliflower. Almost any food with zinc in it also has copper.

Special Points: It is everywhere in the body, just like zinc, only on a smaller scale. Only one-third of copper intake is utilized; the rest is excreted. Copper lack can cause anemia, even with plenty of available iron, B_{12}, folic acid, and vitamin C.

Indications of Copper Deficiency: Weakness, skin lesions, diarrhea, anemia, slowed growth, low white blood cell count, and respiration problems. (Sprue or high zinc intake can cause copper deficiency.) Toxic amounts, over 35 milligrams per day, impair all the zinc reactions in the body, lowering immune system function, interfering with insulin activity, slowing down growth and healing, and interfering with DNA production and energy metabolism.

Fluorine

Useful element. (fluoride is chemically active form). RDA: 50 to 70 micrograms per kilogram body weight.

Activity in Body: Reduces cavities, hardens teeth. Necessary for skeletal system.

Principal Sources: Abundant in all foods in small amounts. Present in some public drinking water sources naturally, and added to many (not all) public water supplies when natural mineral is lacking.

Special Points: Combines easily with calcium. Stored in spleen, eye structure, and elastic tissues. Eliminated from foods when heated, destroyed by too high temperature. Spleen stores and uses large amounts of fluoride. Raw goat's milk contains the highest content of fluoride foods.

Iodine

Essential trace element (iodide is chemically active form). RDA: 150 micrograms.

Activity in Body: Used in thyroid to form thyroxine hormone. Metabolism normalizer in body. Prevents goiter.

Principal Sources: Seafoods (including nori, kelp, and dulse), and in many other foods where iodine is found in the soil. Iodized salt or natural sea salt (containing iodine) is needed in all areas where iodine is lacking in the soil, particularly in most mountain regions.

Indications of Iodine Deficiency: Infants—mental deficiency, neuromuscular problems, cretinisro (severe mental retardation, spastic muscle movements). Adults—goiter, fatigue, impaired work productivity, lowered mental ability, lowered fertility. No problem with excess toxicity *except* in people who have been chronically deficient.

Iron

Essential trace element. RDA: 10 milligrams daily. Women need 18 milligrams.

Activity in Body: Essential in blood as oxygen carrier, and is stored in muscles and liver. Promotes vitality. Works with copper, sodium, vitamin B_{12}, and folic acid to keep up blood supply and prevent anemia.

Principal Sources: Liver and other organ meats, green leafy vegetables, blackberries, black cherries, egg yolk, oysters, raisins, prunes, meat, poultry, and fish.

Special Points: Iron attracts oxygen.

Indications of Iron Deficiency: Children—impaired learning. Adults—Fatigue, lassitude, pale skin, cold extremities, anemia. Surveys show that over 60 percent of Americans are deficient in iron. Excess intake of iron causes liver damage, increased risk of infection.

Magnesium

Essential element. RDA: men 350 milligrams; women 280 milligrams.

Activity in Body: Active component of enzymes. Essential electrolyte works with calcium and phosphorus to build bones. Relaxes nerves. Refreshes system. Prevents and relieves constipation and autointoxication. Keeps most common type of kidney stones from forming. Regulates heart. Converts foods to energy.

Principal Sources: Grapefruit, oranges, figs, whole barley, corn, yellow cornmeal, wheat bran, coconut, milk products, and eggs.

Indications of Magnesium Deficiency: Temper, migraine headaches, chronic asthma, apathy, depression. Deficiency caused by diarrhea, diuretics, diabetes, poor diet, alcoholism, kidney problems, and some drugs. Excess magnesium depresses respiration and central nervous system, which can result in coma or death.

Manganese

Essential trace element. RDA: 2 milligrams.

Activity in Body: Involved with carbohydrate and fat metabolism. Increases resistance to disease. Found and needed mostly in nervous system and brain. Helps bones grow. Supports nerves and pancreas, aids muscle function. Needed by enzymes. Memory mineral.

Principal Sources: Nuts, cereals, dried fruit, tea, vegetables, meat, poultry, fish, and dairy products.

Special Points: Works with calcium, magnesium, phosphorus, copper, and zinc to build bones.

Indications of Manganese Deficiency: Weakened bones, skeletal problems, impaired growth, lower reproduction performance, pancreas problems, reduced glucose metabolism, increases fatty deposits in liver.

Molybdenum

Essential trace element. RDA: 75 micrograms.

Activity in Body: This trace element is available in almost all plant and animal tissues. It is an active part of two essential enzymes. More is stored in the liver and kidneys than anywhere else in the body. Molybdenum is active in the essential enzyme xanthine oxidase, which helps transport iron from the liver and changes it from a lower electric charge (ferrous state) to a higher electric charge (ferric state). It is also active in aldehyde oxidase, which oxidizes fats. Molybdenum interacts with the sulfur-containing amino acids and aids in producing urine.

Principal Sources: Meat, poultry, fish, dairy products, legumes, and cereal grains contain all we need of molybdenum. Most of us don't need it in supplement form.

Special Points: Over half a milligram of molybdenum intake blocks assimilation of copper. Molybdenum helps prevent anemia and works to prevent cavities. Sulfites, used to preserve freshness in fruits and vegetables, block intake of molybdenum. Molybdenum deficiency may cause male impotence. As an antioxidant, molybdenum slows the aging process.

Indications of Molybdenum Deficiency: Quickened breathing, rapid pulse, headache, nausea, mouth and gum soreness, vomiting, coma, and death. Toxicity symptoms (which are extremely rare) are depressed growth, anemia, copper deficiency, elevated uric acid in the blood, and increased risk of gout.

Phosphorus

Essential mineral salt. RDA: 800 milligrams for adults.

Activity in Body: At cell level, phosphorus is involved with lipids, proteins, and nucleic acids—also critical to cell energy production. Needed in four hormonal messengers, including one that regulates oxygen release by hemoglobin. Regulates many enzymes needed to control kidney production of the hormone calcitriol. Necessary for nervous system. It is a brain and bone mineral.

Principal Sources: Sea foods, milk, asparagus, eggs, garlic, grains, seeds, nuts, brewer's yeast, cheese, and dried fruit. All protein foods are rich in phosphorus.

Special Points: 80 percent of phosphorus goes to bones and teeth. Most B vitamins and many enzymes only activate in presence of phosphorus. Present in every cell in the body.

Indications of Phosphorus Deficiency: Weakness, appetite loss, bone pain, stunted growth, irregular breathing, and softening of bones. Extreme loss causes stroke or seizures.

Potassium

Essential element. DRV: 3,500 milligrams.

Activity in Body: Regulates blood pressure. Necessary (with magnesium) for heart health. Found and needed in all cells and body fluids. Always found with sodium. Neutralizes metabolic acids. Creates grace, beauty, good disposition. Helps carbohydrate and protein metabolism.

Principal Sources: Potatoes, bananas, tomatoes, whey, greens, all fruits, all vegetables, nuts, and seeds.

Special Points: Primary electrolyte, helps control acid/alkaline balance, supports heart.

Indications of Potassium Deficiency: Appetite loss, fatigue, irregular heartbeat, depression, weak pulse, nausea, vomiting, diarrhea.

Selenium

Essential trace element. RDA: men 70 micrograms; women 55 micrograms.

Activity in Body: This trace element is mostly found in the body as a structural part of two sulfur-containing amino acids—selenomethionine and selenocysteine. Selenium is found mostly in internal organs, less throughout the muscle structure of the rest of the body. The two sulfur-selenium–containing amino acids just mentioned function as coenzymes and parts of other proteins. These amino acids are powerful antioxidants that seem to be able to take the place of vitamin E or partner with it in destroying free radicals. They play a strong defensive role against several diseases. A powerful protective selenium-activated enzyme called glutathione peroxidase protects the cell membranes in the heart, liver, kidneys, lungs, and other organs from damage. Other selenium-activated enzymes regulate thyroid hormones. One selenium protein binds the heavy metal mercury and removes it from the body.

Principal Sources: The amount of selenium in foods depends on how much is in the soil, and there are wide variations in soils around our planet. In our country, good food sources of selenium include fish, liver and other organ meats, whole cereal grains, raw nuts and seeds, and all fruits and vegetables grown in this country.

Special Points: Essential for reproduction; sperm cells contain a lot of it. Selenoproteins are powerful antioxidants and protect cell membranes along with vitamin E. Deficiency of both selenium and iodine causes much worse goiter than iodine deficiency alone. Protects from cancer, heart disease, emphysema, arthritis, and cirrhosis of the liver. Pancreas function is strongly influenced by selenium. It is believed to slow down aging.

Silicon

Useful element. No RDA. Recommended intake is 200 milligrams daily.

Activity in Body: Needed most by connective tissues. Helps make hard teeth, glossy hair, and strong bones and nails. Tones system. Daily needs met by most diets.

Principal Sources: Oats, barley, brown rice, rye, corn, peas, beans, lentils, wheat, spinach, asparagus, lettuce, tomatoes, cabbage, figs, strawberries, rice polishings, oat straw tea, seeds, coconut, prunes, raw egg yolk, pecans, cod liver oil, and halibut liver oil.

Special Points: Silicon provides agility in body for walking and dancing.

Indications of Silicon Deficiency: None known. Excess: From inhalation in mines, silicosis, which can lead to cancer.

Sodium

Essential element. RDA: 2,400 grams.

Activity in Body: Youth maintainer in body. Influences blood pressure, needed for nerve transmission, an important electrolyte, assists in bone formation. Gland, ligament, and blood builder. Counteracts acidosis. Needed in digestive system. Found in saliva, bile, pancreatic juices, and all body fluids.

Principal Sources: Table salt is the highest source, but natural sources are better for us. They include okra, celery, carrots, beets, cucumbers, string beans, asparagus, turnips, strawberries, oatmeal, raw egg yolk, coconut, black figs, spinach, sprouts, peas, Roquefort cheese, goat cheese and milk, goat whey, fish, oysters, clams, lobster, milk, lentils; it is highest in raw egg white.

Special Points: Intestinal flora need organic sodium. Flexibility of tendons is due to sodium. Most Americans use too much salt—try natural salt substitutes, such as vegetable seasonings, herbs, and spices. Excess sodium produces dehydration, fever, vomiting, and diarrhea.

Indications of Sodium Deficiency: Irritability, restlessness, depression, and nervousness; loss of appetite, thirst, muscle cramps, nausea, and vomiting. Extreme deficiency produces convulsing and coma.

Sulfur

Essential element. No RDA because sufficient sulfur is supplied with adequate protein intake.

Activity in Body: A unique, nonmetallic element present in amino acids methionine, cystine, cysteine, taurine, and in the B vitamins thiamin and biotin. Sulfur helps make up lubricants for the joints and is involved in the body's response to inflammations caused by allergic reactions. It is essential in insulin, a blood-sugar regulator, and heparin, a chemical in the liver that prevents coagulation. Sulfur does not primarily function alone as an electrolyte anywhere in the body but may be found in small amounts in organic sulfates and sulfides. Found mostly in the brain, liver, kidneys, and muscle tissue. Sulfur and selenium have an affinity for one another, and the sulfur-containing amino acids combine easily with the trace element selenium, a powerful antioxidant. All sulfur-containing amino acids are antioxidants, which help prevent cancer.

Principle Sources: Almost all proteins—meat, poultry, fish, dairy products, eggs, and tofu—are the richest sources. Lesser contributors are the sulfur-containing vegetables such as cabbage, cauliflower, leeks, onions, garlic, turnips, and legumes. Fruits including apricots, plums, prunes, peaches, nectarines, papayas, and melons offer small amounts of sulfur.

Special Points: Important ingredient in collagen in skin, nails, and hair. Helps sustain waves and curls in hair. Stimulates bile production. Diets lacking protein may lead to sulfur deficiency. Sulfur-rich foods may help arthritis.

Zinc

Essential element. RDA: men 15 milligrams; women 12 milligrams.

Activity in Body: Zinc's role in developing DNA and proteins emphasizes its special importance in growth and development of children and in the process of healing. Zinc is a critical part of over two hundred enzyme reactions that play a vital part in our health and well-being. Our senses of taste and smell depend on zinc. Insulin production by the pancreas depends on zinc, which is also required for testosterone production. Also needed for prenatal growth, immune system, protein synthesis, energy production, skeletal support, and skin maintenance.

Principal Sources: Three ounces of steamed oysters provides over fifteen times the RDA for zinc! Significant amounts are also provided by clams, crab, fish, meat, poultry, and dairy products are the primary sources. There is a little zinc in just about every vegetable, fruit, legume, and raw nuts and seeds.

Special Points: 95 percent of zinc is inside the cells of the body. Alcohol in excess depletes zinc (as well as B vitamins and other nutrients). Older persons given zinc supplements quickly showed a buildup in T_4 immune system cells. When zinc is lacking, toxic cadmium may take its place in enzymes, causing cell damage.

Indications of Zinc Deficiency: Loss of appetite, smell, and taste. Reduced physical growth, hypogonadism, and slowed mental processes signal zinc deficit in children up to young adults. Reduced sexual interest in adults of both sexes. Excess produces nausea, cramps, and diarrhea; extreme excess causes bleeding and anemia.

CARBOHYDRATES

Carbohydrates are composed of sugars, starches, and cellulose. They produce energy in the body when glucose unites with oxygen in the cells in a series of enzyme reactions.

The conversion of starches into sugars begins in the mouth, where the process of chewing mixes them with a digestive enzyme in the saliva. Grain and cereal starches are insoluble in plain water and cannot be assimilated until they are broken down by pancreatic digestive enzymes. Starch digestion is completed in the small intestine.

The percentage chart that follows is a handy guide to the selection of carbohydrates. You cannot live without eating some of the foods listed in the 5 percent column, which are the least starchy. The 10 percent, 15 percent, and 20 percent lists are increasingly starchy, and excess starch can produce excess weight, just like foods with excess fat content. In cases of overweight and deficiency of minerals and trace elements, it would be well to select all your carbohydrates from the 5 percent column. Whenever heavy starches from the 20 percent column are eaten, be sure to eat foods from the 5 percent column to maintain balance in your meals. All fresh fruits and vegetables are vitamin-rich and mineral-rich, but be careful not to get carried away with too many starchy vegetables.

PERCENTAGE CHART FOR CARBOHYDRATES

5 percent	*10 percent*	*15 percent*	*20 percent*
Vegetables	**Vegetables**	**Vegetables**	**Vegetables**
Artichokes	Beets	Green peas	Baked beans
Asparagus	Carrots	Lima beans	Bread
Beet greens	Kohlrabi	Parsnips	Brown rice
Broccoli	Onions		Green corn
Brussels sprouts	Pumpkin	**Fruits**	Potatoes
Cabbage	Squash	Apples	Shell beans
Cauliflower	Turnips	Apricots	Lentils
Celery		Blueberries	Lima beans
Cucumber		Cherries	Navy beans
Dandelions		Currants	Soybeans

(Continued)

PERCENTAGE CHART FOR CARBOHYDRATES

5 percent	*10 percent*	*15 percent*	*20 percent*
Vegetables	**Fruits**	**Fruits**	**Vegetables**
Eggplant	Blackberries	Huckleberries	Shredded
Endive	Gooseberries	Pears	whole rye
Leeks	Lemons	Raspberries	
Lettuce	Oranges		**Fruits**
Mushrooms	Peaches	**Nuts**	Bananas
Okra	Pineapple	Almonds	Plum
Radishes	Strawberries	Beechnuts	Prunes
Rhubarb	Watermelon	Walnuts	
Sauerkraut		(English)	**Nuts**
Sea kale	**Nuts**		Chestnuts
Sorrel	Black walnuts		(40% fat)
Spinach	Brazil nuts		Peanuts
String beans	Filberts		
Swiss chard	Hickory		
Tomatoes	Pecans		
Vegetable			
marrow			
Watercress			
Wheat			

Fruits
Ripe olives (20% fat)
Grapefruit
Nuts
Butternuts
Pignolias

CHOLESTEROL

Cholesterol is a valuable sterol needed by every cell of the body and a necessary component of many hormones. Most of it is made by the liver, but we also pick it up from meat, dairy products, and eggs. Of course, it is possible to have too much cholesterol. When we have an excess amount of cholesterol in the blood, it can be deposited on arterial walls, causing a hardened plaque that is the basis for cardiovascular disease, also known as arteriosclerosis. Cholesterol, however, is also needed by every cell of the body. Bile is made in part from cholesterol and helps digest fats. Sex hormones and vitamin D are made from a close relative of cholesterol.

We need a certain amount of the fatty substances for the maintenance of our body's health, which include the sterols, fatty acids, and glycerol. Triglycerides are formed by one molecule of glycerol combined with those molecules of fatty acids. Also, fatty acids are the basis for prostaglandins.

When doctors find the blood cholesterol too high (over 200 milligrams per $\frac{1}{10}$ liter of blood), they try to bring it to a normal level. This can be done by having the patient lose weight, which inevitably involves change in diet.

The Trappist monks in Canada are vegetarian. But Benedictine monks consume a good deal of meat. Researchers have checked out both of these orders and find that the Trappist order does not have the high cholesterol level in their blood like the Benedictine brothers do.

I believe that cholesterol can become too high in the body when we consume an excess of the fatty foods of animal origin, such as eggs, butter, milk, cream, as well as the fatty meats. There are cholesterol-lowering drugs, but the main issue in high

cholesterol, as it is in obesity, is lifestyle. The problem is too little exercise (carlorie burning) and too much of the wrong kinds
of food (high fat, high salt, low fiber, high sugar, for example).

For one reason or another, people nowadays seem to
think they can eat anything they want to eat in whatever
amounts they feel like. That is very dangerous. It is said that
the larger the waistline, the shorter the life line. We should avoid
overweight, and avoid the foods that cause it. We should all be
eating less meat, more cereal grains, more salads, and more fresh
fruits and vegetables.

Greens are especially good in aiding the metabolism of fats,
and most of us do not have enough of these greens in our salads and other foods. Many of us would be much better off if
we used vegetable oils instead of the animal fats in our diets.
Excessive cholesterol is the result of poor living habits, and it
goes hand in hand with lack of exercise and obesity.

To decrease cholesterol and body fat, it might be well to go on
a low-fat diet now and then, eliminating the use of all concentrated
fats and oils. If oils are used, make sure that they are cold-pressed
and unheated. Avoid fried foods. Use lots of salad vegetables and
lots of greens. Have green herbal teas, such as comfrey and dandelion. Also use a lot of whey in your diet; it is high in natural sodium
and is capable of dissolving calcium deposits and spurs. Lecithin in
the diet helps lower the free cholesterol in the blood. Lecithin
keeps cholesterol in solution. Cocktails made of celery juice,
cucumber juice, or spinach juice in place of alcohol-containing
cocktails served at bars will aid in decreasing cholesterol.

Find a healthy way to live; find exercises that help keep the
liver in a good operating condition. A sedentary occupation can
build fat storage in the body. We must find a way of changing
our lives, a way to balance our daily routine, a way to preserve
health and a reasonable high quality of life.

SUPPLEMENTARY FOODS

We should never consider a natural remedy or a food supplement as a complete correction for any ailment in the body. We should first learn to live correctly and seek good guidance for nutrition. You may want to seek out professional advice as to what nutritional shortages exist in your body, especially if you have a chronic condition. I have never found anyone who would not benefit from the daily addition of the following supplementary foods. Keep them available. They can, of course, also be added to any liquefied drink, morning cereal, salad, dessert, and so forth.

Blackstrap Molasses

This is an excellent source of iron and B-complex vitamins.

Brewer's Yeast

Brewer's yeast is a good source of B-complex vitamins.

Desiccated Liver

This helps to build the bloodstream. It is high in iron, copper, and the various trace elements.

Nova Scotia Dulse

Take ¼ teaspoon a day (or one tablet). Only minute quantities of iodine are required by the body, and dulse, being a high iodine food, supplies this need. Iodine keeps us from getting goiter. It helps prevent wrinkles. Lack of it causes mood swings, tiredness, brittle hair, and dry skin. Dulse is the highest natural source of iodine for the thyroid gland.

Here's how you can prepare the dulse: Take possibly two or three big leaves of dulse and cut them up fine enough to put in a liquefier. Grind them up in hot water. Let the mixture stand for half an hour, then strain the liquid. Use about 2 ounces of this Nova Scotia dulse liquid in about 2 quarts of water. It can be flavored with a little honey. This liquid can be added to broths, soups, or vegetable juices. Just take a little bit every day—one cup daily is plenty—and you will get the benefit you need.

Rice Polishings

Use a teaspoonful a day. Rice polishings are high in B-complex vitamins—for nerves, brain function, appetite, and muscle coordination—and the mineral element silicon, which is the youth element. Silicon is the "cutter" in the body, cleaning out all toxins and debris. It is necessary for beautiful hair, nails, and skin. For cold feet and skin problems, take extra silicon.

Sunflower Seed Meal

Use 1 teaspoonful three times a day. This is one of the finest vegetarian proteins you can use and a good source of lecithin and vitamin E. If the body is protein-starved, use this to feed the brain and nervous system. All edible seeds are good for the glands, too. Like rice polishings, sunflower seeds are high in silicon.

Wheat Germ

Use 1 tablespoonful daily. This is high in vitamin E, the specific vitamin for the heart. It gives tone to the muscle structure, strengthening the veins (varicose veins) and helping circulation.

Wheat germ also feeds the glands and nerves and is a good source of B-complex vitamins.

Whey

This is one of the finest of foods. Be sure you always have a container of the powder or liquid on hand. A very good habit to develop is to take a glass of whey at each meal. It is one of our best organic sodium sources. Sodium is known as the "youth element," allowing our joints to remain supple. It also aids digestion and builds the blood. Whey is friendly to the acidophilus baccilli in the intestinal tract, which are important to good intestinal management. It also has calcium, the tone-builder and strengthener, and chlorine, the cleanser. People on slimming diets need not be afraid of whey. Taken before meals, it partially appeases hunger.

SUPPLEMENTS AND FORTIFIERS

Tablets, powders, protein and amino acid preparations, mineral and vitamin supplements, oils such as wheat germ oil capsules (discard the "shell"), medicinal herbs, and other necessary supplementlary preparations can be added to liquefied drinks so that you can't tell they are there. Their taste can be camouflaged with a counteracting flavor.

Here are some of the tablets and powders that can be used for health enhancement by including them in liquefied drinks:

Alfalfa Tablets	For alkalinizing.
Green Kale Tablets	For extra calcium.
Lecithin	Keeps cholesterol from depositing in the arteries.

Okra, Celery Tablets	High natural sodium content.
Papaya Tablets	For digestion.
Parsley Tablets	For the kidneys.
Peach Powder	Good for its laxative effect.
Prune, Apricot	Good for its laxative effect, vitamins A and C.
Pycnogenol	Rich in antioxidants.
Watercress Tablets	For the heart (high in potassium and magnesium).
Whey Powder	High sodium and potassium content.

Vitamins are now accepted and established as necessary for health and well-being. Biochemists and medical researchers now clearly understand the roles of the different vitamins in the body.

Vitamins seem to offer the "kick" to the minerals that enter our bodies. They work with enzymes, or as parts of enzymes, to create and control the energy and protein by-products of cells. They work with minerals and hydrocarbon molecules building and maintaining a perfect body.

I do not believe in artificial vitamins made from coal tar, vitamin dosages at many times the needed amount, or those that are made from abnormal or inorganic substances. Prostituted supplements may cause other problems in the body; the future will tell.

To make up for deficiencies in the body, remember these points:

1. Follow a healthy daily eating regimen.
2. Consult with a doctor who knows how to determine chemical deficiencies in the body, or learn how yourself.
3. Find out the natural foods that are high in the minerals and vitamins you are deficient in and make them a regular part of your food regimen.
4. Make sure that everything you eat is whole, pure, and natural.

CHAPTER 14

THE HEALTH FOOD STORE

The other day one of my employees walked into what had been an ordinary small town grocery store and found a new sign on the entrance saying "WE NOW OFFER OVER 300 ORGANICALLY GROWN NATURAL FOOD PRODUCTS." He was so excited he could hardly wait to tell me, and I was glad to hear it. For nearly seventy years I've been telling people, "If you'll change your food regimen to emphasize whole, pure, natural, fresh foods, you'll have far fewer doctor bills and you'll live longer."

Forty years ago, if you weren't familiar with a city, you'd have to ask where the local health food store was. Now, there are not only lots of large, attractive, state-of-the-art health food stores or co-ops in every major city and many small towns, but every supermarket, Wal-Mart, and large drugstore seem to have a natural foods department. Some supermarkets advertise that they sell only pesticide-free produce. They actually pay a chemistry lab to test samples of the produce they purchase at the wholesale level, so they are sure there are no pesticides on the foods they sell. Organic farming has reached a stage where farmers may be certified by an independent private or local government agency. The certification guarantees that their food products have been grown on nutrient-rich soils, without pesticides or chemical sprays or artificial fertilizers, using environmentally sound practices. Organic foods in 1998 topped $4 billion in sales.

Two generations ago, people who insisted on natural, organic foods for their diets were regarded as eccentric "health nuts." Now, the natural food boom includes several million consumers who buy organics because they want to make sure they are getting more nutrients and pesticide-free food. A survey of college students in a recent year showed that 79 percent of the college students bought organic foods "at least occasionally." Their reasons for buying organic products included concern for personal health (63 percent), better quality food (51 percent), environmental concerns (44 percent), support for small or local farms (40 percent), increased availability (25 percent), and better taste (14 percent). Many people come into contact with organic foods initially through the popular "farmer's markets" that have sprung up across the United States since the 1960s. However, many farmer's markets do not require that only certified organic foods be offered for sale by vendors.

Health food stores and the many other stores that feature health-related products (not all natural or organic) carry a much greater range and variety of products than were available even ten years ago. Vitamins, minerals, and daily "multiple vitamin-mineral" supplements are usually allotted significant shelf space. So are herbs, both Western traditional and Oriental traditional. Products like aloe vera juice, powdered natural plantago or psyllium seeds, soy lecithin granules, omega-3 oils, lactobacillus acidophilus, honeybee pollen, whey (powder or liquid), grape seed extract, and many others are being purchased by consumers who have read or heard about what these products do, and buy them in order to improve their level of health or to cope with a chronic problem that conventional medicine does not seem to be able to improve. I would guess that at least 60 percent of health product consumers are very well informed about what they are buying.

Some products have generated short-term fad sales that tend to tail off later. These include natural remedies that promise or imply they will improve sexual performance, restore youthfulness, reduce arthritis pain, improve memory, grow hair (or restore natural color), or improve immune system function. Some products, such as chlorella, spirulina, and blue green alga (the other two are also algae), have been extensively researched at universities, hospitals, and various private institutions, and have been demonstrated to be effective in enhancing health in specific ways, such as detoxification and immune system support. Many of the products have only become available in recent times.

Individual amino acids are relatively new, as are the antioxidants that destroy cancer-producing free radicals. Condensed essences of vegetables are recent products, said to be an adequate substitute for eating normal portions of actual vegetables. DHEA, an acronym for dehydroepiandrosterone, is another new product, claimed to keep biological processes in balance in the body, to increase sex drive, and, for men, to help lose fat and gain bigger muscles. DHEA is a natural substance produced by the body that begins to diminish after age twenty-one, and is alleged to account for some symptoms of aging. There are lots of people taking it, but I feel that the jury is still out on this product. There are many new products being offered to the natural health market, and all of them have to prove their worth if they are going to continue being manufactured.

The severe flu epidemics of the past few years have been the occasion for a herbal combination of goldenseal with echinacea, a product that has been praised by many people, including doctors, for reducing symptoms and shortening the course of the flu. Ginseng, a distinguished Chinese tonic herb, continues in its popularity with large numbers of long-term users. Vitamin C isn't new, but taking large amounts, up to 7 or 8 grams daily, is still relatively new and is relatively controversial. Some doctors claim that large amounts of vitamin C interfere with the assimilation of many minerals and trace elements, excepting iron. It has been proved that taking an iron supplement with a small glass of orange juice doubles the amount assimilated. My problem with megadoses of any natural product is that megadoses don't occur in nature's foods. Only when a genetic weakness in the body creates a chronic shortage of some vitamin or chemical would I agree that an abnormally large amount of the nutrient be given.

Among my favorite places in natural food stores are the bulk food bins, where you can scoop up your own brown rice, millet, prunes, legumes, granola, raw nuts and seeds, and other great bargains. I never have liked paying extra for containers when all I really wanted was the contents. Of course, people who work for me grow a good deal of the fruits and vegetables in my organic gardens and orchards.

I have enjoyed goat's milk as an alternative to cow's milk, which many of my patients have been unable to tolerate. But there are now many other alternatives to cow's milk in the markets and health food stores. I've used soy milk on many occasions, and my cooks have used it as a substitute for animal milk in recipes, with good success. Rice milk has a pleasant flavor, as do the nut milks and seed milks. You can get sesame seeds with hulls removed now, so that making sesame seed milk no longer requires straining out the hulls. The only good reason for drinking animal milk is its high calcium content, but if you drink it for that reason, limit yourself to a glass or two per day. The average American has 40 percent milk and milk products in their diet, which is far too much. We need to work toward a balance in our food regimen.

However, while we are learning about new foods and health products, let us keep an open mind. Often the store itself has a good selection of health books packed with knowledge about some of the latest products. They may not all express the same principles, but they all uphold the basic truth that natural, unsprayed, organic foodstuffs are superior. And they describe the latest supplement discoveries and offerings.

IT'S TIME FOR A CHANGE

Anyone who is sick or gets sick often knows it is time for a change. One thing we have to change is our eating habits. Food is not an easy problem to tackle because most of us have well-established cooking and food preferences, and our family backgrounds and customs make it very difficult for us to change. It seems that we seldom recognize the importance of the relationship between our food and our health. We find it difficult to conceive of an actual relation between the food that goes into our bodies and what happens in our liver, or what happens to our stomach or heart. We do not seriously consider that what's in our bloodstream depends upon what we eat. We do not know that what we eat today is going to walk and talk tomorrow. We do not thoughtfully consider what we eat actually becomes the cell structure of the body. But it's true: If we do not change our faulty ways of eating, we can never expect a permanent turn for the better in our health.

YOUR LIFE IS IN THE LABEL— HOW MUCH DO YOU KNOW?

There are many people who give serious consideration to the labels on food containers these days because of the nutrition information required by law. I think this is a wonderful thing. We need to know what the contents are.

No selection of food should be made without first thoroughly examining the list of ingredients, which indicates their proportionate quantity, and the inert (inactive) components, if any. You should have a working knowledge of the terms commonly employed. You will also need a working knowledge of the processes involved, the conditions under which the food is prepared, the additives it contains, and the effects of these things upon the food's nutritional qualities.

We should know what is meant on a label when it mentions ingredients such as wheat flour, sugar, raw sugar, fats and oils, eggs, milk products, artificial coloring, and preservatives. If properly labeled, every product containing additives would bear a skull and crossbones symbol, and we would carefully store that product in our medicine cabinets with our other poisons. The carcinogenic factor is inherent in all artificial products of coal-tar compounds, which is the common source of these additives. Consumption of these products should be carefully avoided. Methods of processing would soon change if we voiced our objections and refused to purchase these commodities.

Know What's Behind Your Label

We need to learn as much as possible about what happens to the contents before they find their way into their attractive containers. Labels are a very important medium in the business of selling. But remember, "All that glitters is not gold." Fields and factories should be open for inspection to all, so that we may learn how these processes are carried on. Let us find out some things for ourselves.

The result of our learning to read labels more intelligently will bring us produce in its whole natural state, and it will be labeled to identify production by natural methods.

Such products—based on cultivation of crops on naturally fertilized soils—will preserve the vital life elements in the soil. The less we depend upon those varieties that are subjected to the different manufacturing and packaging processes, the better are our expectations for adequately nourishing our bodies.

Learn to Choose "Real" Value

In all commodities, we must depend largely upon the integrity of the manufacturer whose label is on the product. The conscientious manufacturer guards the quality of his products, and he labels them to assure the consumer that the standard is maintained. We should choose those products that have a reputation for good quality. This should be the primary criterion in our selection of foods. Dollar-saving is of little importance as a guideline.

First, we need to learn who are the most dependable processors and packagers. Then we should select those as often as we can afford them—keeping in mind that this is our most important investment.

We have a right to expect our government to establish and maintain controls that will ensure its citizens the highest-quality products, free of any pressure from trade groups or industrial influence. Our best insurance, however, is to demand more and more foods in their natural form, under growers' labels that reflect natural production methods. This will help decrease the consumption of processed foods.

READING THE LABEL

When you start reading the labels you may not be sure what they mean. Of course, we need to educate ourselves, but here are a few very common ingredients from labels to get you started.

Term	Definition
Wheat Flour	This is white flour, from wheat, milled to remove all the vital life elements. The outer coating, bran, rich in mineral content, is bleached to make the flour "pure" white—"real" flour is not "pure white."
Sugar	This is crystallized sugar cane or sugar beets. Sugar, in its natural form, is a rich source of minerals and other nutritive factors. But these are lost by being subjected to prolonged heat and further impaired by bleaching, and so on.
Salt	This is processed to crystallization by extreme heat, leaving a lifeless residue concentrated to such a degree that it is hardly assimilable in the digestive process.
Eggs	In prepared products, eggs have been dried and reduced to powdered form. Generally they are

prepared from eggs in which the germ of life necessary to produce the embryo of a chick never existed because of lack of fertility. Generally they are the product of fowl never allowed to range on the ground, injected with various antibiotics, and force-fed concentrated feed, which is accessible to them around the clock.

Fats	These are fats changed to solid form by a process of hydrogenation, which completely alters the fat molecular structure, rendering it unassimilable in digestion. The new fat structure tends to be cholesterol forming and contributes to hardening of the arteries.
Oils (unless labeled "cold-pressed")	These are extracted from various sources and subjected to heat that alters the minute fat globules, rendering them more carcinogenic in tendency.
Special Preservatives, Artificial Colorings, Flavorings	These are additives, usually of coal-tar derivation, that are carcinogenic in nature; flavorings also perhaps having a high alcohol content.
Vinegar	This is distilled, processed quickly by chemicals, as opposed to the slow aging of pure cider or other natural fermentation process.
Processed	As applied to the making of cheese, this is similar in action to that of hydrogenation, which alters the fatty structure, rendering it more chemically reactive (carcinogenic).

FOODS FROM ANIMAL SOURCES

Let us consider some of the basic foods. We need to be most particular in regard to food from animal sources. We should accept no compromise on most of these. There are animal products that have been contaminated by injection of growth-stimulating hormones in livestock, or meat exposed to radiation or unsanitary processing. Special study is required for knowledge of product handling and processing. Many new factors and scientific developments, such as genetic engineering, may enter into the production and processing of animal products, and it is unsafe to assume our customary trust in the safety of foods may be continued without question.

GRAINS, CEREALS, AND BAKED GOODS

No class of food is subjected to processing to the extent used on grains. They should come to every consumer's hands whole, just as they are harvested. Destruction of their vital life substance begins with their being hulled and continues through the processes of grinding and milling that renders them unspoilable. Destruction also occurs in the additional processes they go through to make them into prepared cereals and baked goods. Little nutritional value is left in these prepared foods, notwithstanding so-called "enriching" additives, unless they are freshly prepared from whole grains, particularly the sprouted grain.

If you would derive maximum returns for every dietary dollar expended, read the labels of prepared and baked products and compare them with those for natural whole grains. Be governed accordingly. You will soon want to invest in an appliance that will enable you to grind the whole grains in your own kitchen when you are ready to use them. You can learn methods that require only tenderizing, and methods of baking that will ensure greatest nutritive benefits. These will be found so satisfying that you will be able to reduce the consumption of carbohydrates, which generally is far too great for balanced nutrition.

FATS

In processing, fats undergo extensive development so that the natural structure is altered, the fatty elements being subjected to what is known as hydrogenation, making them incapable of digestion. And when something is taken into the body that cannot be digested, it becomes harmful to you. Have you learned to select oils that have been subjected only to low temperature?

The furor regarding the cholesterol-forming tendency of these processed fats has made the public more aware of their potential dangers: They increase the incidence of heart disease.

FRUIT JUICES

For breakfast and other meals as well, children and adults should avoid the various popular beverages which purport to contain fruit or resemble a fruit juice but are often loaded with additive substances, dyes, sugar, sugar substitutes, acids, and oils. Foods containing synthetic food dyes and artificial flavors are particularly to be avoided.

ICE CREAM

Among dairy products, the one usually considered the most delectable is ice cream. But ice cream has been reduced in commercial manufacture to the most inferior of foods, containing many artificial ingredients with little nutritive value. When made of natural ingredients, it is most wholesome. How can the consumer evaluate the quality except by demanding more explicit labeling?

CANNED FOODS AND THEIR EFFECT ON THE DIET

The container that bears the label should also be seriously considered. The invention of the tin can revolutionized food processing and contributed to extensive changes in the dietary habits of people. Nowadays, the can opener is one of the most essential kitchen gadgets. The consumption of canned foods is so great that an electrical device has been developed just for this purpose. If the contents are vegetables, they usually are subjected to a cooking process to have greater taste appeal. Prepared and packaged seasonings are added; and they are often immersed in hot fat, which in itself is productive of causes involving metastasis—that change in tissue structure that becomes malignant. Notwithstanding all the evidence and confronted with the increasing prevalence of metastasis, medical science still claims not to have discovered proof of the cause. Why not look in the frying pan or in those foods preserved by artificial means to retard spoilage and to assure a long shelf life? With proper caution on the label regarding the prompt use of any perishable item, the consumer would then assume responsibility for the use within the period designated. The objective should be the quickest possible turnover of all foods, not a long shelf life.

CLEANING PRODUCTS

These factors are not limited to commodities taken internally only. They also apply to those used externally on the skin to keep the body clean and well groomed; also, to the cleaning preparations that contribute to the attractiveness and sanitation of our eating utensils, homes, offices, stores, and shops. Do you know what effects may and do come from the use of detergents? Harsh soaps also can affect the normal health and function of the skin.

SALT

We have both winter foods and summer foods. We should know what the best summer foods are and how to live during the summer. Do you know how to live during the hot weather? It has been discovered that the use of table salt, or salt tablets, replaces salts in the body lost through excessive perspiration. But we should be aware that salt is attracted to certain tissues of the body and can result in hardening of the arteries. Do we have to go from one bad condition to another by taking salt to replace that which has been eliminated from the body? Learn to take care of such conditions in a way that will not cause trouble in the future.

SOME ITEMS YOU'LL WANT FROM YOUR HEALTH FOOD STORE

Herb Teas

Alfamint	Oat Straw
Fennugreek	Peach leaf
Huckleberry	Shavegrass
Mint	Strawberry

Dairy and Substitutes

Cheese of all kinds	Soy milk

Seeds

Guatemala squash

Pumpkin

Safflower

Sesame

Sunflower

Cereals, Grains, and Legumes

Barley

Beans

Brown rice

Cornmeal

Lentils

Millet

Oats

Peas

Rice polishings

Seven grain

Soybeans

Wheat germ

Whole grain wheat

Oils

Olive

Peanut

Safflower

Sesame

Soy

Sunflower

Tahini

Powders

Banana

Coconut

Dulse

Whey

Breads

Millet

Rye

Whole grain

Fruit Juices

Apple

Black cherry

Concord grape

Fig

Pineapple

Pomegranate

Prune

Nuts

Almonds

Cashews

Pine nuts

Pecans

Coconut

Walnuts

Malted nuts

Brazils

Peanuts

Nut Butters

Almond

Peanut

Cashew

Salts

Celery salt

Mineral salt

Garlic salt

Vegetable salt

Herbs

Basil

Rosemary

Flaxseed

Sage

Paprika

Thyme

Natural Sugars

Corn sugar

Maple sugar

Date sugar

Molasses

Honey of many kinds

Raw sugar

Dried Fruits

Apples

Peaches

Apricots

Pears

Dates

Prunes

Figs

Raisins

Olives

Other

Gelatins

Meat substitutes

Lecithin granules

Salad dressings

Lecithin spread

One of the most important principles in obtaining all the vitamins, minerals, and trace elements the body needs is to increase the variety of foods you eat. Most people are locked into a routine food regimen that simply repeats a few basic menus and a dozen or so foods, with no further variety. Bacon, eggs, and toast, with coffee, every morning. At lunchtime, a sandwich, perhaps a carrot and a celery stick, an apple or banana, and two cookies. For dinner, meat, potatoes, peas, corn, or carrots—once in a while with a salad. This is too restricted, too lacking in variety, a diet inviting a disease.

The next time you go to the health food store or supermarket, spend more time than usual in the fresh vegetables area and the fresh fruit area. Check out vegetables you haven't cooked or eaten before. Look over fruits you haven't tried. You might want to ask the vegetable clerk how to prepare what you've picked out. It takes effort to break routines and develop greater variety in foods, but it pays off by adding new foods for you and your family to enjoy.

A food cannot be expected to contain minerals or trace elements that were never in the soil the food was grown in. Talk to the vegetable and fruit clerk about where the various items you are purchasing were grown. Then use your telephone to call around to agricultural agencies and find out what minerals and trace elements are lacking in those soils. You can develop a food-buying plan that incorporates geographical variety as well as food product variety, if you choose to do so.

CHAPTER 15

NATURAL FOOD AND
HEALTH TIPS

In a recent year I was presented with the
President's Award from the National Nutritional Foods Association for my influence in turning the
American public's attention to the importance of nutritional
foods. I can't tell you how many frustrating years I spent as a
nature cure doctor, wondering if our country would ever catch
on to the connection between our state of health and the quality of foods we eat. I think 1998 was the year in which the food
industry got its wake-up call from the people of this country. I
was just as surprised as anyone else.

Sales of natural foods in 1998 jumped 79 percent from the
previous year to a total of $25 billion, while dietary supplement
sales added another $10 billion. Those are the most recent fig-
ures I was able to get. Since the early 1930s, I have been telling
lecture audiences and patients, "If you don't spend money now
buying the best and most nutritious foods, you'll spend it later
on doctor and hospital bills." Now, I knew what I was talking

about because I had been operating health spas since the early 1950s, and I have seen thousands of people get rid of their diseases and chronic conditions by turning to natural, organic foods and getting into a balanced food regimen. I, personally, am delighted to see the American people set their sights on better health through better nutrition.

Our country has been diet-crazy since the 1950s, and we have found out the hard way that nearly all weight-loss diets lead to vitamin and mineral deficiencies. In turn, nutrient deficiencies pave the way to diseases. I feel we need to get off diets altogether, and get into a natural, balanced food regimen that leads to nutrient sufficiency and health. In the last decade of the twentieth century, I believe our nation turned the corner toward that goal.

I think there are many people still who, unknowingly, are on an arthritis-producing diet. I think there are many other people on a diabetes-producing diet, and others on a cardiovascular disease diet. They haven't yet learned their lesson. I sincerely hope they do, in time to avoid the distressing consequences.

In this chapter, I am going to bring you a potpourri of health and nutritional tips that I have discovered in my work with patients over the years. I suggest that you write down those that relate to you and consider incorporating them into your lifestyle for better health.

SPECIAL NUTRITIONAL TIPS

Oils as Nutrients

I believe in minimizing both saturated fats and unsaturated oils in the diet. Saturated fats lead to heart disease while unsaturated oils increase your risk of cancer. If you must cook with oil, use olive oil. If you must have oil in your salad dressings, I encourage you to use flaxseed oil. You cannot, however, cook with flaxseed oil. The natural oils in the fish we eat reduce the risk of heart disease. Don't take mineral oil internally. It is derived from petroleum, which I don't believe is safe, and we find that it dissolves and carries off fat-soluble vitamins—vitamins A, D, E, and K. All of us get enough fat from the foods we eat without taking in extra fats and oils.

Overeating

This is the primary cause of being overweight. Weight-loss diets are not acceptable as a counterbalance to overeating. I mean, it doesn't work to overeat a few months, then diet a few months, then overeat some more—because your weight will slowly creep upward. Try lifestyle changes. Program more activity and exercise and less sitting into your lifestyle. Don't rise up from dinner, turn on the TV, and sit for the next three hours while your dinner turns to body fat. Get creative and come up with enjoyable physical activity. Whatever happened to dancing?

Salt

Table salt is sodium chloride, a concentrated mineral processed at high heat that behaves like a drug when used to excess, and most Americans sprinkle many more times the amount their bodies need onto their food daily. Oversalting has been linked to overeating. Not everyone has a problem with salt, but for some the risk of high blood pressure increases. There are some wonderful salt-free seasonings out there. Experiment—try some of them, including my popular broth powder.

Raw Salads

Raw salads cannot be easily digested by some. Cooked vegetables and raw vegetable juice together are almost the same as eating a raw salad. In many cases, this combination eliminates gas.

Egg Whites

Egg whites should always be beaten to a froth and aerated well before eating. An omelet is best when the egg is beaten well.

Waffles

Waffles considered as a starch are permissible occasionally when made of whole grain flours. They should be eaten with a little butter and covered with honey or maple syrup. However, lean toward cooked whole grain cereals, not breads or waffles.

Colorful Meal Planning

Meals should be planned with the idea of putting together as many attractively colored foods as possible. A natural appetite is not stimulated with unattractive fried, charred, overcooked, greasy foods.

Juices from Vegetables

If you have no vegetable juicer, vegetables may be run through a food grinder. Then put the pulp into a muslin bag and squeeze out the juices. Carrots and beets should be shredded or grated first.

Cell Salts

Cell salts are found most abundantly in the peelings or outer layers of fruits and vegetables. Do not be afraid to eat cucumber peelings. They are not poisonous. Needless to say do not eat orange peelings, banana peelings, and pineapple skins.

Taro Root

Many years ago, I saw a healing take place in a particular lady. She was troubled with a bleeding bowel due to colitis. She had been to the Seventh-Day Adventist Loma Linda Hospital in Southern California, and had the best treatment available. However, she came to my office and wanted further bowel care by natural methods. What do you suppose I recommended? I used a remedy I had learned from a Seventh-Day Adventist minister in the South Pacific, where bowel troubles, parasites, and other tropical disturbances are so common. It was there that a missionary taught me the healing properties of taro root. It is the most soothing thing for the intestinal tract. I used taro root and bananas with great success for her condition.

FOODS AND THEIR INFLUENCE ON THE BODY

Fattening Foods

Good: Nuts (pine nuts and almonds are best), avocados, dried fruits, honey, yellow corn, whole grains (well-cooked), cream.
Bad: Refined starches such as cream of wheat, white bread, white rice, white sugar, chocolate, concentrated oils, fatty meats.

Thinning Foods

Good: Citrus fruits (grapefruit and lemon are best), pineapple, tropical fruits, berries, melons, vegetable juices, tomatoes, leafy vegetables, nonstarchy vegetables, skim milk, whey, and health teas such as strawberry, pine needle, and so on.

Bad: Spices, stimulating foods, coffee, tea, fried foods, distilled vinegar, patent medicines.

Gas-Producing Foods

Sulfur foods, such as cabbage, cauliflower, onions, eggs, and so on. Unsoaked dried fruits, fats, fibrous foods, sometimes raw foods (especially lettuce), fried foods, wrong combinations, such as acids with starches or starches with proteins.

Constipating and Disease-Producing Foods

Cheese, fried foods, pasteurized milk, candies; all denatured, refined, spiced, concentrated, salted, unnatural, or hot foods; all rich, heavy, hard-shelled, or heavy cellulose foods, such as tops of vegetables and legumes. Canned, burned, fermented, processed food and practically any food wherein man has tried to improve over nature.

Laxative Foods

Good: Berries (except blackberries), all fruits, natural sweets, such as soaked dried fruits, honey, and so on, nonstarchy vegetables. Fruit and vegetable juices, tropical fruits. Whole grains are laxative to those who need them.

Bad: Mineral oil, over-the-counter drugstore laxatives, spiced foods, wine with meals.

Blood-Purifying Foods

Fruits, berries, vegetable and fruit juices, tops of vegetables, broths, health teas, skim milk, and goat whey. Tropical fruits, nonstarchy vegetables.

SPECIAL HEALTH TIPS

Comb to Relieve Pain

We can sometimes relieve pain by placing a comb in the palm of our hand and holding the teeth of the comb firmly against the tips of the fingers.

A Golf Ball

Because of its curve, a golf ball is a fine thing to be used for exercising the metatarsal arch, working the foot back and forth on it. If we could learn to walk with the soles of the feet turned in, we would find some degree of relief for lower back pain.

A Vegetable Skin Brush

This will help bring on relaxation when used on the soles of the feet at night before going to bed. Four or five minutes of light brushing, especially by another person, will bring relaxation.

Spine-Easing Exercise

Walking pigeon-toed a little every day as an exercise is especially good for correcting a curvature of the lower part of the spine.

Charcoal

It may be appropriate in some cases of indigestion or toxic bowel conditions to use activated charcoal to absorb problematic gases and toxins in the bowel. Absorption means to take in a gas or liquid as a sponge takes in water. It is used in hospitals for poisoning cases and drug overdoses, along with gastric lavage (pumping out the contents of the stomach). It is also claimed that, taken internally, it is excellent for acid dyspepsia, fermentation, heartburn, and colic due to fermentation in the decomposition of foods in the stomach and bowel. It is a valuable remedy that is able to bind to toxic substances in the stomach and bowel to prevent them from entering the bloodstream.

Charcoal can be made out of willow, coconut shell, pine, and many other woods. Charcoal treated with oxygen becomes extremely porous, "activating" the charcoal by greatly increasing its surface area so it can absorb a greater amount of toxic material. If it is going to be used for any length of time, you should use a vitamin A supplement.

Water Packs

Many times joint pain may be relieved by wrapping the area in a towel wrung out in cold water, then wrapping with a dry towel to hold in the moisture. This will also help to relieve stiffness in the joints.

Hot Water Bottle

To make a substitute hot water bottle, fill a bag made of flannel with hot, dry bran.

Flaxseed Poultice

A poultice is a hot, moist mass sandwiched between layers of cloth, applied to the body to relieve pain, congestion, or inflammation. A flaxseed poultice is one of the finest. (Others are linseed and mustard.) It can be mixed with warm water, applied as warm as can be tolerated, and kept hot with water baths or an electric pad.

Elimination Diet

An excellent five-day elimination and cleansing regimen has been devised to improve bowel tone and improve transit time. For the first three days drink juices of any kind (except citrus) and take 1 teaspoon of high-fiber powder such as ground psyllium seed (Metamucil is fine) five times daily in a glass of water or apple juice. (The fiber in psyllium also reduces blood levels of cholesterol.) During the next two days, eat only fruits, vegetables, and juices, and have a fiber drink three times daily. Always follow the fiber drink with a second glass of water only. On the sixth day, return to your regular health and eating regimen continuing the fiber drink three times daily for another week. Drink additional water (as much as three quarts daily) throughout the regimen.

Enemas

Plain, warm water enemas are the best to empty the lower bowel. If there is a little inflammation or irritation, add flaxseed tea (½ pint), to the enema water. If the flaxseed tea is very thick and heavy, dilute with additional warm water. The knee-chest position is the best, on the average, for taking enemas.

Colemas are bowel-cleansing procedures more thorough than enemas but not as risky as colonics. A special board with a hole at one end and a splashboard fits over a toilet while the other end rests on a chair. A five-gallon bucket is placed on a tall stool, and surgical tubing carries water into the bowel via a narrow diameter plastic insert in the rectum. Five gallons of water are run into and out of the bowel, flushing out fecal wastes, and so forth, and bringing chlorophyll or coffee water to cleanse the bowel walls. While the client lies on his back, water provides deep cleansing, filling a portion of the bowel with the chlorophyll water or the coffee water. The fecal debris and water empty into the toilet.

CHAPTER 16

NATURAL REMEDIES

W hen we consider high-level wellness for the body, the first thing we have to realize is that the body needs nutrients for every different kind of cell. Each cell has own nutritional requirements. They must have different minerals to express differently. A liver cell does not perform the same work as the cell in the prostate gland. The bone cells do not do the same things as the blood cells. Each part of our body is fed according to the "master plan" for mineral and vitamin requirements that is built into these different tissues, perhaps in the cellular DNA.

DISEASES AND REMEDIES

There seems to be thousands of natural remedies for the various known diseases! In the prescription drug system, we have many thousands of prescription and over-the-counter drugs. This is not counting all the remedies we have now for the different diseases in other systems of healing such as aromatherapy, polarity therapy, acupuncture, homeopathy, and so on. In the realm of mechanical treatments, people have been punched, pulled, massaged, and squeezed to a point where every part of the body has been manipulated in every possible way we can think of.

But treatment in itself is not the cure. It is not getting at the root of the trouble. For instance, if a person is living on a diet of coffee and doughnuts, he could receive every treatment under the sun and those treatments would do no more than manipulate a strung-out nerve structure and stimulate the circulation of an impoverished bloodstream. Treatments do not cure disease. Only food and right living will cure disease, or, in the case of the worst genetic dysfunctions, alleviate the symptoms.

ABNORMAL FOODS, ABNORMAL BODIES

Different food patterns produce different bodies. We can produce almost any kind of disease—from heart trouble (lack of magnesium and potassium) to diabetes (overuse of fatty foods, white sugar, and white flour). Diseases are produced from abnormal diets. It should be of paramount interest to everyone, therefore, to get foods that will rebuild and rejuvenate the body.

Natural medicines are found in our fruit and vegetable juices, including apricot, peach, tomato, and the greens of our vegetables. These foods contain vitamins and minerals. In the vitamins, we have highly specialized nutrients necessary to put minerals in their proper place and proper function. There are many things to consider besides food, but let us stay as close to good food as we possibly can. We know that sleep, good blood circulation, pleasurable walks, happiness, relief, relaxation, a proper philosophy, and right spiritual attitude are all necessary requirements if we are to have real health.

Our eating habits must also be good. We cannot eat at any old time and expect the bowels to carry on a rhythmic action for us, even with the best of foods. We must learn to eat slowly and chew our foods well.

A NATURAL BODY HANDLES ALL FOODS WELL

Consider what you are doing, especially if you are not well. A well person can take any natural food and find that it is neither too laxative or binding. A natural body handles all foods well. It is only the sensitive, run-down, irritable body that overreacts to laxative foods, such as prune juice and fig juice, while other foods—certain cheeses, milk, and blackberry juice—become constipating.

SODIUM TO STAY YOUNG

The youth element, sodium, is stored in the body mostly in the joints, and is the most important electrolyte. When a person says he is getting old or stiff, we know he is lacking sodium. There is such a thing as premature old age caused by a lack of sodium. Sodium is highest in okra, celery, and citrus fruits. People sick with an acid stomach do not tolerate citrus fruits well. Therefore, sodium in this fruit is of no use to them. They will need to get their sodium in other ways.

When a person has arthritis, hardening in the joints, or spurs on the spine, he needs sodium. Sodium is the dissolver. If sick blood is flowing through the body, it contaminates every cell, thereby making the cell sick. Sodium helps to prevent that; it keeps calcium from depositing on the walls of our arteries. When the joints become hard, if you put sodium into the body the calcium in the joints will be drawn back into solution and the joints will become limber again.

As an example, there was a little lady who came to me with her head down below her hips with arthritis of the spine. She had a double curvature with spurs on the vertebrae as large as her thumbnail. She had been told by a doctor that she was going to be in a wheelchair for the rest of her natural life. She came to me for help, and I increased her sodium intake and put her on a natural diet. In one year's time, this lady's spine straightened out; we later had a report from Magnolia Hospital in Long Beach, California, that there was no more arthritis of the spine.

Whey is high in sodium. The whey that we use in the office has one hundred times as much sodium as anything else you can use. Taking 1 teaspoon of this whey means taking something very vital. While I do not believe you can live on this, if you have cheated your body of sodium for years, you had better pay yourself back as quickly as possible. Goat whey can do it.

SILICON FOR THE NERVOUS SYSTEM

Silicon keeps the hair and skin from becoming dry. A person who is extremely tired and says that nothing interests him any more lacks silicon. A dancer has to have a lot of silicon in his body or he cannot dance. Silicon helps nerves transmit messages over the nervous system. If you do not have all your nerve tissue in good working order, you become slow. You cannot bend your fingers. You suffer fatigue. You have underactivity in every organ in the body. A tonic that each of us should have is oat straw tea; its homeopathic name is Avena Sativa.

When a horse has been working hard all day, he comes in fatigued and tired. We do not give him an injection for a pickup; we give him a tonic—oats. It is the finest thing that I know of for building up the body. Drinking a cup of oat straw tea revives the nervous system. We treat our horses better than we do our own bodies.

Horsetail tea is another herb tea high in silicon.

MANGANESE FOR THE BRAIN

Manganese is required by the nerve and brain systems. A lack of this element is one reason why some women do not have the ability to produce milk for their babies. Manganese is needed by the bones, pancreas, and enzymes involved in energy production. One of the best sources of manganese is Missouri black walnuts.

MAGNESIUM FOR THE BOWEL

Magnesium is a bowel element we all need. One of the foods highest in magnesium is yellow cornmeal. It is far better than white cornmeal. For many people, yellow cornmeal is better than wheat. Greens are rich in magnesium, which is one of the most important electrolytes in the body, also needed by the bones, heart, and kidneys (to prevent kidney stones).

HONEY FOR THE HEART

One of the finest tonics for the heart is plain white clover honey. Take it three times a day, 1 teaspoon in a glass of water. If you have heart trouble, your disturbance is on the left side of the body. The left side is the negative side. Carbohydrates, starches, and sugars are negative. Proteins are positive and must be used sparingly. If the left side is broken down and the negative factors are worn out, the best and quickest way to get this negative side rejuvenated is with honey and water. Brown rice is also an important negative food in support of the heart.

POTASSIUM FOR THE MUSCLES

Muscles could not function without potassium, second only to sodium as an important electrolyte. Potassium is a healing element, the same as sodium. We need a lot of potassium because our body is made up mainly of muscles, most importantly, the heart. Potassium is found in most of our greens, wild lettuce, dandelion greens, endive, and olives.

Probably one reason people do not have enough potassium is because vegetables containing lots of it are bitter to the taste. But we do need it. Take eight or ten dried olives, steep them in a teapot like a regular tea for about ten minutes, skim off the fat or oil that may have come to the top, and drink. This is a good potassium tea and does wonders for the heart and the muscle structure. Take dried olives and chew them, allowing the saliva to work on them and extract the potassium from them. This is a slow way to procure olive oil, and it is not particularly tasteful, but it is a fine way to get your potassium. Olives do more to revive tired muscle structures than a chocolate bar.

LECITHIN FOR BRAIN
AND NERVE ENERGY

Lecithin is a brain and nerve food. We should take it when we become tired and fatigued, when we lose our alertness and cannot respond readily and easily to suggestions, when we find a lack of memory. It is necessary to have lecithin in abundance before vitamin B can be held in the body. All the vitamin B that people are taking today does very little good if they don't have enough lecithin to retain it.

If we are using our brain and nervous system to the extreme, it is beneficial to take soy lecithin capsules for a short time. In a natural form, lecithin is found best in olives, egg yolk, and avocados. The olives should be ripe and sun-dried. This source of lecithin is better than any we can get in tablets. It takes nearly 1 quart of soybeans to make a dozen lecithin tablets. It is difficult to get all the lecithin your body needs in today's world. In our time, civilization demands more nerve and brain energy than ever before.

SALTS FOR THE FEET

The health stores sell "sea salt." If you use this in your foot baths, it may help tremendously. The foot bath will help break down uric acid crystals that have settled in the feet. Epsom salts (magnesium sulfate) are a wonderful aid for relaxation of the muscles in a nice hot bath, but they also make a refreshing foot bath. Barefoot walks in sand help to "massage" the feet and improve blood circulation.

IODINE FOR THE THYROID GLAND

The best way to get sufficient iodine to the thyroid gland where it is needed to make thyroid hormone is to use Nova Scotia dulse, Japanese Mori (edible kelp), clams or clam juice, or foods grown within a hundred miles of the ocean. I much prefer using natural food sources of iodine over getting it in iodized salt, an unnatural product.

The quickest way of getting iodine into the body is by drinking clam juice. Clam juice can be mixed with any of the vegetable juices. We can even make a little clam broth with warm milk. Take ½ cup of clam juice two or three times a week. This will help supply you with the iodine you need (also calcium, iron, magnesium, phosphorus, sodium, and potassium).

RAW FOODS

Live foods carry the germ of life in them, but the germ of life is usually destroyed when we cook, stew, boil, fry, and pressure them. We receive the greatest good from raw tonics and from raw foods or foods that require the least amount of heat in their preparation. If we live on crullers, dumplings, and doughnuts, we are going to have a very inactive body. For strength, youthfulness, and longevity, it is necessary that we have in our bodies the life-giving energies found in live foods.

The nutrients in raw foods must get into our bloodstream for vital energy. The life-building qualities of these nutrients is what is going to rebuild our bodies. To recharge our tired and failing batteries and bring the blush and bloom back to our cheeks, to have the charm of life and graciousness in our movements, it is necessary that we get all the vitamins and minerals back into our body that we burn out in everyday living. It is impossible to build a good body when we are forced to live on the nutritionally deficient flours that we have today. These devitalized foods do not have the nutrients necessary for body building. So many of our foods are not conducive to long life and good health.

The germ of life in food is depleted when we pasteurize milk, polish rice, and mill or bleach flour. When we look at these food-devitalizing processes in the commercial world today, we can definitely see how so many people become unable to live or work at their marriages by eating these lifeless foods.

A good thing to remember is the proportion of foods we should have in our everyday diets. We should eat four to six vegetables, two fruits, one starch, and one protein daily. Always get the most natural food, the food that is closest to what God made for us. Remember: Use simple combinations! When you are sick, take small meals; perhaps more meals a day, but at least a small amount at a time. A weak digestive system cannot handle a heavy meal. When babies come into this world, mothers give them a small meal many times a day.

Tracing the Cause of Sickness

In choosing tonics for the body, we must first consider what part of the body is affected, then look deeper. For instance, a person may have poor hearing, but it can come from a depleted nervous system, so they should use nerve tonics. Hearing may be depleted because of an excess amount of catarrh settled in the ears. For that, I would then advise catarrhal remedies.

DRIED FRUITS

Prunes, even though they are acid, are rich in vitamin A, potassium, and magnesium. Don't miss them. Most dried fruits have four to six times as much sugar as when fresh. This extra sugar is easy to assimilate and will provide more energy than fresh fruits.

I believe the apricot is the best of the dried fruits. It is higher than the others in vitamin A, iron, magnesium, and potassium, and has a little copper and iron as well. Dried fruits have less vitamin C per gram than fresh fruits, except for pears.

There is almost twice as much vitamin C in dried pears as ripe, raw pears.

FOOD ALLERGIES

The person who is almost always well has fewer allergies than the person who is often sick. I have tested this fact where allergies to certain foods existed. Patients are less likely to react to allergens when they have a healthy body. I might point out that food intolerances should not be confused with allergies. Lactose intolerance among milk drinkers causes symptoms because the person lacks lactase, the enzyme for breaking down lactose. Milk allergy, on the other hand, causes release of immunoglobulin E, which releases chemicals that cause hives and itching. There are foods to which people react with allergic symptoms because of a psychosomatic response, mimicking allergy, but involving no release of immunoglobulin E. There is, however, a very reliable way to sort out food allergens and intolerances.

Many people under my care who had extreme allergies or intolerances have successfully overcome their allergic reactions (or intolerances) by fasting. By introducing one food at a time after fasting, they can eliminate from their diets all foods that trigger allergic, or intolerance, reactions. After eliminating food allergens, however, they may still be allergic to camel hair or dust, and they may spend a great deal of effort trying to keep away from dust and the camel hair clothing.

People are more allergic with a poorly mineralized body than with a fully mineralized body. I believe that allergies have a lot to do with mineral deficiencies in the body; these may be adjusted through proper eating habits. Studies have shown that magnesium is often deficient in asthmatics and people with allergies.

It is foolish to include in allergy questionnaires whether or not regular vinegar is an allergen for you—or pepper, salt, white flour products, and many popular cereals. These things should never go into the human body anyway. We are all "allergic" to them.

Try to avoid the following foods when you have allergies: Wheat and anything made from wheat; all canned foods; all dairy products; citrus fruits (unless organically grown and tree ripened); all sugar and salt; all processed foods.

Also, watch for trouble from mattresses, wool, cleaning chemicals for the home, and dandruff or hair from cats and dogs.

PROTEINS

There are times when the body is going too slow and we need to speed it up. Food can do that. In my experience, proteins are very stimulating to the body; starches are more soothing. Many people have difficulty sleeping after eating too much protein before bedtime. The protein may influence the sleep-awake cycles established in the medulla of the brain. It is better to take proteins at noon and starches at night. We should have vegetables and a starch for the evening meal, especially vital vegetable drinks or vegetable salads, since they are very soothing to the nervous system and are conducive to sleep. Carbohydrates increase levels of serotonin, which aids in getting to sleep.

LEARN FROM YOUR AILMENTS

An ailment can be a blessing in disguise. Your ailment can be the best thing that ever happened to you; it may motivate you to change your lifestyle and do better. It may help you to grow and develop inwardly. Unless you continually develop and grow, you stagnate. When you have gone through a period of disturbance, irritation, or sickness, you seek peace, harmony, and health. Disease moves us to act and so do disturbances and dissatisfactions.

We have to consider ailments from the spiritual side. The spiritual "body" has to be fed just as your physical body does. We can actually "serve tonics" to the spiritual mind just as we serve tonics to the physical body. I believe that the person who is devoid of love is as ill as the person who lacks calcium in his body. The person with a calcium deficiency does not have the tone in his body and the power to accomplish the things he should do physically. The person who is without love is not well in his spiritual body and is handicapped in relationships to God and people.

We have a definite means for taking care of the spiritual body, just as we have definite means to care for the mental and physical bodies. There are things we must know and understand mentally in order to be in good mental health. We need to look at the three-fold man and work out tonics for all parts: physical, mental, and spiritual.

I look at our health problems with a multidimensional vision. Never look at the healing arts in one dimension only. The healing arts are made up of many systems. We have "mind healers," all kinds of physical healers: masseurs, chiropractors, osteopaths, medical men, surgeons—and there is a place for every one of them. I do believe that there is a big place for the chiropractor, and that he has the greatest scope of any branch of the healing arts. When chiropractors learn to incorporate balanced nutritional support into their approach to patient care, they will find that many more complete healings take place. No therapy can build new tissue unless it includes a nutritional component.

We must ascertain our greatest need. If we have trouble with those who are handling our finances, we may need an accountant or attorney, and he will prove to be the best doctor for the moment. When your doctor sends you to Arizona for your health, you should bring a complete healing program with you. It is not enough to just go and absorb the sunshine and get the benefit of the dry climate while you go on living on coffee and doughnuts.

Teaching a person to live correctly is far more important than any doctor's treatments. You must decide whether you want only temporary relief, or whether a visit to the right doctor is going to lead to the root of the problem and offer a solution. To get absolutely well, you must consider starting from the deepest spot within your body and cleanse and work outward, whether the problem is a boil on the outside or a boil on the inside.

We must realize that all foods are made up of many chemical elements that support different activities in the body. You may have seen magnesium flares used by policemen to direct traffic after an accident on the streets. When ignited, they flame brightly. Magnesium is one of the necessary chemical elements in our intestinal tract and is required by every cell of the body. It flares up in the body and creates good muscle tone and moves toxic material along. Other chemical elements may slow down the activity of our glands and muscles.

CHAPTER 17

KNOW YOUR LIQUIDS

I am often asked what kind of water is best. I don't know what a good water is, from a health standpoint. I don't think anyone does!

I can come to only a couple of conclusions as far as water is concerned. All the old men I've met in my worldwide travels used highly mineralized mountain water, and they lived (the last one I saw was 153 years old) without arthritis. No one was there to measure the water to see how much of each mineral was in the water, and they didn't, in their ignorance, care. They were long lived, and they were healthy.

HOW MUCH SHOULD WE DRINK?

We should all drink at least 2 quarts of water daily, regardless of how much juice or herbal tea we may be taking in. On hot days, we should drink 3 or more quarts, depending on the activity level. The color of the urine is a good indicator of sufficient water intake. It should be light or clear. Otherwise, we are not eliminating toxins properly.

We hear of people curing themselves of some ailment by drinking carrot juice or grape juice or going on a water fast. What was responsible for the cure? Was it the grape juice or the carrot juice or the water? I don't think so. I think the cure came from the body taking a vacation from food. I believe *that* cures.

WATER REMEDIES

Sitz Baths

Water should come up five inches on the body. The feet should never be in the water. The baths are only for the pelvis and pelvic organs. This is wonderful for congestion in the pelvis and sluggish bowels. These baths are best taken in the evening just before going to bed. However, they can be taken the first thing in the morning before going to work.

The cold sitz bath is an effective, though violent way of stopping bedwetting. Take cold water and sit in it four to five minutes every morning before going to school or before beginning your daily program or routine. This will help with bladder and prostate problems in general. A gentler approach is to take two sitz baths every morning. The first for one minute, hot; the second for one-half minute, cold. Do this for five changes, going from one to the other. The treatment should continue for a period of three months.

Foot Baths

Alternate, five times, one minute hot, one-half minute cold.

WATER FACTS

Did you know water softeners are not purifiers? They do not kill bacteria or take out organic impurities. They "do" add sodium to the water in exchange for calcium and other minerals, so no one on a sodium-free or restricted diet should drink "soft water." Soft water has also been related to heartbeat irregularity and heart attacks.

Did you know that distilled water is a perishable product and should be consumed in two or three days? The container should be tightly closed immediately after distilling and stored or refrigerated. Before using the stored water, shake the container several times to oxygenate the water.

Our government, scientists, newspapers, television networks, radio stations, and magazines are constantly warning us about the extreme hazards of water pollution. Our sources of water supply, such as rivers, lakes, and streams, are becoming polluted with poisonous chemicals, insecticides, pesticides, sewage, mercury, cadmium, lead, harmful bacteria, viruses, and other sources of waterborne diseases. Small, rural water systems serving less than 10,000 people are especially impacted by pollution, and these constitute 94 percent of the total number of public water systems. In California, during a recent year, one-third of all rural systems contained illegal bacterial contamination, while in Pennsylvania, 90 percent of rural systems were in violation of pollution regulations. Current research is seeking cost-effective means of filtering out microorganisms such as cryptosporidium, giardia, and viruses.

Some interesting and little known facts about water are told by Anthony Smith in his book, *The Body.* He writes:

> An average human being doing light work in a temperate climate loses nearly five pints of water a day—and must replace it.
>
> He can take in six-tenths of a pint at each meal without drinking at all because about half of ordinary food is water.
>
> A man at rest is losing over half an ounce of water through his skin every hour.

The maximum possible daily loss and replacement of water ever recorded was about fifty pints.

A 156-pound man possesses seventy to eighty pints of water within his frame, and about half of the water will have been lost and replaced every ten days.

A woman has less water within her than a man of equal weight.

Even under ideal conditions, a man without food or water will die when he loses 15 percent of his body weight, usually within ten days. With water, he can survive for two months!

With water but no food, a 168-pound man can drop to less than eighty-four pounds and still live.

Without any water, he'll be dead well before he has reached even 140 pounds.

THE WONDERS OF RAW VEGETABLE JUICES

There has been much in the media about vegetable juices, and I believe much good can be done through their use. In order to get the minerals in their original ionized, electrical form, it is necessary to separate the vegetable juice from the cellulose that makes up much of the vegetable structure. When this is done, the fresh raw juice should be taken as soon as possible to get the most good from it. We find that a wonderful change for the better is seen in our bodies. To meet all the body's vitamin and mineral needs, a variety of juices should be used.

While I was visiting the Bircher-Benner Sanitarium in Zurich, Switzerland, I was shown one of the first juicers ever made, consisting of a motor, a grinder, and a pressing machine that old Dr. Benner had improvised many years ago. Before juicing machines came into their present-day use, vegetables were chopped finely, the leaves cut crosswise through the veins and arteries to get the bleeding liquid from the leaf structure;

then they were soaked in distilled water for three to four hours, then squeezed to extract as much juice as possible. Originally, the juice was used with wonderful results for asthma and many other bronchial and catarrhal conditions.

Proper rest and the use of raw vegetable-derived minerals will go far toward rebuilding the body. Many doctors are using juices along with nutritional therapy and rest to help their patients get well. If a doctor knows his foods, he can vary the juices to help the various systems in the body.

The body systems can be flooded quickly with raw fruit and vegetable juices which will provide all the needed vitamins and minerals. Fruit juices stir up the toxins and metabolic wastes in the body and bring them quickly to the various organs of elimination. Quicker healing will take place when minerals in solution get into the bloodstream.

We can see an example of the benefits of vegetable juices by discussing carrot juice. Infectious conditions of the body respond to the use of carrot juice, since it is very high in vitamin A. The orange color of carrot juice is from carotene, a pro-vitamin A that is not always broken down well by the liver cells. Extensive use of carrot juice may impart an odd color to the skin, but this is harmless. Eyes benefit by the use of carrot juice, but not all eye problems are helped by it. We think of carrot juice for sties, inflammation of the eyes (especially when there is catarrhal elimination from the eyes), or loss of night vision.

If we cannot adjust our eyes well from a bright light to dim light, in a theater for instance, it is a sign we can use more vitamin A. Night blindness, or a glare blindness from auto lights, shows a lack of vitamin A. Many accidents could be prevented if those who are thus afflicted would use more vitamin A. Vitamin A is exceptionally good in all the tissues needing fortification against infection. All mucous membranes in the body need a large amount of this vitamin. A lack of vitamin A can affect the bladder, the kidneys, the alimentary tract, the mouth, the tonsils, the tongue, the tear ducts, and the eyes. Many nursing children can be given carrot juice during the weaning process. I recommend a combination of carrot juice and milk, which makes a fine weaning formula for children three to four months old.

Nursing mothers should drink plenty of carrot juice, since it is also high in calcium, which helps build resistance to infections. One 6-ounce glass of carrot juice will provide nearly 50,000 IU of vitamin A, which is ten times the daily requirement.

The Food and Nutrition Committee of the National Research Council has established a scale for the minimum daily requirement of vitamin A as follows:

Infants	1,500 IU
Children under four years	2,500 IU
Children over four and adults	5,000 IU
Women during pregnancy and lactation	8,000 IU

There are many tasty juice combinations your family will enjoy. Carrot juice and apple juice make a wonderful cocktail. Mint may be added for flavoring. Carrot juice can be made into ice cream. Vegetable juices can be made into aspic salads and gelatin molds. Many vegetable juices can be used as a base in liquefying your combined health foods. Use vegetable juices in cooking instead of water. Some good juice combinations for health in general are carrot and comfrey juice, or beet, comfrey, and pineapple juice. Carrot, soybean, and carob make a flavorful juice. Carrot juice with flaxseed tea helps an inflamed condition of the bowel. We use a lot of celery juice, sometimes adding a little parsley. All vegetable juices should be used within two or three hours after they have been extracted from the vegetables.

It has been said that many juices have a special therapeutic value because of the ease of their digestion and assimilation. I believe that the greatest value comes in the fact that the crystalloid minerals in these vegetables can be absorbed very quickly, with very little digestion. Crystalloid minerals dissolve immediately in liquid and can be assimilated right away. Furthermore, I believe that because juices fill the stomach for the moment, they diminish the appetite for heavy foods that are not as easily digested. Vegetable juices give the digestive system a rest. Two or three glasses a day can be taken in an ordinary diet regimen; however, 2 or 3 quarts a day can be used for cleaning the intestinal tract or for getting rid of mucus or catarrhal problems in the body.

Raw juices can be considered an internal bath. They tend to cleanse and wash the tissues, revitalizing the organs of the body. We need fluids to carry away waste material and bring the various nutrients to the tissues. Minerals from juices enter the bloodstream in thirty minutes. (Never use canned juices.)

Going a day, two days, even three days on raw vegetable juices is one of the finest rejuvenating methods there is for developing a new body and cleansing the old one. It is good to take teas often during a juice diet. Shavegrass tea is one of the finest cleansing teas we have, and it also helps to supply the body with the proper amount of silicon. Three or four cups should be taken each day.

Use fruit juices sparingly. Fruit juices stir up toxins that must then be carried off by the eliminative organs. Citrus juices are the worst offenders in this regard. For relaxation, use vegetable juices.

None of the juices offers specific relief for any one disease. In fact, I do not believe in treating a disease or any one organ that may be the source of symptoms. When we have an illness of any kind, it affects the whole body. My approach, following the nature cure program, is to strengthen the whole body, to cleanse the whole body, so that all organ systems lift and strengthen and support the part of the body afflicted by disease or dysfunction. The whole body is involved in the healing process.

During a fast, avoid having too many other kinds of treatments. I believe that they interfere with the vital energies of the body. Enemas are the only adjunct we should use in addition to fasting measures. Fasting is a matter of physical rest, psychological rest, and spiritual rest. Fasting requires *resting* to get its full benefit.

Celery and prune juice together are said to be good for the nervous system. Celery juice contains sodium for neutralizing acidic toxins. You may use head lettuce juice to promote sleep. Beet juice is very good in helping the bile flow more freely through the gall duct. Adding extra parsley to the juices helps the kidneys. A blend of celery and carrot juices is very good for dissolving stones in the gallbladder or the kidneys or any hardness in the joints. The slickage found in comfrey juice is very good for colitis, inflammation of the bowel, and mucosa in the walls of the stomach. One teaspoon of lemon juice five minutes before meals is a good appetite tonic.

Alfalfa juice is the most alkaline of all the juices. Green juices are great blood builders, since they contain chlorophyll, iron, magnesium, and potassium. A balance of vegetable juices is good.

Cucumber juice with whey is high in sodium and is a very cooling drink for the blood. It is also very good in high blood pressure cases. Watermelon and cantaloupe juices are also good cooling summer drinks.

Many times diarrhea is experienced while taking vegetable juices. In most cases, it is normal and necessary, as nature is doing a little housecleaning. To bathe the tissues in your body with these juices will, in time, cleanse them and then rebuild, rejuvenate, and feed a starved body.

Most people lose weight when taking juices. However, in making a new body, you must sometimes lose weight in order to rebuild.

Make your vegetable cocktails in proportions pleasing to the taste. Usually any juice mixed with an equal proportion of another juice will be about right. However, when you mix fruit juices with vegetable juices, such as pineapple and tomato, it is best not to mix them with starches. Acid fruits and starches do not combine. Vegetable juices go best with starches, and all starches should have vegetable juices with them.

There are many combinations of health cocktails you can make. A bitter green taste can be made palatable by adding sweet vegetables, honey, pineapple juice, coconut milk, a little sweet cream, or concentrated juices such as grape and apple.

Cabbage Juice Considered Ulcer Cure

Drinking a quart of cabbage juice daily has proved the fastest natural cure for uncomplicated peptic ulcers. It isn't the easiest way to go because cabbage juice is strong-flavored and far from pleasant. Peptic ulcers are caused by bacteria named *Helicobacter pylori* (or *H. pylori*). In 1996, it was discovered that the antibiotic Biaxin would destroy *H. pylori*. Unfortunately, like all antibiotics, Biaxin destroys beneficial bowel bacteria along with the ulcer-causing bacteria. I recommend the cabbage juice approach. Mix it with carrot juice to improve the taste. The fresh cabbage juice ulcer cure was reported by Dr. Garnett Cheney, San Francisco, in 1949. The cabbage juice cure for stomach ulcers has been confirmed by many doctors all over the world.

HEALTH COCKTAILS

Many disorders of the body can best be aided by using a vegetable cocktail or combination of juices as directed (see Table 17.1). Nearly every disorder responds quicker by adding vegetable juices. Celery, parsley, and carrot juices are good for any condition. They can be mixed any way or can be used alone. The juices suggested for a specific body disorder may be used separately or in combination with each other.

MILK SUBSTITUTE DRINKS

The proper diet must be considered, since everything that goes into the mouth should be a remedy. If it does not nourish the body, it is not a remedy. Nutrition begins with blood building, and the most vital thing in this connection is a diet with the proper amount of protein. Also, we must have nerve fats such as found in egg yolks, nuts, nut butters, and seeds of all kinds. When you want to rebuild the body, think of seeds. All the elements of the mature plant are represented in the seed. There are many ways these can be used in the form of milk substitute

Table 17.1. Suggested Cocktails for Specific Disorders

Disorders	*Cocktail*
Anemia	Blackberry and parsley juice; parsley and grape juice
Arthritis	Celery and parsley juice
Asthma	Celery and papaya juice; celery, endive, and carrot juice
Bedwetting	Celery and parsley juice
Bladder ailments	Celery and pomegranate juice. Pomegranate juice is the best for the bladder. Also, shave-grass herb tea
Blood ailments	Blackberry juice, black cherry juice, parsley juice, dandelion juice. Tomato juice and desiccated liver
Blood pressure (high)	Carrot, parsley, and celery juice; lime juice and whey powder; grape juice and carrot juice
Blood pressure (low)	Parsley juice, also capsicum and garlic
Bronchitis	Juice of 2 lemons, 3 tablespoons honey to 1 pint of flaxseed tea. Use 1 teaspoon every hour. Or bake a lemon, juice one-half of it, and add to 1 cup of oat straw or boneset tea; then go to bed and perspire
Cararrh, colds, sore throat	Watercress and apple juice with ¼ teaspoon pure cream of tartar
Circulation (poor)	Beet and blackberry juice; parsley and alfalfa juice with pineapple juice; grape juice with 1 egg yolk

(Continued)

Table 17.1. **Continued**

Disorders	Cocktail
Colds and sinus	Celery and grapefruit juice; watercress and apple juice with ¼ teaspoon pure cream of tartar; coconut milk and carrot juice; celery and grapefruit juice with ¼ teaspoon cream of tartar
Colitis, gastritis, gas	Coconut milk and carrot juice
Complexion (yellow)	Grapefruit juice
Complexion problems	Cucumber, endive, and pineapple juice; 1 tablespoon apple concentrate, ½ glass cucumber juice, and ½ glass water
Constipation, stomach ulcers	Celery with a little sweet cream; spinach and grapefruit, cabbage juice (1 quart daily)
Diarrhea, infection	Carrot and blackberry juice
Eczema, scurvy	Carrot, celery, and lemon juice
Fever, gout, arthritis	Celery and parsley juice
Gallbladder	Radish, prune, black cherry, and celery juice; carrot, beetroot, and cucumber juice; prune, black cherry, celery, and radish juice
Gallstones	Beetroot and radish juice; green vegetable juices
Glands (for building)	Pineapple juice with 1 egg yolk, 1 tablespoon wheat germ, ¼ teaspoon powdered Nova Scotia dulse—take daily between meals; ¾ cup carrot juice, ¼ cup coconut milk, 1 tablespoon wheat germ, 1 teaspoon rice polishings or rice bran syrup, 1 cup tomato juice, 1 tablespoon cod roe

Disorders	Cocktail
Glands and nerves	1 tablespoon cherry concentrate, 1 teaspoon chlorophyll, and 1 egg yolk
Glands, goiter, impotence	Celery juice, 1 teaspoon wheat germ, and 1 teaspoon Nova Scotia dulse
General house-cleaning	Celery, parsley, spinach, and carrot juice
Gout	Celery juice; combination of celery and parsley juice
Heart	Carrot and pineapple juice with honey; liquid chlorophyll (alfalfa); parsley, alfalfa, and pineapple juice
Hair (to improve)	1 tablespoon cherry concentrate, 1 teaspoon oat straw tea to a cup of boiling water, steep 10 minutes then add cherry concentrate
Indigestion, underweight	Coconut milk, fig juice, parsley, and carrot juice
Infections	Carrot and blackberry juice
Insomnia (sleeplessness)	Lettuce and celery juice
Jaundice	Tomato and sauerkraut juice; 1 glass every day for a week.
Kidneys	Celery, parsley, and asparagus juice; carrot and parsley juice
Kidneys (bladder problems)	Black currant juice with juniper berry tea; pomegranate juice and goat's whey; celery and pomegranate juice
Liver	Radish and pineapple juice; black cherry concentrate and chlorophyll; carrot, beet, and cucumber juice

(Continued)

Table 17.1. **Continued**

Disorders	Cocktail
Memory (poor)	Celery, carrot, and prune juice and rice polishings
Nerve tension	Celery, carrot, and prune juice; lettuce and tomato juice
Nervous disorders	Radish and prune juice and rice polishings
Neuralgia, neuritis	Cucumber, endive, and pineapple juice; cucumber, endive, and goat's whey
Overweight, obesity	Beet greens, parsley, and celery juice
Perspiration	Celery and prune juice; cucumber and pineapple juice
Rheumatism	Cucumber, endive, and goat's whey
Rickets	Dandelion and orange juice
Sinus	Sip lemon juice with a little horseradish; sip mixture of cayenne powder in a cup of water
Teeth (poor)	Beet greens, parsley, and celery juice with green kale
Thyroid	Clam juice with celery juice
Vitality (to increase)	1 tablespoon apple concentrate, 1 tablespoon almond nut butter, and 1 cup celery juice
Weight (reducing)	Parsley, grape juice, and pineapple juice
Youth (retaining)	⅔ cup oat straw tea, ⅓ cup celery, prune, or fig juice with ¼ powdered Nova Scotia dulse to each cup cucumber, radish, pepper (⅓ cup each); ⅔ cup Concord grape juice and ⅓ cup pineapple juice, with 1 egg yolk

drinks. There are five basic types: soy, sunflower, sesame, rice, and nut milks. Soy milk can be made from soy milk powder or commercial brands may be purchased at your health food store or supermarket. Sunflower seed, sesame seed, and nut milks, such as almond and cashew, are easily made by putting the seed in water, liquefying it, and straining it, as necessary. Rice milk can be bought at most health food stores. Tahini, nut butters, or sunflower seed meal may even be blended with an egg beater and made into a satisfactory drink. Add flavorings, such as cherry and apple concentrate, dates, and carob powder, to your substitute milk drinks as desired. Honey makes a good sweetener. Instead of water, try herb teas or soy milk as a base. These drinks we call catarrhal-eliminating drinks.

Many people don't realize that catarrh can be produced from cow's milk, mainly because of the difference between the milk's chemical structure and the body's needs. The body has to take care of this improper balance, reacting to the irritation from chemical substances in milk by producing catarrh. Following are some substitutes to help you avoid that problem, including a recipe for my preferred drink.

Doctor Jensen's Drink

1 tablespoon of any good brand of sesame seed meal or butter
1 glass liquid (may be fruit juice, vegetable juice, soy milk, rice milk, broth, or water)
¼ avocado
1 teaspoon honey

Blend 30 seconds.

Sesame Seed Milk

Seeds and sprouts are going to be the foods of the future. We have found that some of the seeds carry the hormone values of male glands or female glands. Seeds carry the living germ for many years, often as long as they are enclosed by the hull. Seeds found in tombs, and known to have been there for thousands of years, have grown when planted. To get the nutritional values of these seeds into our body in the form of a drink gives us the finest form of nutrition.

For sesame seed milk, take ¼ cup hulled sesame seeds to 2 cups water, raw goat's milk, or soy milk. Place in blender and run for one and one-half minutes.

Add 1 tablespoon carob powder and six to eight dates. For flavor or added nutritional value, any one of the following may be added to this drink: banana, stewed raisins, apple or cherry concentrate, date powder, or grape sugar. Your own imagination or taste may dictate other combinations of fruits or juices. Whenever adding anything, run through blender again to mix. This milk may also be used as the basis for salad dressings.

I believe that sesame seed milk is great. It is a wonderful drink for gaining weight and for lubricating the intestinal tract. Its nutritional value is beyond compare since it is high in protein and minerals. This is the seed used in the making of tahini, a sesame seed oil dressing. This also is the seed that is used so much in the Middle East and India.

Almond Nut Milk

Use blanched or unblanched almonds. Other nuts may be used also. Soak nuts overnight in apple or pineapple juice or honey water. This softens the structure of the nut meats. Then put 3 ounces of soaked nuts in 5 ounces water and blend for two to two and one-half minutes in the liquefier. Flavor with honey, any kind of fruit, concentrates of apple or cherry juice, strawberry juice, carob flour, dates, or bananas. Or it can be used with any of the vegetable juices.

Almond nut milk can also be used with soups and vegetarian roasts as a flavoring. Use over cereals, too.

Almond milk makes a very alkaline drink, high in protein and easy to assimilate.

Sunflower Seed Milk

Sunflower seeds are the vegetarian's best protein. The same principle as used for making nut milks can be employed to make sunflower seed milk: soaking overnight, liquefying, and flavoring with fruits and juices. Use in the diet the same way as the almond nut milk. It is best to use whole sunflower seeds and blend them yourself. However, if you do not have a liquefier, the sunflower seed meal can be used. Use hulled raw seeds.

Soy Milk

Soy milk powder is found universally in health food stores.

Add 4 tablespoons of soy milk powder to 1 pint of water. Sweeten with a raw sugar, honey, or molasses, and add a pinch of vegetable salt. For flavor, you can add any kind of fruit, apple or cherry concentrate, carob powder, dates, or bananas. You can add any other natural sweetener.

Keep in refrigerator. Use this milk in recipes just as you would regular cow's milk. It closely resembles the taste and composition of cow's milk and will sour just as quickly. Therefore, it should not be made in too large quantities or too far ahead of time.

If you bathe the tissues of your body by taking these juices, you will in time cleanse them, and then rebuild, rejuvenate, and feed a starved body. Don't get the idea you should live on them entirely. Take them with meals and between meals. For the best results, drink at least 1 pint a day.

THE BENEFITS OF BLENDING

The liquefier has been a godsend in the health drink field. Now we can blend delectable beverages from natural ingredients, often incorporating supplementary foods such as rice polishings, dulse, yeast, sunflower seeds, flaxseeds, and wheat germ. We can now make a drink that will pass the critical taste of even a child. Whole fruits and vegetables can be liquefied, as can whole melons, with the seed hulls strained out afterward.

If you have tooth or gum discomfort or a chewing disability, it may be better to take your meal in liquid form. There are drinks for those who need to stress the protein side of their nutrition, others with a starch nature.

All of our health drinks are suitable for children, but some will appeal more than others. Delicious milks, milk shakes, and eggnogs can be made from genuine ingredients.

Although a program dedicated to health has no place for coffee, tea, or cocoa, their fans are not left completely comfortless. We dare not suggest that any coffee substitutes can pass undetected, but our "coffee taste" drinks are thoroughly enjoyable as well as nutritious; herb teas can be zipped up with lemon and honey, and the delicious carob makes a drink that amazes chocolate connoisseurs.

Here are a few "dressed up" drinks for that special party or dinner. Try one the next time you entertain.

ALFA-MINT TEA

1 tablespoon Alfa-mint
1 cup boiling water

Steep 5 minutes. Sweeten with honey if desired, and serve with a wedge of lemon.

"ICED" TEA

1 tablespoon peppermint
1 cup boiling water
1 tablespoon honey
1 tablespoon orange juice

Mix peppermint in boiling water and steep 5 minutes. Add honey and juice. Pour over ice cubes in a tall glass and garnish with mint leaves.

BROTHS AND SOUPS FOR SPECIFIC CONDITIONS

The following broths and soups can be used at any time, since they are made of nutritious basic foods. However, when your body needs to be revitalized or needs to overcome some special disorders, you may add these broths to your meals. In specific cases, these broths may be taken between meals. These, as all foods, should be prepared and cooked in glass, stainless steel, enamelware, or earthenware.

Veal Joint Broth

Rich in sodium. Excellent for glands, stomach, ligaments, and digestive disorders. Helps to retain youth in the body.

VEAL JOINT BROTH

1 fresh, uncut veal joint
1½ cups apple peelings,
   ½ inch thick
2 cups potato peelings,
   ½ inch thick
1 small stalk of celery, chopped
½ cup of fresh and frozen okra
   or 1 teaspoon powdered okra

1 large parsnip, chopped
1 onion, chopped
2 beets, grated
½ cup parsley, chopped

In a large pot, place all ingredients and cover half with water. Simmer for 4 or 5 hours. Strain off liquid and discard solid ingredients. It should yield about ½ quart liquid. Drink hot or warm. Keep in refrigerator.

Vital Broth

This wonderful broth is excellent for elimination and is an important part of the Eleven-Day Elimination Regimen discussed in chapter 20.

VITAL BROTH

2 cups carrot tops
3 cups celery stalks
2 cups beet tops
1 teaspoon vegetable broth powder
2 cups potato peelings, ½ inch thick

2 cups celery tops
2 quarts distilled water
Add a carrot or onion for flavor
   if desired

Finely chop or grate vegetables. Bring slowly to a boil. Reduce heat and simmer approximately 20 minutes. Just use broth, after straining. Take 1 cup twice daily.

Fish Broth

Excellent for the nervous system and nerve tissue. It is rich in iodine and phosphorus. (Use only when directed.)

Remove bones from fish, including head, and boil for thirty minutes in parchment paper. Add vegetized salt to taste. Use vitaminized salt, powdered celery, powdered chili, and powdered onions for a delectable flavor.

Potato Soup

Excellent for uric acid, kidney and stomach disorders, and mineral replacement.

Cut peelings of six potatoes ¾-inch thick and simmer twenty minutes to one-half hour in a covered kettle. Strain off the liquid and drink every two or three hours. Do not make it too strong in a convalescing diet. Celery may be added to change flavor if desired. Add powdered okra if the stomach is irritated.

Potassium Broth

Excellent for poor heart conditions and digestive disorders, for building muscle and skin, and for healing sores. Same directions as for Potato Soup with the following addition:

Steep twelve sun-dried olives for ten minutes in 1 pint of water. Strain though five or six thicknesses of cheesecloth to catch the oil, since it should not be in the remaining liquid that you drink. Add this to the potato broth if desired or flavor with celery juice.

Calcium Broth

Excellent for bone conditions, lack of tone, and transverse colon prolapsus. Needed in general throughout the structural system.

Grind eggshells or chicken bones to powder, using them separately or together. Use ½ cup of grindings to 2 quarts of water, bring to a boil and simmer thirty to sixty minutes. Strain and add raw celery juice to flavor. Drink one to two cups two or three times daily.

High Sodium/Potassium Broth

For high sodium broth use beets, celery, carrots, and turnips. For broths high in both sodium and potassium, try apple peelings, or better yet, the jelly from veal joints. This veal joint broth will do more for arthritis and rheumatism than all the other foods combined. The sodium that has been made from the gelatin of the bones of the animal is virtually the same as that found in the joints of the human body.

MORE VALUABLE
HEALTH- BUILDING TONICS

Oat straw tea is very high in silicon and can be made very pleasant by adding apple concentrate to sweeten.

Egg yolk contains natural lecithin, one of the finest brain and nerve fats. When added to green juices or cherry it will not upset the liver or cause intestinal distress. Lecithin keeps cholesterol in solution.

Avocado also contains natural lecithin, and a little may be added to the preceding drink. It can be used in soy milk, rice milk, or raw milk to fortify it with minerals.

A quick energy drink can be made from liquefied yogurt and persimmons. You can even use frozen persimmons. (Did you ever think of freezing them? Try it!)

Brain cocktail sounds interesting to anyone. For the brain-building side, grind some Missouri black walnut meats into powder and use a tablespoon of them in the drink. Black walnuts are considered high in manganese, a brain and nerve nutritional supplement.

Wheat germ is a wonderful item to add to our diet. It is high in vitamin E. It develops tone in our tissues, quickens our circulation, and the vitamin E is an antioxidant.

Carob flour is another fine addition and may be added to any of the juices. It is splendid for giving a chocolate-like flavoring to goat's milk, soy milk, and rice milk, nut milk, and seed milk drinks.

CLEANSING COCKTAIL

Carrot juice   *Parsley juice*
Celery juice   *Spinach juice*

Vary proportions to suit preference.

COMPLEXION COCKTAIL

Cucumber juice   *Pineapple juice*
Endive juice

Mix to taste.

CHLOROPHYLL WATER
(Internal Cleanser)

1 teaspoon liquid chlorophyll in a glass of water

This replaces fresh green juice.

JADE-ADE
(Cooling Summer Drink)

¼ cup cucumber juice   *¼ cup watercress juice*
¼ cup celery juice   *¼ cup tomato juice*
¼ cup parsley juice

Blend.

GREEN COCKTAIL
(Blood Builder)

1 cup mint tea   *1 tablespoon lemon juice*
½ cup young spinach   *½ teaspoon dulse powder*
½ cup yogurt   *A little honey*
1 teaspoon vegetable seasoning

Blend mint tea and spinach until fine. Add remaining ingredients and blend briefly to mix. Serve in a tall glass with a slice of lemon.

MIXED COCKTAIL
(Energy Pickup)

1 cup oat straw tea   *1 carrot, diced*
2 leaves comfrey   *3 to 4 dates, pitted*
1 tablespoon coconut powder

Blend in liquefier.

RADIANCE COCKTAIL
(Catarrh Cleanser)

1 teaspoon raw almond butter   *½ cup each of celery and orange juices.*

Whip.

YOUTH BLOOM COCKTAIL
(Liver Cleanser)

⅓ cup beet juice   *⅓ cup spinach juice*
*2 tablespoons blackberries
   to smooth cocktails*

Whip

MULBERRY COCKTAIL
(Urinary System)

1 cup fresh mulberries   *½ cup whey*

Blend.

WHOLE MELON COCKTAIL
(Energizer)

Juice one melon, skin, flesh, and seeds. Squeeze in a press or strain through a sieve to remove the seed hulls and coarse fiber. In this way, the chlorophyll from the skin and all the vital elements of the seeds are used.

BEET APPETIZER
(Liver Stimulant)

2 cups oat straw tea

1 tablespoon lemon juice

1 cup raw diced beets

Sprig of fresh mint.

¼ slice lemon

1 teaspoon vegetable seasoning

1 teaspoon honey

Blend until smooth.

APERITIF
(Thyroid Support)

1 glass tomato juice

1 tablespoon aged apple
  cider vinegar

1 teaspoon vegetable seasoning

Dash of dulse powder

Beat together and chill.

SPECIAL DRINKS

PROTEIN DRINK
(Tissue Repair)

1 cup acidophilus milk

1 tablespoon sunflower seed meal

1 egg

2 prunes, pitted, revived

Blend until smooth.

STARCH DRINK
(Energy Lift)

1 cup soy milk

¼ teaspoon dulse

Few drops pure vanilla

4 tablespoons cooked cereal

Honey to sweeten

Blend until smooth.

MEAL IN A DRINK
(Nutritional Support)

½ cup mint tea

1 cup apple juice

½ cup orange juice

1 pitted prune, revived

¾ cup cashew nuts

½ cup carrots, diced

½ celery stalk

2 sprigs parsley

2 comfrey leaves

½ cup fresh fruit

½ ripe banana

1 egg

2 teaspoons wheat germ

Blend for 3 minutes. Sip very slowly.

HERCULES PUNCH
(Strength/Energy)

½ cup apple juice

1 teaspoon wheat germ oil

2 tablets oyster shell

1 teaspoon skim milk powder

½ cup papaya juice

1 teaspoon lecithin granules

1 teaspoon brewers yeast

Blend until smooth.

NERVE VERVE
(Nerve Support)

1 cup prune juice

2 teaspoons rice polishings

6 radishes

Blend in liquefier.

VITALITY DRINK
(Kidney Cleanse)

1 tablespoon apple concentrate

1 cup celery juice

1 tablespoon almond nut butter

Blend in liquefier.

CHAPTER 18

ALL ABOUT FOODS

We should learn more of the *universal* sciences that surround us. Sea foods—including the various kelps—contain iodine, as well as sodium, magnesium, and many other minerals. We should know what foods are available from the sea and what foods are available from the land. We should know soil types and how to replenish depleted soil. We cannot study agriculture from only one point of view. Foods can only be as nutrient-rich as the soils that support them.

We must learn that we cannot use drugs or any treatment that will compromise future health by leaving toxic residues in the body. Nature has the upper hand when it comes to healing. Let's see that she has a "free" hand.

God has given us food to meet every need of the body. It is up to us to learn these different food categories and how we can remedy specific conditions by specific foods. We have to learn the best ways to prepare these foods and cook them in such a way as to leave as much food value as possible. All vegetables should be slightly undercooked.

What a blessing it would be to us to learn to use highly nutritious foods, get plenty of rest, lots of fresh air, and just enough sunshine every day. It is foolish to live in a way that compromises our health.

Of course, the first bottle of soda pop is not going to harm us. The first cigarette isn't going to produce cancer. It isn't the eating of any one food that produces a disease any more than the first drop of water will wear away a stone. It is the continuation thereafter that does the damage. Too much fried food, too many dumplings, condiments, or processed foods wear away the good in our bodies.

Some years ago I visited a mental institution. I saw patients served fried foods, mashed potatoes, and gelatin made of white sugar, artificial flavoring, and colored with an extract of coal tar. Is there a relationship between poor nutrition and mental health?

In the 1999 Surgeon General's Report on Mental Health, it is claimed that, "This report recognizes the inextricably intertwined relationship between our mental health and our physical health and well-being." Yet, after going over this nearly 500-page report, I found the subject of nutrition was conspicuous by its absence. It is my understanding that neither good physical health nor good mental health is possible when nutritional principles are misunderstood or ignored.

Yet, the Surgeon General's Report states that "21 percent of children ages nine to seventeen receive mental health services in a year," and "15 percent of the adult population use some form of mental health services in a year." The report predicts that "Disability due to mental illness in individuals over sixty-five years old will become a major health problem in the near future . . . In particular, dementia, depression, and schizophrenia, among other conditions, will all present special problems in this age group." It seems that overall costs of mental health care in 1999 were well "over one hundred billion dollars, and yet prevention or treatment by nutrition was apparently neglected. If better nutrition only helped 10 percent of all persons using mental health facilities in 1999, it would have saved ten billion dollars and greatly improved the quality of life for millions of persons.

What we eat can make a tremendous difference in how we experience life and how we cope with problems and relationships. We all need to know our foods and how they contribute to health and well being.

FOODS THAT SERVE A PURPOSE

Almond Nut Butter. A teaspoon of finely ground almond nut butter is good to add to a drink or a small piece of cheese. Proteins of this kind are digested better in these combinations and make good tissue builders. Nut butters and seed butters can be made from any nuts or seeds.

Many people are thin because they consume more juices than solid food. They are on too much of an eliminative diet. Add a little protein to your juices or fruit to hold your weight. Dried prunes that have been "revived" contain one of the most wonderful nerve salts available; it acts as a laxative and can be added to celery juice or whey for greater laxative qualities. Liquefy if possible. Papaya is good in a laxative drink and is a drink noted for its effect on the digestion.

Celery Juice. This makes what I like to term a "dissolving cocktail." It keeps calcium out of the joints or from forming stones. Celery juice is one of the finest food dissolvers we can introduce into the body. Using it with a tablespoon of plain gelatin is wonderful for the joints. This is a high-sodium cocktail and is also a protein cocktail. Another terrific drink is celery juice and whey. It is a cooling drink for that hot summer day.

Bananas. These are a good building food. Thin people can add a little banana or dried fruit or a little soybean meal to the juices to avoid reducing. For those wishing to reduce, this fruit should be omitted.

Gelatin. A good protein to use is gelatin, and it is recommended in a molded form, not in a concentrated powdered form. This gives few calories and at the same time tends to fill the stomach and remove any feeling of hunger. Gelatin can be made with tomato, grapefruit, or apple juice. No sweetening, please.

Sesame Seed. Sesame seed drinks are wonderful for constipation and for lubricating the bowel. Combine a half cup of sesame seed with one cup of water; put in liquefier and run for about two minutes. Remove and strain out the hulls. This uses the inside of the seed, which carries the oil. Hulled raw sesame seeds are available at most health food stores. The oil carries the lubricating qualities of the sesame seed. Anything else can be added as desired in the liquefied drink: fruits, bananas, pineapple juices, dates, or others.

Pomegranate Juice. This is good for bladder disturbances.

FOOD AS MEDICINE

Let us look to natural remedies for the relief of many small ills. Here is a list of some foods that can be used, and their values and remedial qualities. Palliative drugs have the power of giving temporary relief from pain and may even reduce the suffering caused from nutritional starvation—but it is food alone that contains the necessary elements to restore a normal condition. All vegetables contain a little of nearly all B-complex vitamins, except B_{12}, as well as potassium and sodium.

Artichokes. The Jerusalem artichoke supplies 10 percent of the iron and vitamin C we need but otherwise does not have much nutritional value. It is one food, however, that diabetic people can take because it contains a natural insulin. To use Jerusalem artichokes as a remedy for diabetes wouldn't be the proper thing to do, but all those who have a pancreatic weakness can handle them much easier than they can potatoes, either white or sweet. I know of no other starch that is better for the body.

Asparagus. This is a wonderful fiber food, high in chlorophyll. One-half cup contains 20 percent of the RDA for folic acid. The best way to eat it is to break it off right from an asparagus bed in the garden and eat it *raw.* It tastes better, however, if you steam it.

Beet Greens. These greens contain oxalic acid (not so much as spinach and Swiss chard), a little vitamin C, and quite a bit of vitamin A. Use them raw in salads or steamed. The stems contain more iron than the leaves. They are also good for cooking: To prevent burning of food cooked in stainless steel pans, place raw beet leaves in the bottom of the pan.

Broccoli. This winter vegetable is high in sulfur and vitamin A, and contains a little folic acid. Half a cup provides about 90 percent of the vitamin C we need. If you don't want it to produce intestinal gas, steam it in parchment paper or eat it *raw*.

Brussels Sprouts, Cabbage, and Cauliflower. These are good winter vegetables containing sulfur. All three have high amounts of vitamin C. There is 40 percent more iron in the green base of the cauliflower than in the bleached head, so make sure to use the greens surrounding the head.

Cantaloupe and Watermelon Seeds. The cantaloupe has a "throwaway" seed with real nutritional value. This is one of the finest foods you can eat because of its high calcium content. Liquefy it in the same manner you do sesame seeds: with a little water, tea or pineapple juice, and honey, if desired. If you want a wonderful drink for kidney disturbances, make a milk out of watermelon seeds. However, strain off the seed hull material after liquefying either of these seeds to avoid possible bowel irritation.

I knew a Canadian family that traveled to Florida each winter so that a daughter who suffers from nephritis could have fresh watermelon. This family considered the benefit worth the effort—and it was! There is nothing better for kidney disturbance, nephritis, and Bright's disease than watermelon and its seeds. This is especially so for children. If you can't make annual trips to Florida, take ten or fifteen watermelon seeds and run them in the liquefier with some liquid and sweetening. Strain off the seed hulls, and you'll have a nice drink.

Celery. Early Olympic game winners were awarded celery as a prize. It was considered the greatest thing they could receive since it was the one thing that rejuvenated them more than anything else after a long run or some other arduous competitive game. Celery is the most cooling vegetable you can have in the body. Today it is one of the foods you must be most careful of because it is one of the most sprayed vegetables we have. Wash it well and brush it well. A wonderful food remedy that can be used in the summertime to keep you cool is celery and pineapple juice together. It replaces the salts lost in perspiration on an extremely hot day. This may be mixed with prune juice, especially for those who need nerve salts to help the nervous system.

Cucumbers. Don't forget to eat the peeling, unless it disturbs you. You can get the equivalent value in other foods, especially greens. No drinks are better in summer than cucumber and celery, cucumber and whey, or cucumber and pineapple. In summer they tell us to keep as "cool as a cucumber."

Cucumbers are high in sodium and silicon (in peeling) and are good for the blood.

Dandelions. These should be used for the gallbladder and liver. A fine beverage I enjoy is made of roasted dandelion root. Learn to use this in place of coffee.

Endive. This is a wonderful food, very high in potassium, not bad in calcium. But avoid head lettuce; it has almost no nutritional value. It is very gas forming and contains an opium by-product that slows down digestion. Leaf lettuce has one hundred times as much iron as head lettuce.

Fish. Fish has long been called a "brain food." Most fish contain omega-3 oils that help protect the heart. People who eat fish twice or more each week have fewer heart attacks than those who eat fish fewer than twice a week. Seafood is high in phosphorus, needed by the brain and nerves. All fish have B-complex vitamins, including B_{12}, which is not found in fruits or vegetables. Clams and oysters are very high in B_{12}.

Leeks. Classified with onions, leeks are good because of their powerful effect in driving bacteria from the body. Onions also have the wonderful ability to rid the body of catarrh. Onion packs are an excellent remedy for chest conditions.

Lemon Juice. This is nature's most powerful antiseptic, used internally and externally. Apply to corns, on scalp, on sores; gargle it; brush teeth with it; drink it to purify the breath.

Malva. This herb is highest in vitamin A, an anti-infection vitamin. There are about 50,000 IU of vitamin A to every pound of malva.

Mulberries. Those who are chronically inclined to fevers should eat mulberries because they help bring down high temperatures in the body. They are also good in cases of stomach disorders, such as ulcers. The juice of mulberries reduces the heat of the body without causing perspiration. Mulberries also contain a lot of natural sugar.

Mushrooms. Mushrooms have very little nutritional value, but they are low in calories and combine well with other foods. Like radishes, they grow fast. A rapidly growing vegetable doesn't have the same food value as a slow-growing variety, generally considered.

Noncooked Cereals. These are rich in silicon and especially good for bowel activity. The ingredients are usually one-half cup of flaked rolled oats, one heaping tablespoon of dried raisins, one heaping tablespoon of dried apples or finely cut apricots, one tablespoon of shredded almonds, and one teaspoon of date sugar. Before serving, soak for ten minutes in two-third cups of water and then add fresh fruit such as peaches or bananas; then add cream. Vary the cereal with ground and chopped sunflower seeds, sesame seeds, coconut, and cashews. Add natural supplements or rice polishings, flaxseed meal, and wheat germ for extra vitamins and minerals.

Nuts. The almond is the king, highest in alkalinity. Black walnuts are the highest in manganese, which is the nerve element. Pine nuts are one of the highest in fat content (49 percent). They make a nice salad dressing, best mixed with fruit, especially with apricots.

Papaya. This fruit is a very good remedy for stomach troubles. Make a tea of the seeds; they contain natural papain, which is needed by the stomach as a digestant. Tablets are good for pyorrhea. Papaya tablets disintegrate proteins when they are soaked overnight in the juice. This is why papaya tablets are so wonderful when left in the mouth to dissolve slowly after a meal. They break down toxic protein deposits on the teeth, such as occur in pyorrhea, and should be used after each meal. Following this, use a gargle of liquid chlorophyll, which is a wonderful mouthwash.

Peapods. These make a wonderful vegetable juice and may be mixed with celery and carrot to make a very tasty drink. Put in soup for flavoring (they may be discarded) or with any vegetable while cooking. There is a lot of value in them.

Pumpkin Seeds. They are an excellent food and a good source of vegetable protein. Fresh pumpkin seeds may be liquefied into a juice or strained and combined with other foods that would impart flavor. Use a suitable sweetening agent.

Radishes. Whether they contain much mineral value or not, radishes add fiber and flavor. Black radish and horseradish have a beneficial effect on sinus disturbances and gallbladder troubles. Powdered horseradish is used as a remedy for gallbladder catarrh.

Squashes. This is the mildest vegetable you can have in your diet. When baking squash, leave seeds in for flavoring. Never remove seeds unless you save them for planting.

Turnips. They come under the classification of a sulfur food. Since they are so high in vitamin A, they will fight any catarrhal trouble in the body.

FOODS TO LIMIT IN YOUR DIET

Rhubarb, Cranberries, and Plums. These foods contain oxalic acid, and all dietitians say to leave them out of the diet excepting for rare use on holidays. Prunes, however, contain a beneficial nerve salt and have a natural laxative quality, so in spite of having a high acid factor I recommend them, especially fresh prune plums.

When you have any joint trouble, avoid high oxalic acid foods such as cranberries, rhubarb, cooked spinach, and cooked Swiss chard. Whole, fresh cranberries may be used for cranberry sauce at holidays. If you must eat cranberries (it doesn't hurt if you use them once or twice a year), don't use too much sweetening. Raisins or apples are good sweeteners, added after cooking. (This applies to all cooking: *Add sweetening agent after cooking.*) There is an average of six times as much natural sugar in dried fruits as in fresh fruit.

UNFAVORABLE FOODS

Avoid unfavorable foods at all times. My list of unfavorable foods includes sugar, white flour, white rice, foods with chemical additives, pickled or smoked foods, and any foods significantly altered or depleted of nutrients. One single reckless meal of unfavorable foods may undo the work of a year's careful diet. Be careful of the directions you are taking and watch your habits. Do live moderately, carry out this regimen, and you'll be healthy. You *will* see favorable results.

There is something good in everything in nature. There is a remedy from everything in nature: weeds, skins, flowers, stalks, bark, roots, and leaves.

We should eat foods that do not have many bugs or pests on them. These foods have elements that keep us from getting sick. You seldom see worms in beets or garlic. You will find that if you have a body with all the resistance elements in it, germ life will not live there either.

We have a life force, and we must feed that life force.

You will find many remedies in foods, but you will never get well in less than a year, and for some people two years or even five years is needed. The value comes only through persistence.

FOODS FOR ARTHRITIS

Alfalfa. Alfalfa-mint tea and alfalfa seed tea are good for arthritic conditions.

Celery and Okra. Celery and okra tablets may be used as a remedy for arthritis. Take four of each four times a day. Or get extra okra and celery juice in your diet. These are very high in sodium, which is what arthritic conditions need. If you have an extreme heart problem, you have to be a little careful, because then we try to withdraw some of the sodium and increase the potassium.

Broth. Take a tablespoon of whey, a tablespoon of lecithin, and a teaspoon of broth powder in a cup of hot water. If arthritis is bad, take two cups a day for three to six months.

Potato Peeling Broth. Another broth for extreme rheumatism and arthritic problems, excess catarrh in the body, and neutralizing the body's acids is potato peeling broth.

This is a high potassium broth. Use two good-sized potatoes and one and a half pints of water. Simmer for fifteen minutes, strain, and drink just the broth. Take one or two cups a day over a period of a month. I have seen many rheumatic pains leave with this.

Veal Joint Broth. Veal joint broth is a wonderful remedy for arthritis. People who have broken down the joints in their bodies need this joint material if there is going to be rebuilding. Take the shoulder of a young beef and cook the jelly off the bone. See page 340 for a more detailed recipe.

Lecithin. In the 1950s, it was found that certain kinds of injuries to the brain were greatly helped to heal by lecithin. Concussions and traumatic brain injuries improved in a matter of weeks instead of months when lecithin was given in a dry form.

Lecithin is found in all foods that contain cholesterol; it is high in fish, and can be made from soybeans. It acts by emulsifying the fats in the body, arteries, and veins by supplying an easily digestible and easily absorbed choline. It also increases the peristaltic action of the intestine. When you feel you just can't carry on any longer, when you feel exhausted, fatigued, and rundown, lecithin may be just the thing to lift you up again. Since lecithin does not have to undergo digestive enzymatic action, it is carried directly to the bloodstream, where it can be used for the brain and nerve system.

There are many benefits from lecithin. It provides energy for the brain and nervous system. It helps in giving us a longer life span because it keeps arteries soft. It helps to cleanse the liver and keep fats in solution. It purifies the kidneys, increases brain power, and is especially good in preventing hardening of the arteries. In treating arteriosclerosis, many methods have been tried to get rid of the fatty contents of foods. Lecithin helps to keep cholesterol in solution. Lecithin is part of the structural material in every cell of the body, and is especially important in the brain and nervous system.

It has been determined that when there is a decrease in the intake of lecithin, there is an increase in cholesterol. Patients are reducing cholesterol by taking lecithin. Lecithin is also good for dissolving excess oils in the body. Take a tablespoon of granules or two or three capsules of lecithin every day. Everyone over the age of fifty should use lecithin in their diet.

Soybeans. The soybean has been "the beef" of China. Many a child has been raised to adulthood in Asia on only the milk beverage made from soy powder. Soy milk is low in fat compared to cow's milk. It is low in carbohydrate, calcium, phosphorous, and riboflavin, but is high in iron, thiamin, niacin, and has a little zinc. It is good to add honey to soy milk for flavor. Honey also raises the carbohydrate content. Soy oil will increase fat content and should be blended to give the consistency of cream.

Soy Milk. To make soy milk, take one pound of dried soybeans, soak in two quarts of water overnight in a cool place. Pour off the water in which the beans have been soaking. Grind the beans in a food mixer very finely. Add fresh, pure water to the mixture, three times the volume of the soaked beans. Mix thoroughly and filter with cheesecloth. The milk passes, leaving only the pulp. You can bring the milk to the hot point without boiling. Skim off the surface froth, and cool. Stir frequently to prevent the formation of soy milk skim. If you add other things to the soy milk for flavoring, blend in the liquefier.

BRAIN FOOD

When any part of your body is not working properly, take care of your brain first. To feed the brain properly, we need certain foods to provide lecithin, phosphorus, amino acids, and glucose. Raw egg yolk and raw goat's milk are the best sources of all of these. Meat protein does have phosphorus for the brain, but many people want to avoid meat.

The brain must be well supplied with oxygen. Alfalfa sprouts, vitamin E, and hawthorne berry tea all help bring oxygen to the brain, but exercise is the most important way to get more oxygen in the blood and to improve blood circulation.

Brain food can accomplish and do things, but it is not the food that goes into the person that is most important, it is the kind of person the food goes into.

CALCIUM TONICS

If you lack calcium, you should learn how to make and use a calcium tonic, a calcium broth, and a calcium soup. One of the finest soups we have is from Denmark. It is a barley and green kale soup called "Grunko." This soup has the highest calcium content of any soup I know. Every mother should use this for her children while they are growing up. Both kale and soaked or sprouted whole barley can be liquefied and served raw, warm, or cooked. For additional calcium, use the liquid from boiled egg shells in a broth or blend oyster shell tablets into fruit and vegetable drinks.

Cramps in Legs

Take a Kneipp bath every day as described elsewhere in this book. Use the calcium foods in broths, soups, tonics, bone meal, kale, and barley. Take calcium lactate supplements (there is a vegetarian calcium lactate). Many times, lack of sufficient calcium causes cramps.

FOODS FOR CHOLESTEROL AND OTHER DEPOSITS

Alfalfa sprouts are among the greatest remedies available for dissolving cholesterol and other deposits that settle in the arteries. Researchers at the University of Vancouver, British Columbia, have found that some chemical substance in alfalfa sprouts is great for dissolving the deposits that cause hardening of the arteries.

People who have increasing cholesterol deposits in the body should cut out using heated oils or fats for cooking. Oils are concentrated, and the body does not have sufficient digestive juices to take care of concentrated oils.

You have to recognize that the human body was made to digest and assimilate foods available in nature, not foods that are manufactured, altered, or concentrated in such a way that eating them is injurious to the digestive system, the detoxifying organs, the immune system, and the tissues the blood delivers them to. Concentrated oils, table salt, granulated sugar, excessively spicy foods, and many good tasting snack foods are only creating disease-inviting conditions in the body.

Sprouts are a rich source of vitamins, magnesium, and chlorophyll. Sprouts of buckwheat, mung beans, soybeans, alfalfa, and sunflower seeds are all wonderful with a nice dressing such as tomato sauce or a little Roquefort dressing. Sunflower seed sprouts are coarser than most but are a good source of zinc. They need to be picked before they have grown too high or too coarse, then served with tomato sauce or nut butter dressing.

FOODS FOR THE HEART

Liquid Chlorophyll. Liquid chlorophyll is a great deodorizer and cleaner. For bad breath (which usually comes from the stomach), take ½ teaspoon chlorophyll in ½ cup water before breakfast. Chlorophyll also reduces body odor.

Liquid chlorophyll is also one of our heart remedies. It is high in potassium and is a great blood builder.

Dried Olives. Dried olives are one of the highest sources in potassium, and the heart needs potassium. You can take ten dried olives, steep them in boiling water, take off the oil on top, and drink the remaining broth.

Whole Wheat. This is another good remedy for the heart. Grind ¼ cup whole wheat berries into a rough cereal form, then add ½ cup hot water. Put this into a wide-mouth thermos bottle, close it, and leave overnight. This is a splendid food for heart support. Use it every morning for three months.

FOODS FOR HYDROCHLORIC ACID DEFICIENCY

Most chronically ill persons lack hydrochloric acid, the agent needed to curdle milk. Clabbered milk, already curdled, is therefore a more available protein for the body than milk, since it doesn't require much hydrochloric acid to break it down. Use lemon juice, some clabber from a previous culture, or kefir for clabbering milk (see recipe on p. 162).

FOODS FOR HYPOGLYCEMIA

There are a lot of people with hypoglycemia who should be taking a supplement for pancreatic support. They should also be taking an adrenal gland substance. Many of these hypoglycemia cases develop mental illness symptoms. They are sometimes actually classed as mental cases when they should be taken care of as hypoglycemic cases. I wonder how many people in mental institutions today could be better taken care of from an adrenal gland and pancreatic standpoint than from a mental standpoint. They need nerve supportive foods. When you feed the nerves, the same foods feed the glands also.

In hypoglycemia, I think it is good to have two protein meals and one very small starch meal a day. Depending on the severity of the case, we might even cut down the starches to a minimum, because the needed carbohydrates can be picked up in vegetables. We might even cut out fruits to avoid the load of sugars they put on the pancreas. Of course, all sugars are cut out. (See the hypo-glycemic diet in chapter 20, Special Diets for Special People.)

FOODS FOR THE NERVES

I have a broth I use as a remedy for people who are very sick, very irritable, have nerve depletion, and are on edge. I find it a very nourishing drink for the whole body. Take carrots, celery, parsley, a potato, beets, and maybe beet greens. Chop up very fine and put into a pint or quart of water and liquefy. Then add water, if necessary, to make a nice broth, and simmer for two or three minutes. This gives the least amount of heat, the shortest time of cooking, and keeps the foods as raw as possible, while taking off the acids that can cause a lot of the extreme elimina-tion we find in raw foods. When the broth is just about finished, add a couple of tablespoons soy milk powder, which neutral-izes some of the acids. Strain, and drink the broth.

This is a wonderful nourishing food and soothing drink for the nervous system. It is a good building drink, and at the same time an eliminative drink.

Nerve Drinks

I have a drink that takes the place of a meal. Many times if I cannot eat, I just ask for my drink. My drink is a glass of raw goat's milk, often mixed with a teaspoon of sunflower seed but-ter, sesame seed butter, almond butter, or other nut butter; a tea-spoon of honey; and a nice sliver of avocado. This is a whole meal, and it is all raw. It is a good protein meal, and it feeds the nervous system. This is my favorite.

Apples and Prunes

The apple is charged with malic acid and glucose, both of which are wonderful for the neurogenic aspects of the body. They are wonderful for the nervous system because of the nerve salts they contain. Another excellent food is prunes. Because of their acid, prunes are sometimes not recommended, but I do recommend them. Like the apple, they contain a high content of nerve salt. Apples and prunes are valuable for growing children because of their benefit to the bowels. They are also helpful in cases of colic. Prune and celery juice together make a wonderful nerve food, and an egg yolk in black cherry juice also works well as a nerve tonic.

FOODS FOR THE LIVER

I believe that liquid chlorophyll is one of the great remedies in all liver troubles. Chlorophyll is nature's greatest cleansing agent. Black cherry juice helps the liver to produce bile and keep it moving along. Beets are cleansing to the liver, and I often advise adding grated beets, about 2 tablespoons, to every garden salad.

ACID/ALKALINE BALANCE

To form an electrical current, we have to have a positive and a negative. The body, too, has to have acid and alkaline conditions. Enzymes that control the sequence of chemical reactions in the body that result in functional activities only operate at a particular temperature and level of acidity or alkalinity. The pH of the blood must remain at from 7.35 to 7.45 for many enzyme reactions to work. The body is constantly rebalancing acidic or alkalinic reactions to bring the pH to normal. If elimination has not been good, we may have too many acids. The person who does not exercise enough to produce sufficient acids in the body becomes too alkaline. We have to be aware of acid-forming and alkaline-forming foods.

The body needs 80 percent alkaline and 20 percent acid foods. The starches are the acid-forming foods, as are sugars and proteins. The rest of our foods are alkaline. They are the builders, the foods for regeneration and rejuvenation. However, you also need the acid foods. When you don't have a good balance, a variety of adverse conditions may develop in your body. Exercise helps one to have that balance. If we ingest a lot of alkaline, then we exercise. Every time we use our muscles, we produce lactic acid, which eventually initiates tissue. It needs to be neutralized with sodium, potassium, or calcium. A *too* alkaline body is not good for the bowels.

The more proficient you become in your food routine, the more exercise you must do because your body tends to become more alkaline. Lactic acid is good acid to have in the body. It gives us the balance we need to keep going. It gives us a good "body battery." If you want to recharge your battery, you have to exercise. You can also eat a few of the acid foods, but make sure that you balance your day's eating.

Some people who are overalkaline take cider vinegar to help balance themselves, but I believe that that practice is risky. Some people have thrown their acid/alkaline balance off, perhaps permanently, by using apple cider vinegar for too long a time without more natural means of balancing themselves.

Fruits and vegetables are alkaline-forming as a rule, while starches and proteins are acid-forming. The body is constantly adjusting its acid/alkaline balance to create the necessary conditions for chemical reactions our body must carry out if we are to live. One starch and one protein daily, with the rest of the meal consisting of fruits and vegetables, will give us a good 80/20 balance.

The following Table 18.1 is from Ragnar Berg of Germany. Foods are integrated into the body chemistry after assimilation and processing by the liver in such a way that the acid/alkaline balance is just right for chemical reactions and enzyme activities to take place.

Table 18.1. **Acid/Alkaline Foods**

Column 1: Nonstarch Foods

AL	Alfalfa	AL	Artichokes
AL	Asparagus	AL	Beans (string)
AL	Beans (wax)	AL	Beets (whole)
AL	Beet leaves	AL	Broccoli
AL	Cabbage (white)	AL	Cabbage (red)
AL	Carrots	AL	Carrot tops
AL	Cauliflower	AL	Celery knobs
AL	Chickory	Al	Coconut
AL	Corn	AL	Cucumbers
AL	Dandelions	AL	Eggplant
AL	Endive	AL	Garlic
AL	Horseradish	AL	Kale
AL	Kohlrabi	AL	Leeks
AL	Lettuce	AL	Mushrooms
AL	Okra	AL	Olives (ripe)
AL	Onions	AL	Osterplant

(Continued)

Table 18.1. **Continued**

Column 1: Nonstarch Foods (continued)

AL	Parsley	AL	Parsnips
AL	Peas (fresh)	AL	Peppers (sweet)
AL	Radishes	AL	Rutabagas
AL	Savory	AL	Sea lettuce
AL	Sorrel	AL	Spinach
AL	Soybean (products)	AL	Sprouts
AL	Summer squash	AL	Swiss chard
AL	Turnips	AL	Watercress

Column 2: Proteins and Fruits

AC	Beef	AC	Buttermilk
AC	Chicken	AC	Clams
AC	Cottage cheese	AC	Crab
AC	Duck	AC	Eggs
AC	Fish	AC	Goose
AC	Honey (pure)	AC	Jello
AC	Lamb	AC	Lobster
AC	Mutton	AC	Nuts
AC	Oyster	AC	Pork
AC	Rabbit	AC	Raw sugar
AC	Turkey	AC	Turtle
AC	Veal	AL	All berries
AL	Apples	AL	Apricots
AL	Avocados	AL	Cantaloupes
AL	Cranberries	AL	Currants
AL	Dates	AL	Figs
AL	Grapes	AL	Grapefruit
AL	Lemons	AL	Limes
AL	Oranges	AL	Peaches
AL	Pears	AL	Persimmons
AL	Pineapple	AL	Plums
AL	Prunes	AL	Raisins
AL	Rhubarb	AL	Tomatoes

Column 3: Starchy Foods

AL	Bananas	AC	Barley
AC	Beans (lima)	AC	Beans (white)
AC	Bread	AC	Cereals
AC	Chestnuts	AC	Corn
AC	Cornmeal	AC	Crackers
AC	Gluten flour	AC	Corn starch
AC	Macaroni	AC	Lentils
AC	Millet rye	AC	Maize
AC	Peanuts	AC	Oatmeal
AC	Peas (dried)	AC	Peanut butter
AL	Potatoes (white)	AC	Potatoes (sweet)
AC	Rice (brown)	AL	Pumpkin
AC	Roman meal	AC	Rice (polished)
AC	Sauerkraut	AC	Rye flour
AL	Squash (Hubbard)	AC	Tapioca

Note: Foods preceded by the letters AL are alkaline forming; foods preceded by the letters AC are acid forming.

Using the Acid/Alkaline table

For people with weak digestion, it is best to make food combinations as simple as possible. Follow the suggestions on how to combine foods. Combine foods found in columns one and two, or in columns one and three. Never combine columns two and three. All foods in column one will combine with all foods in column two.

Fruits. Citrus fruits cause extreme alkalinity. Citrus fruits, when broken down, release alkaline chemical ions that begin to change the acid/alkaline balance in the body. (The brain monitors this balance and is able to counter any destabilizing influence.)

Sometimes these citrus fruits stir up the body acids so rapidly that their effect is considered to be bad. Should the eating of fruits cause you distress, you may be misinterpreting your symptoms. You may be eliminating toxic wastes. But, if that is not what's happening, I would say you are very ill and require the advice of a specialist in natural healing.

In general, remember that fruits should be eaten in natural harmony. Oranges, grapefruits, tangerines, and lemons, the acid fruits, go nicely with other acid fruits like pineapple and strawberries. They do not combine well with the sweet fruits or the dried ones, like prunes, figs, raisins, dates, and grapes. Berries and melons should always be eaten alone. There is no more disagreeable surprise for your stomach than watermelon eaten in conjunction with another food.

The subacid fruits mentioned, such as apples, persimmons, pears, plums, peaches, and apricots combine fairly well with the acid fruits, but I do not recommend the combinations. The safest procedure is the *simplest* one.

You can use cream, if you must, but never sugar. White sugar is a poison to your system, no matter how much energy you seem to get from it, and brown sugar is like gilding the lily. The fruit itself is plentiful with sugar and you do not need to put sugar on your sugar.

In general, too, remember that sweet milk goes best with the acid fruits, while sour milk, like clabbered, yogurt, or even cottage cheese, goes best with the subacid fruits. In other words, a glass of milk at orange time is a permissible combination. Again, keep your diet simple.

Columns one and two will combine very nicely, as will columns two and three. Columns one and three never mix. Do not combine acid fruits with sweet dried fruits. Berries and melons are best eaten alone.

Fruits can also be classed into three columns:

Column 1	Column 2	Column 3
Acid Fruits	*Subacid Fruits*	*Sweet or Dried Fruits*
Oranges	Apples	Fruits
Grapefruit	Plums	Dates
Lemons	Grapes	Raisins
Limes	Pears	Figs
	Peaches	
	Apricots	

GOOD FOOD COMBINATIONS

I would rather you have natural foods wrongly combined than manufactured or processed foods properly combined. If it "raises the roof" in the house, forget it. If you are concerned with loss of weight, you may disregard the principle and combine natural carbohydrates and proteins. Every food contains a certain balance of these elements. Acid and alkaline foods, however, should be taken separately, if possible. Proteins may be used with acid foods, and carbohydrates with alkaline foods.

Whenever you have a starch, you should have a green vegetable with it. You will not be constipated, nor have a dry stool if you have at least twice as much vegetable material as starch.

With meat or protein foods, you should have sulfur food in order to drive the brain and nerve fats into tissue.

Most natural foods are generally good. Have a full variety and you can take care of the whole body as you go along. We need all the elements in proper proportion to build a well-balanced bloodstream.

For the various systems of the body that may be run down or need certain chemicals for repair and maintenance, select your foods for the greatest variety possible, according to the growing seasons. Vegetables as fresh as possible from the garden are best. Discover all possible ways of using raw foods. Foods in their natural state are alive and should be our chief source of nutrition.

If you must use fruits and vegetables that have been sprayed, when washing, use a solution of 1 teaspoon Clorox to 1 gallon water (this is high in chlorine, which is the cleanser, but it is like gas and leaves the liquid rapidly). Allow food to remain in this solution for five minutes, then rinse in clear, cold water for another five minutes. This is the cheapest and best way of handling the spray residues.

CHAPTER 19

MY HEALTH AND HARMONY FOOD REGIMEN

The following is a general diet regimen that many of my students and patients follow with wonderful, happy results.

BALANCED DAILY EATING REGIMEN

Make a habit of applying the following diet regimen to your everyday living. This is a healthy way to live because, when you follow it, you do not have to worry about vitamins, mineral elements, or calories.

The best diet, over the period of a day, is two different fruits, at least four to six vegetables, one protein, and one starch, with fruit or vegetable juices between meals. Eat at least two green leafy vegetables a day. Fifty to 60 percent of the food you eat daily should be raw. Consider this regimen a dietetic law.

RULES OF EATING

1. Do not fry foods or use heated oils.
2. If you are not entirely comfortable in mind and body from the previous mealtime, you should miss the next meal.
3. Do not eat unless you have a keen desire for the plainest food.
4. Do not eat beyond your needs.
5. Be sure to thoroughly masticate your food.
6. Miss meals if you are in pain, emotionally upset, not hungry, chilled, overheated, or experiencing acute illness.

IMPOSITIONS FOR GETTING WELL

1. Learn to accept whatever decision is made.
2. Let the other person make a mistake and learn.
3. Learn to forget and forgive.
4. Be thankful and bless people.
5. Live in harmony—even if it is good for you.
6. Do not talk about your sickness.
7. Gossip will kill you. Neither speak it nor listen to it. Gossip that comes through the grapevine is usually sour.
8. Be by yourself everyday for ten minutes with the thought of how to make yourself a better person. Replace negative thoughts with uplifting, positive thoughts.
9. Skin brush daily. Use a slant board daily.
10. Have citrus fruits in sections only, never in juice form.
11. Have only a limited amount of bread. If you have a lot of bowel trouble, have no bread.
12. Exercise daily. Keep your spine limber. Develop abdominal muscles. Do sniff breathing. Have a daily set of exercises.

13. Grass walk and sand walk for happy feet (and better circulation).

14. Retire to bed at 9 P.M. at the latest, if you are at all tired, fatigued, and unable to do your work with vigor. If you are sick, you must rest more. If possible, sleep out of doors, out of the city, in circulating air. Work out problems in the morning, don't take them to bed with you.

FOOD HEALING LAWS

1. Natural food—50 to 60 percent of the food eaten should be raw.

2. Your diet should be 80 percent alkaline and 20 percent acid. Look at the acid/alkaline chart on pages 369–371.

3. Proportion—Six vegetables daily, two fruits daily, one starch daily, and one protein daily.

4. Variety—Vary sugars, proteins, starches, vegetables, and fruit from meal to meal and from day to day.

5. Overeating—You can kill yourself with the amount of food you eat.

6. Combinations—Separate starches and proteins. Eat one at lunch and the other at supper. Have fruits for breakfast and at 3:00 P.M.

7. Cook with the least amount of water. Cook without high heat. Cook without air touching hot food. Use unsprayed vegetables if possible and eat them as soon after being picked as possible.

8. Bake, broil, or roast—If you eat meat, have lean, no fat, no pork.

9. Use stainless steel, low-heat cooking utensils—It is the modern, health-engineered way of preparing your foods.

BEFORE BREAKFAST

One-half hour before breakfast, take any natural, unsweetened fruit juice, such as grape, pineapple, prune, fig, apple, or black cherry. Liquid chlorophyll can be used; take 1 teaspoonful in a glass of water.

You can have a broth and lecithin drink, if you desire it. Take 1 teaspoonful of vegetable broth powder and 1 tablespoonful of lecithin granules and dissolve in a glass of hot water.

On doctor's advice, you may have citrus fruits, such as orange, grapefruit, lemon, or tomato.

Between fruit juice and breakfast, follow this program: skin brushing, exercise, hiking, deep breathing, or playing. Shower. Start warm and cool off until your breath quickens. Never shower immediately upon arising.

BREAKFAST

Stewed fruit, one starch, and a health drink, or two fruits, one protein, and health drink. (Starches and health drinks are listed with the lunch suggestions.) Soaked fruits, such as unsulfured apricots, prunes, or figs. Fruit of any kind—melon, grapes, peaches, pears, berries, or baked apple, which may be sprinkled with some ground nuts or nut butter. When possible, use fruit in season. To reconstitute dried fruit, cover with cold water, bring to a boil and leave to stand overnight. Raisins may just have boiling water poured over them. This kills any insects and their eggs.

Suggested Breakfast Menus
Monday
Reconstituted dried apricots
Steel-cut oatmeal, with supplements
Oat straw tea

Add eggs, if desired

or

Sliced peaches

Cottage cheese, with supplements

Herb tea

Tuesday

Fresh figs

Cornmeal cereal, with supplements

Shavegrass tea

Add eggs or nut butter, if desired

or

Raw applesauce and blackberries

Coddled egg, with supplements

Herb tea

Wednesday

Reconstituted dried peaches

Millet cereal, with supplements

Alfa-mint tea

Add eggs, cheese or nut butter, if desired

or

Sliced nectarines and apple

Yogurt, with supplements

Herb tea

Thursday

Prunes or any reconstituted dried fruit

Whole wheat cereal, with supplements

Oat straw tea

or

Grapefruit and kumquats

Poached egg, with supplements

Herb tea

Friday

Slices of fresh pineapple with
shredded coconut
Buckwheat cereal, with supplements
Peppermint tea

or

Baked apple, persimmons
Chopped raw almonds
Acidophilus milk, with supplements
Herb tea

Saturday

Muesli with bananas and dates
Cream, with supplements
Dandelion coffee or herb tea

Sunday

Cooked applesauce with raisins
Rye grits, with supplements
Shavegrass tea

or

Cantaloupe and strawberries
Cottage cheese, with supplements
Herb tea

Whole Grain Cereal

To cook properly with as little heat as possible, use a double-
boiler or thermos-cook your cereal.

Supplements

About a teaspoonful of sunflower seed meal, rice polishings,
wheat germ, and flaxseed meal (can be added to cereal or

fruit). Even a little dulse, with some broth powder, may be sprinkled in.

10:30 A.M.

Vegetable broth, vegetable juice, or fruit juice.

LUNCH

Raw salad, or as directed, one or two starches, as listed, and a health drink. *Note:* If you are following a strict regimen, use only one of the first seven starches daily. Vary the starch from day to day.

Salad Vegetables

Use plenty of greens. Choose four or five vegetables from the following: Leaf lettuce, watercress, endive, spinach, beet leaves, parsley, alfalfa sprouts, cabbage, young chard, herbs, any green leaves, cucumbers, bean sprouts, onions, green peppers, pimentos, avocados, tomatoes, carrots, turnips, zucchini, asparagus, celery, okra, radishes, and so on.

Starches

Yellow cornmeal, baked potato, baked banana (or at least dead ripe), barley (a winter food), steamed brown rice or wild rice, millet (have as a cereal), or banana squash or Hubbard squash.

Other starches include steel-cut oatmeal, whole wheat cereal, whole wheat bread, rye bread, soybeans, corn bread, bran muffins, or Ry-Krisp.

Drinks

Vegetable broth, soup, coffee substitute, buttermilk, raw milk, almond milk, rice milk, soy milk, oat straw tea, alfa-mint tea, huckleberry tea, papaya tea, or any health drink.

SUGGESTED LUNCH MENUS

Monday
Vegetable salad
Baby lima beans
Baked potato
Spearmint tea

Tuesday
Vegetable salad—with health
mayonnaise, if desired
Steamed asparagus
Very ripe bananas, or steamed,
unpolished rice
Vegetable broth or herb tea

Wednesday
Raw salad plate
Sour cream dressing
Cooked green beans
and/or Baked Hubbard squash
Corn bread
Sassafras tea

Thursday
Salad—French dressing
Baked zucchini and okra
Corn-on-the-cob

Ry-Krisp

Buttermilk or herb tea

Friday

Salad

Baked green pepper, stuffed with
eggplant and tomatoes

Baked potato and/or bran muffin

Carrot soup or herb tea

Saturday

Salad

Steamed turnips and turnip greens

Baked yams

Catnip tea

Sunday

Salad

Lemon and olive oil dressing

Steamed whole barley

Cream of celery soup

Steamed chard

Herb tea

3:00 P.M.

Health cocktail, juice, or fruit.

DINNER

Raw salad, two cooked vegetables, one protein, and a broth or
health drink if desired.

Cooked Vegetables

Peas, artichokes, carrots, beets, turnips, spinach, beet tops, string beans, swiss chard, eggplant, zucchini, summer squash, broccoli, cauliflower, cabbage, sprouts, onion, or any vegetable other than potatoes.

Drinks

Vegetable broth, soup, or health beverage.

Proteins

Three Times a Week: Meat—use only lean meat. Never pork, fats, or cured meats.

Vegetarians use meat substitutes or vegetarian proteins such as soybeans, lima beans, cottage cheese, sunflower seeds, and other seeds, also seed butters, nut butters, nut milk drinks, and eggs.

Twice a Week: Cottage cheese or any cheese that breaks.

Once a Week: Fish—use white fish, such as sole, halibut, trout, or sea trout.

If you have a protein at this meal, health dessert is allowed but not recommended. Never eat protein and starch together.

You may exchange your noon meal for the evening meal, but follow the same regimen. It takes exercise to handle raw food, and we generally get more after our noon meal. That is why a raw salad is advised at noon. If one eats sandwiches, have vegetables at the same time.

SUGGESTED DINNER MENUS

Monday
Salad
Diced celery and carrots
Steamed spinach, waterless-cooked
Puffy omelet
Vegetable broth

Tuesday
Salad
Cooked beet tops
Steak, broiled
or ground beef patties with tomato sauce
Cauliflower
Comfrey tea

Wednesday
Cottage cheese
Cheese sticks
Apples, peaches, grapes, nuts
Apple concentrate cocktail

Thursday
Salad
Steamed chard
Baked eggplant
Grilled liver and onions
Persimmon whip (optional)
Alfa-mint tea

Friday
Salad
Yogurt and lemon dressing

Steamed mixed greens

Beets

Steamed fish, with slices of lemon

Leek soup

Saturday

Salad

Cooked string beans

Baked summer squash

Carrot and cheese loaf

Cream of lentil soup or lemongrass tea

Fresh peach Jello

Almond-nut cream

Sunday

Salad

Diced carrots and peas, steamed

Tomato aspic

Roast leg of lamb

Mint sauce

CHAPTER 20

SPECIAL DIETS

I have seen my potassium broth bring back patients who were just this side of death. Once I sat all night at the bedside of a lady almost comatose, spooning my potassium-rich potato peeling broth a teaspoon at a time into her mouth. She could just barely get her mouth open enough for me to get the spoonful of broth far enough in that it would trickle down her throat in case she couldn't swallow. In the morning, she looked at me and almost got a smile going. She whispered, "I think we're going to make it, Doctor." And she did make it—walked out of her room carrying her own suitcase and got into her daughter's car.

I don't believe in drugs or surgery except as a last resort. I believe in nutrition as a first resort, and I have seen hundreds of lives saved with special diets. Sometimes it's a high-protein diet, sometimes a fat-free diet, high in complex carbohydrates—fruit, vegetables, and juices. I know of a nurse who got rid of her breast cancer by living on a diet of grapes only for a month or so. I had a patient with extreme bowel problems that thrived on raw goat's milk.

When my patients have decided to use a special diet to try to get rid of a chronic or degenerative disease, I encouraged them to telephone their doctors and tell them what they were going to do. I wanted the doctors to learn about the healing power in foods. I knew that most doctors didn't believe foods could heal, so I wanted to confront them with evidence that foods really do heal, in one of their own patients.

In following the idea of yin and yang, the polarities of life from an Eastern point of view, I considered carbohydrates a left-side (or negative) diet for the purpose of responding to any heart or spleen condition. Proteins, on the other hand, were a right-side (positive) diet, helpful for liver and gallbladder. Brown rice is wonderful for the heart, and I want to start out this chapter with a left-side diet good for heart conditions.

THE BROWN RICE DIET

The diet that does the greatest amount of good for high blood pressure and for the heart is the Brown Rice Diet. I have known for many years that adding more starches to the diet helped regulate and protect the heart. I believe that many heart disturbances are caused by diverticuli conditions in the descending colon, aggravated by the putrefaction of undigested proteins. I learned also that starches get rid of much of the gas developed in the descending colon. Too much meat in the diet seems to cause the gas formation that develops in the descending colon.

It would be a good idea to have a medical checkup before beginning the Brown Rice Diet; then have another after three or four days on the diet. If the body shows no abnormal signs, such as swelling in the extremities, excess gas, or other abnormal symptoms, continue with the diet. Have checkups every three or four days throughout the diet. I have had patients going on this diet in a modified way for many months until the body has been normalized.

DAILY MENU

Breakfast: Steamed brown rice, using stewed fruit for seasoning; tea.

Lunch: Salad, and one or two cooked vegetables, if you wish. Cottage cheese one day, egg the next day (in the form of an egg omelet). Nut butter on the third day. Then repeat.

Dinner: Vegetable salad, cooked vegetable, steamed brown rice again.

To modify this diet, have fresh fruit and protein for breakfast, and salad and vegetables for lunch, with more or less starchy vegetables, such as squash, carrots, or beets. At the evening meal, you can have steamed brown rice and vegetables again, or steamed brown rice and stewed fruit (dried fruit that has been reconstituted).

I have seen as much as a 60-point drop in the blood pressure in one month's time by using this diet. In addition, overweight people have lost as much as ten to fifteen pounds in one month. It is a matter of normalizing the body weight and getting the pressure off the heart that helps.

DIET AND DIABETES

Diabetes mellitus is a group of diseases that have in common high levels of blood sugar (glucose) that originate from defects in insulin secretion from the pancreas, reduced insulin activity, or both. In a recent year in this country, 15.7 million people had diabetes—10.3 million diagnosed and 5.4 million undiagnosed. There are 798,000 new cases diagnosed each year. Death rates are twice as high among middle-aged people with diabetes as middle-aged people without diabetes. Adult onset diabetes (non–insulin dependent) is the most common type (90 percent or more of all diabetics), often diagnosed after age forty. Juvenile onset diabetes, diagnosed before age thirty, is insulin dependent, meaning that those who have it produce no insulin at all and are dependent upon periodic insulin intake, often by injection, to regulate their blood sugar. Some women develop prenatal diabetes that disappears after the baby is born, but they are at increased risk for adult onset diabetes.

The complications of diabetes are distressing. Adults with diabetes have two to four times the death rate from heart disease as nondiabetics, and two to four times as many strokes. Over 60 percent of diabetics have high blood pressure. Diabetes-related damage to the retina causes 12,000 to 24,000 new cases of blindness every year. It's the leading cause of blindness in adults. It's also the leading cause of end-stage kidney disease, 40 percent of all new cases, most of whom require kidney dialysis. Over 60 percent of diabetics acquire nerve system damage that results in impaired sensation (or pain) in the hands and feet, slowed digestion, carpal tunnel symptoms, and other nerve problems. Later, the lower limbs may develop gangrene sores. More than half of lower limb amputations each year are performed on people with diabetes.

What can nutrition do under the circumstances of diabetes and its complications? I believe we can do a lot. Our first concern should be optimum nutritional support of the person's general health. I believe it is just as important to take care of the body parts not directly involved in the disease as the parts that are. Second, we should give thought to nutritional means of keeping blood sugar levels as normal as possible. We need to stabilize blood triglycerides and the good cholesterol at a healthy level while keeping bad cholesterol as low as possible. We should try to reduce to a minimum the short- and long-term complications of diabetes. I believe that all of this can be done, if the patient is willing and motivated to do what it takes to bring the diabetes and associated conditions under control.

One study (*New England Journal of Medicine,* 329:97–986) with 1,441 insulin-dependent diabetics has already shown that good progress can be made if intensive care is given to maintaining close control of blood sugar levels. Insulin administered to members of this study group was closely matched to the dietary intake of carbohydrates, and, at the same time, the right amount of carbohydrates (based on the person's metabolism, lifestyle, and weight) was assigned to each diabetic in the study. Protein and fat intakes, I believe, were simply based on the RDA at that time. The results were spectacular.

Risk of retinopathy (and blindness) was reduced by 76 percent as compared with conventional therapy. Risk of kidney failure was reduced significantly, and nerve damage (that would eventually lead to amputations) was reduced by about 60 percent. However, many patients in the test gained weight, and there were problems with blood sugars dropping too low. The doctors who conducted the experiment stated they believed that close blood sugar control would also improve the general health and lower the risk of complications in the non-insulin-dependent diabetics.

Although slender persons can get adult onset diabetics (non-insulin-dependent), most who get it are overweight. We know that overweight persons tend to be more insulin resistant, higher in blood cholesterol and triglycerides, with higher blood pressures, more likely to get premature heart disease, stroke, and nerve damage. Several research studies have shown that when non-insulin-dependent diabetics lost from fourteen to forty-four pounds, they had better blood sugar control, lower cholesterol, and lower triglycerides. The best way to lose weight is by a combination of exercise and lower intake of calories (doesn't apply to insulin-dependent diabetics).

Non-insulin-dependent diabetics appear to have more options for improvement than insulin-dependent diabetics, but diet considerations apply to both.

DIETARY CONSIDERATIONS

The days when all diabetics were offered the same diet are gone. With the help of their doctor or a nutritionist, each person with diabetes should have their own tailor-made diet for maximum health, based on their overall health profile, type of diabetes, medications being taken, activity level, food preferences, weight, and other lifestyle issues. Sometimes doctors are too lenient on bad lifestyle habits, but I feel it is of great importance—when health and quality of life are at stake—to give up alcohol, all nonessential drugs (legal or illegal), smoking, caffeinated drinks, and granulated sugar. I realize that recent studies have shown that blood sugar levels are not any more disturbed by sugar than they are by starchy vegetables, beets, corn, apples, peaches, and other complex carbohydrates. Sugar should be eliminated for other reasons, such as the destruction of B-complex vitamins, interference with calcium metabolism, and its contribution to fermentation in the bowel. Researchers have found that stabilizing the blood sugar level is more productive of health than trying to keep it low.

To get blood sugar under control so it stays as stable as possible, it is very important to have meals and snacks at exactly the same times every day—for example, breakfast at 7 A.M., snack at 10 A.M., lunch at 12:30 P.M., snack at 3:30 P.M., supper at 6 P.M., and last snack at 8 P.M.

The amount, type, and variety of carbohydrates in the daily food regimen are also extremely important in fine-tuning blood sugar control with food intake, rate of calorie use in work and play, and amount of insulin if needed. Diabetics with kidney disease should keep their protein intake at 0.36 grams per pound of body weight each day to slow the process of kidney breakdown; those without kidney disease should keep protein intake at 10 to 20 percent of total calories. Proteins and carbohydrates are each 4 calories per gram while fats are 9 calories per gram, and you should keep a written record of food intake (and calories) if you are aiming (as I hope you will be) at optimum well-being, not just "getting by." With 20 percent protein meals, you and your doctor or nutritionist will have to work out the relative percentages of carbohydrates and fats in the remaining 80 percent of calories.

I want to caution you on making your fat intake too low. We would expect that lowering dietary fat intake would lower blood lipids and cholesterol, but because of the way body chemistry works, that doesn't happen. Going as low as 20 to 25 percent dietary fat intake drives up the triglycerides, reduces the "good" cholesterol, and drives up the after-eating levels of glucose and insulin, without reducing the "bad" cholesterol at all. This, as we know, increases the risk of coronary heart disease instead of decreasing it, which is already two to four times more common in diabetics. In these circumstances, the diabetic should be tested for a month by taking chromium picolinate (chromium chloride is also okay) to find out if it lowers blood lipids, cholesterol, or glucose. Chromium is a key component of glucose tolerance factor, and if this is deficient, taking a chromium supplement can be very encouraging. Another important supplement for the diabetic is 400 IU of vitamin E daily, which reduces oxidation of "bad" cholesterol. Larger vitamin E daily doses (900 IU) were used in a University of Naples study with insulin-resistant, overweight, elderly patients with angina pectoris. During the four-month, double-blind study, after-meal glucose and insulin levels dropped 23 percent, triglycerides dropped 20 percent, and the ratio of bad cholesterol to good cholesterol dropped 28 percent—which is good. The *Journal of Nutritional Medicine* (1995; 4:431–439) carried an article about twenty-one non–insulin-dependent diabetics going on a vegan diet for twenty-five days—a high-fiber, low-fat (10–15 percent) diet. Of these, seventeen reported complete relief of pain in four to sixteen days. They all lost weight, numbness was reduced, fasting blood glucose dropped 35 percent for eleven patients with the highest baseline levels. Insulin needs dropped for half the patients, triglycerides dropped an average of 25 percent, and blood cholesterol dropped an average of 13 percent.

Obviously, the last word is not yet in regarding dietary improvement of diabetes and its complications. My Health and Harmony Food Regimen can be altered to fit diabetic needs.

ELIMINATION DIETS

The purpose of elimination diets is to stimulate the body to release and get rid of toxic wastes, which are usually settled in the fatty tissues; the inherently weak tissues, glands, and organs; lymphatic tissue; and along the bowel walls, especially that of the colon. Elimination diets are what I call "one-sided" diets. Unlike a balanced diet, they are not meant to build and repair tissue along with eliminating unwanted substances from the body.

For your own protection, I advise that you consult your doctor when you intend to use an elimination diet or fasting procedure. It is best to be under the supervision of a doctor or nutritionist for any elimination diet or procedure lasting more than three days, especially if you have any chronic diseases or are over fifty years of age.

Eleven-Day Elimination Regimen

I want you to know that there are many procedures we can follow in detoxifying the body. Most people do not drink enough water, eat enough fiber foods, or get enough exercise to prevent bowel stasis and clogged lymph systems, so the body's natural and normal means of ridding itself of toxins is not adequately taken advantage of. There is no great secret to elimination diets and procedures. By using less food, more liquids, simpler foods, and simple food combinations, we simply make it easier for the body to do what it should do naturally.

In outline, our plan for the eleven-day regimen is to begin with water and juices for the first three days; graduating to a diet of fruits, juices, and water for the next two days; then six days on citrus and other fruits, salads, broth, and steamed vegetables. I want you to take a hot bath before going to bed each night.

Gather the foods you will need in advance. They should include lots of fruits and vegetables.

The fruits you may select from are citrus, grapes, melons, tomatoes, pears, peaches, plums, and other fruit in season. Reconstituted dried (unsulfured if available) fruits, such as prunes, figs, apricots, and peaches, may be used. To reconstitute the dried fruit, cover with water in a saucepan, bring to a boil, and let soak overnight. Salads should be garden salads (avoid iceberg lettuce) made with fresh leaf lettuce, sprouts, raw spinach, radishes, celery, green onions, cucumber, raw zucchini, tomatoes, and parsley. A little raw shredded parsnip, carrot, or beet may be sprinkled on top. If you can take the salad without dressing, that would be best. If you need to use dressing, use it sparingly—no more than a tablespoon or two. The last six days you may steam fresh vegetables, such as broccoli, carrots, peas, squash, corn, cauliflower, and snow peas. Vital broth is also an important part of this regimen. The recipe is on page 340.

Before I present the schedule for the Eleven-Day Elimination Regimen, I want you to be prepared to use enemas for the first four or five days if you are not having bowel movements. It is not unusual for bowel movements to stop when you cut back on the amount of food you are eating. You may want to take a nap or rest every afternoon of the eleven days. Drink 2 or 3 quarts of water each day—eight to twelve 8-ounce glasses per day (one every hour or so) in addition to juices. When you get to the sixth day, eat slowly so that you don't overeat.

Days 1 to 3

To start your day, drink two 8-ounce glasses of water. After a half hour to an hour, have your first glass of grapefruit or orange juice, and continue drinking a glass every four hours. The reason I want you to use citrus juice is because it stirs up acids and toxins better than any other juice, and the water helps carry this unwanted material off. Remember to drink a glass of water every hour or so until you've had eight to twelve glasses. Take a hot bath before bed.

Days 4 and 5

Drink two 8-ounce glasses of water upon rising. For meals, eat fruit only, breakfast, lunch, and dinner. You may also drink

is desired; when hips get too large; when joints get stiff; if constipation is present; if you have any symptoms of catarrh. When you finish the regime, be sure to always use one of my transition diets.

TRANSITION DIETS

After being on a fast or juice diet, it is necessary to come back onto a regular regimen gradually in order to get the full benefit from this period without food. I offer two transition diets here. Either may be used after a two- or three-day fast or eleven-day elimination period on juices with a bulk cleanser. When one has been on a water fast for a longer period, it is advisable to make the transition more slowly as suggested in my seven-day transition diet.

The Three-Day Transition

FIRST DAY

Vegetable or fruit juice, one glass every two hours.

SECOND DAY

Breakfast:	Steamed dried fruit, or fresh fruit in season.
10:00 A.M.:	Glass of vegetable juice.
Lunch:	Finely shredded carrot steamed for three minutes.
3:00 P.M.:	Glass of vegetable juice.
Dinner:	Finely shredded carrot steamed for three minutes; one cooked vegetable.

THIRD DAY

Breakfast: Steamed dried fruit, or fresh fruit in season.

10:00 A.M.:   Glass of juice.

Lunch: One cooked vegetable; fruit or vegetable salad.

3:00 P.M.:   Glass of juice.

Dinner: Fruit or vegetable salad; one cooked vegetable; cottage cheese.

The Seven-Day Transition

FIRST DAY

One glass of juice every three hours—half pineapple juice and half water. (If diabetic, take half grapefruit juice and half water.)

SECOND DAY

Glass of carrot juice every two hours.

THIRD DAY

Breakfast: Steamed dried fruit, or fresh fruit in season.

10:00 A.M.:   Glass of vegetable juice.

Lunch: Finely shredded carrot steamed for three minutes.

3:00 P.M.:   Glass of vegetable juice.

Dinner: Finely shredded carrot steamed for three minutes; raw fruit.

FOURTH DAY

Breakfast: Diced orange and/or steamed dried apricots.

10:00 A.M.:   Juice of any kind, vegetable preferred.

Lunch: One cooked vegetable; a fruit salad.

3:00 P.M.:   Juice of any kind, vegetable preferred.

Dinner: Vegetable salad, sour cream, or yogurt dress-
                   ing; one cooked vegetable; a baked potato.

FIFTH DAY

Breakfast: Diced orange and/or steamed dried apricots.

10:00 A.M.:   Juice of any kind, vegetable preferred.

Lunch: One cooked vegetable; fruit salad; yogurt.

3:00 P.M.:   Juice of any kind, vegetable preferred.

Dinner: Vegetable salad; one cooked vegetable; cot-
                   tage cheese.

SIXTH DAY

Same as fifth day, except add an egg yolk to breakfast menu.

SEVENTH DAY

Regular diet.

DIET FOR HYPOGLYCEMIA

On arising: Medium orange, half grapefruit, or juice.

Breakfast: Fruit, one egg (two slices of ham or bacon,
                   optional), one slice of bread or toast with

plenty of butter, milk, decaffeinated coffee or weak tea made with a tea bag (not brewed).

Two hours after breakfast:	4 ounces of juice.
Lunch:	Meat, cheese, or fish, salad (lettuce, tomato, raw vegetable, with mayonnaise or French dressing made without sugar), vegetables, one slice of bread or toast with plenty of butter; sugar-free dessert; beverage.
Three hours after lunch:	One glass of milk.
One hour before dinner:	4 ounces of juice.
Dinner:	Soup, if desired (not thickened with flour), vegetables; liberal portion of meat, fish, or poultry; one slice of bread, if desired; sugar-free dessert; beverage.
Two to three hours after dinner:	One glass of milk.
Every two hours until bedtime:	Juice, nuts, cheese, or milk.
Allowable vegetables:	Asparagus, beets, broccoli, Brussels sprouts, cabbage, carrots, cauliflower, celery, cucumber, eggplant, onions, radishes, squash, string beans, tomatoes, turnips.
Allowable fruits:	Apricots, avocados, berries, grapefruit, melons, oranges, peaches, pineapple, tangerines.

	May be raw or cooked, with or without cream, but without sugar. Canned fruits must be without sugar.
Juices:	Any unsweetened fruit or vegetable juice except grape juice or prune juice.
Beverages:	Weak tea, Postum, Sanka. May be sweetened with saccharine. Sugarless soft drinks, except colas.
Avoid absolutely:	Sugar, candy, and other sweets, pie, cake, pastries, sweet custards, puddings, ice cream. Caffeine and cold beverages. Peas, potatoes, rice, corn, grapes, raisins, plums, pears, figs, apples, dates, bananas. Spaghetti, macaroni, noodles, and other pasta. Cream sauces and gravies made with flour. Wines, cordials, cocktails, beer, and other alcoholic beverages.

STOMACH ULCERS

The cause of painful stomach ulcers is now known to be the bacteria *Helicobacter pylori*. Medical doctors cure it with the antibiotic amoxicillin. Chronic constipation is really the beginning of ulcerous conditions, whether they are of the stomach, skin, bone, or any organ of the body. The clogging of the lower colon can delay the passage of the food through the stomach and into the small intestine. Constipation may cause putrefaction of bowel contents, multiplying undersirable bacteria.

Prolapsed organs cause acid puddles to remain in the stomach, which stagnates food and irritates and inflames the stomach walls. Over time, this draws the bacteria that cause ulcers.

Constant use of drugs may weaken the lining of the stomach and bowl, increasing the likelihood of ulcers. Aspirin and other analgesics can cause ulcers.

Many people are constipated. To discover whether or not you are having the proper elimination, swallow a few activated charcoal tablets (drugstores have them) before a meal and check the clock. When the charcoal appears in the stool, check the clock again and calculate the bowel transit time. Your breakfast should not stay in the body any more than thirteen to fifteen hours, your lunch seventeen to twenty hours, and dinner fifteen to twenty hours.

Blood would not take in toxins and multiply bacteria that would damage the body if bowel transit time was regular and the bowel was clean. A high-fiber vegetable and whole grain diet is nature's own regulator, and we can have this if we so desire. Diet alone has not succeeded in the healing of stomach ulcers, but diet and bowel cleansing have done the job in most cases.

Dr. S. Bergman reported after working for years in Ethiopia that most of the natives suffered from ulcers. He traced this condition to the native habit of using pepper sauces at every meal. Most of their meals consisted of sour bread drowned in this stomach-damaging sauce that is 50 percent cayenne pepper. Meat, peas, and beans supply the rest of their diet, which is insufficient to counteract the formation of stomach ulcers. Harsh condiments definitely can cause irritation of the stomach, although not everyone is equally vulnerable. However, you wouldn't put pepper in an open sore, would you?

In the past, milk seemed to be the ideal diet for stomach ulcers. However, I am not interested in just allaying inflammation and relieving pain; I am interested in building a new stomach. We must try to accomplish four things:

1. Stop smoking, alcohol use, and wind down the stress.
2. Rest the stomach and allay inflammation.
3. Restore mineral and vitamin content to the body.
4. Promote regular elimination of waste.

In severe cases, following a hemorrhage, for instance, it is best to eat or drink nothing other than an alkalinizing vegetable liquor. (Check with your doctor before trying this.) Follow this with a combination of raw goat's milk and soaked peeled dates. The milk should be diluted half and half with water, and the dates should be soaked overnight, then peeled before eating. Eat three dates and a half glass of milk every hour and a half. In severe cases, follow this regimen for three days, then increase the amount of food to one glass and four or five dates every three hours, with vegetable liquor in between.

Enemas must be taken morning and night. Sunbathe, if possible, every day for ten minutes to build up the calcium of the body. (Sunlight on the skin creates vitamin D from sterol under the skin, and vitamin D is necessary to accumulate calcium.) Stay away from bicarbonate of soda, for this only relieves hyperacidity. In severe cases, it is best to be under the direct supervision of a doctor.

After extreme inflammation has subsided, you can take soft, sweet fruit, stewed fruit mashed through a sieve, well-cooked vegetables, vegetable broths with a little cream in them, spinach toast, raw meat juice from young beef, and an occasional egg. Eat often in small amounts. One food at a time is best. Add one of the above foods to the regular regimen each day. Taking well-beaten egg whites in food or drinks fifteen or twenty minutes before lunch and supper is good. Also helpful are buttermilk, parsley, and diluted parsley juice. When you get to the place where you are having a variety of meals and larger portions, try the following suggestion (no seeds, no peelings, no skins):

8:30 A.M. Soy or rice milk and dried fruits (steamed or pureed), or goat's milk and dates (soaked and peeled).

9:30 A.M. Veal joint broth or raw vegetable juice with milk and plain gelatin.

11:00 A.M. Egg yolk and pineapple juice with beaten egg white on top.

1:30 P.M. One pint of raw cabbage juice; vegetable broth and gelatin.

3:00 P.M. Stewed peaches or stewed apricots (or water-packed fruit) with milk, if desired.

4:30 P.M. Another pint of raw cabbage juice and milk or yogurt and apple concentrate.

6:00 P.M. Spinach or beet greens pureed and served on soy bread toast. Baked potato and pureed vegetable.

7:30 P.M. Aloe vera juice, and carrot juice mixed with raw, fresh goat's milk.

9:00 P.M. Milk and dates (date milk shake); four dates to a glass of milk.

Take 1 tablespoon of gelatin three times daily. Take a duodenal substance (available at the health food store) every two
hours for the first week, then reduce to three times daily.

Take daily enemas using 1 teaspoon powdered whey to
1 pint of water. Take bulk-forming powders orally, at least to see
if they help.

Later, begin to add other things to your diet, such as baked
apple with cream or nut butters in fruit or fruit juices. Eat pureed
soybeans, lima beans, or peas, with any other vegetable during the
diet also. Avocados and an omelet may be added at this time,
too. Use plenty of fruit juices, such as cherry, apple, and prune
juice after the diet regimen is underway. No citrus fruits.

Sometimes using a teaspoon of olive oil every two hours
will help ulcer conditions. But remember: All this is not a
whole remedy and you should be under a doctor's care.

From this limited stomach ulcer diet, gradually work up to
a bland diet that is based on my Balanced Daily Eating
Regimen (see chapter 19).

NERVOUS INDIGESTION

The mind has an enormous influence over the body. Scientists
definitively observed this at the beginning of the twentieth century with the work of Ivan Pavlov, the Russian physiologist.
Using various animals, such as cats and dogs, researchers gave
them enough barium with their meals that the digestive organs
could be clearly outlined. Under the fluoroscope, the living animal's stomach and bowel could be observed operating quite
smoothly. But the moment the animal was frightened (as a cat
might be by the presence of a dog in the room), a marked
change would occur. The digestive organs would cease their

operations. The normal peristaltic movements of the stomach and intestine would stop—a clear indication of the effect of emotional stress on the digestive tract.

The same thing happens to human beings. Much of the digestive distress of which many people complain arises from adrenaline-driven nervous tension. This applies not only to adults, but also to little children. Nervous stress within the family is a common cause of dyspepsia and digestive upsets. Such conditions may be temporarily relieved by taking pills, but they will not be cured by medicines. Only by smoothing out the annoying situation will the condition be fully solved.

BLAND FOOD DIET

A program in which the nutritional needs of the whole body is addressed is the foundation of good health. When we cannot take the foods necessary for health in their normal form and are using the blender as an aid, we must not forget that a balanced daily eating regimen is still required. It is no use living on milk and mush to soothe stomach ulcers while starving the rest of the body. Good health depends on balanced nutrition. When we are sick, we often have to favor a weak organ, but we cannot neglect all the other needs of the body.

Here is a program in which we are following the dietetic law of balanced eating and using the blender almost exclusively. Do not forget that *chewing well* is necessary for a healthy body. Even though the food is liquefied, it must be chewed to mix with saliva.

Use the foods raw, in liquefied salad form, wherever possible; if necessary, have them cooked and liquefied; or cooked, liquefied, and then strained for severe colitis or ulcer cases.

People on a bland diet usually don't get all the variety that healthy people do. Have daily four to six vegetables, two fruits, one starch, and one protein, with juices or liquids between meals.

DAILY MENU

On arising:	Take any natural, unsweetened fruit juice.
Breakfast:	Fruit (protein or starch).
10:30 A.M.:	Liquid or fruit.
Lunch:	Two vegetables (one starch); tea or drink.
3:30 P.M.:	Fruit juice; tea or fruit.
Dinner:	Two vegetables (one protein); tea or drink.
Fruit juice suggestions:	Black cherry, fig, grape, prune, papaya, pineapple. Do not eat starch and protein together. Eat them at separate meals.

REDUCING DIETS

These diets should be followed for only two weeks. Then return to my Health and Harmony Daily Eating Regimen for at least two weeks (see chapter 19). Alternate three or four times according to weight loss goal.

The meats used may be lamb, fish, lean beef, turkey, or chicken. Never have fats or pork. Bake, broil, or roast fish and meat. The fish should be a white fish (one that had fins and scales).

Always have ripe, fresh tomato slices (canned only in an emergency), or grapefruit when you eat meat or fish.

If you do not use meat, then use the other proteins: eggs, cottage cheese, gelatin mold, skim milk, soy milk, tofu, low-fat yogurt.

All vegetables should be from the 5 percent carbohydrate list (see below).

Drink in-between meals only. This should be one hour before or two hours after meals. Use Cleaver's tea (2 cups daily). (Cleaver's tea eliminates catarrh and detoxifies the blood, the liver, and the kidneys and stimulates perspiration to increase skin elimination.)

---

5 PERCENT CARBOHYDRATE VEGETABLES

Artichokes	Cucumber	Radishes	String beans
Asparagus	Dandelion	Rhubarb	Swiss chard
Beet greens	Eggplant	Sauerkraut	Tomatoes
Broccoli	Endive	(not	Turnip tops
Brussels	Escarole	canned)	Vegetable
sprouts	Leeks	Sea lake	marrow
Cabbage	Lettuce	Sorrel	Watercress
Cauliflower	Mushrooms	Spinach	
Celery	Mustard	Sprouts	
Chard	greens	(alfalfa,	
Chicory	Okra	mung, etc.)	

Regular Reducing Diet

ONE WEEK MENU

Breakfast: One fresh fruit; one or two eggs or cottage cheese.

Lunch: Brown rice; one vegetable and salad.

Dinner: Meat or fish with tomato or grapefruit, one vegetable (if desired).

Other meal suggestions include:

1. One cup skim milk, 1 tablespoon sesame seed meal, ⅓ avocado, and one fruit. Blend.
2. One cup skim milk; watercress or romaine lettuce (blend), or salad with fish and tomato. (Or use four to six watercress tablets per meal.)
3. Fruit and cheese.
4. Apples and cottage cheese.

You may use rice cakes or Ry-Krisp once in a while. Bananas are a reducing starch. There are four starches that I consider using: millet, rye, yellow cornmeal, and brown rice.

Strict Reducing Diet

USE ONLY THIS MENU

Breakfast: One fresh fruit; one or two eggs.

Lunch: Vegetable; salad.

Dinner: Meat or fish with tomato or grapefruit.

Many people can use this diet for a whole month, others less. It is best to be under a doctor's care.

Vegetarian Reducing Diet

Follow this diet for two weeks. Then, return to the Balanced Daily Eating Regimen (see chapter 19) for two weeks. Alternate.

Drink in between meals only. This should be at least one hour before or two hours after meals. Use KB-11 or Cleaver tea (2 cups daily).

Always use sliced ripe tomato or grapefruit sections with proteins at dinner. Use canned tomatoes only when you can't find fresh ones.

Use proteins such as eggs, cottage cheese, gelatin, soy tofu, and low-fat yogurt.

All vegetables should be from the 5 Percent Carbohydrate Vegetable chart on page 410.

ONE WEEK MENU

Breakfast:	One fresh fruit and one or two eggs or cottage cheese.
Lunch:	Brown rice and one vegetable and salad.
Dinner:	Protein with tomato or grapefruit and one vegetable, if desired.

Other meal suggestions include:

1. One cup soy milk or skim milk, 1 tablespoon sesame seed meal, ⅓ avocado, and one fruit. Blend.
2. Fruit and cheese.
3. Apple and low-fat yogurt.
4. One cup skim milk, watercress or romaine lettuce (blend), or salad with cottage cheese and tomato. (Or use four to six watercress tablets per meal.)

You may use rice cakes or Ry-Krisp once in a while. Chlorella tablets will help balance every meal.

BULK PROGRAM FOR CLEANSING

This program is best done under a doctor's supervision because it is a type of fast which could be risky for persons with existing health problems. It is a good elimination program to carry out at home any time. You are going to be on juices for the first three days. Acceptable juices are apple, pineapple, grape, and carrot juice. Have carrot juice at 10:00 A.M. and 3:00 P.M. You may have a different juice each time. Apple concentrate or black cherry concentrate can be used. You may use a liquid chlorophyll drink in place of any of the juices at anytime.

First Three Days

Do not take any food supplements. Take 1 teaspoonful of bulk in a glass of juice five times during the day. After each glass of juice, with bulk added, take a glass of water. Do not eat any food. (A good way to mix the bulk with the juice is to put them into a container, seal, and shake.) Take enemas daily for six days, as long as bulk is being taken.

Fourth Day

Do not take any food supplements.

Breakfast:	Fruit, fresh in season, or steamed dried fruit.
10:00 A.M.:	Glass vegetable juice or fruit juice.
Lunch:	Finely shredded carrots, steamed for three minutes only.
3:00 P.M.:	Glass of vegetable juice or fruit juice.
Dinner:	Finely shredded carrots, steamed for three minutes only, and one other lightly cooked vegetable.

Take 1 teaspoon of bulk in glass of juice or water, followed by a glass of water, three times daily.

FIFTH AND SIXTH DAYS

Do not take any food supplements.

Breakfast:	Fruit.
10:00 A.M.:	Juice of any kind.
Lunch:	One cooked vegetable and a fruit or vegetable salad.
3:00 P.M.:	Juice of any kind.
Dinner:	One cooked vegetable, cottage cheese, and fruit or vegetable salad.

Take 1 teaspoonful of bulk in glass of juice or water, followed by a glass of water, three times daily.

SEVENTH DAY

Take supplements, if prescribed. Resume the Balanced Daily Eating Regimen (see chapter 19).

Ask doctor if bulk and enemas should be continued and, of course, consult your doctor for advice anytime you have problems with this program.

CLEANSING GRAPE DIET

Of course, I don't believe that there is a single cure (silver bullet) for any disease, nor do I believe in panaceas. But thousands of people might be cured of various ailments, and many diseases might be prevented by merely taking an annual "grape fast." For centuries, the cleansing property of grapes has been utilized in Europe, but it was only since the publication of *The Grape Cure* by Dr. Johanna Brandt of South Africa in 1928 that it became generally known in this country. (The book is available as a reprint.)

In Europe before World War II, thousands of people from many countries flocked to the grape-growing districts of central Europe during the grape season and took "the cure." A friend of mine was passing through the French grape-growing districts on a bus. She noted a heavy fragrance and inquired of the driver what it was. "It's grapes," he said. "This is the grape season, and every hotel, boarding house, and even private home is filled with people taking the grape cure."

In America, the grape diet is used as an elimination diet to alleviate or reverse various ailments such as arthritis, liver problems, migraine headaches, rheumatism, skin problems, and stomach ulcers. Doctors and patients report that the grape diet eliminates considerable quantities of impurities. If we cleansed the body at intervals, serious diseases would be far less likely to develop.

Almost everyone can profit by the grape diet. Here's how to make it work best:

Enemas should be taken once or twice daily for the first week of dieting. Don't use laxatives or drugs. If possible, have marathon bath or hydrotherapy treatments to aid in elimination. Continue skin brushing and moderate sunbathing throughout the grape cure (ten minutes daily).

Get plenty of sleep; frequent a congenial environment. Avoid heavy exertion, *but* exercise daily as prescribed and practice slant board exercises twice daily.

Eat 3 to 5 pounds of dark-skinned grapes daily. Do not eat seeds. (Grape seed extract may be taken.) Concord, Fresno Black Beauty, or even Muscat or Malaga grapes are preferable to Thompson Seedless or Ladyfinger. Skins may be eaten and grape juice may be drunk along with eating the grapes. Eat approximately five grape meals per day.

If you tire of grapes, change to one day of raw salads or different kinds of fruit. Take a glass of grapefruit juice occasionally. You should enjoy the grapes to reap the greatest good.

Should a crisis develop, get professional advice immediately.

Before going back to a regular diet, first eat raw fruits every other meal for about two days. Next eat raw vegetable salads every other meal for about two days, then eat raw vegetable salads every other meal one day more unless otherwise directed. In any unusual condition, it is good to consult your doctor. After completing the diet instructions, follow my Balanced Daily Eating Regimen (see chapter 19).

The grape diet will not make you weak. You should gain strength. However, almost everyone goes through an elimination process. In such cases, your energy will be temporarily taken away and what is inside your body that doesn't belong will be cast off, sometimes with miserable effects. But whatever symptoms you may go through, you have gone through them before at some period of your life. What is actually happening is a breaking down of chronic settlements in your body resulting in an active acute eliminative condition. This purification process is the only means of actually making a correction, whether it be through following the grape diet or following any other natural food regimen.

INTERNAL WATER TREATMENT

In the morning, water treatment is very effective.

Take two or three glasses of warm water before breakfast as follows: Take the first glass of water half an hour before breakfast. Ten minutes later, take the second glass of water; the third glass of water should be taken ten minutes later.

You may use 1 teaspoon liquid chlorophyll in one of the glasses of water. Also, in place of one glass of water, you may take a health tea.

This water treatment flushes out the kidneys and genitourinary tract. It helps to move the gas and promote a natural bowel movement.

Exercise and warm water should be taken before breakfast. Stay on your regular health-building diet. The water is just in addition to regular meals. This water treatment should be taken for one month.

TABLE SUPPLEMENTS

Use about a quarter teaspoon a day of Nova Scotia dulse (high in iodine) if the doctor advises and you desire. Use 1 teaspoon of rice polishings daily (high in vitamin B and silicon). Use 1 tablespoon of wheat germ daily (high in vitamin E). All these can be mixed with whole grain morning cereals.

If you are constipated, or your bowels are irregular, use 1 or 2 teaspoons each meal of ground flaxseed meal. Be sure you drink water with this; otherwise it will stick in your throat.

VEGETABLE JUICES

Vegetable juices should be taken twice a day, at 10:00 A.M. and at 3:00 P.M. For those on regular health-building regimens, raw vegetable juice is a good substitute for raw vegetable salads if desired.

Vegetable juice diets are also good, in some cases. Juices are taken every two hours. Get specific instructions and advice from your doctor. One teaspoon of liquid chlorophyll in a glass of water is equal to one glass of raw vegetable juice.

SPECIAL BROTH FOR SICK PEOPLE

Take four to five vegetables. Liquefy in blender. Bring to a boil. Add soy milk powder and simmer three or four minutes. Strain. This is my special life-giving broth.

NORMALIZING WEIGHT

If you are concerned with gaining or losing weight, remember it is more important to have a healthy body than to be a few pounds over or under the standard weight chart. No one knows for sure how much you should weigh. The weight chart is made from the average weights of heavy, medium, and thin people of the same age. However, no two people are alike. Your parents may be thin or tall or fat or broad-chested or thin-legged or bony or nervous or one of many possible types. The old saying that an apple cannot be any better than the tree from which it fell holds true in the human family as well. You cannot make a race horse out of a dray horse, neither can you, by diet, change a person's basic body structure.

Work to normalize the functions of every organ in the body, and the weight normalizes itself. The same applies to gaining weight. Start a "right living" program and nature automatically adjusts you without further assistance.

When you are underweight, do not overdo on cleansing diets to the exclusion of other foods. When you are overweight, do not indulge in rich, concentrated foods, even though they are natural.

Overweight

Exercise is the best tonic. Say "No" to the second helping of food. Keep the bowels open, learn to swim—and swim. Take Nova Scotia dulse tablets daily, three or four a day. Follow the

Eleven-Day Elimination Regimen (see page 395). Go on a heavy protein diet. Eat plenty of greens and liquid foods. Stay away from fatty and starchy foods.

Get a high-protein supplement to use along with the fruit juice and use that as a meal. Skip one meal a day until you bring yourself down to a normal weight, making sure you have a well-balanced diet. Many can get good results by eating wisely at breakfast and supper, then eating only 1 tablespoon of cottage cheese and two prunes for lunch daily for one month. A lunch of just yogurt and fresh fruit is also very good, or select a low-calorie diet from the vegetable kingdom.

Try exercising in a sweat shirt and perspire. If you perspire a lot, or if the body needs a lot of sodium, increase your water intake (you should be drinking at least 2 quarts of water daily, no matter what else you are drinking), take about four okra and four celery tablets with each meal.

Those with weight problems usually need a chlorophyll supplement to keep the bowel clean. Also use watercress, which is high in chlorophyll and potassium salts. Use alfalfa tea for trace element support.

Rye, millet, rice, and yellow cornmeal are four reducing whole cereal grains that can help you meet your need for carbohydrates but will not add weight. Wheat puts on fat and rye puts on muscle.

An herb tea combination that helps with losing weight is chickweed, licorice, saffron, gotu kola, mandrake, echinacea, black walnut, hawthorne, and fennel.

Epsom salts baths also may be taken once or twice a week to help you reduce unless they prove too weakening. Use about 3 cups of Epsom salts to the average bath water. Five to seven minutes in the tub is long enough, or until the body has begun to perspire. Always follow these baths with a cold towel treatment, then with a brisk rubdown. The Epsom salts, plus the water, stimulates elimination of toxic wastes.

Follow the Eleven-Day Elimination Regimen (see page 395). In most cases, that additionally takes off weight from five to ten pounds. Omit all bread and rolls and use Ry-Krisp in its place.

Follow the Balanced Daily Eating Regimen (see chapter 19) after the elimination regime. Eat no more than one slice of bread a day, if you eat bread at all. Drink no milk. When using cream, dilute it with water. Eat only a fruit breakfast and work toward the purification process or healing crisis. Use the skin tonic bath. Always leave the table a little hungry. Do daily exercises and eat plenty of fruit and vegetable salads. There are times when glandular foods will help in losing weight.

There is one exercise that works better than all others for losing weight: After you have eaten two-thirds of what was on your plate, place both hands on the edge of the table and push away.

Underweight

To gain weight, go through a cleansing process by following the Eleven-Day Elimination Regimen (see page 395), then follow with the Balanced Daily Eating Regimen (see chapter 19). Play every day. Hike, swim, or exercise at least one hour daily. Exercising in the open air is most helpful in gaining weight. All trouble, cares, and worries should be forgotten. Picture yourself as the filled-in jovial, "happy-go-lucky" man or woman that you would like to be. Get plenty of sleep by going to bed at nine o'clock at night. Cut down mental activity and eyestrain. If you are nervous, use deep breathing exercises.

Eat weight-building foods: bananas, sunflower seed meal, soy milk, and dried fruits with stewed fruit, goat's milk, and soy milk between meals. Take flaxseed tea before each meal (1 cup).

Weight loss sometimes indicates a vitamin A deficiency. Parsley, carrots, and all other green or yellow vegetables are rich in vitamin A.

Typical Meals for Gaining Weight. Baked potatoes with butter, spinach, broccoli, carrots, and other cooked vegetables. Omelet, salads, and custard. Drink a glass mixed with one-half goat's milk and one-half water. Use the Balanced Daily Eating Regimen as a base. Use cream on fruits in the morning. A combination of celery, apples, and cottage cheese or goat cheese is a good weight builder, or combine celery, nuts, and dried fruits, such as raisins, dates, and figs. Sometimes glandular foods are necessary to add to the regular meals. Seek professional advice regarding glandular foods.

Never consume high-calorie foods without vitamins. Ice cream, doughnuts, and pastries may be fattening, but there is nothing healthy about this kind of weight. Get on the regular Balanced Daily Eating Regimen with a bias toward the weight-building foods. Have a good whole grain cereal for breakfast. Put a little flaxseed meal, sunflower seed meal, dulse, and rice polishings on it, and cream or butter. Have a glass of goat's milk or buttermilk.

Choose more from the sweet and dried fruits; citrus fruits are for slimming or detoxifying. Take a spoonful of nut butter with them. Have between-meal snacks of nut milk or sesame drinks, using carob, dried fruits, banana, or honey for flavoring. Take a dish of yogurt with fruit. A small whole grain sandwich with stuffed celery sticks occasionally will help. Rich cocktails of fruit or vegetable juices with an egg yolk and other supplements added will help, or a drink of milk with fruit and cheese. On your lunch salad use a cream or oil dressing, sometimes adding an egg yolk. Favor more of the root vegetables, but don't neglect the greens! Choose a cream or legume soup or a soup thickened with barley or whole rice. Nibble on raw nuts and sunflower and pumpkin seeds at odd moments. Don't skimp on proteins. Drink cocktails with a flaxseed tea base. Before bed a hot carob-milk drink is permissible.

One cup of flaxseed tea twenty minutes before each meal also helps in gaining weight. Rather than using fresh fruit juice in drinks, use reconstituted dried fruits with soybean milk, nut butter, and so on. When using raw vegetable juices, add 1 tablespoon sunflower seed meal or 1 tablespoon sesame seed meal so the drink will add weight to the body.

Weight gaining is not all food. Get plenty of exercise. Sleep and rest are especially important if you are the thin, worrying type. Live as much as possible out in the open air and sunshine.

The best weight-building foods are lean meat, poultry, fish, tofu, bananas, sunflower seed meal, soy milk, and dried fruits.

SIGNS OF A CHEMICALLY BALANCED BODY

Everyone knows what disease looks like. These are signs of health:

- General appearance of good health.
- Active, alert, vigorous.
- Skin clear, smooth, soft, slightly moist, and somewhat pink.
- Weight proportionate to age and height; a pleasing carriage.

- Hair plentiful, lustrous, having no indication of being brittle or excessively dry.
- Eyes bright and clear with no dark rings or circles under them.
- Muscles firm and strong.
- Tongue pink and not coated. Breath sweet. Posture straight and upright. Nerves steady. Joints limber, free from deposits and stiffness.
- Organs working well without sensations of pain, soreness, fatigue, discomfort, heaviness, swelling, or pressure.
- Willing to do things, able to do them, and glad to be alive.

CHAPTER 21

HEALING AND COOKING WITH HERBS

T here are many wonderful herbs available to help you reverse a disease or prevent a disease state from developing, but like anything else having to do with your personal health, you need to know what you're doing. The use of herbs and spices in cooking is also important to explore not only because of the flavors they impart but also because of the healing properties they offer. This chapter on herbs will get you started on the right foot.

HERBS FOR HEALING

Herbs are among nature's greatest healers, and I feel everyone should get acquainted with them. In my bout with prostate cancer over the past few years, I give essiac tea some of the credit for driving the cancer into remission. Herbs seem to be directed by their DNA and messenger RNA to draw to themselves particular minerals from the soil that, transformed by cellular chemistry, form biologically active substances with cleansing or healing properties. In fact, a significant number of prescription medications are derived from herbs.

Herbs are an easy-to-use natural remedy resource. I would encourage you to learn how they are used in teas, tonics, tinctures, infusions, and extracts, and I will get you started in this chapter. Many homeopathic remedies are made from herbs. Most modern health food stores have a wonderful selection of herbs, some freshly picked, some processed commercially and sold in containers as powders, capsules, or tablets. These days you can even buy them on the Internet.

We find that herbs have a long and commendable history. They were used in China at least a thousand years before Christ, and are often prescribed today by modern Chinese doctors. People in many countries seem to have their favorite herbal remedies and often grow certain herbs in their gardens. I feel that our regular food regimen should be supplemented with herbs, as the occasion for their need arises.

How to Make Herb Teas

Use 1 heaping teaspoon of your favorite tea to 2 cups of water. Bring the water to a boil in a stainless steel pot, add the herb or herbs you want, and let stand till cool. Strain it and drink the tea, cool or reheated. You may flavor it with a little honey. If you don't want to drink it right away, refrigerate it. This recipe will work for most herbal teas.

CATALOG OF HEALING HERBS

Alfalfa Leaf. Stimulating for kidneys, bowels, appetite, and digestion. Highly alkaline. Use for peptic ulcers.

Alfalfa Seed.　Rich in silicon. Liver cleansing. For arthritis and similar joint pains.

Alfa-mint (Alfalfa Mint).　Rich in minerals and vitamins. Good for arthritic conditions, digestion. An antacid—very alkalinizing. Alfa-mint should always be on your shelf. Alfalfa is one of the greatest alkalinizers we can put into our body. Mint is a gas driver. It is great for toning up the intestinal tract. Both are very high in chlorophyll.

Angelica.　Use for bronchial problems, colds, indigestion, colic.

Balm.　Helps to soothe nervous headaches, toothache, hysteria, earache, chlorosis.

Balsam.　Balsam tea with ginger can be used to help expel gas. It is also used for cramps and colic. Can be given to children.

Basil.　Stimulates circulation and helps eliminate catarrh.

Bay.　Used as a skin tonic for skin problems.

Blueberry.　Tea from blueberry leaves is specific for alleviating hypoglycemia.

Blue Violet.　Leaves and flowers are good for lymph gland drainage, catarrhal conditions, severe cough, healing sores. High in vitamin C; the leaves are especially high in vitamin A.

Borage.　Used for palpitations, hysteria, adrenal problems; to increase mother's milk.

Buchu. Good for the kidneys, genitourinary tract, uric acid gravel, and the lungs. Stimulant and diuretic.

Burdock. Used to reduce weight and as a blood purifier. A renal cleanser.

Burnett. Use for throat infections and to control hemorrhages.

Catnip. Diaphoretic (prevents gas), carminative (increases perspiration), and tonic. Relaxes nerves. Used as a tranquilizer. Relieves fevers, pain, flatulence, and colds.

Chamomile. Aids digestion. Clears complexion. Good for flatulence and gas. Soothing for colic. Discharges catarrh; soothes inflammation; has potassium and calcium. A wonderful tonic for children and for all ages. Antispasmodic, relaxant; take before bedtime.

Chickweed. For acne and a good all-around tonic.

Chicory. Is used to help jaundice. Roasted chicory is a good and healthful substitute for coffee.

Comfrey Leaves. Use for external poultice only (see cautionary notes about herbs on page 439).

Cornsilk. Kidney and bladder; genitourinary tract; mucous linings. Rich in magnesium. Dried cornsilk makes a wonderful kidney tea, especially for one who has a tendency to have gravel in the kidneys and bladder. It helps to dissolve the gravel and break it down.

Curly Cabbage. In Germany, they use curly cabbage, chopped up fine, for varicose ulcers, milk leg, phlebitis, and leg ulcers.

Dandelion. Purifies blood; contains iron; rich in calcium; diuretic. Good for cold, dyspepsia, diabetes, tuberculosis, rheumatism, arthritis, kidneys, gallbladder, and liver. Dandelion tea is especially good for the gallbladder and the liver. Leaves and flowers help the bile to flow.

Echinacea. Immunostimulant, wards off colds, flu; mild antibiotic activity; use with goldenseal or vitamin C; anti-inflammatory. Echinacea is effective in relieving arthritis pain, indigestion, fighting infections, strengthening immune system.

Ephedra (Ma Huang). Used in China and India for several thousand years to relieve bronchial asthma. Relief from nasal congestion and reduction of allergy symptoms. (Not effective for weight loss, despite rumors.) Should not be used by those with heart conditions, high blood pressure, diabetes, or thyroid problems.

Elderberry. For catarrhal conditions, colic, diarrhea. Good for the blood and kidneys. Elderberry tea is a fine tonic for ovarian problems and menstrual disorders and the sexual orifices. Use leaves and berries for teas. Blossoms may be used in omelets. Can be used to lighten freckles.

Essiac Tea. Combination of burdock root, sheep sorrel, red clover, watercress, blessed thistle, kelp, rhubarb root, and slippery elm bark. Detoxifies, cleanses, removes heavy metals, stimulates cell repair, increases energy level, supports immune system. Essiac tea was originally developed by the Ojibway Indian tribe. Sometimes used for degenerative diseases. Buy at health food stores.

Eyebright. Tonic; astringent; clears and tones; for gastric trouble and eye beauty.

Fennel. Used for gas problems and colic.

Fenugreek. Soothes mucous surfaces; for ulcers, sore throats, poor digestion, fevers. Very healing. If you have a weakness in the bronchial tubes, fenugreek helps remove the catarrh.

Feverfew. Claimed to reduce migraine headaches.

Figwort. For blood-clotting problems.

Flaxseed. Demulcent; for constipation; tea enema for bleeding bowel. High in silicon and vitamin E. Flaxseed tea with 1 teaspoon liquid chlorophyll three times per day is very good for stomach ulcers.

Fo Ti Tieng. Fo ti tieng is known in Chinese medicine as the elixir of life. It is said that the Chinese herbalist, Li Chung Yun, who died at the age of 256, used this herb in particular. In *Nature's Medicines,* authored by Richard Lucas, Fo ti tieng is claimed to be the finest of all herbs, tonics, and nutrients. It appears to have no equal in the treatment of debility and general decline—digestion is strengthened, foods are better absorbed, and metabolism improves.

Garlic and Onions. I observed while visiting Armenia that they wrapped garlic in comfrey leaves and dried it for the wintertime. The Armenian people also use it in a soup. I asked a mother why she used it, and she told me that it helped her children to be free from colds and kept her husband on the job without any sickness. Both garlic and onions contain a chemical substance called allicin that acts as a germicide. Garlic is a traditional remedy for high blood pressure.

In Russia, they have discovered an antihistamine reaction from garlic extract. When I look at all the herbs and foods, I think that garlic and onions are the two best and most powerful of them all.

For asthmatic contractions and bronchitis: An onion pack on the chest may be helpful for alleviating asthmatic contractions and works well in cases of bronchitis and catarrhal congestion of the chest.

For glandular congestion: I have seen the onion pack work well on swellings on the neck apparently caused by thyroid disturbance. I have seen it reduce lymph gland congestion in which swollen lymph nodules on the neck were relieved.

For tuberculosis: In the Bircher-Benner Clinic in Zurich, Switzerland, garlic and onions were used therapeutically to treat tuberculosis.

For worms: Garlic oil capsules may be used for getting rid of worms in children. You can take three or four garlic oil capsules three or four times a day for three days, and you will find that most of the worms will leave the body. Worms cannot stand garlic. Reducing food intake will hasten the elimination of the worms. Or use 1 teaspoon of either garlic oil or garlic powder in 1 quart of warm water and apply as enema. You may also take onions and garlic for three days by mouth. Repeat in twenty-seven days and repeat again in another twenty-seven days.

For tapeworms: Use garlic for a period of three days. It takes about three days for the garlic to saturate the bowel and the body. Then the worm begins to detach itself. At that time, I recommend using a strong laxative, then have the patient sit in warm milk. Do not have any air between the bowel passing and the milk, because if you do, the worm will cut itself off. The tapeworm comes in three- to six-inch sections, and if you do not get the head, it keeps on growing.

Geranium Green Leaves. Astringent.

Ginko Biloba. Improves memory, stimulates mental activity, improves blood circulation to brain.

Ginseng. Tonic herbal root dating back to ancient China. Adaptogen, normalizes body conditions, normalizes blood sugar in nondiabetics, supports sexual system, helps prevent hypoglycemia, improves energy.

Gotu Kola. Known for its rejuvenating qualities, believed to lengthen lifespan.

Goldenseal. Stimulates gastric juices, speeds up and aids digestion. For all mucous membrane problems. For colitis, catarrhal discharge problems, nasal drip.

Goldenseal is more effective for colds and flu when mixed with echinacea. It also appears to be a catalyst to make other herbs work better. You will find that both alfalfa and shavegrass are more effective when they are mixed with goldenseal. Try first for correcting any condition of the body.

Hawthorne Berry. Hawthorne berry tea is one of the finest remedies for the heart. It acts as a tonic. (This remedy comes from a sanitarium in Germany.) Hawthorne berries are said to increase oxygen and bring oxygen to the brain.

Hops. A bitter herb for soothing sleep.

Horsetail. Diuretic. High in silicon and calcium.

Huckleberry. Antispasmodic. Good for the pancreas in cases of diabetes. Helps in the digestion of starches, for lowering high blood pressure, and stopping diarrhea.

Hydrastis. Very good for indigestion.

Juniper Berries. Father Sebastian Kneipp started with two berries in a tea and built up to fifteen berries on the tenth day, then reduced the number of berries back down to two a day. This really cleans the kidneys. Juniper berry tea is also good for liver and blood cleansing, weak stomach, foul breath, gas, urethral infections, and bladder stones.

Lavender. Good for nervous headache, both blossom juice and as a tea.

Lemon Balm. Calms nerves, mild antibiotic effect. Europeans use on cold sores (herpes simplex).

Lovage. For indigestion, colic, scurvy, and as a diuretic.

Marigold. Used for scarlet fever. Direct applications help to smooth scar formation on skin.

Marshmallow Root. Combine with slippery elm for skin.

Milk Thistle. Used for liver conditions such as cirrhosis and hepatitis.

Nasturtium Juice. Used for itching skin, as an antiscorbutic, and as a blood purifier.

Oat Straw. High in silicon. Soothes, stimulates, tonic, mineralizer, potent solvent.

Oat straw tea has been used for years for all kinds of skin troubles including psoriasis, pimples, acne, and pustules. It is one of the best substances for getting silicon back into the body. Silicon is in the skin. If you use 2 cups oat straw tea every day for a year, you will see the benefits to the skin, hair, and nails.

An oat straw tea pack is good for varicose veins. Oat straw is a potent solvent, and it soothes as it stimulates. It must be boiled twenty minutes to release the silicon from the oat straw shaft. Oat straw tea rejuvenates the glands.

Papaya. Digestion of protein, dyspepsia, stomach weakness, pyorrhea. Hold papaya tablets in mouth to dissolve tartar on teeth.

Papaya tea helps to digest protein. If your doctor says you lack hydrochloric acid, then use papaya tea. If you have papaya seeds, dry them and make tea out of them. Use a tablespoon of the seeds to a cup of hot water. If you want to simmer the mixture for two minutes, you will get more papain out of it. Papain is found more in the leaves; pepsin is found more in the seed.

Papaya–Mint. The mint adds a nice flavor and is also a digestant.

Parsley. Best diuretic; also a mild laxative. Rich in iron and manganese. Parsley root, when dried, makes a wonderful tea for the kidneys. It is also good for gallstones, diabetes, jaundice, and rheumatism. Parsley seed tea is used for fevers.

Parsley juice is used for genitourinary tract infections, urine retention, iron deficiency; boiled parsley roots are used for epilepsy, adrenal deficiency, and thyroid deficiency. Eat parsley with onion and garlic to get rid of odor.

Pennyroyal (Mint). Combined with ginger helps to expel gas and helps with colic and cramps.

Peppermint. Antacid; aids digestion, circulation of blood; eliminates toxins; rich in manganese. Peppermint and spearmint can be used interchangeably. Both are good for colic and cramps, especially soothing for children.

For flatulence, use four drops of oil of peppermint to a cup of hot water.

Persimmon Leaf. Very high in vitamin C.

Pine Needle Tea. High in vitamin C.

Primrose. For sense of well-being, poise, and calmness.

Raspberry. For poor circulation. Tones female organs; reduces menstrual cramps and pain.

Red Clover. One of the wonder herbs. Rich in iron and vitamin C. Cleansing tea for drug residues; used for diarrhea.

Rice Tea. Used for congestion, acute head pain, nausea, fainting, difficult breathing, stomach cramps, colic, worms. Also used as a sedative. The liquid is used as a disinfectant.

Rose Hips. High in vitamin C. Used for kidneys and bladder; bladder stones.

Rosemary. Very soothing to the brain. Combined with rue, it is a good disinfectant.

Rue. Used for nausea and head congestion.

Sage. Blood cleanser, astringent (gargle), clears complexion, sedative; used for eye diseases; good for heart, liver, and kidneys; strengthening. For longevity and memory problems. For menstrual flow stimulant, use red sage tea. Helps combat night sweating.

St. John's Wort. Relaxant, mild tranquilizer, relieves menstrual problems, helps insomnia, nervous conditions, and anxiety.

Sarsaparilla. Rich in iodine; purifies blood; good for rheumatism. Researchers at Penn State University found that sarsaparilla contains saponin, a chemical similar to the male hormone, testosterone. They also found progesterone, a female hormone. Sarsasparilla is generally used for building up and maintaining the vitality of the body. Sarsaparilla taken three times a day in an eight-grain capsule stimulates mental alertness, boosts the physical strength, and helps to feed the glandular system.

Sassafras. Purifies blood, spleen, liver; digestant; reduces catarrh.

Savoy. Used for lethargy, colic, digestion problems, tonsillitis, bee stings, and an herb bath.

Saw Palmetto. This is one of the finest herbs for the prostate gland. For sexual impotency, it can be combined with damiana and kola nut. Use 1 ounce each of these dried herbs, simmer in 2 pints of water until 1 pint is left. Strain and cool. Take a wine glass full of the mixture after meals.

Senna. Purgative; cleanses digestive tract; relieves constipation.

Shavegrass. High in silicon. Good for kidneys, bladder, gas, varicose veins, mucous membranes.

Shavegrass is high in silicon, one of the elements we need most in our bodies. A lack of silicon may show up as rashes of the skin and in the nails.

Shavegrass tea is one of the finest herbal teas I have used with patients. It removes toxic material efficiently from the body. It is a mild diuretic, not irritating, and does not overwork the kidneys. It is especially helpful with ulcers, skin problems, psoriasis, wounds, and sores. Use the leaves as a poultice on wounds and sores and cover with a wet cloth.

Slippery Elm. For inflammation of mucous tissues, colitis, diarrhea. Slippery elm can be used in the form of small chips. Pour 1 pint of boiling water on a ½ ounce of chips and let it stand for half an hour. You can then take as much tea as desired and sweeten it with honey. It has wonderful, healing virtues. It counteracts acidity and soothes the membranes of the stomach and intestines.

In cases of duodenal and stomach ulcers, slippery elm is unsurpassed. The kidney and bladder are improved through its use. The weakest stomach can take it when possibly no other food can be tolerated. For troubles of the bowel and stomach, it can be mixed with rice gruel.

Slippery elm combined with marshmallow root is very soothing for the skin.

Sorrel Tea. For ulcers of the mouth and throat, use sorrel tea with honey. A stimulant; used for catarrh, stomach, blood problems, and ridding worms.

Spearmint. Diuretic. Contains iron. Good for nausea, vomiting, flatulence. Antidote to feverish conditions.

Strawberry. Diuretic. High in sodium and iron. Good for liver; blood purifying; heals mucous membranes. With woodruff is used as a cleansing medicine.

Uva Ursi. Diuretic. Useful for kidney complaints.

Valerian. Natural tranquilizer, relaxes nerves; relieves despondency, pessimism, head congestion, coughs, insomnia. Valerian root tea is very soothing for epilepsy. Use ½ cup of warm milk, ½ teaspoon of molasses, and ½ cup of valerian tea for a soothing tranquilizer.

White Oak. Rich in iodine and potassium. Use for diarrhea, dysentery, bowel problems, and for enemas.

Woodruff. For duodenal ulcers, internally, and as a wash. Used for liver, kidney, and abscesses. With strawberry leaf tea, woodruff is used as a cleansing medicine.

Yellow Dock. As a tea, used for acidosis, eczema.

CAUTIONARY NOTES ABOUT HERBS

I am not saying that you should not use the following herbs, but I am warning you to be careful. I recommend using herbs under the supervision of someone who knows herbs well, at least until you know enough to take care of yourself. The greatest mistake people make with herbs is the same mistake many people make with dietary supplements, such as vitamins and minerals. That is, people suppose that if a little of a certain product helps, then a much larger dosage would help much more. That is not true. Many products have safety limits, beyond which toxic effects begin to show up. The following listed herbs should be used with caution and wisdom, if at all. Get advice from a doctor who knows herbs before you use any of them.

Borage. Large amounts may cause liver damage. It contains alkaloids known to cause cancer and liver poisoning. Long-term effects of small amounts may be just as harmful as large doses over the short term.

Broom. Another herb containing alkaloids. Sparteine is the main alkaloid. Why take chances? Broom is usually taken for its diuretic effects. Use KB-11 from your health food store instead.

Chaparral. This herb was removed from the FDA's GRAS (generally regarded as safe) list in 1968. It has produced liver necrosis.

Coltsfoot. Japanese researchers found the dangerous alkaloid senkirkine in the flowers and leaves of coltsfoot. In tests with laboratory rats, cancer tumors developed in their livers. Don't take a chance.

Comfrey. This has been one of America's favorite herbs. Russian comfrey has the most toxic alkaloid contents, but many other comfrey species also contain enough of the alkaloid echimidine to cause liver damage. The roots contain ten times the amount of toxins as the leaves. Several cases of liver failure in the United States have been traced to comfrey. Several cases of atropine poisoning from comfrey have been documented. The leaves of the deadly nightshade are loaded with atropine and look similar to those of comfrey. An inexperienced gatherer could confuse the two. *Comfrey is perfectly safe to use as an external poultice on infections, boils, and wounds. It is not safe taken internally in any amount.*

Foxglove. A powerful toxin to the heart.

Juniper. Dangerous to pregnant women or persons with kidney disease.

Licorice Root. Licorice has a chemical ingredient named glycyrrhizin, which is very similar to aldosterone, the hormone released by the adrenal glands to get the kidneys to reabsorb sodium. Large amounts of licorice eaten or used over several days can cause the same effect as an overdose of aldosterone. This causes headaches, fatigue and weakness, loss of potassium, increased sodium and water, and increased blood pressure. It can cause heart failure. There are several medical cases on record of people eating too much licorice, or chewing too much tobacco laced with licorice as a sweetener. The relatively small amounts taken in licorice root capsules may not cause problems, but be on the lookout for cumulative effects.

Pennyroyal. Both American and European pennyroyal contain dangerous amounts of the toxic chemical pulegon, which destroys liver tissue. As little as a half teaspoon of pennyroyal oil produced convulsions and coma in one case in the medical records. The herb and the oil are used in animal flea collars. It has been used to promote abortions, but since it takes a nearly lethal dose to do it, many young women have died, not knowing how much to take. Let's leave this herb alone.

Pokeweed. Pokeroot and pokeweed have been praised for healing everything from athlete's foot to festered eyebrows, so to speak. In reality, it works as a cathartic and emetic only because it is poisonous. It doesn't have any track record for healing or helping anything. It sells on the basis of hearsay only, along with the mistaken recommendations of a very few herbalists who have probably never used it with a client.

Rue. May sensitize skin to damage from ultraviolet in sunlight.

Yohimbe or Yohimbine. Advertised as a sex stimulant, it contains a chemical that becomes toxic when combined with another chemical (phenylpropanolamine) found in cheeses, red wines, liver, and other foods. It should not be used by persons with kidney disease, high blood pressure, hepatitis, cirrhosis, or heart disease. Use only under supervision of a doctor.

HERBS AND SPICES FOR COOKING

In ancient days, herbs and spices were not only used for flavoring but were also used in foods as a general preventive therapy. There was no refrigeration in those days, and food spoiled quickly. People found that they felt better when they added the herbs and spices, which, of course, also offered a great variety of flavors. Their medicine was taken with their foods. At one time in history, the spice market influenced world commerce in the same way that the oil market influences ours today.

Today, using herbs and spices as seasoning and flavoring is a custom that is so universally accepted that we think only of these properties and have forgotten the original purpose. You will note that most of their healing properties relate to the stomach, aiding digestion, relieving gas, and so forth.

Allspice. Sauces; steamed puddings; pumpkin, raisin, and other pies; fruit salads and fruit cups; spiced cakes and cookies.

Healing properties: Wild allspice is used as a fever-breaker in colds.

Aniseed. Used whole or crushed in fruit and vegetable salads, cakes, breads, and rolls.

Healing properties: Comes from the anise plant native to Egypt. Very good for stomach upsets and baby's colic.

Basil. Salads: tomato, mixed greens, cucumber, cheese and fruit; sauces; vegetables; egg and cheese dishes.

Healing properties: Basil is of the mint family. For flatulence.

Bay Leaves. Vegetable and tomato soup, tossed green and vegetable salads, French dressing, potatoes, carrots, dessert custards, and creams.

Healing properties: Soothing to the stomach; relieves flatulence.

Caraway. Cheese dishes; coleslaw, cucumber, potato, and tomato salads; crushed in salad dressings; vegetables.

Healing properties: Use for stomach gas and colic, hair problems, and vision problems.

Cardamom. Cardamom cakes, cookies, and breads; with honey to flavor fruit, whipped cream; with spices in pies, puddings, and desserts.

Healing properties: The spicy seeds of this East Indies herb are used medicinally for soothing relief to digestive system.

Cayenne (Red Pepper or Capsicum). Adds color and wonderful taste to vegetables, broths, soups, meat and fish, cheeses, and salads.

Healing properties: A well-known natural stimulant, has less reaction than many, and can be used frequently with no ill effects. It increases the efficiency of all organs, stimulates the secreting organs, helps the digestion. Can be used with utmost safety.

Celery Seed. Breads; butter and spreads; dips, ground in egg and cheese dishes, vegetable juices, salads, and salad dressings; sauces; vegetables.

Healing properties: Celery seeds, leaves, and stems are especially indicated for stomach disorders.

Chervil. Egg dishes, sauces, soups, salads.

Healing properties: An herb of the carrot family. Can be used as a poultice for bruises.

Cinnamon. Good in beverages—hot spiced fruit drinks, hot chocolate, eggnogs, milk shakes, spiced tea, or fruit punches;

desserts and puddings; fruits. Use whole cinnamon "sticks" in hot drinks.

Healing properties: Astringent; stimulant; as a tea, soothing for intestinal tract.

Cloves. Whole in fruit punches, when cooking fruit; ground in spiced cakes and cookies, egg dishes, sauces, and vegetables—beets, sweet potatoes, and tomatoes.

Healing properties: Used as an anesthetic; for flatulence; oil of cloves for toothache.

Dill. Seed: Cream cheese dips and spreads, butter, vegetables—cooked green beans, cabbage, squash, and turnips. Herb: Rich sauces, appetizers, vegetables as above; salads—avocado, cucumber, vegetable, coleslaw; soups.

Healing properties: Use for hiccoughs and as a sedative.

Garlic. Appetizers; salads—green and vegetable, potato; dressings; sauces; soups; entrées; butters. Now available as salt, powder, and chips.

Healing properties: Cleansing, purification, high blood pressure. See previous chapter for its many healing properties.

Ginger. Grind in tiny quantities in vegetables, salads, savory rice, and most Chinese recipes. Whole dried: some cooked fruits. Ground: Ginger cookies, cakes, and puddings; fruit sauce, winter squash, glazed carrots, onions, and sweet potatoes.

Healing properties: Can be used to help expel gas, in colic and cramps, and can be given to children in peppermint or balsam teas.

Horseradish. Sauces, dips, spreads, salad dressings, vegetables.

Healing properties: Is a stimulant for sinuses, mucus, and phlegm problems. Bruised horseradish is used as a poultice for sciatica. Gets the bile flowing, clears out the gallbladder and the liver.

Mace. Whole: In cheese sauce, cooked apples, prunes, apricots, fruit salads, sauces, and marinades. Ground: Breads and cakes, "chocolate" puddings, fruits, and vegetables.

Healing properties: Mace is made up of the hulls of nutmeg. Cleansing and detoxifying.

Marjoram. Soups—spinach, onion; cream sauces; egg dishes; vegetables—mushrooms, carrots, peas, spinach, zucchini.

Healing properties: Used as an antiseptic, stimulant, purifier, for headaches, irregular menstruation, and skin diseases.

Mint. Appetizers; fruit and gelatin salads; coleslaw; vegetables—carrots, peas, potatoes, zucchini, cabbage; mint sauce; fruit, gelatin, and ice desserts; beverages—hot and iced teas, hot chocolate, fruit punch.

Healing properties: Digestant, antispasmodic, diuretic, vomiting, asthma, colic.

Mustard. Whole: Salads—coleslaw, salad greens, vegetable and potato salads; vegetables—cabbage, buttered beets. Ground: Salads, dressings, sauces, butters, vegetables.

Healing properties: A stimulant for sinuses, croup, coughs. Poultices are used with whole wheat flour and white of egg for rheumatism chest congestion, and hot foot baths for headaches.

Nutmeg. Beverages—milk shakes, eggnog, spiced hot drinks, hot chocolate; breads, cakes, pies, desserts. Fruits—grated over applesauce, compotes, mincemeat.

Healing properties: One-half nutmeg crushed and steeped in a cup of hot water is good for insomnia. Helps indigestion and nervous stomach. The aroma of this warm spice soothes a headache. Must be used in small doses.

Oregano. Vegetables—zucchini, eggplant, tomatoes; hot sauces.

Healing properties: Aids digestion and is soothing to stomach.

Paprika. Appetizers, cheese, salad dressings, sauces, butters. Adds color to foods.

Healing properties: Stimulates appetite.

Parsley. Salad dressings, sauces, cheeses, fish, meats.

Healing properties: Good diuretic. Contains iron, magnesium, and manganese. Helps kidneys, gallstones, diabetes, jaundice. Fresh parsley helps eliminate food odors.

Pepper (black). *Do not use.* This is seventeen times more irritating to the liver than alcohol.

Saffron. Adds color to rice dishes, vegetables, and sauces. (Drawback: costs $55 to $170 per ounce.)

Healing properties: Antispasmodic; used for scarlet fever.

Sage. Soups—cream and chowder; salads; vegetarian stuffings; vegetables—lima beans, eggplant, onions, tomatoes.

Healing properties: An antiseptic. Used for eye diseases, longevity, memory problems, as a blood cleanser, astringent (gargle); for menstrual flow stimulant use red sage tea. Helps correct night sweating.

Savory. Soups—bean and lentil, consommé; salads—mixed green, vegetable, potato; sauces—horseradish; vegetarian stuffings.

Healing properties: Savory is a very aromatic herb of the mint family. It is so pleasing to taste and smell that the phrase "a savory meal" came from this herb.

Tarragon. Mixed green and fruit salads; sauces; egg dishes.

Healing properties: Soothing for eczema and scurvy.

Thyme. Tomato salad, aspic; tomato juice; sauces; vegetables—onions, carrots, beets.

Healing properties: After meals, aids digestion. An antiseptic for ptomaine poisoning. Helps to relieve phlegm and mucus, bronchitis, whooping cough. Is a good relaxant and can be used in bath.

Turmeric. Salad dressings; cream soups and chowders; for coloring; scrambled eggs.

Healing properties: A stimulant, prevents gas formation. Helps remove phlegm and mucus; protects gallbladder.

CHAPTER 22

CONCLUSION

In my ninety-two years, I have lived to see the people of the United States and the federal government and its agencies embrace my philosophy of disease prevention through proper nutrition, exercise, and a healthy lifestyle. Organically grown foods are often now found in supermarkets, not just small "natural food" stores. The natural food industry and alternative health care are both thriving, multibillion-dollar-per-year industries, with strong consumer support. I wonder if people will remember what a tremendous struggle was necessary to overcome the extreme and widespread prejudice against the natural health movement and its teachings from the 1930s to the 1970s. I was once thrown in jail for telling a man with cancer about the benefits of fresh vegetable juices. (Fortunately, a wise judge dismissed the charges against me.) Young people today would hardly believe that could happen in a democracy.

These days, clinical nutrition plays a very important part in preventing and even reversing disease. Herbal remedies like

Echinacea and special foods like garlic and various algae are valuable in addressing particular symptoms in a gentle but effective way. The physiological needs of the body that support health and protect against disease are better understood so that conditions like osteoporosis and heart disease can be improved by exercise and by using more of certain foods instead of relying only on drugs, which have undesirable side effects.

I am pleased to see all the wonderful herbs and other natural health products available, not only in health food stores but in supermarkets, drug stores, and sources like Wal-Mart, Costco/Price Club, and the Internet. There are specialty goods like acidophilus cultures, omega-3 fatty acids, and CoQ10 that help keep certain tissues healthy. I am greatly encouraged that so many people are taking it upon themselves to learn about natural remedies and to use them instead of drugs. There are many excellent companies competing with one another for consumer preference in the natural health field.

What encourages me most, however, is that ordinary people are becoming motivated enough to educate themselves on the subject of staying healthy. They are taking responsibility for their own health, and I expect this concern for better health to spread to more people in this new millennium.

Many great discoveries in medicine and health have been made in my lifetime. In the year I was born, Elie Metchnikoff in Russia and Paul Erlich in Germany shared the Nobel Prize for their research into the workings of the immune system. In 1929, Christian Eijkman was credited with the discovery of the first B vitamin. In the 1940s, antibiotics were discovered. Watson and Crick determined the structure of DNA (deoxyribonucleic acid) in 1962, and in the year 2000 the structure of the genome was finally completely mapped. Our biochemists are now working on ways of curing diseases by changing the very genetic structures that are responsible for inherent weaknesses in the human body as well as diseases caused by specific genes (or lack of them). All of the preceding discoveries have had a tremendous influence on the way health and disease are understood and on the various ways the healing arts are administered in taking care of patients.

What I hope for in the future more than anything else is that useful discoveries in the natural health realm will continue to have such an impact on health care professionals that they will eventually consider nature's remedies as the initial treatments of choice in all possible cases before resorting to drugs, radiation, chemotherapy, surgery, and other invasive therapies that can reduce the quality of life and possibly the length of life.

All truly valuable discoveries in health and medicine involve deeper insights into the nature of body functions, as we see in the amazing discoveries going on now in microbiology and biochemistry. Each living cell in the human body is a treasure chest of health secrets that are gradually being revealed so that we understand more and more of what we can do to develop healthier bodies and live longer lives. The future of health care holds wonderful (I almost wrote *miraculous*) possibilities.

I hope that this book has added to your reservoir of knowledge about staying healthy and happy. I find that most of my patients have felt that longevity is only desirable if we are able to sustain a certain essential quality of life. My mother often said, "A long life lived is not always good enough, but a good life lived is always long enough." In my view, she was right.

INDEX

A

abdominal exercises, 178–180, 193, 197
acid/alkaline balance, 5–6, 24, 224, 367–373
acid/alkaline food table, 369–373
acidophilus bacteria, 35, 160–161, 174, 224–225
addictive behaviors, 115–116
adrenal glands, 148, 196
affirmations, 127
air, 3–4, 13–18, 75, 128, 230
    about, 13–18
    composition of, 13–14
    purification of, 15, 21
air baths, 28, 43, 186, 187
air pollution, 14, 15, 16–18
air pressure, 20–22
alcohol addiction, 116
alfalfa, 108, 132, 152, 163, 279, 328, 359, 363, 426, 427
alfalfa leaf, 426
Alfa-Mint Tea, 293, 339, 427
allergies, 230
    food, 316–317
    inhalant, 18
allspice, 442
almond nut milk, 336–337
almonds, 351
aloe vera, 164–166, 182
altitude, 18, 20, 21–22, 29, 41, 46, 71
    about, 22–23
    air and, 15
    circulation and, 136–137

Alzheimer's disease, 114, 116–117
amino acids, 117, 130, 283
anemia, 145–147, 250, 263, 265
angelica, 427
angina, 151–152
aniseed, 442
Apertif, 346
apples, 367
apricots, 184, 315
    seeds, 38
Armenia, 35
aromas, 124, 125
arthritis, 3, 298, 310
    foods for, 359–362
asthma, 228–233, 325, 431
    herbs for, 232
    treatment of, 231, 232
    turnip diet, 238–239
    types, 228
attitudes, 216
    brain health and, 113–114
avocado, 343

B

Balanced Daily Eating Regimen, 375, 416
balm, 427
balsam, 427
bananas, 352
barley, 5, 36, 44, 47, 146, 173, 215, 363
basil, 427, 442
baths, 187, 211–212, 313
    about, 187–191
    cold, 188–189

baths, *continued*
    cold water, 190–191
    hot and cold, 140
    Kneipp, 139–140, 363
    Russian, 189
    sitz, 140, 212, 322
    warm, 128
bay leaf, 87, 427, 442
beauty, 40–41, 124
beef, 136
bee pollen, 44
Beet Appetizer, 346
beets, 146, 175, 300, 328
behavior, and foods, 68–69
beliefs, spiritual, 8–10
Berg, Ragnar, 369
Bergman, S., 404
Bible, 59–61
bile, 171
biotin, 251
blackberry juice, 146, 171–172
black cherry juice, 75, 146, 172, 367
blood, 135–156
    food remedies, 154
blood circulation. *See* circulation
blood pressure, 25, 147–151
    high, 149–151
    low, 148
blueberry, 427
blue violet, 57, 427
Blum, Kenneth, 115
body
    chemical elements of, 242, 243,
        258–272
    rebuilding with foods, 6, 80
body heat, 28–29
borage, 427, 439
bowels
    abdominal exercises,
        178–180
    breathing exercise, 197
    magnesium and, 311
    managing, 160–180
    sensitive, foods for, 171–178
    squatting posture and, 167
brain, 73, 111–133, 312–313, 343,
    360–361
    about, 111–113
    addictions and, 115–116
    best foods for, 130–133
    foods for, 8, 362
    glucose and, 112, 114–115
    headaches and, 101

    health of, and attitude, 113–114
    sleep and, 124–127
Brandt, Johanna, 414
breakfast, 378–381
    pre-breakfast routine, 378
breathing, 29, 139
    altitude and, 22–23
    catarrh and, 222–223
    chest, 159
    correct, 14
    exercises, 194–201
    increasing capacity, 200
    outdoors, 137
    techniques, 141
brewer's yeast, 277
broom, 439
broths
    barley and kale, 36
    for nerves, 366
    potato peeling, 39–40
    for sick people, 418
    for various conditions, 339–342
Brown Rice Diet, 388–389
buchu, 428
burdock, 428
burnett, 428

C

cabbage, 146
cabbage, savoy, 329–330, 429
calcium, 26, 68, 215, 259–260
calcium broth, 342, 363
calcium tonics, 363
calendula, 90
canker sores, 91
caraway, 443
carbohydrates, 272–274, 393
    percentage in foods, 273–274
carbon dioxide, 14, 15, 24
carbon monoxide, 16
cardamom, 443
Carrel, Alexis, 131
carrots, 91, 150, 300, 325–326
catarrhal conditions, 77, 99, 135–136,
    160, 217–239, 325
    defined, 217
    development of, 218–219
    diet and, 226–228, 232–233, 315
    disease and, 224
    ears and, 95, 96–98
    eliminating, 158–159
    as elimination process, 217–218
    milk and, 335

nasal remedies, 237–238
remedies, 225–239
skin care, 235–236
symptoms, 219–221
what to do about, 222–226
catnip, 428
cayenne, 226, 443
celery, 28, 55, 328, 351–352, 354–355, 443
cell salts, 301
Cernan, Eugene A., 10
chamomile, 428
change, 45, 118–119
chaparral, 439
charcoal, activated, 304, 404
cheese, 37
chemical elements of body, 242, 243,
    258–272
Cheney, Garnett, 330
cherries, 47, 142
chervil, 443
chewing, 91, 95
chickweed, 428
chicory, 428
children, 219
China, 36
chlorine, 260
chlorophyll, 5, 57, 67, 68, 90, 92, 93,
    132, 136, 158, 159, 182, 221, 239,
    306, 328, 344, 364, 367, 417
    about, 93–94
Chlorophyll Water, 344
chocolate, 161
cholesterol, 151–152, 261, 275–276, 361
    foods for, 363–364
choline, 361
chromium, 260–262, 393
cinnamon, 443–444
circulation, 193
    breathing exercise, 198–199
    exercises, 203
    food remedies, 152–154
    foods and, 141–142
    improving, 136–142
    vein problems, 142–145
clam juice, 314
cleaning products, 292–293
cleansing body, 223–225
Cleansing Cocktail, 343
cleansing diet, 412–416
climate, 18, 19–20, 24–25, 46, 71
    about, 18–22
    effects on body, 29–31
    extremes of, 31

cloves, 444
cobalamin. *See* vitamin B_{12}
cobalt, 262
coconut, 41, 42
cod liver oil, 26, 42
coffee, 161, 338
    enema, 177, 224, 306
cognitive abilities, 114–115
cold, common, 233–235
    remedies, 233–235
colon, 89–90
color, 7, 120, 121–123, 125
    in meal planning, 300
coltsfoot, 439
combining foods, 371–374
comfrey, 43, 440
comfrey leaves, 428
Complexion Cocktail, 343
constipation, 168–170, 302, 403
containers, food, 292
cooking, herbs and spices for, 441–447
copper, 262–263
cornsilk, 428
cough syrup, 226
cucumber, 97–98
cucumbers, 5, 28, 184, 329

D

Daily Diet Regime, 206–207
daily habits, 74
dairy products, 130, 228, 237, 291–292
dandelion, 142, 429
dates, 37, 55, 174
deep breathing exercises, 194–201
Denenberg, Herbert, 48–49
depression, 114
diabetes mellitus, and diet, 298, 389–394
diarrhea, 171–172
    vegetable juices and, 329
diet(s)
    all-cleansing, 7–8
    bland, 168, 408–409
    blood pressure and, 150
    Brown Rice Diet, 388–389
    catarrh and, 226–228
    cleansing, 412–416
    diabetes and, 389–394
    elimination diets, 305, 316,
        394–399
    Health and Harmony Food
        Regimen, 375–386
    hypoglycemia, 401–403
    migraine and, 104–105

diet(s), *continued*
    for nervous indigestion, 407–408
    oxygen need and, 15
    for peptic ulcers, 403–407
    for reducing, 409–412
    special, 387–423
    transition diets, 399–401
    variety in, 295–296
digestants, 163
dill, 444
dinner, 383–386
diseases
    catarrh and, 224
    foods and, 308–309
    versus healing crisis, 77–78
    natural remedies, 307–308
    sexually-transmitted, 123
    toxins and, 71–72
diverticulitis, 171
Doctor Jensen's Drink, 335
drinks, blended, 335, 338, 343–347, 366
    health cocktails, 330, 331–334
dulse, Nova Scotia, 46, 108, 264, 277–278, 313, 417

E

ears, 95–100
    catarrh, 95, 96–98
    hearing problems, 98–100
eating habits, 285–286, 309
echinacea, 429
eggs, 131–132, 228, 300
elderberry, 429
elder flower tea, 153
elderly, 43, 255
    changes and, 45, 119–120
    cognitive abilities, 114
    healing crisis in, 72
    meals of, 44–45
electromagnetism, and water, 3
Eleven-Day Elimination Diet, 395–399
elimination diets, 394–399, 415
elimination processes, 217–218. *See also* catarrhal conditions
    Vital Broth for, 340–341
eliminative organs, 224, 230. *See also specific organs*
emergency storage of food supplies, 57–59
emotions
    circulation and, 137–138
    color and, 121–123
    emotional balance, 8
    music and, 120–121

enemas, 168, 177–178, 305–306, 328, 405
    cleansing, 224, 306
    coffee, 177, 224, 306
    retention, 177
energy, 65
enzyme supplements, 163
ephedra, 429
essiac tea, 425, 429–430
eucalyptus honey, 239
exercise(s), 4, 40, 174, 193–216
    aerobic, 14
    Alzheimer's disease and, 116–117
    for blood circulation, 203
    for bowel problems, 178–180
    circulation and, 138–139, 143
    deep breathing, 194–201
    ears and, 97, 98
    eyes, 201–203
    leg, 211
    mule kick, 209
    muscle tension/relaxation, 204–205
    outdoor, 33, 42, 46, 74, 128
    for prolapses, 206–208
    side roll, 208–209
    sitting, 210
    slant board, 207–208
    spine, 303
    standing, 210–211
    tai chi, 212–213
    wrestler's stance, 209
eyebright, 430
eyes
    circles under, 85–86
    exercises, 201–203
    eye bath, 190
    infected/irritated, 86
    natural remedies, 85–86
    problems, 325

F

face exercises, 201
faith, 8–10
fasting, 7–8, 231, 316
    about, 78–80
    healing crisis and, 78–80
    under medical supervision, 79
    rest and, 328
    transition diets, 399–401
fatigue, 218, 230
fats, dietary, 275–276, 289, 291, 298–299, 393
fatty acids, 275

feet, warm, 141
fennel, 430
fenugreek, 430
feverfew, 430
fiber, dietary, 169–170
figs, 176
figwort, 430
fish, 38, 130, 355–356
fish broth, 341
flaxseed, 56, 92, 175–176, 224, 305, 430
fluorine, 183, 263–264
flu remedies, 235
folic acid, 247, 250, 251
food allergies, 316–317
foods, 4–7, 349–374. *See also* natural
    foods; organic foods; raw foods
        acid/alkaline, 5–6, 369–373
        for arthritis, 359–362
        behavior and, 68–69
        blood-purifying, 303
        body chemistry and, 5–6
        for bowel problems, 171–178
        for brain, 8, 362
        carbohydrate percentage chart,
            273–274
        catarrh-producing, 228, 230
        circulation and, 141–142
        for circulatory system, 152–154
        color of, 122–123
        combining, 371–374
        concentrated, 54
        constipating, 302
        devitalized, 9
        disease and, 308
        fattening, 301
        gas-producing, 302
        hair and, 108
        health and, 66–69
        from health food stores, 293–295
        increasing variety, 295–296
        influence on body, 301–303
        labels on, 286–289
        laxative, 302
        to limit in diet, 358–359
        live, 3, 34
        for lungs, 159–160
        non-catarrh producing, 228
        processed, 34–35
        remedial qualities, 353–358
        seasons and, 5, 6, 25–28
        storage for emergencies, 57–59
        supplementary, 277–279
        for survival, 54–56

        thinning, 302
        unfavorable, 359
        whole, 4–5, 6
foot baths, 190–191, 313, 322
fo ti tieng, 36, 44, 430
Fowler, Edmund P., 99, 100
foxglove, 440
fruit juices, 7, 27, 291, 325. *See also kinds
        of fruits and fruit juices*
        caution, 327–328
fruits, 6–7, 38, 164, 296
        cleaning, 372
        dried, 315–316
        laxative formula, 176–177
Funk, Casamir, 245

G
garlic, 95, 159–160, 431–432, 444
gelatin, 172, 352
germs, 223–224
Gerson, Max, 177
Gesser, Charles H., 234
ginger, 444
ginkgo biloba, 117, 432
ginseng, 36, 44, 284, 432
glucose, and brain, 112, 114–115
Gold, Paul, 114
goldenseal, 432
gotu kola, 36, 44, 432
grains, 290–291, 300, 357
grape diet, 150, 414–416
grape juice, 43, 109, 110
gravity, 36–37
Green Cocktail, 344
Green Drink, 152
greens, 67–68, 75, 93, 94, 132, 133, 146,
        215, 276
gums, about, 90–91

H
hair, 106–110
Halpenn, Stephen, 125
hawthorne berry, 432–433
hay fever, 226–227, 228, 229
headaches
        acute, 100, 101
        causes, 100–102
        chronic, 100, 101
        migraine, 101–102, 104–106
        natural remedies, 102–104, 105
healing, herbs for, listed, 425–441
healing crisis, 71
        bringing on, 72–73
        disease versus, 77–78

healing crisis, *continued*
    elimination of toxins during,
        77–78
    fasting and, 78–80
    Law of Cure, 72, 76–77
    as reversal process, 72–73, 76–77,
        78
Health and Harmony Food Regimen,
    375–386
    breakfast, 378–381
    dinner, 383–386
    lunch, 381–383
health cocktails, 330, 331–334
health food stores, 281–296, 426
    recommended items, 293–295
health/wellness
    food healing laws, 377
    Health and Harmony Food
        Regimen for, 375–386
    maintaining after age forty, 46–47
    maintaining in old age, 44–45
    nutrition and, 66–69
    rules of eating, 376
    signs of, 422–423
    tips, 303–306
hearing problems, 98–100
heart. *See also* circulation
    breathing exercise, 194
    foods for, 153, 311–312
hemorrhoids, 167–168
herbs, 43, 56, 73
    asthma and, 232
    cautions, 439
    for cooking, listed, 441–447
    for healing, listed, 425–441
herb teas, 293, 338–339, 426
Hercules Punch, 347
Hering, Constantine, 72, 76–77
Hering's Law of Cure, 72, 76–77
hobbies, 46
honey, 39, 41, 86, 110, 153, 184, 239,
    311–312, 335
hops, 433
horseradish, 87, 225–226, 445
horsetail, 433
huckleberry, 433
humidity, 19, 21, 23–25
Hunt, Roland, 123–124
Hunzas, 38, 93
hydrastis, 433
hydrochloric acid deficiency, 365
hypertension, 149–151

hypoglycemia, 365–366, 401–403
hypotension, 148

I

ice cream, 28, 291–292
"Iced" Tea, 339
identity, sense of, 117
immune system, 64–65, 114
indigestion, nervous, 407–408
intrinsic factor, 250
iodine, 38, 40, 46, 57, 69, 264, 277,
    313–314
iron, 4, 68, 145, 146, 264–265

J

Jade-Ade, 344
jogging, 40
joints, 309–310, 358
    tai chi for, 213
    water packs for, 304
joy, 119–120
juices, 27–28. *See* drinks, blended; fruit
    juices; vegetable juices
juicing machines, 324–325
juniper berries, 433

K

kale, 5, 36, 55, 94, 279, 363
kidneys, 7, 24, 97
    care of, 157–158
Kneipp, Father Sebastian, 433
Kneipp bath, 139–149, 363

L

labels, reading, 286–289, 292
lavender, 124, 125, 433
laxative foods, 175–177, 302
lecithin, 47, 107, 130, 131, 132, 276, 278,
    279, 312–313, 342–343, 360–361
legs
    calf stretcher, 211
    circulation problems, 143–145
    cramps in, 363
lemon balm, 433
licorice root, 440
lifestyle, 299, 319, 392
lightning, 18, 20
linseed oil, 86
liquids, 321–347. *See also* broths; drinks,
    blended; fruit juices; health cocktails;
    juices; milk; soy milk; vegetable juices;
    water
    recommended intake, 321–322

liver, 194, 223
liver in diet, 367
    dessicated, 277
longevity, 54, 431
    obtaining, 33–49
lovage, 433
love, 73, 137–138
Lucas, Richard, 430
lunch, 381–383
lungs
    breathing exercise, 196
    care of, 158–160
    food for, 159–160
lymph glands in neck, draining, 211

M

mace, 445
magnesium, 105, 214, 265–266, 311, 316, 319
manganese, 130, 266, 311
marigold, 433
marjoram, 443
marshmallow root, 434
mastoiditis, 96
Meal in a Drink, 347
meats, 150, 161, 228, 289–290, 362
Meecham, William C., 129–130
melanin, 30
melatonin, 124
mental health, 73
mental illness, 350–351, 365
migraine headaches, 101–102, 104–106
milk, 159, 230, 259, 285, 404
    allergy to, 316
    clabbered, 35, 41, 45, 173, 365
    clabbered, preparing, 162
    coconut, 232
    enemas, 224
    goat's, 47, 117, 230, 284, 387
milk packs, 86
milk substitute drinks, 330, 335–338
milk thistle, 434
Mills, Clarence A., 24–25, 31
minerals, 214–215, 242, 243, 316, 327.
    See also specific minerals
mint, 445
Mixed Cocktail, 344
molasses, blackstrap, 277
molybdenum, 266–267
mouth, 87–95. *See also* teeth
mouthwash, 190
mucous membranes, 219, 326

Mulberry Cocktail, 345
multidimensional approach, 318–319
muscles, 312
music, 120–121, 125
mustard, 445

N

nasal douches, 221
nasal remedies, for chronic catarrh, 237–238
nasturtium, 434
National Nutritional Foods Association, 297
natural food industry, 449, 450
natural foods, 281–296, 297, 314–315
natural food stores, 281–296
natural remedies, 307–319
    fads, 283
    gradual effects of, 70–71, 76
    at health food stores, 282–284
    from other countries, 35–44
    value of, 64–65
neck, breathing exercise for, 195–193
Nerve Verve, 347
nervous system, 311, 312–313
    colds and, 236
    foods and, 133, 366–367
    nourishing, 128–130
    silicon and, 310–311
niacin, 97, 142, 152, 248
nitrogen, 14, 20
noise pollution, 129–130
nuclear radiation, 56–57
nutmeg, 446
nutrition, 297–303
    cellular requirements, 307
    mental illness and, 350–351
    survival and, 51–59
    tips, 298–303
nuts and seeds, 42, 43–44, 335, 351, 357, 366
    blended drinks, 335–337
    storing, 57–58

O

oats, 44, 144–145, 310, 311, 342, 434
obesity, 276
oils, 298–299
okra, 40, 55, 309
olives, 39, 313, 364
onions, 159–160, 226, 239, 431–432
oregano, 446
organic foods, 281–284

organization, 73
outdoor exercise, 42
overeating, 65, 299
overweight, 418–420
oxalic acid in foods, 358–359
oxygen, 3–4, 14, 15, 22–23. *See also* air

P

packs, hot and cold, 212, 221
pancreas, 199–200
pangamic acid, 252
pantothenic acid. *See* vitamin B₅
papaya, 42, 90–91, 280, 357, 434
papaya-mint, 434
paprika, 446
parathyroid gland, 193
parsley, 28, 44, 93, 97, 108, 152, 280, 328, 435, 446
Pauling, Linus, 245
pennyroyal, 435, 441
pepper (black), 446
peppermint, 435
peptic ulcers, 329–330, 403–407
perspiration, 186–187
pesticides, 281–282, 323, 374
phosphorus, 267–268
pine needle tea, 436
pituitary gland, 196, 199
plants, 4, 18
pokeweed, 441
pollutants, 14, 15, 78, 129–130
pomegranate, 352
posture, 215–216
potassium, 39, 268, 312
potassium broth, 341–342, 387
Potassium Cocktail, 153
potato packs, 86
potato peeling broth, 39–40
potato soup, 172, 341
poultices, 305
preventive remedies, natural, 35, 64–65.
      See also natural remedies
prolapsed organs, 102, 403
      exercises, 206–208
prostate trouble, 47, 425
protein, 130, 317
Protein Drink, 346
prunes, 172, 328, 385, 367
psyllium, 305
pycnogenol, 280
pyridoxine. *See* vitamin B₆

R

Radiance Cocktail, 345
radiation exposure, 56–59
radon, 17–18
raspberry, 435
raw foods, 161, 300, 314–315
      vegetable juices, 323–330, 331–334
RDA, 245
red clover, 435
reducing diets, 409–412
relaxation, 40, 43, 124–125, 213–214, 216
respiration rate, 14–15
rest, 180, 325
retirement, 46
riboflavin. *See* vitamin B₂
rice, 150, 173, 247, 312
      Brown Rice Diet, 388–389
rice bran syrup, 97, 142
rice milk, 285, 335
rice polishings, 278
rice tea, 436
Rocine, V. G., 110
rose hips, 436
rosemary, 436
rue, 436, 441
rutin, 144
rye, 37

S

SAD. *See* seasonal affective disorder
Sadler, William S., 155
saffron, 446
sage, 87, 436, 446–447
St. John's wort, 436
saliva, 88
salt. *See* sodium
sarsaparilla, 436
sassafras, 436
sauerkraut and tomato juice, 37–38
savory, 447
savoy, 437
saw palmetto, 437
scalp massage, 108, 109
seasonal affective disorder, 19
seasons, 18
      foods and, 5, 6, 25–28
seaweed, 40
seeds and nuts. *See* nuts and seeds
selenium, 255, 268–269
self-esteem, 117–118
senna, 437

serotonin, 317
sesame seeds, 43–44, 335, 336, 352
sex, 123
sexuality/sexual system, 152
    climate and, 30, 31
shavegrass, 97, 327, 437
showers, 191
silicon, 68, 130, 135, 144, 146, 182–183,
    214, 269–270, 310–311
sinuses
    natural remedies for, 87
    sinusitis, 24, 221
sitz baths, 140, 212, 322
skin, 181–192
    suntanning, 185–186
skin brushing, 43, 129, 151, 187, 231,
    235, 303
    technique, 191–192
skin care, 182–183
    for catarrhal conditions, 235–236
    complexion remedies, 184–185
slant boards, 179. 168, 207–208
sleep, 46, 230, 317
    brain and, 124–127
    breathing exercise, 198
    unclothed, 126
slippery elm, 176, 177, 437–438
Smith, Anthony, 323–324
smoking, 18, 74, 228
snoring, 126–127
sodium, 3, 21, 68, 270, 293, 299,
    309–310
    broths, 340, 342
soils, 4, 39, 242, 244, 250, 296
sorrel tea, 438
soups, for specific conditions, 339–342
soybeans, 361–352
soy milk, 36, 55, 225, 230, 284–295,
    335, 337–338, 362
spearmint, 438
spices, listed, 441–447
spine, 193, 303, 310
    exercise, 204–206
spiritual beliefs, 8–10, 59–60
spirituality, 8–12, 75–76, 154–156, 318
spleen, breathing exercise for, 194
sprouts, 132–132
Starch Drink, 346
Stepaniak, Joanne, 250
strawberries, 27, 47
strawberry, 438
strokes, 142

sugar, 392
sulfur, 270–271, 302
summer, 26–28
sunbaths, 189–190, 405
sunflower seeds, 278, 335
sunlight/sunshine, 1–2, 7, 18–19, 26, 27,
    43, 45, 75, 148
suntanning, 185–186
supplements, 279–280
    table, 417
surgery, unnecessary, avoiding, 48–49,
    387
survival
    of fittest, 53
    foods for, 54–56
    nutrition and, 51–59
symptoms, defined, 219

T

tahini, 336
tai chi, 212–213
taro root, 301
tarragon, 447
teas
    Alfa-Mint, 339
    elder flower, 153
    essiac, 425, 429–430
    for headaches, 103–104
    herb, 293, 339
    herb, making, 426
    "Iced," 339
teeth, 91–95
thiamin. *See* vitamin B_1
throat
    exercises, 200, 201
    natural remedies, 87, 239
thyme, 102, 124
thyroid gland, 28, 195, 196, 313
tofu, 130
tomatoes, 28
tongue, 89–90
tonics, 315, 332–334, 335, 342–347
    calcium, 363
tonsillitis, 221
toxemia, 230–231
toxins
    eliminating, 7–8, 187
    healing crisis and, 71, 77–78
trace elements, 242, 244
triglycerides, 275
L-tryptophan, 115–116
turmeric, 447

turnips, 159, 238–239, 358
Tyler, Varro E., 252

U

ultraviolet radiation, 2, 185
Uman, Martin A., 20
underweight, 420–422
uva ursi, 438

V

vacations, 45, 47–48
vagus nerve, breathing exercise for, 197–198
valerian, 124, 126, 438
varicose veins, 143–144, 153
veal joint broth, 348, 360
vegans, 250
vegetable juices, 300, 324–330, 331–334, 417
    cocktails, 343
    crystalloid minerals in, 327
    diarrhea and, 329
vegetables, 6–7, 296. *See also kinds of vegetables and vegetable juices*
    bowels and, 164
    cleaning, 374
    dehydrated, 55
    remedial qualities, 353–358
vegetarians, 275
vein problems, 142–145, 153
vibrations, and water, 3
vibratory state of body, 7
vital broth, 340–341
Vitality Drink, 347
vitamin A, 75, 99, 100, 234, 325–326
    about, 246
vitamin B complex, 100, 214–215, 246–252
vitamin B$_1$ (thiamin), 247
vitamin B$_2$ (riboflavin), 247–248
vitamin B$_3$. *See* niacin
vitamin B$_5$ (pantothenic acid), 248
vitamin B$_6$ (pyridoxine), 249–250
vitamin B$_{12}$ (cobalamin), 250–251, 262
vitamin C, 75, 99, 100, 144, 234, 252–254, 284
vitamin D, 2, 26, 254–255
vitamin E, 47, 144, 255–256, 278

vitamin K, 256–257
vitamins, 244–259, 280, 282
    about, 244–245
    best natural sources, 257
    fat-soluble, 244
    water-soluble, 244
vitellin, 131
vocal cords, 200–201
von Braun, Wernher, 10

W

walking, 47, 74, 136, 138–139, 140, 203
Walsh, Michael J., 92
water, 2–3, 158, 170, 182
    amount in body, 243, 258
    distilled, 2–3, 47, 56, 170, 323
    facts about, 322–324
    vibratory, 3
watercress, 146
watermelon, 5
water softeners, 322–323
water treatments, 38, 73, 128, 139–140, 140, 144, 187–192, 211–212, 322. *See also* baths
    internal, 170, 416–417
weather. *See* climate
Weger, George, 79
weight, normalizing, 418–422
wheat, 54, 159, 230, 365
wheat germ, 278–279, 343
whey, 5, 97–98, 109, 210, 279, 280
White, Ellen G., 83
white oak, 438
Whole Melon Cocktail, 345
Williams, Roger, 245
winter, 25–26
withdrawal symptoms, 102
woodruff, 438
work, enjoyment of, 119–120
worms, 431–432

Y

yellow dock, 438
yogurt, 41, 42–43, 161, 215
yohimbe, 441
Youth Bloom Cocktail, 345

Z

zinc, 246, 263, 271–272